The Price They Paid

The Price They Paid

Slavery, Shipwrecks, and Reparations Before the Civil War

Jeff Forret

NEW YORK
LONDON

Published in the United States by The New Press, New York, 2024
Distributed by Two Rivers Distribution

ISBN 978-1-62097-886-3 (hc)
ISBN 978-1-62097-899-3 (ebook)
CIP data is available

The New Press publishes books that promote and enrich public discussion and understanding of the issues vital to our democracy and to a more equitable world. These books are made possible by the enthusiasm of our readers; the support of a committed group of donors, large and small; the collaboration of our many partners in the independent media and the not-for-profit sector; booksellers, who often hand-sell New Press books; librarians; and above all by our authors.

www.thenewpress.com

Composition by Westchester Publishing Services
This book was set in Adobe Caslon Pro

Printed in the United States of America

2 4 6 8 10 9 7 5 3 1

Contents

Abbreviations

BNAN	Bahamas National Archives, Nassau
GA	Georgia Archives, Morrow
NAMS	National Archives Microfilm Series
NARA	National Archives and Records Administration
NAUK	National Archives of the United Kingdom, Kew, Richmond
NCDAH	North Carolina Department of Archives and History, Raleigh
NOPL	New Orleans Public Library
RSPP	Race and Slavery Petitions Project
SCDAH	South Carolina Department of Archives and History, Columbia
SCL	South Caroliniana Library, University of South Carolina, Columbia

Cast of Characters

American slave owners, shippers, and civilians

Charles Allen
Capt. John S. Chattin
George Mason Chichester
Antonio Della Torre
Franklin & Armfield
Amédée Gardanne
Henry Grimké
Gabriel Holmes
Jonathan and Juliet Lemmon
Nathan Morse
Sylvester W. and Mary E. Mudd
Joseph W. Neal
Antonio Pacheco
Capt. Paschal Sheffield
Oliver Simpson
Capt. Elliot Smith
Capt. Isaac Staples
John and Henrietta Strohecker
Henry N. Templeman
Col. Charles P. and Ann M. Tutt
John Waddell

Enslaved people

The Douglass family
George Hammett
Henry
Jack

Joe
Nelson Lemon
Lewis
Summerset Nutter
Matilda Ridgely
Susan and her baby
Toby Vincent

U.S. politicians, officials, and diplomats

John F. Bacon
Alexander Barrow
Joshua Bates
Thomas Hart Benton
John C. Calhoun
Charles M. Conrad
Edward Everett
Millard Fillmore
John Forsyth
Joshua Giddings
George Huyler
Andrew Jackson
Edward Livingston
Louis McLane
Alexandre Mouton
Andrew Stevenson
John Storr
Nathaniel G. Upham
Aaron Vail
Martin Van Buren
Daniel Webster

British officials

Lord Aberdeen
George Campbell Anderson
Lord Ashburton
Blayney Townley Balfour
Thomas Butterfield

Sir James Carmichael-Smyth
Sir Stephen Remnant Chapman
Sir Francis Cockburn
William Melbourne Fox
Lord Goderich
Edmund Hornby
Alexander MacVey
William Vesey Munnings
Lord Palmerston
Thomas Pindar
William Rothery
Thomas Spring Rice
Thomas B. Wylly

Introduction

Throughout the age of American slavery, enslaved men and women took heroic steps to escape the horrors and oppression of bondage. Some devised creative, elaborate plans to elude their owners. Frederick Douglass disguised himself as a free Black sailor and boarded a train from Baltimore to the North. Enslaved in Virginia, Henry "Box" Brown had himself mailed in a cramped wooden crate to abolitionists in Philadelphia. William and Ellen Craft, an enslaved couple in Georgia, pulled off a successful masquerade that bent the social rules of race and gender and exploited a feigned disability to their advantage. Countless other fugitives fled to inhospitable swamps, sought refuge with Indigenous peoples, or sneaked onboard an outbound ship from port to take a maritime Underground Railroad to freedom. Still more absconded with no firm plans, desperate to flee unbearable situations and conditions. They chose to survive by their wits and hoped for the best. Whatever form their bids for liberty took, enslaved people seized the opportunities available to them in attempts to improve their lives in the North and in Canada or southward in Mexico.[1]

Other emancipations were the consequence of a perverse form of good luck. In the following pages, weather, wind, rough seas, reefs, and shallow, difficult-to-navigate straits set in motion events that upended the status quo between enslaver and enslaved. To take just one example, on January 2, 1831, the brig *Comet* crashed into a reef near the Abaco Islands, in the Bahamas, and sank. The *Comet* had departed Alexandria, in the District of Columbia, on December 18, carrying a shipment of Black captives bound for the New Orleans slave markets. The maritime route to the Crescent City was a customary one in the fully lawful domestic slave trade that redistributed surplus bondpeople from the Upper South to the cotton frontier of the Old Southwest. But this particular journey did not proceed according to plan. The *Comet* strayed off course, drifted among the rocks in shallow Bahamian waters, and suffered a gash ripped into its hull. Miraculously, all

Map by Joe LeMonnier.

on board, including the valuable cargo of 165 enslaved men, women, and children, managed to survive the shipwreck. British authorities seized the Black captives, and the Vice Admiralty Court in Nassau set them free, much to their erstwhile owners' consternation.

This might seem like a singular stroke of good fortune for these enslaved people, but over the next nine years, three similar incidents, involving the U.S. slaving vessels *Encomium* (1834), *Enterprise* (1835), and *Hermosa* (1840), resulted in the emancipation of more than 150 additional enslaved captives who inadvertently landed in a British Atlantic colony. In all four cases, by holding everyone on board captive to the power of nature, environmental forces enabled the literal captives, bound in chains, to gain liberty. Almost all of the more than three hundred total prisoners on the four slave ships chose freedom when British authorities offered it. Through the fortuitous intervention of colonial officials, they achieved emancipation without weapons, violence, or murder and went on to forge new lives in their adoptive island homes. Though an infinitesimally small portion of the millions enslaved in the American South, news of their emancipations, and the issues they raised, roiled the nation.[2]

Particular slave ships, such as the *Hare*, *Antelope*, *Amistad*, and *Clotilda*, have become well known in the literature on Atlantic slavery. All of these vessels participated, legally or illegally, in the transatlantic slave trade. A less visible but still significant part of the waterborne slave trade was domestic, facilitated by vessels that plied the waters off the U.S. coast, shuttling captives from Upper South ports such as Baltimore, Alexandria, or Richmond to those in the Lower South, most notably New Orleans. Scholars have devoted extensive study to only a few coastwise maritime incidents involving enslaved people from the United States, all of which occurred after the dramas of the *Comet*, *Encomium*, *Enterprise*, and *Hermosa*.[3]

These four slave ships were not the first U.S. vessels to wind up unexpectedly in a British Atlantic colony. Some, like a craft containing 101 enslaved people bound for New Orleans that accidentally ended up in the Bahamas in 1818, produced no controversy whatsoever and continued on their way. Other incidents generated friction between the United States and Great Britain. For instance, in 1819, the captain and crew of the *Francis and Eliza*, flying the Union Jack, "were compelled by absolute want to send a boat on shore to procure provisions" in New Orleans, in violation of the terms of a U.S. navigation act. In consequence, a U.S. district court ordered the British vessel condemned and sold. An appeal to the U.S. Supreme Court resulted in the overturning of the district court ruling and an order to restore the ship to its British owners, but because the master of the vessel could not instantly secure "the security required to stay [the] execution" of the original decision, the *Francis and Eliza* was sold anyway, despite the Supreme Court's intervention. In what one British newspaper called "the grossest injustice that could be committed by the Government of one civilised country upon the subjects of another," the British claimants received only the proceeds of the sale rather than the ship itself. The owners of the vessel were still seeking indemnity from the United States for legal expenses and lost freight years later, by the time the cases of the *Comet*, *Encomium*, *Enterprise*, and *Hermosa* cropped up between 1831 and 1840. Issues of compensation arising over maritime disputes—a frequent source of longstanding international grudges—were nothing new. What set the four U.S. slaving vessels apart was the chronologically rapid succession of the disasters that befell them, precisely at a time when a radical abolitionist movement in the United States was gaining traction and abolitionists abroad had successfully struck at slavery in the British Empire.[4]

Abolitionists on the home front had mobilized overwhelming public support in Britain for emancipation as early as the late 1780s. In time, the British government joined the antislavery cause, abolishing its participation in the international slave trade, but not slavery itself, in 1807. Government opposition to slavery as an institution grew more pronounced in the 1820s, and slave revolts in the British Atlantic, capped off by the large-scale rebellion in Jamaica in December 1831, pushed the Crown toward full abolition. In colonies such as the Bahamas, officials reflected the Crown's increasing hostility to slavery even if white residents did not necessarily share their governing authorities' mounting antagonism toward the institution. Some were slave-owning whites who had resettled in the Bahamas after the American Revolution with their enslaved property. Others were British slaveholders. The disjuncture between some white Bahamians and their colonial government became evident after the wreck of the *Comet.* Great Britain's passage of the Slavery Abolition Act of 1833, which called for the immediate emancipation of enslaved people under age six and the gradual emancipation of other bondpeople in the West Indies, set the stage for the collision between British abolitionism and the United States' thriving coastwise domestic slave trade.[5]

Slavery was waning in the British Atlantic as it waxed in the American South. With the 1830s ushering in the "flush times" in the Old Southwest, slave owners poured into Alabama, Mississippi, and Louisiana to make their riches through cotton and cane planted and harvested by enslaved labor. Collectively, the number of captive laborers at owners' disposal could not match the size of their ambitious dreams. The appetite for property in enslaved people seemed insatiable. A professionalized domestic slave trade worked to meet that demand by sending surplus bondmen and bondwomen from the Upper South to bustling slave markets in New Orleans, Natchez, and lesser hubs of the Lower South. Although slave dealers sometimes traveled overland with the enslaved chained in coffles, the *New York Journal of Commerce* also explained that "a brisk trade in human flesh is carried on, by sea, between the Northernmost slaveholding States and the Southernmost." Although the United States prohibited participation in the transatlantic slave trade effective January 1, 1808—only a little more than nine months after Great Britain—the acceleration of the pace of the domestic "*American* slave trade" kept the transport of enslaved captives by sea very much alive.[6]

In the 1830s, the business of coastwise domestic slave trading was as dangerous as it was thriving. Outbreaks of disease and the possibility of shipboard uprisings were constant threats. Moreover, despite U.S. government pleas in the 1820s to convince Great Britain to erect lighthouses in the

Bahama Islands, at night, safe paths through the archipelago remained shrouded in darkness, presenting challenges to even the most seasoned navigators. Absent a network of lighthouses to illuminate the maritime hazards off the Bahamian coast, ship captains piloting slavers through perilous channels jeopardized the lives of their human cargoes. One U.S. government official informed a British dignitary that, regrettably, the necessary coastwise journeys to redistribute the enslaved labor of the Old South involved "taking a course which unavoidably carries them into the waters of the British islands at the entrance of the Mexican Gulf, where, from the dangers attending the navigation of those seas, they are exposed to such disasters" as befell the *Comet*, *Encomium*, *Enterprise*, and *Hermosa*. No one, either free or enslaved, perished in any of the four incidents that follow, although it is possible that injuries sustained in the crashes may have led to the deaths of a small number of captives shortly thereafter.[7]

Unlike the *Antelope* or the *Amistad*, which were illegal transatlantic slavers, the *Comet*, *Encomium*, *Enterprise*, and *Hermosa* all sailed legally, under the terms of the same U.S. statute that forbade the traffic in enslaved Africans across the ocean. And whereas the cases of the *Antelope* and the *Amistad* eventually landed before the U.S. Supreme Court in 1825 and 1841, respectively, those of the enslaved captives held prisoner aboard the U.S. slavers were heard in British colonial courts of vice admiralty or the Supreme Court of Bermuda. From the outset, the British courts were more partial to freedom than were American ones, and they never seriously considered re-enslaving the captives who had been made free when they arrived in a British Atlantic colony. The larger question—the one at the heart of this book—centered on whether their owners would be compensated for the loss of their enslaved property.[8]

U.S. claims to recompense for the enslaved captives lost to freedom revealed slavery's role in promoting the growth of the economy and capitalism nationally, not merely of the South. One important pillar supporting capitalist ventures was insurance, because insurance companies offered, through their policies, a mechanism of protection to mitigate against entrepreneurial risk. Insurers underwrote temporary policies on the enslaved people transported coastwise by their owners or by slave dealers to protect their valuable investments in human merchandise while in transit. Through those policies, insurance companies functioned as the agents of capitalism but also, as businesses themselves, labored to protect their bottom line. On each of the fateful voyages of the *Comet*,

Encomium, *Enterprise*, and *Hermosa*, at least some, and sometimes nearly all, of the enslaved captives on board were insured. Companies sometimes paid on the policies they issued without undue trouble for the claimants, but they sometimes objected to making payment. Disgruntled owners took them to court in disputes over whether seizures by a foreign government qualified as a covered risk.[9]

Insurers whose profits plummeted when they paid on their policies joined slave owners with uninsured human merchandise aboard the four U.S. vessels to plead with the federal government for assistance. Their sense of entitlement was clear. All those invested in slavery expected unquestioned compliance with their demands for aid on their behalf, and the federal government readily mobilized to defend slaveholder interests. The U.S. government in the early nineteenth century was small, not prone to the passage of sweeping programs of governmental aid as would become more common a century later. But in the antebellum decades, white Southerners played pronounced roles in the federal government, and they used their disproportionate influence to deploy that government in service to slaveholding. The common tie of slave owning led to close cooperation with a government that expended extraordinary diplomatic efforts to benefit enslavers and their allies in business.[10]

American enslavers and the insurance companies that protected them commandeered U.S. foreign policy to preserve their investments in slavery. The diplomacy surrounding the cases of the *Comet*, *Encomium*, *Enterprise*, and *Hermosa* raised thorny issues complicated by international borders, geopolitics, and questions of the legal jurisdiction of vessels on the high seas. Between the first of these shipwrecks, in 1831, and the last, in 1840, Parliament passed the Slavery Abolition Act, changing the British law of slavery that applied to that portion of the Crown's empire near American shores. The new statute provided justification for resisting U.S. demands for compensation for the bondpeople confiscated from U.S. slave ships on the grounds that slave laws were operable only in slaveholding regions and did not enjoy extraterritoriality when foreign vessels either wrecked or were carried by "stress of weather" into British ports. A series of American officials pressed slaveholder demands, arguing that the British were tampering with the United States' legal coastwise domestic slave trade. U.S. diplomats insisted that the seizures of the enslaved cargoes by the British government violated the "law of nations." According to them, since slavery was not forbidden under international law, Britain possessed no right to impose its laws upon U.S. vessels forced by shipwreck or storm into a British port. The U.S. position maintained that masters' rights to their enslaved property were neither lost nor diminished on the high seas and that the Crown was therefore obligated to supply restitution.

Throughout the quest for indemnity, from 1831 to 1855, the federal government's consistent role in supporting the business of slavery, across the eight presidential administrations spanning from Andrew Jackson to Franklin Pierce, revealed the extent to which antebellum slavery must be understood not merely as the "peculiar institution" of the South but as a national institution—one defended by all the expertise and resources the U.S. diplomatic corps could muster. By 1804, all the states north of the Mason-Dixon Line had either abolished slavery outright or enacted gradual emancipation laws. The agonizingly slow process of liberation was not yet completed in some of the purportedly free states by the time the *Comet*, *Encomium*, *Enterprise*, and *Hermosa* met their respective fates, but it was underway. Nevertheless, Northern-born diplomats such as Martin Van Buren of New York defended slaveholder rights on the high seas as ably as did the Southern-born U.S. minister to the United Kingdom, Andrew Stevenson of Virginia. Regardless of their respective birthplaces, they both represented the interests of a fundamentally proslavery government at a time when hostility toward slavery was growing in the Atlantic world.

Inevitably, the voyages of the *Comet*, *Encomium*, *Enterprise*, and *Hermosa* entered the contentious discourse between abolitionist and proslavery forces in U.S. domestic politics. The radical abolitionist movement was taking shape as the *Comet* sank in January 1831, one day after the publication of the first issue of William Lloyd Garrison's *The Liberator*. The *Encomium* wrecked in the Bahamas and the *Enterprise* hobbled into Bermuda years before South Carolina senator John C. Calhoun repudiated the abolitionists in 1837 by declaring slavery a "positive good," yet it was Calhoun who emerged as the loudest, most aggressive voice in Congress in favor of indemnification for Southern slave owners and insurers. His greatest congressional foil, Joshua R. Giddings of Ohio, who in 1838 took a seat in the House of Representatives, opposed compensating slave owners and the Northern complicity implied by the U.S. government's quest for restitution. Giddings was likely the author who wrote under the pseudonym PACIFICUS in the *Western Reserve Chronicle* to protest that "the spirited manner in which our Government espoused the cause of the slave dealers . . . brought upon the people of the free States all the ignominy attached to the supporters of the slave trade." Giddings saw as clearly as anyone the Slave Power conspiracy at work as the government labored to secure payment, while he labored in the House to obstruct it, much to slave owners' frustration.[11]

Would indemnification be granted? And if so, how much would be paid? The U.S. government had pressed Great Britain for compensation before. After the American Revolution and the War of 1812, it pursued payment for enslaved people emancipated during the military conflicts with the Crown. The 1814 Treaty of Ghent included a provision to compensate U.S. owners for lost slave property, but Britain construed the clause narrowly to evade financial responsibility. In 1826, after many years of negotiations, Britain finally agreed to make "a lump sum payment" totaling £250,000, or 1.2 million U.S. dollars, "in satisfaction of all American slaveowner claims." A mad rush to file for a share of the indemnity ensued, but many claimants received nothing before the available funds dried up in 1828. Just a few years later, the controversy over recompense for Southern masters was renewed.[12]

The chapters that follow recount the little-known history of the *Comet*, *Encomium*, *Enterprise*, and *Hermosa*, while underscoring the persistent questions of reparations that they raise. Part 1, "Disaster as Opportunity," details the voyages of the first three vessels, initial insurance company and slave owner demands for restitution, and the decisions made by Black captives and rescuers. Part 2, "Law, Diplomacy, and Politics," examines Great Britain's belated decision about indemnification for the first three U.S. ships and Sen. John C. Calhoun's stalwart defense of Southern slaveholding interests founded on his interpretation of the law of nations and his unflinching belief in slave owners' property rights. The wreck of the *Hermosa*, occurring five years after the *Enterprise* incident, further complicated relations between the United States and Great Britain. Part 2 also chronicles the financial resolution of the conflict, abolitionists' objections to restitution, the slave-owning men and women overlooked by the outcome, and the final efforts to settle their claims.

The correspondence of U.S. diplomats to the United Kingdom stated explicitly that they were pursuing, on behalf of Southern slave owners and their insurance companies, "indemnity," "compensation," or "restitution" from the British Crown. They used these terms interchangeably. Their lexicon also included the word "reparation," a term familiar to students of international law at the time. The law of state responsibility, not formally codified until the early twenty-first century, determines when a nation has breached international obligations and covers the possible remedies for damages inflicted by a wrongful act. Today, according to United Nations guidelines adopted in 2006, reparation may take the form of "restitution, compensation, rehabilitation, satisfaction [measures to acknowledge the violations] and guarantees of nonrepetition," all of which were designed "to restore the *status quo ante*." U.S. diplomats could not realistically expect the re-enslavement of the captives emancipated by the British in the 1830s and 1840s (although they did raise that prospect), but they relentlessly pressed for payments so that the finances of the affected slave owners and insurance companies would be made whole, as if the emancipations had never occurred.[13]

How the nineteenth-century usage of "reparation"—singular—in the language of international relations transitioned to the plural "reparations," more commonly used by the twenty-first-century public with relation to African Americans, is a legacy of the story recounted here. Whereas the historical narrative details the transatlantic efforts to secure reparation for losses incurred from the *Comet*, *Encomium*, *Enterprise*, and *Hermosa*, the epilogue reframes it within the modern-day debate over reparations for African American descendants of slaves. The analogy is of course imperfect. Although a quest for compensation is common to the discussions of both reparation (singular) and reparations (plural), the intended recipients of payments diverge markedly. In the United States prior to 1865, the clamor for payments was almost always for monies due to white slave *owners* deprived of their human property, not to the enslaved or formerly enslaved themselves. In the antebellum decades, only a few abolitionists, monitoring news of these four slave ships, declared publicly in the press that, if reparations were paid at all, they should go to the liberated captives, rather than to the distressed owners or the insurance companies whose pockets had been lightened by paying on their policies. Abolitionists detected a moral imperative to compensate those freed from bondage. The U.S. government, meanwhile, pursued indemnification for the owners. Contrasted with modern calls for reparations for the descendants of slaves, the pursuit of compensation for enslavers or those in service to them is arresting, a mirror image or perverse reflection of reparations' true purpose of remedying a historical wrong. Another important difference over time concerned the responsible party. The cases of the *Comet*,

Encomium, *Enterprise*, and *Hermosa* inspired calls for a settlement between competing state actors, not between a state and its citizens or subjects—a meaningful distinction that determined whose money was at stake.[14]

Despite the evident differences from the nineteenth century to the twenty-first, this book provides useful context for present-day discussions of the reparations issue. Before and even during the Civil War, the U.S. government voiced no qualms against pursuing compensation when white slave owners and white-owned insurance companies stood to benefit. To the contrary, officials actively and enthusiastically labored to subsidize them for their losses, not unlike the financial rescue of the banks deemed too big to fail during the Great Recession. In highlighting the contrasts in the nature of reparations battles over time, the epilogue invites readers to grapple with the legacies of slavery and the commonplace miscarriages of justice to which enslaved Americans and their descendants have been routinely subjected. Today we hear increasing calls to compensate the descendants of the enslaved because the historical injustices their ancestors suffered have continued to manifest generations later in myriad ways, including the high incidence of police brutality against Black people, the mass incarceration of marginalized populations ensnared by the prison-industrial complex, the phenomenon of Black landlessness, and the racial wealth gap, among others. With calls for fairness, justice, and genuine equality growing louder, a deeper historical understanding of reparations *should* inform the debate of our own time. History necessarily and inescapably bears on the present, but it is up to all of us to decide how that knowledge is used.

This book interlaces the distinct yet related storylines of the slaving vessels and their captains, slave owners, insurance companies, diplomats, and politicians in a narrative that begins with the wreck of the *Comet* in 1831. Newspapers, combined with a wide range of government records, including governors' papers, secretaries of state correspondence, treasury records, congressional records, census data, state court cases, and petitions, help craft a history that is simultaneously personal and political, intimate and sweeping, and that brings together social, diplomatic, and political history in unusual ways.

While the name, sex, age, height, and complexion of each captive is known from the slave manifests of the voyages, the archival sources for this project discriminate against the enslaved no less than the Southern society from which they were shipped. Enslaved people tend to appear most vividly in historical records for violating laws or for failing to conform to whites' social expectation of obedience. The captives aboard the *Comet*, *Encomium*, *Enterprise*, and *Hermosa* did nothing illegal. They aggravated their owners merely by accepting the offer of liberty in a British colony. Whenever possible, the text identifies the enslaved or formerly enslaved individuals by name and elaborates upon their stories, in spite of the archival gaps and silences that make those opportunities regrettably scarce.

The shortcomings of the surviving sources mean that, counter to the general thrust of twenty-first-century historical scholarship as well as much of my own previous work, the voices of the enslaved are often obscured, drowned out by the complaints of slave owners, insurance company executives, and their representatives who serve as the protagonists here. Those actors ask us to look upon them as objects of pity, wrongfully cheated by a foreign government whose gross misconduct imposed terrible suffering upon them. Some surely did feel the sting in their pocketbooks or the inconvenience in their households, yet in truth, their vehement and protracted protests most underscored a desperation wrought by their dependence on human beings they invested in as property and treated as merchandise.

The separate yet intertwined incidents involving the *Comet*, *Encomium*, *Enterprise*, and *Hermosa* collectively shed some faint rays of light on slavery and its place in the American economy, U.S. domestic politics, Atlantic diplomacy, and international slave law. Yet the overall product is fundamentally that of a social historian curious about slave owners' stranglehold over their national government and the rich irony of enslavers' insistence upon the necessity of reparations in the aftermath of emancipation. They may have received sympathy from the U.S. government, but they do not deserve ours.

1

Disaster as Opportunity

1

The Wreck of the *Comet*

Likely a native of Maine, Capt. Isaac Staples was, at the age of thirty or so, an experienced seafarer.[1] By the fall of 1828, he had become master of the *Comet*, a brig that frequented many of the major ports of the United States and the West Indies. By the time he was anchored again in the port of Alexandria, then within the District of Columbia, in December 1830, Staples had logged countless thousands of nautical miles aboard the *Comet*. He knew the ship well. It took an extraordinary combination of circumstances to disorient him enough to strand his vessel on a Bahamian reef.[2]

On Saturday, December 18, Capt. Staples pulled the *Comet* out of Alexandria, carrying a small crew, an unspecified number of white passengers, and 164 enslaved people bound for New Orleans. The two-masted vessel sliced its way through the broadening Potomac River and into Chesapeake Bay. By the twenty-second, it sailed past Cape Henry, Virginia, and out into the Atlantic, bearing south. All was well with the ship on the thirtieth, when it chanced upon the schooner *Emily Davis* on the open ocean, more than five hundred miles due east of Savannah, Georgia. The next day brought darker skies and "boisterous" severe weather. The *Comet*, though "tight and staunch," encountered relentless "heavy gales and adverse winds." The "unabated violence" of the ferocious winter storm that blew up on New Year's Eve allowed few glimpses of "the sun, or other . . . heavenly bodies" to aid navigation.[3]

Unable to accurately gauge his location, and fighting both head winds and counter currents, by January 2 Capt. Staples did not realize how far the vessel had strayed from his intended course and how dangerously close it had drawn to the Bahama Islands. Normally beautiful, the turbulent blue and turquoise waters surrounding the Bahamas concealed hidden hazards at or just below the surface. The twenty-nine islands of the archipelago were surrounded by more than six hundred cays—low banks of rock, coral, and sand—and thousands of individual jagged rocks reaching up from the ocean

Map of the Bahamas, 1831.

floor. In the darkness, about 11:00 p.m., Capt. Staples didn't notice the breaking waves in time. Still some eight or ten miles from the Abaco Islands, the *Comet* had tacked too far into the shallows and found itself suddenly "encompassed by reefs," instantly crashing onto one. The wooden-hulled ship remained lodged "hard and fast," stuck to a stubborn ridge of rock and coral.[4]

Staples made "every exertion" to extricate the *Comet* from the reef's tight grip. As he and his mate, twenty-five-year-old Stephen Foxwell from Maryland's Eastern Shore, later related, "in order to get her afloat, they threw over the ballast and had recourse to all other resources which practical experience, and the nature of their situation required." Yet their efforts proved fruitless. With every undulating wave, the vessel's hull risked being breached by repeatedly scraping and grinding against the rock and coral. With the ship still intact for the moment, Staples "launched the boats . . . in search of a landing on one of the neighboring Keys, to save the lives of the Crew, [and] passengers." A vague indication of land peeked over the horizon from the site of the wreck. Three or four miles from the reef, a scouting party, consisting of the first mate and two seamen, located a long, narrow strip of land, barely a quarter mile in width, called Spanish Cay. Having located the island, the party returned to the distressed vessel at about 3:00 a.m. By then, the situation had grown increasingly dire. Capt. Staples needed to save those on board, including the valuable cargo of enslaved men, women, and children he had forcibly conveyed out of Alexandria.[5]

Although this voyage of the *Comet* was as a slave ship, the brig often transported not people but more mundane cargoes of sugar, molasses, and tobacco. In 1830 alone, Staples piloted the ship from New Orleans to Alexandria, moving in the reverse direction of the coastwise domestic slave trade. In April, he journeyed to St. Thomas in the Virgin Islands. The return trip carried him to New York City in early June. Later that same month, the *Comet* departed for San Juan, Puerto Rico.

The *Comet*'s frequent runs back and forth to the Caribbean could not lawfully have been made while carrying enslaved human cargoes for sale. Ever since Congress prohibited U.S. participation in the international slave trade starting January 1, 1808, measures had been implemented to carefully monitor waterborne shipments leaving and entering U.S. ports. Manifests were filled out, double-checked, and signed off prior to departure and carefully inspected for accuracy upon arrival. Port authorities noted discrepancies. The same law that forbade the transatlantic slave trade, however, affirmed the legality of the coastwise domestic slave trade, which the *Comet* was engaged in as 1830 drew to a close. In early November, when Staples pulled into port in New Orleans from Richmond, Virginia, he was carrying both hogsheads of tobacco and, no doubt, victims swept up by the domestic slave trade.[6]

Those most likely ensnared in the human traffic were the surplus slaves found in Upper South states such as Virginia and Maryland. There, slave traders from Baltimore, Washington, DC, Richmond, and smaller communities, as well as the various agents they dispatched, scoured the countryside, paying cash for slave owners' excess or unwanted bondpeople, or those sold under economic duress to put quick cash in sellers' pockets. After accumulating a sufficient shipment, the slave dealers then sometimes marched their captives south and west, over land, in chained pairs known as coffles, in order to sell them at much higher prices in the slave markets of the Deep South. But this was a grueling journey of at times hundreds of miles, hard on the human merchandise. Traders often preferred conveying their prisoners southward through the saltwater slave trade, aboard ships like the *Comet*.[7]

The *Comet* was not as large as many of the brigs or barques customarily employed in the antebellum era's coastwise domestic slave trade, with less than 139 tons of cargo capacity. By contrast, some ships boasted 180 to sometimes more than 500 tons. All of these coastwise slave ships were wider and deeper but also slower than the transatlantic slaving vessels constructed to outrun the British patrol ships that prowled the open Atlantic to crack down on the illegal importation of enslaved Africans. Domestic slavers like the *Comet*, shuttling captives from one U.S. port to another and engaging in a perfectly lawful commerce, needed neither high-speed capabilities nor cannon to defend themselves.

If outfitted like other coastwise slavers of its era, the *Comet* would have had a pair of compartments below deck—one for enslaved men, one for enslaved women—separated by a partition. The sleeping quarters would have been cramped, no more than about two feet high, three feet wide, and five or six feet deep. Packing enslaved cargoes like cattle made the air below deck thick and still. The fumes emanating from vomit, urine, and feces produced an overwhelming toxic stench. The conditions facilitated the spread of smallpox and other virulent diseases on board. Domestic slave-trading voyages were only shorter than the transatlantic journeys of an earlier time, but not necessarily any better.[8]

The 164 enslaved captives crammed onto the *Comet* in December 1830 further augmented their number at sea. On December 23, one of the seventy-seven female slaves on board gave birth. Susan was nineteen years old, five feet four inches tall, and "yellow" in complexion, an indication of her mixed-race ancestry. Her unidentified child entered the world a hostage on board a slave ship, presumably destined for a lifetime of unfreedom.[9]

Three-fourths of the *Comet*'s prisoners were being shipped to the Crescent City for sale by the Alexandria-based firm of Franklin & Armfield. Working out of their office on Duke Street, Isaac Franklin and John Armfield were the nation's premier slave dealers from the late 1820s through the mid-1830s, shipping 1,000 to 1,200 enslaved people annually to the Old Southwest. Their profits from slave sales were staggering, approaching the modern-day equivalent of a million dollars per year. Franklin & Armfield supplied 125 of the *Comet*'s captives; Thomas

William Overley of Maryland accounted for the balance. He consigned forty enslaved people on the *Comet* to a member of the Baltimore-based Woolfolk slave-trading clan for whom he may have worked as an agent. In compliance with maritime slave-trading law, Overley and Armfield each swore before the port collector George Brent in Alexandria that the 164 enslaved persons listed on the manifest were "legally held to service or bondage, and that none" had been smuggled unlawfully into the United States since January 1, 1808. Capt. Staples gave an identical oath and verified the manifest's accuracy. With that, the customs house cleared the *Comet* for departure, granting the brig "permission . . . to proceed to the Port of New Orleans."[10]

The largest slave market in all of North America, New Orleans bore witness to the magnitude of a domestic slave trade and forced migration that tore a million people from family and friends in the East. From 1800 to 1860, some one hundred thousand were forced to pass involuntarily through the Crescent City en route to new sites of toil and exploitation.[11] But the captives aboard the *Comet* would never make it there. In the early morning hours of January 3, 1831, they found themselves stranded on a reef 850 miles east-southeast of Louisiana, aboard a ship in peril.

With the *Comet* perched precariously upon a reef, the seven men who navigated the vessel sprang to action. Well before daybreak, Capt. Staples and his crew "occupied themselves in saving a part of the provisions . . . , together with the [several white] Passengers and a part of the Slaves," placing them on the *Comet*'s long boat. First mate Stephen Foxwell piloted them toward land at Spanish Cay. Staples followed in the small boat, carrying "a load of Baggage" belonging to the white passengers and crew. The crew returned to the *Comet* at 5:00 a.m. By that time, after six hours ensnared on the reef, the brig finally bilged. Saltwater sloshed into the hole smashed into the ship's hull, and the *Comet* slowly began to sink. Crew members faced a new urgency to rescue the enslaved people, most of whom remained on board, having been left behind to liberate precious space on the long and small boats for white passengers and their belongings.[12]

At about 7:00 a.m., Capt. Joseph Curry, fishing from his sloop *Sarah*, spied the wreck of the *Comet*. Like other seafarers in the Bahamas for the past century and a half, Curry made his living at least in part through wrecking, the opportunistic salvaging and reselling of valuable cargoes recovered from sunken vessels. Numerous poor white and Black sailors engaged in the practice. Curry steered the *Sarah* and "two other sail Boats" under his command, the wreckers *Carpenter's Revenge* and the *Dash*, toward the *Comet*, set anchor, and gingerly climbed aboard. Finding the slave ship "in a very dangerous state," Curry arranged for his vessels "and a Launch belonging to the Comet, to save the Lives of the Slaves" still teetering unsteadily on a sinking brig. As Curry made preparations, at about 8:00 a.m., the aft of the *Comet* sank beneath the waves. The stern submerged, the desperate captives, who must have been unchained if they had been securely fastened in the hold the preceding night, scrambled to the bow of the vessel. From there, they clambered onto the other boats, and Curry conducted them to Spanish Cay. All were saved. No passenger—white or Black, voluntary or involuntary—perished in the accident. Capt. Staples returned to the *Comet* at 10:00 a.m., followed by the *Sarah*, the *Carpenter's Revenge*, and the *Dash*. They salvaged whatever last provisions from the wreck they could and stripped the brig of anything usable before leaving at 2:00 p.m. to regroup and recover on Spanish Cay. A reflective Capt. Staples understood "that the lives of the Crew, Passengers, and Slaves" had made only the narrowest of escapes. He admitted that, absent "the timely assistance of the Wrecking Vessels, . . . the greater part of the Persons on board the Brig must inevitably have perished."[13]

The *Comet* castaways and their rescuers passed the night on Spanish Cay, but shelter on the island was only a temporary expedient. "This key," which lay five or six miles off the northeastern coast of Great Abaco, according to reports, "is in fact a bare, desert and uninhabited rock, furnishing neither vegetation or fresh water for the use of man or beast." The three vessels under Capt. Curry's command lacked adequate water and supplies for all the people they had saved. So at 8:00 the next morning, the *Sarah*, *Carpenter's Revenge*, and *Dash* shuttled the 165 enslaved captives seventeen or eighteen miles southeast to Green Turtle Cay, another barrier island off Great Abaco. They arrived at about 11:00 p.m., immediately found water, and proceeded to bake bread by firelight. A small town lay nearby. Due to head winds, Curry's three ships and the stranded Americans remained at Green Turtle Cay from January 5 to January 7. During that time, the enslaved captives were allowed to "[go] freely on [the boats], occasionally for a short time to wash their Cloathes & procure refreshments." The *Comet* refugees also got to work laying new floors in the three wrecking vessels and outfitting them "in a more commodious manner for the slaves," adding "the necessary [sleeping] platforms for their comfort and convenience."[14]

Isaac Staples's thoughts turned to those captives. He was the captain of a slave ship, and six different consignees in New Orleans expected the arrival of a valuable shipment. If each bondperson sold on average for $500, the human capital from the *Comet* represented a cumulative market value of $82,500, or about $2.5 million in modern currency. Staples needed to get that living, breathing merchandise to its intended destination. He therefore parleyed with Capt. Joseph Curry and "endeavoured to make terms with the Wreckers to convey the Slaves to Key West or some other Port of the United States." Doing so would take the wrecking vessels away from the Bahamas and out of their jurisdiction, however, so Staples's request was "positively refused." Captains of the *Sarah*, *Carpenter's Revenge*, and *Dash* "insisted on conveying the Passengers, Slaves, and materials of the Wreck to the Island of New Providence," the location of the Bahamas' colonial capital at Nassau. Staples strenuously objected to the plan, but, "having no other means of assistance on hand, and responsibility of the lives of so many persons destitute of provisions devolving on himself," he relented and "accede[d] to their terms." On the morning of January 8, the three wreckers departed Green Turtle Cay with everyone taken off the *Comet*. They proceeded first to Man-O-War Cay, and from there to Little Harbor on Great Abaco Island. Departing Little Harbor at 9:00 p.m. on the ninth, with favorable winds, they skirted Great Abaco, sailing an additional eighty nautical miles to the south, reaching the harbor at Nassau on January 11.[15]

ENTRANCE TO PORT NASSAU.

Entrance to Port Nassau, Bahamas.

When Isaac Staples, his crew, the white passengers, and those held captive aboard the sunken *Comet* reached New Providence in 1831, that one Bahamian island maintained a population of almost 2,500 enslaved people and nearly as many free people of color. In Nassau, Black residents outnumbered the white minority four to one. The islands had a long relationship with the institution of slavery. During the American Revolution, loyalists opposed to the colonies' independence fled the fledgling United States with some six thousand bondpeople in tow, doubling the Bahamas' white population and tripling that of the enslaved. After the British government abolished its participation in the transatlantic slave trade in 1807, the Royal Navy deposited intercepted illegal shipments of captive Africans on New Providence and other islands of the Bahamas as well. Those liberated from their chains and resettled throughout the colony numbered about five thousand in total by the time the *Comet* castaways reached Nassau.[16]

On January 12, the morning after their arrival, daybreak revealed a series of warehouses built of square stone blocks fronting the harbor. Capt. Staples swiftly began making arrangements for the removal of his enslaved cargo to New Orleans. He first went to the United States' consular agency office to consult John Storr, the U.S. commercial agent at Nassau. Storr advanced the captain $4,000 for the acquisition of a new slave ship and "every thing necessary to enable him to proceed to his original port of destination." Staples "without delay" struck a bargain to procure a vessel, a brig of 126 tons, for the resumption of the journey. He and his crew began weighing down the replacement ship with "the requisite ballast" and loading the water and provisions necessary to sustain themselves, the passengers, and the enslaved men, women, and children for the duration of the voyage.[17]

They had scarcely prepared the vessel for its journey when officers from the customshouse at Nassau arrived with a notification for John Storr and Capt. Staples. The directive ordered them to cease readying the ship for departure and commanded that they "detain the slaves until the Governor and Crown Officers were consulted." Word had reached Thomas B. Wylly, solicitor general for the Bahamas, of the arrival of the *Comet*'s enslaved cargo into His Britannic Majesty's realm. Wylly expressed concern to Sir James Carmichael-Smyth, governor of the Bahamas, that the bondpeople's presence in the colony might violate the British Parliament's Act for the Abolition of the Slave Trade. That law, made effective May 1,

1807, ended the slave trade within the British Empire. Even though slavery survived as an institution in the Bahamas, the appearance twenty-four years later of a cargo of enslaved persons in Nassau's harbor was an arresting sight. The *Comet*'s manifest would have shown that the vessel was participating in the United States' lawful domestic slave trade rather than in the forbidden international slave trade, but royal officials needed time to deliberate and consider the proper course of action under British law. They knew of the *Somerset v. Stewart* decision of 1772, which held that enslaved people landed on British soil could not be forced to return to slavery, but the ruling said nothing with respect to bondpeople carried to colonies within the British Empire. Perhaps the human cargo was owed its freedom, "on the ground that these persons had been landed on two of the out Islands of the Bahamas." In the meantime, Gov. Carmichael-Smyth ordered customshouse officials to deny Staples permission to continue his journey. He and his newly purchased slave ship were going nowhere.[18]

Meanwhile, the captives rescued from the *Comet* remained on board the three wrecking vessels and, from their vantage point in the harbor, could probably see Staples's substitute slave ship being equipped for their imprisonment and transport to market. Under the cover of darkness, nine enslaved men decided to jump from their floating jail into the harbor and swim to shore at Nassau the night of January 12. The following evening, two others followed suit. Nineteen-year-old Nelson Lemon, a Black man being shipped by Franklin & Armfield to Isaac Franklin's nephew James in New Orleans for sale, and another enslaved companion, whom he identified as thirty-one-year-old Toby Vincent, "let themselves down in the water" in "the middle of the night . . . and swam to the land." Certainly unaware that British colonial officials were then weighing their fates, these eleven enslaved men resolved to self-liberate rather than resume the forced journey to the American South.[19]

The enslaved people detained in the harbor did not enjoy a magnanimous reception among the white population of New Providence. To the contrary, their presence generated a "good deal of excitement . . . , for fear these negroes would be let loose in the colony." Giving voice to jittery whites' grave concerns about the menacing appearance of enslaved cargoes offshore was the provincial House of Assembly for the Bahama Islands, then in session in Nassau. Speaker of the House Thomas B. Wylly, dressed in his robe and carrying his ceremonial mace, followed by fellow members of the House,

The Government House in Nassau, Bahamas.

strode directly to the Government House on January 14 and submitted a petition to Sir James Carmichael-Smyth, the Bahamas' colonial governor since May 1829. An abolitionist, Carmichael-Smyth demonstrated throughout his tenure as governor sympathies with the enslaved people of the islands. Already he had spearheaded an effort to end the corporal punishment of enslaved women in the Bahamas, the source of just one of the many clashes he had with the Bahamian legislature and certain influential whites in the islands over the issue of slavery in the British colony.[20]

The legislators opened by stating their extreme anxiety over "the Cargo of American Creole Slaves . . . lately cast by shipwreck on our shores" while in transit from one U.S. port to another. Although the lawful slave trade to the Bahamas had long since concluded, slavery remained a fact of life in the Bahamas in 1831, as did the negative racial assumptions held by white Bahamians. They widely considered the enslaved people cast upon their shores a "dangerous . . . class of negroes." According to the memorial, "American Negroes" combined "the characteristic want of thought and foresight, almost inseparable from a state of slavery," with "the intelligence and cunning of the lower order of freeman." It was, in their estimation, a volatile mixture threatening the safety of the Bahamas' greatly outnumbered white population. Adding to legislators' suspicions, the enslaved persons aboard the wreckers had been swept up in the U.S. domestic slave trade, which often selected for sale those whom masters accused of errant behavior or wrongdoing. Bahamian whites assumed that enslaved people's "profligate habits," "vices," and "crimes" were "notoriously" the cause "of the deportation of Slaves from the Atlantic states" to the Old Southwest. They rejected the influx of a population of presumed enslaved ne'er-do-wells in their midst.[21]

The House's petition adamantly opposed granting freedom in the Bahamas to the enslaved individuals detained on board the wreckers in Nassau's harbor. In addition to concerns that possible liberation would imperil the security of white Bahamians, House members upheld masters' right to hold enslaved property. The institution of slavery remained legal in the Bahamas, and British subjects resident on the islands possessed the right to own human capital. As long as that right was "constitutionally recognized, by the laws of the empire," the House could not condone freedom for "the like property of our foreign neighbours" "without a deep sense of humiliation" and feeling of "inhospitable violation of . . . principle." House members were "deeply impressed with a sense of the injustice of the measures" that could be "enforced against the [U.S.] owners of the slaves." Their petition warned that any "severe application of the law, or mistaken principle of moral justice," which might lead to the manumission of the *Comet* slaves, would "spread a general panic throughout the Country." The *Comet* captives must not be "set loose among" us, the memorial implored, and "thrown, in a state of newly acquired freedom," upon the white people of the Bahamas. Instead, they ought to be returned to "their lawful Owners" so that they might resume their journey and thereby "relieve us" of their presence.[22]

House members closed their petition by reminding the governor of a bill that had been introduced during the most recent session of Parliament back in London. One of its provisions stated that "if any slaves, the property of foreigners, should be cast away by shipwreck, at any of His Majesty's Colonies in which slavery is established by Law, the Governor of such colony should, at his discretion, restore such Slaves to their Owners, whenever a claimant should be present on their behalf." The passage of the proposed law had been delayed by the death of King George IV on June 26, 1830, but lawmakers in the Bahamas invited their governor to assume that the measure had already passed and "is probably, by this time, a law of the region." While they rationalized a delay in communication, in truth, the proposed law was never implemented. Nevertheless, House members urged the governor "to prevent any attempt being made, from any quarter, to inflict on the country so serious an evil" as the liberation of those imprisoned on the wrecking vessels.[23]

Sir James Carmichael-Smyth composed a reply to the petitioners the same day that they descended upon his residence. Despite his abolitionist proclivities, he addressed them with the careful words of a politician. The governor expressed an eagerness to comply with its signatories' "solemn and serious" wishes, but he also refused to act in haste. He explained that his course of action "must depend upon the opinion of the Law officers of the Crown" then examining all of the evidence laid before them. The case of the shipwrecked captives might also be referred to the appropriate tribunal for adjudication. Regardless of the eventual outcome, the governor assured the House members that he would continue his "unceasing efforts for the preservation of the public tranquility."[24]

Until a final determination could be made, Carmichael-Smyth relayed instructions to the customs officers. On the afternoon of Saturday, January 15, four days after the shipwrecked slaves' first appearance in the harbor, William Melbourne Fox, His Majesty's searcher and waiter of the customs for the port of Nassau, seized from Capt. Staples "the whole number" of enslaved persons from aboard the wreckers on the ground that landing on two outer islands of the Bahamas violated "an act of the Imperial Parliament of Great Britain relating to the abolition of the Slave Trade." Taking the captives from the *Comet* into custody in Nassau, Fox released the three emptied wrecking vessels from detention.[25]

The customs officer then initiated a legal proceeding known as a salvage or libel suit against the enslaved people in the Instance Court of Vice Admiralty for the Bahamas, alleging that the prisoners should be forfeited under British law. The Crown had empowered vice admiralty courts throughout the British Atlantic world to liberate shiploads of captives rescued from the illegal African slave trade. This case differed in that it concerned a U.S. domestic slave-trading vessel operating legally, but until the date of the upcoming trial, Fox needed to hold the *Comet*'s enslaved cargo

The enslaved captives from the *Comet* were kept on Hog Island, across from Nassau, while British authorities determined what to do with them.

securely. He therefore sent the captives to a place "immediately opposite to the Town of Nassau," known as Hog Island. Later rechristened Paradise Island, in 1831 the 685-acre tract of sand five miles long and less than a mile wide was best known as home to roaming herds of wild pigs. There, the *Comet* prisoners were "quartered in Barracks . . . under the charge of the officers of the Customs" as Capt. Staples filed the first of several formal protests concerning the seizure and libel against his cargo and until the Vice Admiralty Court decided whether he could reclaim possession of the enslaved merchandise.[26]

The captives on Hog Island were fairly typical of those caught up in the U.S. domestic slave trade. According to the slave manifest from the *Comet*, in age, eight were thirty or older; the oldest sixty. But the domestic slave trade generally desired younger, healthy, able-bodied captives capable of enduring the rigors of strenuous labor on cotton and sugar plantations. Almost half aboard the *Comet* were from fifteen to twenty years old. Seventeen were less than ten, including two infants. In complexion, 127 of the original 164 captives were described as black, nineteen as brown, twelve as mulatto, and six as yellow. Three were exceptionally tall for the era, topping six feet. At six feet two and a half inches, the black twenty-one-year-old Arthur Spady stood like a giant among enchained men.[27]

Although Spady and a majority of all the *Comet* prisoners were transported as individuals, entirely separated from loved ones, as victims of the domestic slave trade usually were, this particular enslaved cargo also included seventeen complete or partial family units totaling fifty-three people. Several enslaved parents were held captive with their children. Sixteen-year-old Peggy Irvine had her child, Mary E., with her. Likewise, Eveline Smith had been sent away with a four-month-old daughter named Sarah. The twenty-six-year-old mother Catherine Mapp also had her boys Joe, five, and Nathan, three, at her side. The largest families from the *Comet* were the Douglasses and the Baileys. Richard Douglass and his wife, Hannah, were headed south with their five children: Lydia, age twelve; James, nine; Robert, eight; Martha, five; and Eliza, three. Six Bailey siblings—Lavinia, James, Dick, Lawson, Hamilton, and Matilda—ranging in age from thirteen to six, were transported together as well. Probable siblings Mary and Joshua Jackson and sisters Charlotte and Jane Marshall, all between thirteen and fifteen years old, may perhaps have taken comfort in staying together, although their ties would likely be severed once they reached the slave markets of New Orleans.[28]

As this group bided its time on Hog Island, the eleven who had swum to shore found their initial encounters with freedom fleeting. The two enslaved men who escaped on January 13, Nelson Lemon and the captive he identified as Toby Vincent (but based on police records probably Summerset Nutter, a twenty-two-year-old Black man consigned to John Woolfolk in New Orleans), "walked about [Nassau] until they met a negro man who directed them to go to the Governor," a man with known abolitionist sympathies. Taking the stranger's advice, the pair found their way "to the Government House to claim protection." Carmichael-Smyth directed them to Robert Duncome, police magistrate for the island of New Providence, who took statements from Lemon and Nutter on the thirteenth. Each man knew the name of the respective slave traders transporting them, that Isaac Staples was the captain of the sunken slave ship, and that they were intended for sale in New Orleans. They recounted for Duncome the story of their wreck and rescue, although neither could recall the name of the brig *Comet* specifically. After examining Lemon and Nutter, colonial authorities deposited the escapees in the city workhouse, where they presumably performed forced labor alongside its other inmates. The other nine escapees also apparently entered the workhouse, or house of correction. It is not clear if they, too, had consulted the governor immediately upon reaching Nassau or if they had attempted to live anonymously as free men before being picked up. Either way, these eleven prisoners were excluded from the prosecution pending before the Vice Admiralty Court. In late January, when Carmichael-Smyth wrote Frederick John Robinson, Viscount Goderich, a former prime minister serving as Great Britain's secretary of state for war and the colonies, he shared his intention "not to permit these eleven Men to be taken away as slaves," regardless of the outcome of the *Comet* captives' case. In having dared to plunge into Nassau's harbor and flee to shore, Carmichael-Smyth believed they had earned their freedom.[29]

Among Bahamian authorities, the governor's order to seize the remaining 154 shipwrecked slaves from the wreckers did not meet with unanimous approval. Two customshouse officials on January 20 wrote the Board of Customs in London directly to share their misgivings. Collector James Walker and comptroller W. Webb predicted two possible outcomes, both in their view unfortunate, from the confiscation of the *Comet*'s human cargo. On one hand, if the Vice Admiralty Court overturned the seizure of the enslaved people from the sunken brig, "the cause of humanity itself must suffer" as the captives' mounting "hopes of freedom" would be cruelly dashed. If, on the other hand, the court confirmed the seizure, leading to the manumission of the enslaved men, women, and children temporarily housed on Hog Island, "a serious expense may be entailed on the [Bahamian] public."[30]

Meeting with Gov. Carmichael-Smyth before his decision to seize the captives from the wreckers, Walker and Webb had hoped that he "might entertain similar views" and prevent "all proceedings" concerning the *Comet*. Strong arguments could be made not to intervene in the case of the shipwrecked slaves. The twenty-first section of Parliament's act abolishing the slave trade permitted "the trans[s]hipping, and assisting at sea of any Slave or Slaves that shall be in any Ship or Vessel in distress," as the *Comet* certainly had been. Or, if the governor somehow disagreed with that plain understanding of the law, perhaps he would avoid "interference with the coasting Trade" of the neighboring United States, "a Friendly Power." When conferring with Carmichael-Smyth and Solicitor General (and Speaker of the House) Thomas B. Wylly, Walker and Webb also mentioned the bill known to be circulating in Parliament concerning "the accidental arrival of Slaves" in British colonies—a category of bondpeople

Bahamian whites feared that captives emancipated from U.S. slave ships would end up on the streets and be a burden to the public.

not covered by the act outlawing the transatlantic slave trade. In reply, the governor and solicitor general stated that the proposed measure "was itself a proof" that the present law was "deficient" and could only be remedied by parliamentary action. Further clarity was required.[31]

Walker and Webb further attempted to persuade Carmichael-Smyth and Wylly through the power of historical precedent. They observed that a similar cargo of shipwrecked American slaves in 1818 was allowed entry into Nassau's harbor "and then cleared out at this Custom house for their original destination" without impediment. The two customshouse officers likely referenced the slaving schooner *Young Sachem*, piloted by Lawrence W. Smith, which left Norfolk, Virginia, for New Orleans in April 1818. Like the *Comet*, it wrecked near the Abaco Islands. In that case, William Vesey

Munnings, administering the colonial government during the temporary absence of the governor, authorized two Bahamian wrecking vessels to deliver the captain, crew, white passengers, and 101 enslaved captives to Charleston, South Carolina, for the resumption of their journey. What distinguished the *Young Sachem* from the *Comet* was that Walker and Webb "could not prove" in the earlier case that "any actual landing of the people had taken place in any part of the Bahamas," a crucial distinction that Wylly believed "all such cases must entirely hinge upon." Carmichael-Smyth took his cues from other historical sources: a pair of letters written by Earl Bathurst in 1825 "directing that any Foreign Slaves who arrived in the colony should not be restored to Foreign Masters." That year, Britain had curtailed the intercolonial slave trade between its possessions, giving rise to a range of questions surrounding the slave trade. Until Parliament enacted clear measures for him to follow, Carmichael-Smyth resolved to act on Bathurst's instructions, which were more recent than the *Young Sachem* incident. Walker and Webb left their audience with the governor and solicitor general disappointed and in grudging agreement with the logic of their superiors' decision-making. Even as the customs agents acknowledged their own opinions as "unsound," they still felt compelled to write the Board of Customs to register their dissenting and "contrary views."[32]

The colonial House of Assembly launched its own investigation into the *Comet* disaster, questioning Capt. Staples; mate Stephen Foxwell; Joseph Curry, commander of the wrecking vessels; searcher William Melbourne Fox; and U.S. commercial agent John Storr. The House committee acknowledged on January 28 that, ultimately, the Vice Admiralty Court would decide the fate of the enslaved people from the *Comet*. But its report to the governor clearly preferred the release of the captives back into Capt. Staples's custody, on multiple grounds. First was the economic consequences of detention. If the American owners were denied the return of their slaves, Great Britain would have to absorb the costs of that decision, for surely the shippers deprived of a valuable investment would demand recompense. As the House asked rhetorically, since "our laws recognize the legal right to such property in ourselves, on what just principle can we deny the same to others, whose laws in that respect correspond with our own"?[33]

The committee next turned to the absurdities of the existing slave trade law under which the *Comet*'s human cargo was detained. The statute outlawing the slave trade criminalized the introduction of "foreign Slaves to

[Bahamian] Shores." If the glorified rock of Spanish Cay were generously considered "*land*," committee members posited that Capt. Joseph Curry and his crew, who had rescued the enslaved people from the reef and deposited them there, were technically the guilty parties deserving prosecution under the law. Of course that idea was preposterous: "the monstrous injustice and inhumanity of the idea of punishing a man for saving the lives of unfortunate unoffending sufferers from shipwreck, . . . protected the sailors from prosecution." But by the same "principle of rational equity," the committee asked, why should the equally "unfortunate and unoffending" slave traders suffer the stern application of the law and "a confiscation of their property"? A fateful accident cast the human cargo upon Bahamian shores, and nothing more. Here, the committee underscored the point, also made by Collector Walker and Comptroller Webb, that section 21 of the act forbidding the slave trade authorized the aid of slave ships in distress. Surely it could not be "criminal to accept . . . such assistance" when the alternative was death.[34]

The committee report finally pondered the all-important social ramifications of the governor's seizure. If the enslaved people from the *Comet* had been an illegal shipment from Africa, its enchained prisoners, by law, would be "bound out for a limited time of service among the Inhabitants" of the Bahamas. Since the *Comet* was not a transatlantic slaver making an illicit delivery, the captives, if emancipated by the Vice Admiralty Court, would "almost certain[ly]" be granted immediate freedom, incorporating directly into "the free black and coloured population of the Colony," with no transitional period of apprenticeship.[35]

Apprehensive lawmakers warned that the release of 165 formerly enslaved Southerners onto the island of New Providence marked "a perilous addition" to the Bahamas' "already too numerous class" of free Black people. Their report then exposed white Bahamians' racist assumptions about Black laziness and criminality. "The unconquerable aversion of negroes to voluntary agricultural labour is too well known, and now universally admitted to be doubted of," it read, and in the Bahamas, "a very large proportion of the people" would struggle to find any other form of employment. As a result, should those aboard the *Comet* not be restored to Capt. Staples but instead "be thrown at large upon the community to seek subsistence as they can, there are but very few among them, in the opinion of the Committee, who will not speedily come under the description of common vagrants or worse": criminals. The House committee predicted that their criminal futures would cause them to be transported out of the colony anyway, "if not otherwise got rid of" preemptively. In short, the white Bahamian public did not want the added burden of foreign-born freedpeople on the islands. The House of Assembly called upon Gov. Carmichael-Smyth simply to return the *Comet* captives to their American owners.[36]

The publication of the House committee report in colonial newspapers and the copies that circulated through the British colonial bureaucracy were intended to "prevent the recurrence of a similar evil in [the] future," but they also put Gov. Carmichael-Smyth on the defensive. Though he took the advice of the law officers of the Crown, he ultimately made the controversial decision to seize the enslaved people from the *Comet*. The governor felt compelled to write to the colonial secretary, Lord Goderich, who likewise received a copy of the committee report critical of the governor's handling of the *Comet* castaways. In his missive, the governor underscored the significance he attached to Earl Bathurst's circular of 1825, further citing the instructions Lord Bathurst gave in a dispatch to the governor of Antigua for dealing with "slaves from any foreign Island or state arriving in any of His Majesty's colonies." The governor remained resolute: "the Law till altered must be obeyed and enforced as it stood."[37]

Public interest in the fate of the *Comet* castaways grew not only in the Bahamas but also in the United States. Seafaring vessels carried newspaper accounts of the unfolding story from the Caribbean to U.S. port towns and cities. The citizens of Pawtucket, Rhode Island, read in their hometown paper the recommendation of the Bahamas House of Assembly that the bondpeople be restored to Capt. Staples. On January 30, the schooner *Pomona* reached Savannah, Georgia, with news from the Bahamian press as well as an anonymous white passenger rescued from the *Comet*, who surely offered a gripping firsthand account of the ordeal. Southern slave owners took intense interest in the outcome of the case, as slaving vessels in the domestic slave trade regularly sailed between the Florida coast and the Bahamian archipelago, a distance of as little as fifty miles. Any British refusal to produce the *Comet*'s cargo for its owners boded ill for the future of the South's human trafficking and would demand extra precautions to avoid similar disasters going forward. Suspicious of some Bahamian officials' commitment to slavery, the Southern press scoffed that eleven of the original captives aboard the *Comet* had "been suffered to escape. [T]his has been winked at by those in authority." Abolitionist newspapers in the North took notice of the case as well. William Lloyd Garrison began reporting on the *Comet* less than seven weeks after founding *The Liberator* in Boston.[38]

Outside observers could only speculate as to the outcome of the case. As Sir Carmichael-Smyth told Lord Goderich, "The business is now in a course of legal adjudication & will be decided by the proper tribunal." In the meantime, Capt. Staples registered various protests in Nassau and maintained regular contact with U.S. commercial agent John Storr, consulting him for "advice and protection" against the "arbitrary measures" imposed by the Bahamian government. Storr used his position to press for "all proper claims on behalf of the owners" of the *Comet*'s captives through the presentation of "remonstrances and memorials to the authorities" of the colony, emphasizing the peculiar "hardship of the case, the involuntary landing at the Island" forced "only by stress of weather, and other causes beyond [Staples's] control." These efforts yielded no results. Staples understood there was nothing more for him to do but await the verdict of the Court of Vice Admiralty. Upon the advice and aid of Storr, on January 26 or 27, Staples and most of the white passengers from the *Comet* boarded the schooner *Sarah Jane* in Nassau and sailed for New Orleans, minus the enslaved captives.[39]

In 1831, New Orleans was a city on the cusp of a tremendous boom fueled by cotton and slavery. The flush times of the 1830s would double the city's population to around one hundred thousand over the coming decade, making it the largest in the South, the third largest in the entire country, and the wealthiest in the nation. And it was all because of enslaved people like those Capt. Staples was obligated to leave behind on Hog Island. Upon reaching New Orleans, Staples and his mate, Stephen Foxwell, filed a public act of protest with notary public Carlile Pollock. Their statement documented the loss of the *Comet*, "the illegal seizure, arrest, and detention" of the captives on board, and the fact that Staples invested in Storr "all necessary Powers to prosecute the recovery of said property." The protest, though crediting the Bahamian wrecking vessels for saving the lives of all aboard the *Comet*, criticized the decision to carry the castaways to Nassau, as well as the actions of William Melbourne Fox, other customshouse officials, the governor, and all other colonial authorities for their roles in depriving American owners of their enslaved property. Staples and Foxwell emphasized that their slaving voyage was legal under U.S. law and that only "stress of weather" had accidentally cast them onto foreign soil. Through no fault of their own, their cargo was confiscated and detained. The captain and mate filed their protest on Monday, February 14.[40]

That very same day, hundreds of miles away in Nassau, the Instance Court of Vice Admiralty ruled on the case concerning the enslaved captives. The basic facts about what happened were not contested. At issue was simply whether or not the seizure of the *Comet*'s human cargo was justified under Britain's law abolishing the slave trade. Parties on each side of the question had previously submitted material relevant to the case to Judge William Vesey Munnings, so on February 14, opposing counsel had only to present their final arguments. Once again, the judge heard Staples's position: The prisoners on the slaver were shipped by U.S. citizens in compliance with U.S. law, and their rescue from the *Comet* and removal to Nassau "were acts of necessity arising out of circumstances of misfortune over which no human power had control." U.S. counsel contended that, because the captives did "not come within the intent and meaning of the statute" prohibiting the international slave trade in the British Empire, they were not "liable to seizure, forfeiture, or condemnation." The case should therefore rightfully be dismissed and the enslaved people restored to their American owners.[41]

William Vesey Munnings turned for legal guidance to a nearly thirteen-year-old letter written by Sir Christopher Robinson and the late Lord Gifford to then colonial secretary Earl Bathurst on August 27, 1818, after a famous maritime incident in Britain's Atlantic realm. In 1818, a Portuguese slave ship transporting captive Africans from Mozambique to Brazil, after landing briefly for provisions in Great Britain's Cape Colony, wrecked off the Cape of Good Hope, at the southern tip of Africa. Prompted by that incident, Robinson, then King's advocate and later judge of the High Court of Admiralty, and Attorney General Gifford jointly penned a missive clarifying the British government's legal positions on matters raised by the encounter. First, they determined that the British laws for abolishing the slave trade prohibited His Majesty's subjects in British colonies not only from directly trading in slaves but also from "aiding & assisting" those who did, should they end up in British ports. Second, they found that "a cargo of slaves" should not be regarded as "Africans illegally imported," for whom proceedings in the Court of Admiralty would be appropriate. Rather, they should be "treated as free persons on their landing in the colony, and . . . be provided for and taken care of as other distressed and helpless persons accidentally thrown upon the colony would be." Finally, because shipwrecked enslaved Africans were "free persons" rather than "Slaves illegally imported," colonial governors maintained "no power to deliver" them, "without their consent[,] to the person claiming ownership over them." Bathurst shared the Robinson/Gifford letter with Munnings in 1818, giving him explicit instructions to let their missive "frame [his] conduct" in the future.[42]

Munnings therefore dismissed the libel against the *Comet*'s slaves filed by searcher William Melbourne Fox. As the judge saw it, since the captives were shipwrecked, they could not be considered "Slaves illegally imported." Had he been present, Capt. Staples might have thought he would soon be setting sail for New Orleans with his human cargo. But, Munnings continued, once the castaways "actually landed" in the island chain of the Bahamas, he knew "of no Law under which they may lawfully be dealt with as Slaves within this Colony, or which will authorize their removal to a foreign Country" in the condition of slavery. The governor would have no lawful authority "to deliver up these Persons" to those "claiming ownership over them" without the consent of the enslaved themselves. The bill being considered in Parliament in 1830 that might have empowered colonial governors to return shipwrecked slaves to their owners to resume their journey implied that the governor maintained no such power at the present. With that measure's outcome unknown, Munnings insisted that he had no alternative: captives from the *Comet* "must . . . be treated and considered as free persons."[43]

Munnings understood the controversial nature of his verdict. His courtroom decision enshrined the Robinson/Gifford letter as bold legal precedent. Far from arbitrary, the ruling was consistent with a British Empire that actively policed the international slave trade and would soon begin to eradicate slavery from vast swaths of its territorial holdings. Munnings knew his ruling would be unpopular not only with Bahamian slave owners but also with searcher Fox and with white people throughout the colony, most of whom he understood regarded "an increased population" of Black people set free in Nassau as "onerous." But without statutes guiding him to rule otherwise, Munnings defended, "I am compelled to act according to my own humble judgment." With the full expectation that his decision would be appealed, he directed both parties to the suit to pay their own court costs.[44]

Ships from Nassau soon carried news of the Vice Admiralty Court's ruling to U.S. ports such as Charleston and Savannah, and by the end of

February, the American press circulated reports of the liberated slaves. Lazily republishing stories straight from Bahamian papers, they often described the freedpeople from the *Comet* as having been "turned loose" among the unfortunate residents of Nassau, "contrary to their [white Bahamians'] wishes" and their repeated, urgent appeals to the colonial government. But not all outlets took the same view. *The Liberator* headlined its story the BENEFIT OF A SHIPWRECK. The Baltimore-based *Genius of Universal Emancipation* celebrated the Vice Admiralty Court's decision as a new "obstacle" erected "in the way of prosecuting the *infernal* traffic in human flesh along our coast." But abolitionist publications' celebration of the ruling in the Bahamas proved premature.[45]

2

Insuring Human Merchandise

"I have delayed writing to you a few days," Ann M. Tutt wrote her brother in late January 1831, "with the hope that the servants would arrive." Tutt had recently moved from Loudoun County, Virginia, to Pensacola, where she reunited with her husband, Col. Charles P. Tutt, a U.S. Navy agent employed by the federal government. "I cannot say that I am pleased" with the Florida Territory, Mrs. Tutt confided. "It is the most poverty stricken Country in appearance I have ever seen. Neither do I like the inhabitants, with the exception of two or three." Adding to the difficulties of her transition to her new surroundings was the lack of the enslaved labor force to which she was accustomed. The nine people over whom the Tutts claimed ownership—sixty-year-old Dennis Young, the diminutive bondwoman Milly (only four feet seven inches tall), Richard (Dick) and Hannah Douglass, and the Douglasses' five children—had not traveled with her. Instead, her brother conveyed them to Alexandria, where he placed them aboard the *Comet*, bound for New Orleans for subsequent transshipment to Pensacola to rejoin their owners. "But I have heard nothing from them," Ann Tutt fretted at the end of January, "and feel a good deal of uneasiness on the subject."[1]

At the time she wrote her brother, Dennis Young, Milly, and the Douglass family were watching the hours pass on Hog Island. In another two weeks, Judge William Vesey Munnings determined that they were free persons. The ruling clearly indicated that the Tutt household would not be reunited with its enslaved property, nor would slave traders Franklin & Armfield with their bondpeople shipped on the *Comet* for resale in New Orleans. But all was not lost, financially. U.S. newspapers reported that Franklin & Armfield "had taken the precaution" of getting their valuable cargo "*insured*." "We understand," confirmed customshouse officials in the Bahamas, "that the Slaves were insured & that according to the American

Laws the proprietors will recover," for the "loss . . . will belong to the Underwriters."[2]

Domestic slave traders who carried enslaved people to the Old Southwest by slave ship, as well as slave owners forcibly relocating their bondpeople via waterborne routes, often took out policies to protect their valuable property. Marine insurance companies operating in port cities of the North, including the Nautilus Mutual Life Insurance Company (later New York Life), Aetna, and U.S. Life, offered such products. These policies were even more common in cities of the coastal South, such as Charleston and New Orleans. Dating back to Italian merchants of the Middle Ages, marine insurance alleviated the risks associated with maritime commerce and proved crucial to the expansion of seafaring trade. Such contracts were common during the transatlantic slave trade as a hedge against the unpredictability of any ocean crossing. Slave traders routinely protected their capital investment in the captive Africans they planned to sell in the Americas from the dangers of inclement weather, shipwreck, enemies on the high seas, and outbreaks of disease. Slave dealers deploying vessels in the saltwater domestic slave trade between Southern ports—still legal after 1808—continued the long-established custom of insuring enslaved cargoes through marine insurance firms.[3]

Unlike in England, where private underwriters such as Lloyd's of London drafted marine insurance contracts, chartered joint-stock corporations dominated the U.S. marine insurance industry after about 1810. These companies first appeared in Northern port cities such as Philadelphia in the early 1790s but within the decade found a welcoming environment in Southern ports as well. Domestic slave traders regularly took out policies with these marine insurance firms on enslaved cargoes shipped from the Upper to the Lower South, and slave owners migrating with their bondpeople via sailing vessel followed suit. Shippers paid premiums based on a small percentage of the total value of the lot of captives being transported for a policy that terminated upon completion of the voyage. The policies insured the lives of enslaved people against the many potential hazards of waterborne journeys. Yet maritime slave insurance functioned more as property than as life insurance. Monies disbursed by such policies accrued to owners rather than to a bondperson's family, policy values correlated to commodity prices in the slave market, and the terms of the policies were of short duration. Buttressing the domestic slave trade by design, maritime slave insurance illustrated the connections between slavery and the emerging capitalist world.[4]

The parties shipping human beings aboard the *Comet* had secured insurance on almost 90 percent of them. Altogether, 146 of the original 164 enslaved captives were covered under policies issued by three different New Orleans firms: the Louisiana State Marine and Fire Insurance Company, the Mississippi Marine and Fire Insurance Company, and the Merchants Insurance Company. The slave-trading firm of Franklin & Armfield alone collected tens of thousands of dollars from the policies it had taken out. After landing in Nassau, Capt. Staples promptly consulted John Storr, an "agent or attorney of several Insurance Companies, Underwriters or other Mercantile associations in New York and elsewhere in the United States." He arranged with Storr the financing for the acquisition of a replacement slave ship, but at some point prior to departing the Bahamas, the captain may also have discussed with him the possible ramifications—and future insurance payouts—should the Vice Admiralty Court refuse to restore the *Comet*'s enslaved cargo to his possession. When Staples arrived in New Orleans, he likely visited one or more of the city's insurance offices that stood to lose a substantial sum if the enslaved were not returned.[5]

When word of the court decision reached the Crescent City, insured owners deemed "it useless to make any further exertions to get possession" of their formerly enslaved property and instead pursued payment for their losses under the insurance clause protecting them "against the risk of '*detainment* by foreign Powers.'" Upon receiving the customary "proof of loss," the three insurance companies paid the amounts due under the policies they had issued. Collectively, they shelled out $71,330 (almost $2.2 million today) on covered claims.[6]

It was a terrible financial blow for the firms to absorb, and they did not intend to. Acting jointly, on June 30, 1831, the Louisiana State Marine and Fire Insurance Company, the Mississippi Marine and Fire Insurance Company, and the Merchants Insurance Company appointed New Orleans attorney Nathan Morse to represent their interests. Morse, a member of the board of directors for the Mississippi Marine and Fire Insurance Company, similarly acted as agent for the two individual slave owners without insurance policies on their human capital aboard the *Comet*. Sylvester (or Sylvanus) W. Mudd of Louisiana and Col. Charles P. Tutt, whose wife anxiously awaited the arrival of the family servants, each claimed nine uninsured enslaved people emancipated by the British colonial government of the Bahamas. Morse's instructions were straightforward enough: go to Nassau and "demand the slaves from the authorities of that place." It would have been naïve to assume the Bahamian government would deprive people of the freedom they had been granted, but, on the outside chance they were "delivered up," Morse was "to send them to New Orleans." Since the three insurance companies had already paid on their policies, the insurers may well have planned to sell the recovered chattel in the New Orleans slave markets, rather than swapping them for the cash previously disbursed. Perhaps the insurance companies could even recoup greater sums than they had paid out to ex-owners. More likely, however, Bahamian officials would refuse to hand over the liberated slaves. In that case, Morse was "to have all the necessary documents duly authenticated, and submit them to the Government of the United States."[7]

By the time Morse arrived in Nassau on August 3, 1831, much had happened with the captives liberated from the *Comet*. Three days after the court judgment in February, Customs Collector James Walker and Comptroller W. Webb informed both Attorney General William Martin and Solicitor General Thomas B. Wylly of the verdict and asked for advice on the propriety of pursuing an appeal. In weighing this decision, one important factor the customs officers raised was the desirability of avoiding for the colonial government "the additional expense of maintaining this numerous body of People." From a financial standpoint, the emancipated slaves "should be got rid of as soon as the interest and wishes of the Negroes themselves may render possible." Bahamian whites desperate to head off an influx of foreign ex-slaves into Nassau were already developing colonization schemes to expel them from the islands. They floated proposals to some of the newly liberated freedpeople on Hog Island "that they should remove as free Persons to Mexico or elsewhere"—an idea that was reportedly "favorably received." Similar plans to dispose of the *Comet*'s bondpeople were outlined at the customshouse as soon as the public learned of the Vice Admiralty Court's decision.[8]

The week after Judge Munnings's decision, the Court of Vice Admiralty directed a commission to conduct an appraisal of the emancipated slaves, still housed on Hog Island. The effort to assign monetary values to them would prove useful in the event the court's decision was appealed or if presented with U.S. demands for recompense for the loss of enslaved property. A three-man team crossed the narrow channel to Hog Island on

February 25, arranged the freedpeople into families and other groups, and inspected them to estimate their value. They made the appraisal in dollars rather than pounds, arriving at a total of $20,710. This amount represented only about 30 percent of the $71,330 that the three New Orleans insurance companies had paid out in covered losses.[9]

Compared with the heated market for enslaved people in the Lower Mississippi River Valley, enslaved property in the Bahamas was cheap. Despite a brief flirtation with cotton cultivation after the arrival of slave-owning American loyalists from South Carolina and Georgia in the mid-1780s, the Bahama Islands in the early nineteenth century failed to establish a plantation economy driven by the production of slave-grown agricultural staples. Frustrated planters gave up their lands and instead congregated in Nassau, while surplus enslaved laborers increasingly hired out their own time. Through these self-hire arrangements, they paid their owners a set weekly sum but otherwise were at liberty to seek employment of their choosing at the best rates they could find. With a blurry line between slavery and freedom in the Bahamas, slave prices were depressed. "Prime slaves"—the strongest and fittest, at the peak of their physical condition—"may be had here for one hundred to one hundred and fifty dollars each," declared John Storr, adding, however, that "the slaves wrecked [from the *Comet*], whose characters are unknown, most certainly would not sell for one half that sum." In New Orleans, where enslaved people like those aboard the *Comet* might run as high as $600 on average, these were obscenely low prices. Low valuations notwithstanding, Judge Munnings approved the appraisal on March 4.[10]

Variations in spelling aside, the list of assessed captives that Munnings endorsed matched the manifest from the *Comet*, with only a few exceptions. Three captives on Hog Island—one of the two Hensons, one of the three Lucindas, and one of the trio of Elizas—gave last names that did not match the surnames listed on the manifest signed in Alexandria. Perhaps optimistic about their odds of living as free people, the process of refashioning their own identities was already underway. Another detainee on Hog Island, named Philip, told assessors his last name was Sly, a surname not appearing on any other document. Claiming the moniker Sly implied that the prisoner was pulling one over on his captors by withholding his slave identity. He may have been preparing to reinvent himself as an emancipated man.[11]

Still, the captives' futures were uncertain. The seizure of the enslaved property from the *Comet* sparked internal debate and dissent within the

British colonial bureaucracy itself. Away from the public eye, government authorities debated among themselves whether they had executed the law properly. Their correspondence revealed a host of doubts, divisions, and administrative missteps.

When James Walker and W. Webb wrote the Board of Customs in London in January 1831 to object to the seizure of the *Comet*'s human cargo, they found a sympathetic audience among the commissioners of customs. Relaying Walker and Webb's report to the lords of the Treasury, the Board of Customs concurred that the shipwrecked slaves should have been promptly restored to Capt. Staples and sent on their way. "But as they have been seized under an order from His Excellency the Governor," they deferred to a higher authority, the lords commissioners of the Treasury. Until given commands from them, the Board of Customs "shall refrain from issuing instructions to [British] Officers at Nassau."[12]

Although the Vice Admiralty Court ruled in mid-February that the enslaved detainees should be released as free persons, the captives remained on Hog Island as officials in London debated their fate. For a month between their seizure and their court date, they were held at the Crown's expense, and Gov. Carmichael-Smyth confessed his "anxiety" over it. He did not wish to gain a reputation as a careless steward of His Majesty's fiscal resources. He wrote Lord Goderich, the colonial secretary, in early March to explain that "novel and very unexpected" circumstances had "made it necessary for me to interfere in the case of these American Negroes." But he had "no fault to find" with William Vesey Munnings's court. The decision, the governor admitted, was "perfectly correct and legal" and in "strict conformity" with Robinson and Gifford's letter to Earl Bathurst.[13]

The directives from 1818 that Munnings followed in declaring the *Comet*'s captives free in 1831 seemed clear enough to Carmichael-Smyth once he learned about them. Embarrassingly, he had been unaware of those commands prior to ordering the seizure and detention of the shipwrecked slaves for their appearance before the Vice Admiralty Court. "I had never seen or heard of the existence of such a document," he informed Lord Goderich. "It was not amongst the papers given over to me by Mr. Munnings, upon my arrival in this colony." Writing to the judge to inquire about it, Carmichael-Smyth was shocked when Munnings sent him "an original and duly authenticated" copy of the missing papers. Munnings, a long-serving colonial official, had received the Robinson/Gifford letter in early

1819, along with a circular composed by Earl Bathurst in reply. During the investigation into the absent documents, Robert Duncome, acting customs collector, admitted to having taken them out of Munnings's office, thereby withholding essential knowledge from the governor. Carmichael-Smyth railed against being made to look like a fool in front of his superiors. Had he been aware of the legal opinions given in 1818, he explained to Lord Goderich, "I, of course, would never have permitted the Custom House to sieze [*sic*] the American Negroes whom I should have considered as free Persons; and the expence attending the legal proceedings as well as that necessarily incurred in the case & in the feeding of such a number of People from the 2d January to the present period would have been avoided." To diminish the magnitude of his inadvertent error, he catalogued for Viscount Goderich a series of shipwrecks in the Bahamas dating back to 1818 that also led to legal proceedings and entailed costs for the Crown.[14]

The aggravated Carmichael-Smyth next turned to the issue of appealing the Vice Admiralty Court's decision. Attorney General William Martin and Solicitor General Thomas B. Wylly advanced their opinions to the governor on the matter of the appeal. To Carmichael-Smyth's consternation, they submitted "advice diametrically opposite to each other." The solicitor general stated that an appeal undertaken should go before the High Court of Admiralty of England, that valuations of the castaways should be gathered, and that "the Negroes should in the mean time be kept together by the Officers of the Customs." The attorney general understood that Munnings's verdict was based on the Robinson/Gifford letter and saw "no reason to call in question the correctness of that opinion." He advised against an appeal. The governor concurred.[15]

The decision held significant implications for the formerly enslaved people still biding their time on Hog Island. Carmichael-Smyth's priority was to "reliev[e] the Public from a heavy and useless expence." The governor could imagine no scenario under which the *Comet*'s captives would ever be "restored to Slavery or . . . given back to their former owners." He therefore encouraged the freedpeople "to engage themselves as Servants, as any other free People." As the governor concluded, "The sooner they were allowed to provide for themselves, & the Public . . . relieved from the expence of feeding them, the better." Just to be safe, "in the event of any claim for these Negroes being made, on the part of their former owners, by the American Government," Carmichael-Smyth took the precaution of having them "legally appraised & valued."[16]

On March 5, 1831, the Nassau-based *Royal Gazette* contained a public declaration about the castaways from James Walker and W. Webb: "Persons wishing to engage any of them as Servants are at liberty to proceed to Hog Island, and to make any agreement they may think proper with those whom they may select." Officials highlighted the group's range of available skills: "There are understood to be among them a few Mechanics and sailors, and there are indoor and outdoor Servants of both sexes. There are likewise a good number of promising Boys, and also some very young Gals." The *Comet*'s manifest identified seventeen enslaved children under the age of ten. In a veiled indictment of the American domestic slave trade, the notice added that, since many of the children were "without any parents," "it is hoped respectable people will be induced to take [them] into their service" and help raise them.[17]

The islands' whites proved less enthusiastic than their abolitionist governor about the prospect of hiring formerly enslaved Americans. Colonial authorities were obligated to intervene more directly in the lives of those unclaimed for work, plus those not yet suitable for labor. On March 8, Carmichael-Smyth took it upon himself to appoint James Walker and William Hield, the latter a justice of the peace for the Bahamas, the guardians of all children who "have no Parents with them" and charge them with apprenticing them out "for such a term of years as may to them appear most eligible." By March 19, the governor boasted to Lord Goderich of several placements.[18]

Whereas the abolitionist governor touted the achievement of incorporating former U.S. slaves into Bahamian life, New Orleans insurance company agent Nathan Morse was less impressed by news that various arrangements had dispersed "our Shipwrecked property" across the islands. Morse groused "that the Slaves were suffered to go at large among the Islands in full exercise of their freedom, under the protection of British Laws[,] in search of employment." In March and April, American newspapers complained that the residents of Nassau were "compelled" to give the freedpeople from the *Comet* "employment to keep them from starvation." Upon his arrival at New Providence in August, Morse reported seeing "droves of these miserable creatures in the public streets of Nassau," "in the full enjoyment of their newly acquired freedom, but . . . nothing else, ragged and filthy, begging for bread, and soliciting me to remove them to some Country in which they could procure subsistence by their labour."[19]

With a few exceptions, Morse's assessment of the individual freedpeople's condition was overwhelmingly grim. Capitalizing on a useful set of skills and benefiting from Carmichael-Smyth's abolitionist beliefs, one of the liberated castaways gained employment "as a Chief Cook by the Governor, at $10 per month." In addition, "a few other Mechanics" were earning somewhat lower wages than the chef. The "greater part" of the *Comet*'s cargo, however, labored "for mere subsistence." Like other Black Bahamians, the men may have farmed or fished. Black women often worked as vendors or hucksters, selling produce or handiwork. Two former captives had already died, including the Tutt family's eldest slave, Dennis Young. According to Morse, another "four or five" castaways had "fled from liberty and gone to America with a view of returning to voluntary servitude under their former masters." No available sources specify who those individuals were, or to whom they returned. That they would have opted for their previous lives suggests the hostility of the reception they received in the Bahamas and their difficulties in supporting themselves. Reports of onetime slaves seeking refuge with their old masters, if true, also smacked of slaveholder fantasies about their bondpeople's love for them and a validation of owners' benevolent paternalism. On the whole, Morse's portrait of the castaways' life in the Bahamas diverged sharply from that of Sir James Carmichael-Smyth, who informed Lord Goderich in early 1832 "that all the [former] Slaves [were] gaining their livelihood" and were "very quiet & industrious."[20]

Overall, Goderich agreed with Carmichael-Smyth that the Court of Vice Admiralty had correctly interpreted the law and that no appeal to the decision should be pursued. Doing so would only "subject His Majesty's Treasury to a heavy charge" without meaningfully contributing "to the comfort or security of the negroes themselves." The only exception Goderich could imagine was if searcher William Melbourne Fox, who had physically seized the enslaved cargo, wanted to file an appeal, at Fox's personal expense, "with a view to his interest in the Bounties." Judge Munnings determined that the *Comet* castaways had not been illegally introduced into the Bahamas, but he did not fault Fox for taking them up, noting "that there was probable cause" at the time. Fox later petitioned to receive a bounty for the enslaved people he escorted off the *Comet*, and in 1832, the Crown approved him "one guinea" for each of the 165 captives. His reward for "meritorious Services" totaled £173.5.[21]

For his part, Lord Goderich, himself an opponent of slavery, complimented Carmichael-Smyth's handling of "the Negroes who formed the Cargo of the American Brig" and was pleased to learn of the governor's "protection of the Infants" and of "the Adults . . . gaining their own livelihood." Personally, Goderich favored allowing the liberated slaves "to live in the Bahama Islands in a state of freedom, so long as they should conduct themselves peaceably, and earn their own subsistence," preferably under an apprenticeship. To protect the freedpeople from possible re-enslavement, he recommended that the governor issue "a Certificate of their having arrived in the Bahamas claiming His Majesty's protection" and declaring them free inhabitants of the colony; however, Goderich added, "If they should become burthensome to . . . Society[,] . . . either by pauperism or by any more gross misconduct, they might be removed." If that came to fruition, they would be expelled as free aliens, and not as slaves, and would not be sent anywhere "their personal freedom would be endangered."[22]

Lord Goderich's sole criticism was that the governor had preemptively ordered the appraisal of the *Comet*'s formerly enslaved cargo, which "may possibly be construed into an admission that the British Government are responsible for the value of these Negroes." He urged the governor to keep quiet about it. The viscount favored the emancipation of the enslaved people from the *Comet*, but he did not want to pay for them out of British coffers.[23]

By the summer of 1831, the British government gradually coalesced around a shared interpretation of how best to legally regard the shipwrecked slaves. Lord Goderich was crucial to creating that understanding. The commissioners of customs initially agreed that those enslaved aboard the *Comet* should have been returned to Capt. Staples, but prior to issuing an official reply sought advice from the lords of the Treasury. The secretary for the lords of the Treasury, in turn, wrote Lord Howick, a member of Parliament serving as an undersecretary of state for the colonies. Recognizing the importance of the issue laid before him, Lord Howick consulted Lord Goderich, who immediately sought to squelch any doubts within His Majesty's government over the actions taken in the Bahamas over the court ruling leading to the liberation of the *Comet*'s enslaved merchandise. Approving the outcome of the decision, Lord Goderich intended to silence "the opposite opinions" and directed Lord Howick to have "the Lords Commissioners of the Treasury . . . convey to the Board of Customs such Instructions as may prevent any further collision on this subject" between the customs commissioners in London and "the principal officers of Customs at the Port of Nassau."[24]

Howick passed along Lord Goderich's reasoning to his intended audience. The general thrust of the Act for the Abolition of the Slave Trade, Howick declared definitively, was "that no person shall be sent from any part of His M[ajesty]'s Dominions in a state of Slavery." Although the law did contain exceptions to the rule, none covered the landing of enslaved people on British shores after a wreck. The statute did authorize the "trans[s]hipment of slaves at Sea in case of distress," but for Goderich, the distinction between transshipment and "landing on the shore," as castaways from the *Comet* had done, was "sufficiently plain." This, at heart, marked "the conclusive objection to the compulsory restitution of these negroes to a state of Slavery."[25]

Goderich's emancipationist principles inspired his conviction that the British should "respect the claim of the Alien to protection," even if that meant violating the property rights of others. The shipwrecked slaves from the *Comet* "are Aliens, cast by stress of weather on the shores of His Majesty's Dominions," Goderich declared. "So long as they conduct themselves inoffensively and do not endanger the Peace of Society, they have the same general claim as any other Aliens to a hospitable reception, and to the protection of British Laws." No one would second-guess that position if the castaways had landed in Great Britain, and it should be no different for those who reached the shores of British colonies. Lord Goderich fully understood the consequences of that policy decision. "Foreign Powers," he told Lord Howick, "are, of course, at liberty to retaliate."[26]

By the time Nathan Morse arrived in Nassau in August to press the three New Orleans insurance companies' claims to the *Comet*'s onetime prisoners, the British government's position had hardened. "The subject," wrote one British official, "is of considerable importance in principle." While conceding that the *Comet* had violated no U.S. law or any treaty with Great Britain, the government insisted that the enslaved cargo could not be surrendered to its American owners. The individuals held captive on the slave ship were not "Slaves illegally imported" but accidental "Aliens" owed "a hospitable reception" and the protection of British laws. They could not be compelled to resume their journey to a life of continued bondage.[27]

Reclaiming the liberated bondpeople presented no small challenge to Morse. In ill health upon his arrival, he could not hold face-to-face meetings with Bahamian officials. Instead, he wrote a pair of letters, including one, on August 6, to Sir James Carmichael-Smyth. Identifying himself as the "authorized agent" of the Louisiana State Marine and Fire Insurance Company, the Mississippi Marine and Fire Insurance Company, and the Merchants Insurance Company of New Orleans, as well as of uninsured slave owners Sylvester W. Mudd and Charles P. Tutt, Morse explained that he knew "the Libel against the slaves has been dismissed" by the Instance Court of Vice Admiralty. Asserting that he was "not aware of any other statute . . . that would authorize the further detention of the [enslaved] property from its lawful owners," he informed the governor of his readiness "to receive the slaves provided there should be no further interference to prevent their trans[s]hipment to their original port of destination." Morse pressed the urgency of the case, stating, in a thinly veiled threat, "I am on the eve of my departure from this Island for the purpose of submitting this subject to the Gov[ernmen]t of the U.S." Carmichael-Smyth composed a brief reply that same day stating matter-of-factly that his instructions from the British government were "clear and precise." He simply acted according to the orders of Lord Goderich, the colonial secretary in London, and should therefore discontinue correspondence on the subject.[28]

Morse found a more receptive audience to his plea among other white elites in the Bahamas, especially lawmakers in the House of Assembly. On August 5, he penned a missive to George Campbell Anderson, the new Speaker of the House. Morse began by requesting information "in regard to the situation of these Slaves" and an explanation as to "why they are still withheld by this Gov[ernmen]t from their lawful owners." He peppered the Speaker with a barrage of questions. The U.S. agent wanted to know the British law that entitled "slaves belonging to subjects of a friendly Power" to be forfeited or condemned "when brought into a British Colonial Port" in distress. Did any statute or legislative enactment of either Great Britain or the Bahamas require their emancipation? If not, what circulars, orders, precedents, or proceedings justified such action? Morse wanted to see them. If slaves were freed merely by stepping foot on the shore of a British colony, how could slavery legally exist in the Bahamas or in any of the king's dominions? And since the landing was clearly involuntary, "the result of an unforeseen calamity," should not the owners be treated with "humanity" rather than a spirit of "vengeance"?[29]

George Campbell Anderson sent a long and generous reply to Morse's queries, which Morse received on August 9. The Speaker explained that Great Britain's act abolishing the slave trade was the only law with any possible relevance to the case of the *Comet.* Anderson believed that, because the *Comet* incident "was one of invincible necessity and unavoidable misfortune, . . . which no human foresight could avert, and arose completely from the act of God," it did not fall under "the purview of the statute." The strictest reading of the law, in fact, penalized the wreckers for rescuing the shipwrecked slaves, because they, and not the captain, were actually responsible for landing the castaways on Bahamian sands. Anderson confessed to Morse frankly, "There is not any British statute or other legislative enactment which, in my opinion, subjects Slaves belonging to subjects of a friendly Power to forfeiture or condemnation, when brought into a British Port, under circumstances similar to the Cargo of the 'Comet.'"[30]

Anderson could hardly have been more accommodating in intimating to Morse the aspects of the law upon which the official British position in the case relied and the weaknesses of those arguments. First, he informed the insurer of the Robinson/Gifford letter and Earl Bathurst's circular from 1818 but denied their applicability to the *Comet*'s voyage because the *Comet* was not participating in the outlawed transatlantic slave trade, as the Portuguese slave ship had been. Second, the Speaker of the House pointed out to Morse that, while enslaved people who set foot on the soil of Great Britain, whether voluntarily or involuntarily, became free, that same "rule of freedom" did not apply in British colonies. In the Bahamas and elsewhere, "slavery is not only enforced by colonial statutes, but recognized by the Laws of the Mother Country." Anderson concluded his letter by enclosing, for Morse's convenience, copies of the sections of the British law abolishing the slave trade that best applied to the *Comet.* He specifically noted the section that allowed "the trans[s]hipment of slaves from vessels in distress at sea." Anderson's missive surely would have met with the approval of House of Assembly members opposed to the captives' release into Bahamian society, just as it proved useful to the man sent to retrieve the shipwrecked American slaves.[31]

Nathan Morse found another powerful ally in the Bahamian press. The *Bahama Argus* skewered Gov. Carmichael-Smyth for his "illegal and unjust detention of the Slaves in question from their rightful owners." The bondpeople had only been carried into Nassau in the process of saving their lives. In contrast to the preference of the abolitionist governor and the colonial secretary, white public sentiment in New Providence overwhelmingly favored handing over the captives to continue on to New Orleans. The shrewdest lawyers would be hard pressed "to find any law or statute of Great

Britain, or any of her colonies," to justify anything but the return of the bondpeople, the paper asserted. "We do not want the private instructions of Lord Viscount Goderich, or the opinions of the Abolition Society" to determine policy, the *Argus* hissed, for "these may serve to oppress and, in the end, ruin our own Colonies," by allowing freedpeople rescued from a U.S. slave ship to take up residence. The newspaper ended by smearing Carmichael-Smyth for having a personal, selfish interest in the freedpeople. Not only did one of them serve as "*head cook*" for the governor (with others "now in his employment" as well), but also many of the emancipated slaves' names allegedly appeared on a petition supporting the governor's continued service in that political office. The whole thing smacked of corruption, his critics charged.[32]

News of the *Comet* and the aftermath of the Vice Admiralty Court's decision rippled across the British Caribbean. Outside the Bahamas, it was often met in the press with less vitriol and more measured reason. "The case, divested of . . . twattle[,] is most simple," declared the *Courant*, in Jamaica. The newspaper implored its readers to consider the law of nations: "Whenever an act of nature throws the people of . . . friendly countries on the shores of another, the sufferers are entitled to receive all the assistance and *hospitality* which can be afforded by those on whose coasts they are cast." The nation whose people required aid pays the expenses incurred in helping them, and the victims of the tragedy are "allowed to complete their original voyage." It was a "plain and undoubted principle of international law" that an "accident of nature" does not "give the one nation any right to legislate over the other." That the cargo in this instance consisted of property in people did not change matters at all.[33]

But the reality was not that simple. When the *Comet* wrecked off Abaco, it also produced a second collision between nations on different trajectories with slavery. U.S. commitment to the institution was deepening as the cotton frontier spread westward, while in Great Britain, mounting abolitionist sentiment was close to bearing new legal fruit. Presciently assessing the historical moment, agent John Storr contacted American secretary of state Martin Van Buren within forty-eight hours of the *Comet* captives' seizure by customshouse officials with a pessimistic message for the U.S. shippers. "I have not the most distant expectation that one of the slaves will ever again see the United States," he predicted on January 17. It did not take Nathan Morse long after his arrival in Nassau in August to realize the futility of trying to convince Bahamian government officials to surrender the liberated slaves.[34]

Morse's failure in achieving the restoration of the freedpeople to their former owners struck the insurance agent as the consequence of "an extraordinary and inhospitable exercise of power on the part of the British Government, towards the subjects of a friendly nation," for two main reasons. First, he explained, the *Comet* was "under circumstances of peculiar calamity and distress," with no intention of violating British law. Second, in prior instances in which the situation was reversed, when American ships rescued enslaved cargoes "from British wrecks and uninhabited rocks," the United States never detained the bondpeople from their owners. Morse cited the case of a Nassau-based British schooner lost off the Double Headed Shot Cays, south of Key Largo, Florida, in 1827. Three Black seamen were aboard, two of whom were enslaved.

After their rescue, the two enslaved sailors were delivered to the British consul for restoration to their owners in the Bahamas. Morse wished that Great Britain would extend the same courtesy to Americans. A similar grasp of irony struck many contemporaries who marveled that, after the British stole "black Africans from their native land" for more than 150 years, conveyed them to their North American colonies without inhibition, and profited from the transatlantic traffic in human capital, they now discovered that form of property "so base, that it justifies a violation of the first principles of that code by which Nations are governed."[35]

Observers sensed that the two nations stood on the cusp of something serious. The *Comet* incident, wrote one District of Columbia newspaper, could well "become important to the whole country." It invoked important principles of international law as well as "the Southern right of slave property." It contained all the ingredients necessary to "excite a very hostile feeling between the United States and the British Government."[36]

Rebuffed in his efforts to reunite owners with their lawful property, Morse was tasked by the three New Orleans insurance companies he represented to assemble the relevant paperwork for transmission to Washington, DC. He filed a report with new secretary of state Edward Livingston outlining all the necessary facts "for the purpose of obtaining indemnity of the British Government for the illegal seizure and detention" of the enslaved American property in Nassau. This information, Morse wrote, should "enable you to suggest a prompt remedy for the wrongs which have been so wantonly inflicted on the subjects of the United States." For all intents and purposes, wrote one British official, U.S. insurance companies "now represent, and stand in the same situation as the Owners," as "the parties urging the American Government to claim Indemnification."[37]

Although Morse declared that some of those enslaved on the *Comet* were worth $2,000 individually in the New Orleans slave market, he placed the average value of each bondperson at $600, for a total of $98,400. (That tally, based on the 164 original prisoners on board, excluded the infant born during the voyage, who subsequently died.) As Morse saw it, Bahamian officials had underestimated the human cargo's collective value by tens of thousands of dollars. In submitting the claim on behalf of the underwriters against the British government, he also added his expenses while in the Bahamas and $1,500 for travel to Nassau and, from there, to Washington, where he lobbied in person on behalf of the insurers. Finally, to this figure, he tacked on interest accruing from the January 15 date of seizure. The bill already exceeded $100,000 (more than $3 million today) and was growing with each passing day. But His Majesty's government was unwavering. In late October 1831, Lord Goderich expressed continued approval of the "course adopted" by Gov. Carmichael-Smyth. "Hence," concluded the *Bahama Argus*, "it seems a national question to be settled between the United States and England."[38]

3

Proslavery Exertions

The three New Orleans insurance companies and the two uninsured owners of human capital aboard the shipwrecked *Comet* would have to rely upon U.S. diplomats to seek redress from Great Britain. Some of the politicians negotiating with Britain were from the North, and others from the South, with some more personally inclined toward slavery than others. They were all white men, well acquainted with the institution of slavery and attuned to its significance to the Southern and national economies. At least as important, they understood that vital principles of diplomacy and international relations were at stake. As a result, Northerners as well as Southerners within the diplomatic ranks advanced slave owners' interests. The peculiar circumstances leading to the loss of the enslaved men, women, and children aboard the *Comet* meant that the full force of the U.S. government would cater to the needs of the Southern plantation machine.

The pursuit of reimbursement for lost or damaged human property was nothing new. Masters whose valuable enslaved laborers were injured, maimed, or killed because of another's negligence often filed suit in civil or criminal courts across the South in an attempt to extract compensation from the allegedly responsible party. Aggrieved owners whose economic interests suffered counted on judges or juries, depending upon the state, to provide redress and make things right. The case of the *Comet* was different, however, given its international dimensions. Whereas slave owners normally would have resorted to the legal system within individual counties and states to debate who was at fault, what emerged instead was a contest over the principles that governed maritime clashes over slavery.[1]

Martin Van Buren, recently named U.S. minister to Great Britain as a recess appointment by President Andrew Jackson, spearheaded the initial diplomatic effort to secure recompense from the British government. Secretary of State Edward Livingston relayed Jackson's instructions to Ambassador Van Buren. "On the whole, it is the President's desire that you should take every proper opportunity of urging the right of the claimants to indemnity," Livingston informed him in early December 1831. The secretary of state thought it self-evident that events in the Bahamas had been "injurious to the rights of our citizens," unjust, "unfriendly," and inconsistent with how governments properly handled relations over "this species of property." Not even the most "zealous" abolitionist statesman in England had ever "ventured to propose that other nations . . . should be forced to consent to a general emancipation" if enslaved people landed in British colonies. The British "acknowledge[d] that slaves are property" as well as "the right to hold such property in their colonies." How incredulous it seemed, then, to Livingston that enslaved "property legally held by the citizens of a friendly country" should be stripped away as a result of "the calamity of shipwreck" on a colony where slavery existed by law. No British statute authorized the seizure and liberation of those enslaved aboard the *Comet*; rather, it was merely an "executive comment" that brought about that result. Livingston pressed Van Buren to insist that, even if the British wished to emancipate "every slave cast by . . . shipwreck on their islands," it would be absurd to think that "this scheme of philanthropy should be executed at the expense of the unfortunate citizens of a friendly nation." At the very least, the British government owed "the shipwrecked stranger . . . due compensation." Livingston assured Van Buren that the U.S. government "will be content with a moderate valuation" of the lost human cargo; however, he added in a note of caution, "The magnitude of the sum makes it a matter of importance to the parties interested, and the principle involved is one of considerable delicacy."[2]

Van Buren was perfectly suited for delicate matters. Always the politician, he measured each word carefully, speaking with such caution and precision that, if he desired, his listeners were left to wonder precisely what he had said. In negotiations over compensation for the lost *Comet* cargo, Van Buren would need to be more direct, yet eminently tactful. The British counterpart with whom he would be communicating was Henry John Temple, the 3rd Viscount Palmerston. Lord Palmerston served two decades as the secretary of war before becoming, in November 1830, the secretary of state for Foreign Affairs. Stylistically, Palmerston's renowned abrasiveness contrasted with the American minister's charm. But the dispute between the two countries the men represented was over substance. Van Buren well knew that the "state of public feeling, and the extreme sensibility" over the slavery issue in the United States mandated that he delve thoroughly

Lord Palmerston.

into the matter of the *Comet*. "The arguments in favor of the claim," moreover, must be granted "the fullest consideration."[3]

Van Buren laid out the American claimants' case methodically in an extensive letter dated February 25, 1832. He opened by explaining that the American actors in the drama were blameless. The *Comet* had undertaken a domestic slaving voyage fully authorized by U.S. law. The rescue from the reef and the removal of the people aboard to New Providence "appear to have been acts of necessity, arising from circumstances of misfortune, over which Captain Staples had no control." Staples, in fact, had objected to the plan to go to Nassau, and upon involuntary arrival there, he immediately made arrangements to depart as quickly as possible. The enslaved people were detained, but the Vice Admiralty Court determined the "illegality of the seizure." At that point, Van Buren stated, Staples should have encountered "no further difficulty" in "remov[ing] . . . the slaves to the port of their original destination." Contrary to that "reasonable expectation," British colonial authorities refused to surrender the enslaved individuals and instead released them from their existing relations with their owners. After outlining the monies paid out by the three New Orleans insurers and the efforts made by Nathan Morse in the Bahamas to recover the liberated slaves, Van Buren announced to Palmerston that the "claimants apply to the justice and equity of his Majesty's Government, for indemnity for the heavy losses which they have sustained."[4]

The U.S. minister then delved deeper into the troubling legal points raised by what had transpired in the Bahamas. He dismissed the notion "that the mere fact of landing the slaves upon a bare rock on the Bahama coast, to save them from immediate death, or even touching with them at another island for the sole purpose of saving them from starvation or loss in the small [rescue] crafts" qualified as "landing" on British soil. The only true "landing" occurred in Nassau, "in consequence of the unlawful seizure" by customshouse officials, contrary to the wishes of the U.S. captain and agent. Van Buren agreed with Judge William Vesey Munnings's decision that the enslaved cargo was not illegally imported, but he argued that after that verdict there should have been no impediment to the bondpeople's "immediate *reshipment*" to New Orleans.[5]

Van Buren paused at this juncture to point out to Palmerston that, already, "the liability of his Majesty's Government to redress the injury . . . appears . . . too clear to be disputed." Nonetheless, he continued, concerned with matters of principle, specifically the security of Southern slave owners participating in the coastwise domestic slave trade. Although he lauded Great Britain for its "early and effectual suppression" of the transatlantic slave trade, he expressed his apprehension that the imperial power would "propose the slightest interference with the rights and duties of master and slave in other States" where "domestic slavery was permitted to exist." The same 1807 American law that "rigorously guards against the further introduction of slaves" from abroad protected slave owners' right to "transfer" their enslaved property "coastwise, from one of these States to another." Van Buren reminded Palmerston that their two nations disagreed only over the ability of American slave owners to conduct the saltwater domestic slave trade unmolested.[6]

Reading into British law, Van Buren claimed that the empire's abolition of the international slave trade said nothing about shipwrecked slaves transported "under the laws of a foreign friendly nation." "Cases like the present are neither within the policy of that act, nor embraced in the intention of its framers," Van Buren insisted. If Parliament did not even envision shipwrecked slaves from the United States thrown upon the shores of British colonies, there could be no "just, liberal, and legal construction of that act" that would permit the confiscation of the enslaved people from the *Comet*. Van Buren conceded that the 23rd section of the law did authorize the forfeiture of those enslaved persons, "*by shipwreck* or otherwise," who were "*cast upon*, or shall *escape* to, or *arrive* at, any island or colony" within His Majesty's dominions; however, he quickly added, the text of the law stated that that provision applied only to those "*illegally held or detained in slavery*." Those aboard the *Comet* were Americans lawfully held in bondage and therefore legally ineligible for seizure.[7]

As Van Buren interpreted events, the British government had begun extending its policy toward enslaved people touching foot in Great Britain to its colonies. British courts had long upheld the notion that ownership rights to slaves ceased when enslaved people set foot on English shores, using a long-held phrase that "the air of England had become too pure for a slave to breathe in." Slave-owning nations across the world understood British policy and "conform[ed] to it in their intercourse with her." But, Van Buren continued, Great Britain seemed to be extending that same principle to a colony that still lawfully recognized slavery. The American slave owners requested only "the same protection in regard to their property" as would have been granted to slave-owning British subjects in the Bahamas.[8]

Finally, the U.S. ambassador took issue with Britain's use of the wrecked Portuguese slave ship from 1818 as a suitable precedent for deciding the case of the *Comet*. The Portuguese slaver transported stolen Africans in defiance of British law. In contrast, those enslaved aboard the *Comet* had been "born in servitude in the territories of a friendly nation" equally interested in quelling the transatlantic slave trade. Van Buren conveyed his sincere doubt that British lawmakers intended for the law to function as it just had in the Bahamas.[9]

Overreaching at the conclusion of his letter, the U.S. minister expressed "the strongest confidence" that the British government would fulfill President Andrew Jackson's "just expectation" of the liberated slaves' return, plus "reasonable indemnity" to the American claimants "for the damages caused by the detention of their property" and for those individuals who may not be tracked down for restoration to their owners. If, however, Britain was "unable to comply with this request," which the ambassador surely knew they would not, he proposed an alternative. Van Buren invited Lord Palmerston to pay "all suitable compensation" owed to the U.S. slave owners "for the property taken or detained from them." He repeated Secretary of State Livingston's assurance that the American claimants would be satisfied with a "moderate valuation." Enclosing Nathan Morse's estimate of the total due, Van Buren presented the British government with a bill for about $100,000.[10]

With that, his role in the story abruptly ended. In January 1832, the Senate voted narrowly against confirming Van Buren's recess appointment as U.S. minister to Great Britain. Though out of a job after serving only an eight-month stint as ambassador, Van Buren could not have argued the case for indemnification more strongly than he did. The New Yorker garnered no criticism from slave owners or Southern members of Congress over the performance of his duties. Though slavery was at issue, the *Comet* incident was treated as a national concern. Little about the negotiations over the slave ship seeped into the emerging radical abolitionist press, and the U.S. effort to obtain redress from Great Britain did not yet become a centerpiece for antislavery agitation. Nat Turner's slave revolt in Southampton County, Virginia, which shocked the nation in August 1831, stole the headlines and steered debate in other directions.

Van Buren presented the argument for compensation so masterfully, in fact, that the British government was confounded over how best to respond. According to one note from the Foreign Office, "the question was first referred to the King's Advocate," but, "feeling the difficulty of the case," he "requested the assistance of the other law advisers of the Crown." On January 7, 1833, Lord Palmerston advised the King's advocate, attorney general, and solicitor general to work together to tackle the issue.[11]

Meanwhile, the secretary to the U.S. legation in London assumed the role of chargé d'affaires ad interim in April 1832. Aaron Vail, son of a former U.S. consul and commercial agent in France, would be kept busy at his post in the cosmopolitan hub of a vast global empire and the most populous city in the world. As he began his duties, Vail would have ranked negotiating a satisfactory settlement for the *Comet* disaster as his top priority. During a personal interview with Lord Palmerston that summer, Vail was given assurances that the law officers of the Crown were reviewing the matter and was promised that further inquiries would be made. Vail also regularly pressed Sir George Shee, Britain's undersecretary of state for Foreign Affairs, for updates. By all accounts, he politely and respectfully agitated for a quick resolution to the dispute. Pressure was on Vail to perform. The State Department reminded him that the American slave owners and insurers were "exceedingly anxious to procure a decision of their claim upon the British Government, which they cannot doubt will be a favorable one." Months passed. By mid-November, Vail called at the Foreign Office once again to find out where the investigation stood and to convey the urgency of the question. Undersecretary Shee gave the familiar reply that the law officers of the Crown had yet to reach a decision and repeated his customary pledge "to inquire into the cause of the delay."[12]

By the end of February 1833, U.S. impatience was evident. Secretary of State Livingston shifted away from writing to Vail about the *Comet* specifically—a case he believed "too clear to admit of a doubt"—and to the significant ramifications of its outcome for the slave system writ large in the United States. Any "doctrine that would justify the liberation of our slaves is too dangerous to a large section of our country to be tolerated by us," he declared. If the coastwise traffic in slaves was not secure, slave owners would feel vulnerable. Opportunities abounded for white men with a sizeable-enough enslaved labor force to do the work to make them rich in the Lower Mississippi Valley. Slave owners needed the confidence of knowing that the flow of compulsory laborers from the Chesapeake would not be endangered and that transported workers would not be lost. Livingston directed Vail to take a new tack in his diplomatic efforts. In urging "attention to our application," he advised Vail to give "as a reason for your pressing it . . . the extreme . . . susceptibility of a very large portion of our country on the question which it involves." Livingston punctuated his remarks by noting that President Andrew Jackson was counting on both "the sense of justice of the British Government" and Britain's desire "to remove every unfriendly feeling between the citizens and subjects of the two countries" to bring negotiations to "a satisfactory arrangement."[13]

Jackson embraced the institution of slavery more wholeheartedly than any of his predecessors in the presidency had, without expressing any of their nagging doubts or criticisms. Born of humble origins, he achieved wealth through a combination of sketchy land speculations and the exploitation of enslaved people. He was the only president ever to have made a living, briefly, as a professional slave trader. By the time he rose to the presidency, he counted ninety-five enslaved people among his property holdings on his grand estate in Tennessee. Politically, he pursued policies so that other "common men" like him could rise to greatness on the backs of enchained others. Furthermore, Jackson spearheaded the drive that divested the Indigenous peoples of the American South of their land. By signing the Indian Removal Act into law in 1830, he paved the way for the Cherokee Trail of Tears, the final genocidal flourish of his policy toward Native peoples. Jackson, in short, had done everything in his power to promote the advance of the cotton frontier. The safe transportation of bondpeople via the coastwise domestic slave trade was essential to protecting the ability of other white men like himself to seize the opportunities afforded by land and enslaved labor in the cotton kingdom.[14]

Vail transmitted Jackson's concerns in two letters. In an official note dated March 25, 1833, the chargé d'affaires called Lord Palmerston's attention once again to Van Buren's correspondence, written thirteen months earlier. By this point, more than two years had elapsed since the wreck of the *Comet.* Vail avoided any further discussion of the merits of the American claim. He then related Jackson's wish that the British government "not allow the great loss incurred by the claimants . . . to be aggravated by any unnecessary protraction of the delay which [had] already occurred in the adjustment of their claim." Tight-lipped as ever, Lord Palmerston offered nothing new in reply. The law officers of the Crown were still mulling over the *Comet* claim. Vail, no doubt frustrated at his ongoing failure to deliver news of a settlement, insisted to Secretary Livingston that he was taking advantage of every possible opportunity to make "a fresh appeal" to Palmerston about the *Comet.*[15]

Vail's next formal missive, of April 4, more forcefully emphasized Jackson's desire for a "speedy adjustment of the Claim." He explained to Palmerston that the president understood that "the difficulties and delays . . . owing to the delicate nature" of the case could prolong the investigation and prevent an "immediate adjustment," but the American claimants had already waited "for more than a year." Their "losses . . . are daily increased by every fresh delay," and they have become more "urgent" in their calls for redress, Vail explained.[16]

He then laid out for Palmerston the broader significance of the saltwater transportation of slaves from the Upper South to the Lower. With the cotton frontier laid open, U.S. economic growth demanded "the necessary and frequent removals of portions" of the enslaved population "from one section of the country to another." The "coastwise navigation" route "through the Bahama Channel" was convenient, but "this dangerous thoroughfare remains unsafe." The United States hoped to remedy that situation and avoid any similar incident in the future like that involving the *Comet*.[17]

Vail segued into a note of warning. More than the "individual interests" concerned in the settlement over the *Comet*, the case involved important principles with repercussions for Anglo-American diplomacy. President Jackson assumed that the claim would rightfully conclude in favor of the U.S. claimants. But if it did not, the outcome "would go to establish a doctrine authorizing the liberation of the American Slave whom unavoidable accident may have thrown out of the Jurisdiction of the United States," thereby setting a precedent "too dangerous to a large section of the Country to be tolerated by its Gov[ernmen]t." A commitment to American slave owners was "deeply felt by the President," Vail cautioned, and should be remembered during ongoing talks. A veiled threat issued, Vail clarified that Jackson wished "to remove every unfriendly feeling between . . . the two Countries."[18]

Nonetheless, the responses Vail received differed little from those that came before. Undersecretary Shee stressed "the difficulty of reconciling the principle" the case involved with Britain's "existing laws." He confessed that its "complexity" had become "a subject of much embarrassment to the Crown lawyers." Vail's latest had done nothing to hasten a response. Lord Palmerston replied more than two weeks later with the customary statement that he had transmitted Vail's message "to the King's law officers," along with a promise to prod them into action. Increasingly impatient, Vail suspected the British of stalling. There was nothing more for him to do but hope for "a speedy termination" of the lawyers' difficulties.[19]

The summer brought no new developments for the *Comet*'s claimants. The most significant news on the subject of slavery was Parliament's passage, in August 1833, of the Slavery Abolition Act, which began the process of liberation throughout most of the British Empire, including in the Bahamas, all of the British Caribbean, Mauritius, and the Cape Colony of South Africa. Only the British territories under control of the East

India Company, including India, Ceylon, and St. Helena, were excepted. Effective August 1, 1834, the law emancipated enslaved people younger than six years old. Freedpeople older than that entered a protracted period of apprenticeship, lasting either four years for skilled slave laborers or six for field slaves, en route to eventual freedom in 1838 or 1840, respectively. The British government allotted £20 million in compensation to former slave owners for the loss of their property under the law. The eight hundred thousand liberated slaves, including more than ten thousand in the Bahamas, received no payments whatsoever.[20]

Still Aaron Vail waited. In late September, exactly one month after approval of the Slavery Abolition Act, he contacted Louis McLane, who had succeeded Edward Livingston as U.S. secretary of state. "I have again called the attention of Lord Palmerston" to the American claims from the *Comet*, Vail wrote. None of his communications had yet "had any effect in hastening the labors of the crown lawyers." It "has now been near two years under consideration," he complained in 1834, "notwithstanding my repeated calls, both written and verbal, for a decision." Palmerston continued to plead "the delicate nature of the question, and the intricacy of the case," offering more seemingly hollow pledges to accelerate the review process.[21]

The King's advocate, attorney general, and solicitor general at long last submitted their opinion to Lord Palmerston on April 9, 1834. The Crown lawyers evaluated the arguments made by former U.S. minister Martin Van Buren and "perused" all the documentary evidence he supplied. They ultimately concluded "that the claim is well founded." It took them twenty-seven months. The error that made the British government liable to provide restitution, as they saw it, derived from Bahamian customshouse officers' confiscation of the enslaved captives. The enslaved people were victims of foul weather and a shipwreck, forced by unavoidable circumstances into a British port. Had colonial officials not illegally seized the captives, they "would no doubt have been conveyed to their place of destination." Those individuals liberated from the *Comet* certainly could not be retaken and re-enslaved, but in the collective mind of the Crown attorneys, Bahamian authorities' mistake did constitute "a sufficient ground for the demand of . . . compensation."[22]

At last, all appeared to be moving toward a resolution in favor of the New Orleans insurance companies and the two uninsured slave owners. On May 10, Lord Palmerston transmitted the news to the lords of the Treasury and requested their authority to alert Vail that the American claimants would soon receive compensation for the emancipated slaves. Since the Treasury controlled the money, Lord Palmerston needed permission to spend it. The lords of the Treasury replied on May 28 that further consultation was necessary before they could make that commitment. Among those offering additional input was William Rothery, a veteran Treasury official long relied upon by the Treasury for his legal expertise on "all subjects connected with the Slave Trade."[23]

Rothery habitually wrote thorough and lengthy missives, and his report on the *Comet* proved no exception. He started with the premise that the Crown's law officers had not considered "the whole of the circumstances" surrounding the case. Conducting his own independent review, Rothery recapped the incident in minute detail, from the *Comet*'s departure from Alexandria to the Vice Admiralty Court's judgment, and rehashed the legal arguments made to date. Rothery agreed with Munnings that the enslaved cargo had not been "illegally imported" and that it was best to consider them "Aliens, cast by stress of weather on the shores of His Majesty's Dominions" and worthy of "our hospitable reception." To have done otherwise would have been "contrary to Law."[24]

Rothery then pivoted to the central question, declaring, in a departure from the Crown lawyers' position, that the American slave owners were *not* "entitled to restitution." In his explanation, he homed in on master Isaac Staples. Before the seizure of the *Comet*'s human cargo, Rothery explained, the captain could not have removed the enslaved people from Nassau without violating British law. After the seizure and the Vice Admiralty Court's decree, Staples also could not have legally removed with them, unless they "voluntarily . . . consented to depart as free Persons." The court's decision, in other words, "in no degree altered or affected" Staples's ability to leave Nassau with his Black captives in a condition of slavery. There was no circumstance, then, either before or after the ruling, under which they could have been restored to their owners as enslaved property. "Consequently," Rothery concluded, "there is not the least pretext for claiming Indemnity from the British Government."[25]

Striking a further note of caution, Rothery understood that the case of the *Comet* raised an important issue about foreign slaves shipwrecked within British holdings across the globe. "I apprehend it to be abundantly clear," he explained, "that if Indemnification is to be granted in this case, it must be conceded in all other cases of Shipwrecked Slaves." The financial costs "will of necessity be very considerable, for several instances have occurred besides the present, and no doubt others will." How long was the reach of that slippery slope? What about enslaved people who ran away to the British? Or those who sought refuge on a British ship or safe haven in Canada? Rothery asked the worthwhile question, "If Indemnification be granted for Shipwrecked Slaves," would not "owners of Foreign Fugitive Slaves" who had run away and found "asylum in His Majesty's Possessions, . . . have not a more than equal right to expect Indemnification"? The potential ramifications to British coffers, already strained by the program of compensated emancipation adopted by Parliament in 1833, were profound.[26]

Rothery concluded by stating that any effort to gain reparations "for the value of the Individuals wrecked from the Comet" should have begun with Capt. Staples filing an appeal of the Vice Admiralty Court's decision to the High Court of Admiralty. "The American Master," however, no longer present in Nassau at the time of the verdict, prosecuted "no appeal." Under these circumstances, Rothery explained, "It does not appear to me that any just claim exists against His Majesty's Government to indemnify the Americans for the loss they have sustained."[27]

Just as the lords of the Treasury sought William Rothery's opinion, they also solicited the input of Thomas Spring Rice, who in early June 1834 succeeded Lord Goderich as colonial secretary. After being given the evidence to consider, Spring Rice took his time to mull over the weighty—and potentially costly—decision.[28]

U.S. chargé d'affaires Aaron Vail had no idea that the Crown lawyers had recommended reparation in April 1834 or that the lords of the Treasury had introduced an additional layer of doubt into the process. Already Rothery opposed paying the requested indemnity; perhaps Spring Rice would too. As far as Vail knew, there had been no movement on the question of compensation at all. Pressure on him arrived in the mail, indirectly, from the highest authority.

Andrew Jackson loyalist and slaveholder John Forsyth of Georgia, the new U.S. secretary of state, explained the president's "great regret" and "surprise" at the protracted postponement of any sort of settlement. Jackson reportedly viewed Britain's "disregard . . . to the rights and interests of American citizens" with "painful feelings." On August 1, Vail penned another official letter to Lord Palmerston. He regretted to bother the viscount again, he explained, but the case involved "principles of international law, imparting to the subject an importance which, in the opinion of the

American Government, should recommend it to the early and serious consideration of that of his Britannic Majesty." Although Vail understood from Palmerston's previous replies "that steps had been made towards an adjustment of the claim," he felt obligated to note "the long period of time during which the claimants have been deprived of the use of their property," at this point more than three and a half years since the date of the wreck.[29]

Vail never expressed frustration with Viscount Palmerston. "In all our conversations," he wrote, "his lordship always manifested the best disposition to see" the matter of the *Comet* "satisfactorily arranged," and Palmerston dutifully followed through. He directed Vail's letter to the lords of the Treasury on August 9, with a request for an "early decision upon the subject." In turn, the lords of the Treasury dispatched the message to the Colonial Office on August 22. It was up to Spring Rice to decide whether "compensation should be made." Vail hoped to wrap up the "unfinished business" of the *Comet* quickly, for a second American slave ship had already crashed in the Bahamas.[30]

4

The *Encomium* Runs Aground

"The Packet Brig ENCOMIUM, for New-Orleans, will sail *This Day*, at 1 o'clock," announced the *Charleston (SC) Courier* on February 1, 1834. Ships in the transient trade had previously left port only once they were completely filled with people or cargo, but by the 1830s, packet vessels like the *Encomium* operated on fixed schedules, charging more for the regularity of their service. "Passengers are requested to be on board" by the 1:00 p.m. deadline, the newspaper continued, but "Slave passengers must be cleared *This Forenoon*, at the Custom House."[1]

Sometime that morning, Antonio Della Torre delivered seven enslaved people to the ship, all of them consigned to Joseph A. Barelli and bound for the slave markets of New Orleans. In the hard calculus of slavery's capitalism, the three most valuable of these captives were skilled Black bondmen York, "a first rate Sail maker," age twenty-three; Sam, "a first rate Cooper," age twenty-one; and Anthony, a carpenter, age twenty-four. Each was projected to bring $1,000 at auction. Charleston slave dealer John Hagan predicted that the twenty-six-year-old "prime field hand" Charles would sell for somewhat less, at $850, but it was enslaved people like him whose muscle and know-how cultivated the profitable crops of the Lower Mississippi Valley. As with all others caught up in the domestic slave trade and exploited by the slave system, Charles's stolen labor would line the pockets and augment the wealth of his white buyer. Bidders at auction could snag either of the two women Antonio Della Torre carried to the *Encomium* for less than the price of the men. Georgiana, an eighteen-year-old house servant, and Minda, another "prime field hand" of twenty-four, had anticipated values of $800 and $700, respectively. Della Torre's lot totaled $5,350, excluding Tay, an octoroon or mustee bondman with only one-eighth Black ancestry. Della Torre was shipping Tay on behalf of Capt. Noah B. Sisson, a mariner who, at the time of the *Encomium*'s scheduled departure, was "absent on a coasting voyage" to Savannah,

Georgia. At the more advanced age of thirty-five, Tay, his owner presumed, might fetch a relatively modest $500.[2]

For shipper Antonio Della Torre, slave trading was not his primary profession, as it was for Isaac Franklin and John Armfield. Rather, it marked but one small component of a broad-based, sweeping commercial enterprise. Born around 1780 on the shores of Lake Como in the Lombardy region of Italy, Della Torre as a young man made wine and brandy from the fruits of his father's vineyards. Sometime in the first decade of the nineteenth century, prior to his thirtieth birthday, Della Torre crossed the Atlantic to Charleston to start anew. In doing so, he antedated the arrival of large numbers of Italian immigrants to the United States by almost a century. Only about twelve thousand Italians ventured to the United States between 1783 and 1871, most of them headed to the Northeast or to the Lower Mississippi Valley. The largest number of Italians in the South—a little less than one thousand—could be found in the state of Louisiana. An Italian immigrant like Della Torre living in the Eastern Seaboard city of Charleston was unusual in 1810.[3]

In his first couple of decades in Charleston, Della Torre appeared in newspapers occasionally, perhaps by vouching for individuals, such as fellow Italian immigrant Antonio Barrelli, applying for licenses to "retail Spirituous Liquors." In addition to alcohol, religion supplied immigrants a sense of belonging. In 1823, Della Torre served on Charleston's committee of the Catholic Book Society and as one of the trustees for the Roman Catholic Cathedral. At the first convention of the Roman Catholic Church of South Carolina, Della Torre and Dr. James C.W. McDonnald were among the laymen elected "general Trustees of the Church of the State." Three years later, both men were elected delegates to the South Carolina Convention of the Catholic Church.[4]

The church enabled Della Torre to forge not only spiritual but also business ties with McDonnald. By 1823, Della Torre had already begun to establish himself as a merchant, receiving, along with others, a cargo of deerskins and 324 bales of cotton from the steamboat *Hamburg*. But in 1825, he and McDonnald concocted an ambitious scheme that would, if implemented, alter the entire agricultural landscape of South Carolina. Fearing that their state was too dependent on cotton production, whose center was shifting westward, they proposed to diversify the state's economy through the cultivation of grapevines and olive and mulberry trees. With a knowledgeable "free white body of labourers" acquainted with the arts "of making fine wines, [and] cognac brandy," South Carolina could end the importation of those commodities. Likewise, the state could press its own olive oil and, by providing an ecosystem for silkworms in newly planted mulberry trees, produce fine fabric from their cocoons. All the two entrepreneurs requested was a $40,000 loan from the South Carolina state senate for establishing "a wine and silk manufactory in the interior of the state." Lawmakers denied their request.[5]

Della Torre nonetheless thrived in Charleston's commercial world with a small cadre of Italian countrymen, all members of the Barelli (Barrelli) family. By 1825, he and John Barelli formed the co-partnership of Barelli, Torre & Co., a commission business operating at 65 Broad Street. They shared that physical space with Joseph A. Barelli, the same man to whom Della Torre consigned the seven bondpeople put aboard the *Encomium* the first day of February 1834.[6]

Della Torre established a shop at No. 113 King Street in Charleston, where he specialized in the sale of "ENGLISH FANCY GOODS." By 1828, he advertised pianofortes, mirrors, paintings, mahogany frames, guns, "Gilt and plated Sabres, Swords and Dirks," "Gold and silver Epaulettes," "Lace and Fringe," candlesticks, snuffers, compasses, tableware, "Mathematical Instrument Cases," telescopes, and watches. His inventory only expanded from there, spilling back into the 65 Broad Street location. Della Torre sold spectacles, walking canes, looking glasses, clocks, china vases, and "Alabaster Ornaments from Italy." Ships brought back the "best Spanish Segars [cigars]" from Havana, Cuba, and premium casks of sherry. By 1832, more pedestrian fare entered his store as well: hogsheads of bacon and barrels of salted "mess pork," sugar, and whiskey.[7]

Charleston's newspapers documented the robust business of the Italian commission merchant. Della Torre advertised in October 1830 that the brig *Mary* would soon sail to New Orleans and invited the public to book freight or passage, noting that half the cargo was already loaded. Della Torre did not issue specific summons for enslaved property as professional domestic slave traders did. His business model considered the enslaved one of many different commodities that might end up on a vessel for his profit. Any cargo ship headed to New Orleans during the slaving season, which spanned from the fall to the spring of the following year, was bound to carry at least some chained captives on board. Della Torre's mercantile business did so well that, by 1830, he had accumulated sufficient wealth to claim title to eleven enslaved people of his own.[8]

The seven bondpeople whom Antonio Della Torre hustled onto the *Encomium* cleared customs, and on the afternoon of February 1, the brig departed for New Orleans. Master Paschal Sheffield, a veteran mariner from Connecticut, guided the craft out of Charleston harbor and into the open Atlantic. In his thirties, Sheffield had piloted multiple voyages to New York City and New Orleans as captain of the schooners *Eliza* and *Frederic*, but by the start of 1833 he served as master of "the fine new copper fastened Brig ENCOMIUM," described as a "very fast sailing packet" vessel of a svelte 130 tons cargo capacity. That year, Sheffield steered the *Encomium* on voyages to Charleston, to New York City, and to Newport and Providence, Rhode Island. By early January 1834, the ship was back in Charleston harbor, docked at Gibbs' Wharf, preparing for the reception of freight and passengers. When the brig departed, Capt. Sheffield, mate Richard T. Evans, and a crew of about six carried sixteen white travelers, 46 casks of Lowcountry rice, 200 barrels of tar extracted from Carolina pine forests, mill stones, and "71 Packages Merchandise." Newspapers made no mention of Antonio Della Torre's half dozen enslaved captives, Capt. Noah B. Sisson's one, or the thirty-eight other bondpeople on board.[9]

As one white passenger explained it, the *Encomium* enjoyed "uncommon fine weather" from the moment it set out for New Orleans. Sheffield and Evans documented that "fine breezes from [the] north-east, and East north-east," pushed the vessel along on Monday, February 3, with "all drawing sails set" under cloudy but unmenacing skies. The wind picked up somewhat at about 8:00 p.m., prompting the crew to lower the royal and gaff sails, but there was no indication of gales, raging seas, or towering waves. Yet suddenly, around midnight, just fifty-six hours out of port, the *Encomium* found itself among breakers in the shallows off the Bahamian coast, not far from the graveyard of the *Comet*. The brig "immediately struck" a reef off the northeastern side of Great Abaco Island and got tossed "from one rock to another" by the rhythmic motion of the water. The ship bilged within twenty minutes, a gash ripped into its hull, and saltwater poured into the cargo hold. The *Encomium*'s third night on the Atlantic since leaving Charleston would be its last.[10]

To lighten the sinking brig and perhaps gain a few precious hours for those aboard, at 1:00 a.m. the crew "cut away the main mast" of the ship, which fell "across the deck" and took down with it the fore topmast, topgallant mast, and royal mast. Still the vessel "thump[ed] . . . violently" against the rocks. Capt. Sheffield ordered all on board "to secure themselves, for he said she would not hold together another hour," as "it was expected every wave would dash her to pieces." By 2:00 a.m., water filled the *Encomium* and within minutes it lapped over the deck. The captain, crew, and sixty-one passengers—the sixteen fare-paying whites as well as the forty-five enslaved Black people—confronted dire peril. They clung desperately to the main mast, which the captain and crew had lashed tight to the ship, and the quarter houses, under the assumption that they were living their last moments before slipping into "a watery grave." As one unnamed survivor put it, "Death appeared to us inevitable." All the "*sixty-nine souls*" on board could do was anxiously await the arrival of daylight to reveal a nearby speck of land or to increase their chances of rescue by fishermen in the area.[11]

Another two hours passed. The *Encomium*, victim of the relentless waves, at last "thumped over a ledge of rocks into deep water." The bow sank below the sea, leaving "only a few feet of her stern" peeking "above the surface." At 4:00 a.m., still before daybreak, the vessel's "small boat," or "jolly boat"—its lifeboat—was retrieved from the leeward side of the sunken craft. It twice filled with water as the crew tried to deploy it, but finally, twelve people managed to clamber in: the captain, three members of his crew, four of the white male passengers, and all four white female passengers. Leaving the fifty-seven others, including all of the enslaved, clinging to the wreckage of the *Encomium*, they set off before dawn in search of land. Daylight shone on Fish Cay, "about five miles distant." There they landed, "in an exhausted state."[12]

Fish Cay was "desolate"—"a small island inhabited only by a single family of fishermen." Apprised of the ship's desperate circumstances, Benjamin Curry and his kin set off for the site of the *Encomium* disaster. The poor Bahamian fishermen spent the day rescuing the remaining white passengers, crew, and captives. By 4:00 p.m., the "humane exertions" of strangers landed everyone safely on Fish Cay. Plucked from the wreckage, they remained there for four days, "subsisting on rice . . . drenched with salt water" and, as one survivor recorded, "what [fish] we could catch, having scarcely enough to keep us alive." According to one report, "the Passengers suffered much for want of food, and from the inclemency of the weather, before they were relieved by the wreckers." Two Bahamian wrecking vessels, the schooner *Jasper* and the sloop *Carpenter's Revenge* (one of the same vessels involved in the *Comet* rescue), attempted to save the *Encomium*'s cargo, but because the vessel was now completely submerged, the rice was "all damaged, and not fit for use" and "little of the cargo was recovered." Capt.

Sheffield, it was later reported, "only saved his anchors and chains and some naval stores."[13]

On Saturday, February 8, the wreckers delivered everyone from the *Encomium* to Green Turtle Cay, the same sliver of land where the *Comet* survivors had taken refuge three years earlier. They remained just one day and one night before the *Jasper* and the *Carpenter's Revenge* delivered them in Nassau in mid-afternoon on Tuesday, February 11. As a bedraggled white passenger wrote, "We . . . were brought to this place completely destitute." The most harrowing part of the journey was behind them, but in other respects their troubles were just beginning.[14]

Once in Nassau harbor, the white passengers did not receive the warm and hospitable reception they anticipated as shipwreck survivors. A boat immediately approached from shore, under the command of a visiting health officer in service to the British government. Thomas Pindar was charged with ascertaining the physical condition of those on board the pair of wreckers and preventing outbreaks of yellow fever or other contagious diseases from infiltrating the colonial capital. He found the castaways in generally good health, but passengers informed him that their ordeal had left them "in want of the common necessaries of life" and "worn out by fatigue and loss of rest." Crammed on board the wreckers, they "respectfully requested" that Pindar consult the governor "and obtain permission for them to land," for they desperately needed food. The medical officer departed, noting that he would return "shortly."[15]

Within fifteen minutes after the two rescue ships set anchor in Nassau's harbor, a second boat drew up alongside the wreckers. It carried Alexander MacVey, who had replaced William Melbourne Fox as searcher and waiter of the customs since the *Comet* incident. Realizing the import of the arrival, MacVey ordered the enslaved captives to arrange themselves on the decks of each vessel. He beheld the entire group. Like Antonio Della Torre, Charleston's Robert Eagar had shipped seven bondpeople aboard the vessel: carpenters Prince and Jim, age forty-five and thirty, respectively; Kelly, thirty-five; Tom, twenty-eight; Tom Elmey, twenty-five; and Emily and Grace, each forty years old. No professional slave trader or commission merchant, Charles Allen was traveling on board with his legal property, Billy, Joe, and Peggy, to his home in Missouri. Plantation owner Amédée Gardanne Jr. was in transit with half a dozen enslaved people bound for his lands in Louisiana: Luke, age fifty-two; Jacob, twenty-nine; Sampson, twenty-two; Rose, thirty-nine; Mary, twenty-one; and Nancy, six and one-half, probably Rose's daughter. The other twenty-two enslaved people belonged to passenger John Waddell of North Carolina. Altogether, the *Encomium*'s human cargo consisted of thirty-one male and fourteen female captives.[16]

MacVey seized all forty-five bondpeople "in the name of His Britannic Majesty," King William IV, but for the time being left them on the *Jasper* and the *Carpenter's Revenge.* He informed the masters of the two vessels that they were temporarily responsible for the "Negro Slaves." Despite the passengers' need for subsistence, he instructed them to "hold no intercourse with the shore, not even for the purpose of procuring food" and warned that "if there should be any attempt to communicate with the Town" of Nassau, the wreckers "would be fired into by His Britannic Majesty's sloop of war 'Pearl,' then lying in the harbour."[17]

On his return, medical officer Pindar informed all on board "that they would not be permitted to land until the next morning between ten and eleven o'clock." Expecting greater sympathy, the white passengers and crew complained "that they had been living on rice wet with salt water for several days." At this, Pindar reportedly "laughed heartily, and insultingly replied, that they looked remarkably healthy, that wet rice was good enough for them, and that it would not kill them to live another night on such food." While the white castaways detected perverse delight in the officer's regard for their suffering, they believed him "uncommonly civil to and familiar with the slaves." "Well, my lads," Pindar said to them, "you are now freemen." Pointing to an unnamed "black fellow" in Pindar's own boat, Pindar told the captives, "There is one of your Yankees who was liberated by us about four years go," almost certainly a reference to those freed from the *Comet.* White passengers from the *Encomium* described the "negro" in the boat as "insolent," although they surely recognized in him a frightening glimpse of a future in which their own property was made free to work of their own accord in a foreign land.[18]

Upon Pindar's departure, the free people from the *Encomium*, exhausted by their ordeal and chafing under orders they resented, discussed "the propriety" of disobeying the instructions they had been given and "of going ashore at all hazards." They were still debating the matter when, at 6:00 p.m., an officer from the *Pearl* pulled alongside the wreckers. He commanded "the masters to weigh anchor and lay within pistol shot" of the warship. As though he had overheard the passengers' conversation, he issued a threatening reminder not to interact with anyone on land. A waiting period before contact assured that the overall health of the Bahamian people would not be jeopardized.[19]

The distressed and insulted white people on board finagled permission to debark from the two wreckers, thanks to "the intercession of one of the passengers, a merchant, who had formerly resided on the Island" of New Providence. A British subject and the only non-American aboard the *Encomium*, David Laird of Glasgow, Scotland, "had friends on the island" and made a "manly" plea for his fellow castaways' release. The other white passengers included slave owners Charles Allen of Missouri, Amédée Gardanne "& Lady" of New Orleans, and John Waddell of North Carolina, as well as John's brother Haynes Waddell, fellow North Carolinian L. Curl, and John M. Neal of Virginia. Six of the sixteen hailed from Charleston, their port of departure: Henry Reilley, William D. Smith, John Tate, a W. Anson, and two unmarried women with the surnames Kelley and Johnson. No home was listed for passengers William Dalzell or Mrs. Edwards. After an hour, George Huyler, serving as U.S. consul for the port of Nassau, went on board the wreckers. Precisely what interventions he had made are not clear, but all of the white castaways were allowed off the boats. At about 8:00 or 8:30 p.m., barges shuttled them into Nassau, where they took lodging at Mrs. Fisher's Hotel. The enslaved people spent the night on the wreckers.[20]

On Wednesday morning, February 12, Bahamian officials took the forty-five captives off the wrecking vessels and conveyed them to the Nassau customs or police office. U.S. consul George Huyler, Capt. Sheffield, and slave owners Charles Allen, Amédée Gardanne, and John Waddell, who together owned thirty-one of the captives, were all assembled there as well. The Bahamas' lieutenant governor, Blayney Townley Balfour, had already informed police magistrate Charles Rogers Nesbitt that the enslaved castaways, consistent with Judge William Vesey Munnings's earlier decision on the *Comet*, "were free to stay" in the Bahamas "unmolested, or to depart at their pleasure." It was entirely their choice. That knowledge framed the series of questions that Nesbitt put to each bondperson: What is your name? How old are you? Where are you from? Were you enslaved or free? To whom did you belong? What job or trade did you hold? The magistrate then reached the most important query of all: "Do you wish to remain here and be free or return" to slavery in the United States? All of the enslaved people expressed a preference to remain as freedpeople in the Bahamas, except three. Evidence suggests that one of those willing to return to bondage

View of Bay Street, on the west end of Nassau.

in the American South was Joe, the property of Missouri's Charles Allen. The identities of the other two are unknown. The remaining forty-two bondpersons were "*immediately liberated*" and "declared . . . free and independent subjects of William the Fourth," making them the newest residents of Nassau, welcome to roam the city streets at will.[21]

The proceedings in the police office marked an unconventional means of emancipation, one far more direct and perfunctory than that involving the *Comet* castaways. The interrogation over, Nesbitt directed the newly freed to live in the quarters of a Black regiment at Fort Charlotte, a military installation overlooking the western portion of Nassau harbor. Lt. Gov. Balfour instructed the commissary to issue daily provisions of bread and meat and saw to it that "a person be engaged to attend" the liberated slaves "in the old Barracks, where they are lodged, to prevent them from getting into any scrapes with the [British] troops or others." "I am in hopes that in a very short time," Balfour concluded, "we shall be relieved from any

A Nassau street scene.

trouble or expence, by their finding means to provide themselves with a livelihood." In the meantime, those who were emancipated shall "be taken care of."[22]

Later in the day on Wednesday, Capt. Sheffield, mate Richard T. Evans, and seaman William Richardson of the *Encomium*, along with slave owners Allen, Gardanne, and Waddell, filed a protest with the U.S. consul against the seizure of the enslaved cargo, seeking the restoration of their human property. The complaint held "the officers of Customs, the Civil Authorities and all others" involved in the slaves' liberation responsible "for all loss, costs, damages, and injury" sustained by the Americans. Huyler notified the police magistrate of the protest, but Nesbitt replied that he "was acting legally" and certainly in conformity with his lieutenant governor's orders.[23]

The *Encomium*'s white passengers felt themselves persecuted throughout their brief stay in Nassau. According to the reports shared in U.S.

newspapers, "while walking about the streets attending to their own concerns," they "were insulted in the grossest manner by the free negroes of the town." More likely, the outraged whites—especially the slave owners—were simply unaccustomed to dealing with Black people who were not enslaved and compelled by fear of the lash to acquiesce. Even in places like Charleston Neck, South Carolina, where more than 1,100 free Black people lived in 1830, their subordinate place in the Southern racial hierarchy was nevertheless understood. South Carolina was only a small stretch of ocean but a world away from the Bahamas. South Carolina's commitment to the institution of slavery only grew throughout the 1830s, whereas in the Bahamas, the process leading to the final abolition of slavery was slated to begin in about half a year. Perhaps for that reason, the minority white population on the streets of Nassau, many of whom would have been former slave owners themselves, sympathized with the white castaways' plight. They treated the shipwrecked Americans "with the most marked politeness," offsetting to some degree the perceived offenses committed by free Black Bahamians. White islanders further nourished the Americans' sense of racial grievance when they cautioned the *Encomium*'s white passengers that "if they attempted to chastise" Nassau's free Black residents, "they would be handled severely by the Police."[24]

The next day, Thursday, February 13, slave owners Allen, Gardanne, and Waddell were preparing to leave the Bahamas. According to later U.S. newspaper reports, already within "a day or two" of their emancipation, "several of the slaves" from the *Encomium* who had initially stated their desire for liberty "returned to their masters with tears in their eyes craving pardon, . . . soliciting in the most humble manner to return to the United States with them." Such accounts should be treated with skepticism, but as the newspapers told it, the Southern slave owners were happy to oblige and sought permission to take their bondpeople with them. John Waddell addressed a note to George Huyler and asked if their enslaved property could be retrieved from their temporary quarters at Fort Charlotte. The U.S. consul informed Lt. Gov. Balfour that "some of the slaves were extremely anxious to return with their masters" and inquired "if any impediment exist[ed] to prevent the removal of the said Slaves from the Colony." The lieutenant governor's secretary immediately sent back a brusque reply: "The only impediment against the American Gentlemen removing . . . the forty five persons who landed here, is that, by so doing, they are liable to be hanged."[25]

The vast majority of the enslaved captives from the *Encomium* remained in the Bahamas. Although they had never been in the islands before and could not know precisely what the future held for them, they could at least revel in a freedom denied them in the land of their birth. Huyler commented on their good appearance on February 15. Within a few days, they began their lives at large, outside the protections of Fort Charlotte. Lt. Gov. Balfour noted that "the expence of maintaining the Americans during the fortnight they were here, amount[ed] to about £12." He did not closely track the emancipated slaves but commented that they "are, as I suppose, obtaining by Labour, an honest livelihood, as there have not been any complaints made against them." Freedom suited them just fine. Altogether, Huyler reported on February 24, thirty-five enslaved people from the *Encomium* were "about the Town" of Nassau. The boys Henry, age five, and Jack, three, both the former property of John Waddell, were the youngest captives rescued from a life of forced labor in the Lower Mississippi River Valley.[26]

Ten total captives from the *Encomium* chose to return to bondage in the American South. One was Charles Allen's bondman Joe, whose motivation is not known. Perhaps Joe had family members on Allen's holding in Missouri, or he considered Allen sufferable as far as masters went. Joe likely lived on a modestly sized family farm. If his owner was typical of Missouri slaveholders, Allen was a yeoman farmer who worked side-by-side in the fields with his bound laborers, rather than master of a large-scale plantation. Or maybe Allen issued a direct threat that compelled Joe's return. Fear of violence or harm to oneself, or to a loved one or friend back in Missouri, may have served as a powerful motivator. For whatever reason, Joe did not seize the opportunity to break free.[27]

Allen booked passage for himself and his bondman aboard the American schooner *Thurle* to New Orleans. Most of the white passengers from the *Encomium* reached the Mississippi River port on the same vessel. Capt. Sheffield, mate Richard T. Evans, the crew, Amédée Gardanne "and lady," L. Curl, John M. Neal, Henry Reilley, William D. Smith, John Tate, W. Anson, William Dalzell, Mrs. Edwards, and the "Misses Kell[e]y and Johnson" all docked in the Crescent City on March 1 after an uneventful voyage from Nassau. Thus, reported the *New Orleans Bee*, they "have, after much suffering, privation and insult, reached their port of destination."[28]

Slave owner John Waddell and nine of his bondpeople left Nassau aboard the schooner *Sarah Jane*, bound initially for Key West, in the Florida

Territory. Six of the bondpeople who voluntarily returned with Waddell were estimated at twenty years old. Two, Hales Berry and Solomon Nash, were labeled as "mustees," while the other four were Black: Crawford Nash, John Santee, Lucy Santee, and Elsey Santee. The relationship, if any, between the three Santees is not clear. They may have been related by blood or may have each taken the name of the South Carolina river as their surname. Two other of Waddell's bondpeople heading with him back to the United States were Ned Gibbs, a blacksmith, and Marcellus Paine, "a first rate Carpenter," both twenty-five. Perhaps both men joined their owner because they knew their particular skill sets privileged them over other bondpeople and would likely have kept them away from the hard drudgery of field labor performed by the overwhelming majority of all enslaved people in the American South. Unless he or she was illegally smuggled out of the Bahamas, the last of Waddell's enslaved persons who accompanied him back must have made the decision at the last minute, for the name did not appear on a certificate filed by U.S. consul Huyler prior to their departure from Nassau. Precisely why any of Waddell's enslaved people returned when thirteen others did not remains a mystery.[29]

Newspapers and letters documenting the *Encomium* disaster and the liberation of the enslaved people reached U.S. ports from Nassau more than a week ahead of the *Thurle*. The belated arrival of the castaways and the firsthand accounts of their experiences in the Bahamas added fresh detail, capturing the public's interest when they were reprinted in the press across the country.[30]

Once in New Orleans, the disgruntled white passengers who so narrowly escaped death aboard the sinking *Encomium* complained tirelessly of their ill treatment while stranded in the Bahamas. They groused that the British authorities in New Providence had behaved toward them "in the most insulting and inhospitable manner." Ten "gentlemen" from the brig—Henry Reilley, William D. Smith, L. Curl, Charles Allen, John Waddell, John M. Neal, Haynes Waddell, and Amédée Gardanne, along with Capt. Sheffield and mate Richard T. Evans—issued a formal statement in the *New Orleans Bee*, originally composed while still in Nassau, condemning, "in strong terms, . . . the conduct of the people of that island." They singled out for rebuke searcher Alexander MacVey for seizing the enslaved captives and for threatening to have the *Pearl* fire into the wrecking vessels, health official Thomas Pindar for laughing at their suffering and using "insulting" language toward them, and Lt. Gov. Balfour for threatening to hang them if they "presumed to remove the negroes." One paper recounting these appalling and "disgraceful" actions expressed the hope that the accounts were "highly colored," for certainly no such "wretches" should "be entrusted with authority by the British government, or . . . dare so to abuse it." Assuming the accuracy of the reports, the editor expected that the Crown would condemn the officials' "conduct and discharge them from its service," neither of which happened.[31]

Four of the irate passengers—Henry Reilley, John Waddell, Amédée Gardanne, and William Dalzell—next paid a visit to New Orleans notary public Jules Mossy. On March 11, they filed a formal protest with him. They deposed that they had all been passengers aboard the *Encomium*, that it had wrecked, and that they were carried to Nassau, where the British government seized the enslaved people rescued from the vessel and "set [the] said Slaves at liberty." Having a written legal document of their ordeal could prove useful as the slave owners pursued redress.[32]

At least two of the slave owners, Amédée Gardanne and Robert Eagar, had taken out insurance policies on the people they claimed as property with the Charleston Fire and Marine Insurance Company shortly before the *Encomium*'s departure. On January 30, Gardanne had insured three enslaved men, two enslaved women, and one enslaved child at $500 each, although with individual bondpersons valued as high as $900, his $3,000 policy undersold their total market worth by $750. Eagar insured his seven enslaved people on February 1 for a total of $3,200. He grossly underinsured his human cargo. Given their specialized woodworking skills, enslaved carpenters Prince and Jim were individually appraised by Charleston banker and slave trader Alexander McDonald at $1,600 and $1,200. Altogether, Eagar's policy covered a little more than half of his seven bondpeople's collective market value of $6,150.[33]

The policies issued by the Charleston Fire and Marine Insurance Company to the two slave owners were in standardized forms and boilerplate language, indicative of the professionalization of slave insurance practices by the 1830s. Each policy delineated the quantity of enslaved people covered, the duration of the company's financial protections, and the intended destination. Charleston Fire and Marine insured the "six Negroes" and "seven negroes" whom Gardanne and Eagar placed aboard the *Encomium* only "until the said goods and merchandize shall be safely landed at New Orleans." The insurance company's commodification of enslaved persons could not have been clearer.[34]

The policies spelled out the covered hazards—"the adventures and perils . . . of the seas"—the Charleston Fire and Marine Insurance Company was willing to bear. They listed the traditional range of marine insurance losses caused by "men of war, fire, enemies, pirates, assailing thieves, jet[ti]sons, letters of mart and counter mart, surprisals, takings at sea, arrests, restraints, and detainments of all kings, princes, or people, of what nation, condition, or quality soever, barratry of the Master (not if consignee) and of the mariners, and all other unavoidable perils, losses and misfortunes, that have or shall come to the hurt, detriment or damage of the said goods and merchandize, or any part thereof, for which assurers are legally accountable." An additional clause assured slave-owning policyholders that vessels, during their voyages, may "proceed and sail to, and touch and stay at any port or places whatsoever, if . . . obliged by stress of weather or other unavoidable accident, without prejudice to this insurance." Explicit exclusions to the policies included enslaved people's "natural death and escape."[35]

When the city newspaper declared the *Encomium* "and Cargo a total loss" in its February 20 issue, the Charleston Fire and Marine Insurance Company paid on its policies as contracted, absorbing a significant financial loss. Amédée Gardanne was reimbursed for his six emancipated slaves on April 3, 1834; Robert Eagar for his seven on October 31. Upon receiving payment, both men signed over their "right, title, and Interest" to their bondpeople to the insurance company, "with full power to sue for and recover from the British Government, its Officers or agents" the "negro slaves or their proceeds," plus damages. The Charleston Fire and Marine Insurance Company, in short, became "the sole proprietor" of the financial stake in the emancipated slaves.[36]

Company president John Haslett signed off on the payments, but he also had a $300,000 company to protect. On April 3—the same day he compensated Gardanne—Haslett penned a letter to U.S. secretary of state Louis McLane asking, "What notice has or will be taken of this business by this Government[?]" Implied in the question was the expectation that the U.S. government would labor strenuously to help recoup the monies paid out by the insurer.[37]

Haslett looked to the U.S. State Department to take the lead role in securing recompense from a foreign government and to help him right the company's ledgers. His insurance policies were an important component in the smooth operation of a domestic slave trade whose victims built the

American economy. Surely the government of the United States—a government whose very constitutional structure magnified slave owners' voices—would consider his business too valuable to suffer on account of slave stealing by a foreign power.

Less than six weeks earlier, Charles Harrod, president of the Mississippi Marine and Fire Insurance Company of New Orleans, had also written Secretary of State McLane. Harrod's office had insured a number of the enslaved people liberated from the *Comet* in early 1831, and more than three years later he was still seeking the U.S. government's assistance "to bring the subject to a speedy and favorable termination." The seizure and emancipation of bondpeople from the *Encomium* further complicated diplomatic efforts already underway. "This is the second outrage of the kind upon the persons and property of American citizens whose misfortunes have obliged them to put into Nassau," stormed the *New Orleans Courier*, "and it is confidently expected that the strong arm of the Government will be immediately put forth in order to insure redress."[38]

5

British Indecision

As word of British colonial authorities' conduct toward the *Encomium*'s white passengers spread to port cities across the American South in March 1834, "great complaints" arose alongside "calls for the interference of the American government." The *New Orleans Bee* asserted its belief that the United States would "not allow their citizens to be insulted and abused by the underlings of any power, and more especially too, when cast, friendless and unprotected upon the[i]r shores, by the elements." Reprinted in many Southern newspapers, the *Bee*'s report of the British "outrage . . . excited great indignation in Charleston." The British consul there expressed uneasiness over the hostile state of "publick feeling in that Town." Their collective ire raised, Charlestonians called upon their U.S. congressman, Henry L. Pinckney, founder and longtime editor of the *Charleston Mercury*, "to demand the interposition of the government."[1]

The U.S. government, already embroiled in a three-year-long dispute with Great Britain over the *Comet*, expanded the scope of its action. At the insistence of Secretary of State McLane, U.S. consul George Huyler pressed the Bahamas' Lt. Gov. Blayney Townley Balfour to identify and transmit a copy of the law that guided British authorities' dealings with the enslaved people rescued from the *Encomium*. Balfour's prompt reply, unsatisfying to its American recipient, stated, "There is not, to my knowledge, any positive or distinct enactment of the British Parliament, which declares Slaves landing on our Coasts to be free." Balfour instead cited the "clear and distinctly given opinion" of Sir Christopher Robinson and Lord Gifford, whose contention from 1818—the same one invoked in the case of the *Comet*—was that "Africans cast on the shore of a British Colony, in consequence of the wreck of the Vessel in which they were conveyed, as Slaves, are not to be considered as Slaves illegally imported, but as free persons." Balfour adopted that stance when he informed those enslaved on the *Encomium* "that they were at liberty to stay here or to depart, as they pleased."[2]

Balfour vehemently opposed British compensation for emancipated Southern slaves. The lieutenant governor envisioned all of the possible administrative headaches and social problems for his colony "should the Public Authorities in the United States countenance the idea that the British Government would repay to the Masters, the value of any Slave, who, by touching on our Shore, becomes free." Should indemnification become standard policy, he feared, the Bahamas would serve as a dumping ground for elderly or disabled bondpeople unwanted by their American owners. At the same time, given the widely republished unflattering account of their British hosts given by *Encomium* passengers to the *New Orleans Bee*, Balfour expressed to Huyler his concern that the U.S. government would improperly "conceive that there was a disposition in the Bahamas to treat shipwrecked strangers with harshness or inhospitality."[3]

At least one unnamed white "gentleman" from the *Encomium*—likely John Waddell—communicated his grievances directly to President Andrew Jackson. A correspondent from Washington, DC, informed one North Carolina newspaper "that the President is highly indignant at the insult recently offered by the British authorities at Nassau, to the passengers of the American brig 'Encomium.'" Jackson was not a man to take insults lightly. His personal record of dueling testified to his sensitivity to slights. Word had it that Jackson "intends, as soon as [the U.S.] Minister reaches the English Court, to make through him a peremptory demand of satisfaction," as any offended Southern gentleman would when affronted. The Southern press approved of Jackson's anticipated aggressive diplomatic response to the *Encomium* outrage. "We consider the question involved of vital importance," explained one paper. "Let the principle be once settled, that the owners of slaves shall . . . be protected in their rights—rights which are guaranteed to them by the Constitution." Foreign nations must be divested of the notion that they may "seize our property before our eyes" without suffering "redress."[4]

The task of presenting the American position to British diplomats fell once again to U.S. chargé d'affaires Aaron Vail, whom the new secretary of state, John Forsyth, briefed on the *Encomium* in August 1834. Vail heard a story already familiar to a man who had been grappling with the intricacies of the *Comet* case for more than two years. Again, authorities in the Bahamas defended the liberation of enslaved people on the basis of Sir Christopher Robinson and Lord Gifford's legal opinion from 1818. And the stakes were no less high. "This transaction has produced a strong sensation in the United States," Forsyth cautioned Vail, "and particularly in the

South, where it is viewed as a direct interference with their rights of property." That the seizure and emancipation happened for a second time in three years in about the same place only added to the "unfavorable impression" of British officials' handling of the *Encomium* incident.[5]

Forsyth outlined for Vail the "abundant grounds for . . . dissatisfaction" produced by the case of the *Encomium*. First, he wrote, "The slaves were in the quiet possession of their owners." The captives had not asked "the authorities of the island to interpose for their discharge," and the owners certainly did not invite their interference. British intervention "was wholly voluntary and gratuitous," heedless of the slave owners' legal rights. Second, Forsyth complained that Lt. Gov. Balfour relied on a legal opinion that applied only to Africans, not "to slaves born in the United States, and belonging, for generations, to American citizens, under titles derived from British laws, prior to the separation of the two countries." Authorities in the Bahamas, rather than treating the castaways as citizens of a "friendly nation," showed a blatant "disregard for interests of a great importance to a large portion of the American people." Forsyth concluded by conveying President Jackson's desire that Vail soon take the issue up with the British government. The United States expected "early indemnification . . . in both cases" for the sake of "justice" as well as the maintenance of "friendly relations between the two countries."[6]

On September 20, 1834, Vail penned a voluminous letter to Lord Palmerston. With neither hesitation nor objection, he shouldered the responsibility of defending U.S. slaveholding interests in the face of an empire that had, over time, grown increasingly hostile to slavery. The American diplomat could hardly have been unaware of the difficulty of his task, especially since Britain's Slavery Abolition Act had gone into effect just seven weeks earlier. Yet Vail plowed ahead in service to his government. After reviewing old arguments over the *Comet*, he fulfilled the more recent "duty assigned to him" by submitting "a fresh appeal" to the Crown concerning compensation for the enslaved people liberated from the *Encomium*. President Jackson, Vail explained, was "impressed from the first with a deep sense of the justice of the demand put forth by the claimants" from the *Comet*. After that surprisingly "long delay," for which Vail still awaited an answer, "that regret is now greatly increased by the occurrence of another shipwreck, attended with analogous circumstances."[7]

Vail reiterated to Lord Palmerston the legality and the magnitude of the forced migration of enslaved people across the American South. For the

Encomium, he focused less on the domestic slave trade than on the compulsory relocations with owners who exploited enslaved laborers to set up new "agricultural establishments." "Daily" during the flush times of the 1830s, slave owners traveled with "that species of property . . . through the different States" in search of virgin soils. They "remov[ed] their slaves, by land or by sea, from one State to the other where slavery continues to exist under their respective laws." The enslaved people aboard the *Encomium* were thus transported "under every legal sanction" of the United States.[8]

Vail condemned the British authorities in Nassau for not acting "in obedience to any existing parliamentary enactment declaring the freedom of slaves landing under such circumstances." The only rationale given by the Crown for the seizure and emancipation of the *Encomium*'s human cargo was the legal opinion issued by Sir Christopher Robinson and Lord Gifford in 1818, which in any case was an inapplicable precedent involving the transatlantic slave trade. The *Encomium* was not a transatlantic slaver, and it conveyed people born into slavery, no different than the generations of ancestors who came before them.[9]

The American diplomat, in short, drew a distinction between those actually kidnapped and those descended from the kidnapped. Under the tortured logic of slavery, this mattered, especially in regard to bondpeople's lived experience. The native African taken "by forcible abduction becomes the property of a master who holds them [*sic*], as merchandize, until he can dispose of him with profit," Vail reasoned. The individual stolen directly from Africa was thus "exposed to arbitrary treatment from the Slave dealer, who has but a temporary interest in his welfare."[10]

Summoning all of the paternalistic rhetoric of proslavery apologists, Vail described a completely different situation for enslaved people born in the American South. The African American bondperson living "under a title originally derived from British Laws," he declared, labors "in the Service of a Master bound to protect him," "under the safeguard of laws framed for the security of his person, and for the restriction of the power of his master over him." Legally, the argument could hardly have been more disingenuous. In almost all cases, slave owners functioned as unchecked judges and juries over the bondpeople in their possession. At times, whether intentionally or not, they played executioner on their plantation, murdering an enslaved person through punishments and tortures that exceeded the physical limits of human endurance. When that happened, and the state intervened to hold slaveholders accountable for the offense of killing a slave, they almost always got away with it.[11]

Vail drew a final contrast. Whereas the Portuguese vessel forced Africans "from a land of freedom to . . . one of perpetual bondage," the *Encomium* carried enslaved people from the older slave states of the Atlantic coast to the new cotton frontier, a purported benefit to them. The diffusion argument, popularized during the controversy over the admission of Missouri into the United States fifteen years earlier, maintained that distributing enslaved people more widely to new lands would allegedly increase their standard of living and improve their overall happiness. Vail observed in his note to Lord Palmerston that the enslaved Southerner aboard the *Encomium* "is following the fortunes of his master, [and] a passenger in the same ship with him." They "remov[ed] for the advantages of both, probably," in Vail's telling, "but certainly not for any purpose likely to aggravate the condition of the slave." Forced removal, in other words, was allegedly beneficial to the enslaved. In negotiations with Britain, the chief U.S. diplomat thus employed an argument long favored by proponents of slavery's expansion.[12]

Although Vail discounted the supposed parallels between the cases of the Portuguese ship and the *Encomium*, the next part of his letter assumed for the moment that the Robinson/Gifford position was correct. Their opinion from 1818 considered the question of whether British colonial authorities could lawfully provide "supplies or relief" to the Portuguese slaver. Vail noted that Robinson and Gifford believed such aid to slave ships justified in exceptional "cases of absolute distress," in which landings of enslaved people "arose from stress of weather, peril of the sea, or other inevitable accident." Upon that clause, Vail thought he might "safely rest the title of the [American] Claimants to redress." After the wreck of the *Encomium*, and the loss of all of their property except their enslaved people, the white passengers had a right to expect "the hospitality which, in all other civilized parts of the Globe, awaits persons in their situation." To the contrary, scoffed Vail, they were not greeted with "the kind reception which a stranger in distress has." The "seizure of their property" was "irreconcilable with the ordinary principles of common justice."[13]

Vail then turned to Great Britain's Slave Trade Act of 1824, a statute designed to amend and consolidate all preexisting laws relating to the abolition of the slave trade. Nothing in it permitted the confiscation and liberation "of Slaves belonging to the Citizens of a friendly Power accidentally cast upon the shores of a British Settlement in the prosecution of a lawful

Voyage," Vail wrote. To the contrary, it affirmed that no obstacles were to "prevent the trans[s]hipping and assisting, at Sea, any Slave or Slaves which shall be in any ship or Vessel in distress." For Vail, the message was clear: "With this implied, if not express, warrant to the authorities of the Bahamas to grant to . . . the passengers of the 'Encomium' that assistance which they came to seek at Nassau because it was no where else to be found, it is difficult . . . to conceive" how officials in the Bahamas "could have arrived at the conclusion that they were bound to interfere in any other way."[14]

Whether relying on Robinson and Gifford's legal opinion or the consolidated Slave Trade Act of 1824, Vail believed it abundantly clear that "the Colonial authorities of the Bahamas, in refusing to restore the Slaves who were Passengers in the 'Encomium' to their rightful owners," violated "any public act intended for their governance in such cases." Had he stopped at that point, Vail thought that perhaps the American claimants would receive "justice," but he could not be sure. He continued.[15]

With the Bahamas so close to the Florida coast, separated by a busy maritime corridor, Vail emphasized a desire for "relations of good neighbourhood." When British colonial agents conducted themselves in ways that undermined "friendly sentiments," they jeopardized Anglo-American relations. Already, Vail cautioned, "the case of the 'Encomium' has produced a deep sensation throughout the United States, but especially in the South, where the existence of a large Slave Population has rendered the people more sensitively alive to every occurrence that may tend to disturb the relations existing there between master and Slave." They saw in the events in Nassau a direct affront to their property rights, which they defended more vigorously as the radical abolitionist movement took root in the North in the early 1830s.[16]

American slave owners' complaints of "direct interference" with their enslaved property seemed valid to Vail. The captives from the *Encomium* were "in the quiet possession and under the entire controul of their masters," en route to New Orleans, "when they were forcibly seized and landed" and taken from their owners. The enslaved people had not applied to the colonial authorities for liberation, nor had their owners invited foreign meddling in the master-slave relation. British "interference," Vail charged, "was wholly gratuitous, and uncalled for," a blatant violation of "the rights of foreigners whom misfortune had placed in their power," especially considering "that this was the second time that the same cause of complaint had, from their illegal acts, arisen" in the Bahamas.[17]

As Vail explained to Lord Palmerston, U.S. citizens lawfully transporting "their property, by sea, from one part of the Union to another," had long maintained an expectation of "hospitality" in the event of "shipwreck or other calamity" that forced them into a British port. The "laws of all civilized communities" routinely granted such "protection" in episodes of "misfortune." By denying those protections, Vail implied, Britain excluded itself from the ranks of "civilized communities."[18]

Vail at last circled back to the insurance companies whose pleas spurred governmental action to secure reimbursement. He explained that U.S. insurers calculated marine risks under the assumption of the "just and benevolent policy" of hospitality practiced by foreign actors. If nations such as Great Britain suddenly "declare the forfeiture of property . . . , without previous warning of their intentions," the financial repercussions to American business and commerce would be incalculable, at least until shippers adjusted and changed their "mode of conveyance" or until commercial insurers recalculated the risks of various routes. Not only did the economic costs of the British seizure and liberation affect the owners deprived of their human property but they also reverberated across a U.S. economy permeated by the institution of slavery. The loss of two boatloads of enslaved people posed no danger to the overall production of Southern cotton or other agricultural commodities, but it did threaten the fiscal well-being and survival of the affected insurance companies.[19]

Vail concluded by reminding Lord Palmerston that President Jackson sought "full indemnity to the Claimants" in the case of the *Encomium* as well as for "the persons shipwrecked in the Comet," which the American diplomat still had not heard word about forty-four months after the wreck. Vail urged "no delay," expressing the hope that "a speedy adjustment . . . will prevent the occurrence of similar causes of complaint."[20]

Three days after Vail sent his lengthy missive to Palmerston, colonial secretary Thomas Spring Rice, operating on an independent timeline, offered the first indications of his long-awaited decision on the *Comet*. The issue of reparation for the *Comet* disaster had generated disagreement within the British government. Although the Crown lawyers favored compensation for the liberated slave cargoes, Treasury official William Rothery was not similarly convinced. On September 23, 1834, Spring Rice, too, expressed his belief that the American owners and insurers of enslaved people aboard the *Comet* were not "entitled to compensation." One week later, Lord Palmerston, unaware of Spring Rice's opinion, sent the colonial secretary a copy of Vail's long note of September 20, asking for "a speedy adjustment" of the claim on the *Comet* and introducing the additional claim on the *Encomium*. Palmerston and Spring Rice planned a face-to-face meeting as soon as both were in London.[21]

Spring Rice sent his definitive opinion on the *Comet* to the lords of the Treasury on October 17. He encouraged "the Law Officers" to seek "additional information" before the British government delivered its final judgment to the Americans, forwarding copies of the relevant correspondence in his possession. He took explicit issue with one aspect of the Crown lawyers' initial ruling. The law officers blamed the loss of the enslaved people on the confiscation by customs officers in the Bahamas. Spring Rice disagreed, finding the seizure irrelevant. He concurred with William Rothery that, either before or after the captives were taken up, "the exportation of the Slaves from Nassau would have been equally illegal."[22]

The colonial secretary also underscored an important new reality: Parliament had initiated the process of slavery's abolition in much of the British Empire, beginning August 1, 1834. The passage of the Slavery Abolition Act removed slavery's legal standing in the British Atlantic world, and as a result, any "alien landing in a British Colony," Spring Rice asserted, "can . . . only be considered as a freeman, with the rights of a freeman." If British law no longer recognized the ownership of human beings, British authorities could not be expected to deliver them up to a state of bondage elsewhere. In Spring Rice's estimation, "the circumstance of Shipwreck or accidental importation" did nothing to "vary the case." Therefore, he concluded, "I should . . . consider that any Governor or Officer of the Crown . . . who permitted an Alien negro to be forcibly taken from the British Territories and carried into Slavery, to be guilty of a most flagrant violation of his duty."[23]

Spring Rice's rationale made sense, but the enslaved people aboard the two American ships were confiscated and liberated *prior* to the implementation of the Slavery Abolition Act. The colonial secretary pointed out, however, that even before that time, it was illegal for "a British Subject to remove a Slave from one Colony to another" within the empire. By that principle, he asked, "How . . . could it become lawful for an American Citizen to do so within a British Territory and under British jurisdiction?" Surely the British government could not be expected to provide compensation to Americans for an act that was illegal under British law.[24]

Spring Rice wanted to see no precedent set for reparation due "Foreign States" for enslaved people lost in British territories. It could only "lead to the most serious inconveniences in [the] future." As he saw it, the best way to avert compensation claims was "by maintaining in the broadest and most unqualified manner the right of the Negro, however he may have been introduced into our Colonies, to the privileges of a freeman . . . under the protection of British Law."[25]

Having heard from both William Rothery and Thomas Spring Rice, the lords of the Treasury were equipped to respond to the Crown lawyers, who had been waiting since April for approval of the necessary monies to reimburse American slave owners who lost bondpeople from the *Comet*. After reviewing all the evidence and opinions they had gathered, the lords of the Treasury concluded in November that the *Comet*'s slave owners did not deserve restitution. The case should not have gone before the Vice Admiralty Court at all, but its verdict "did not interfere with any right of the American owners to resume possession of the Slaves," because "no such right" existed. Given the importance of the question, the lords of the Treasury recommended that the law officers of the Crown revisit their original decision, because they felt confident that further review would reveal the "necessary conclusion that the American owners can have no claim upon the British Government for Indemnification for the loss of their Slaves."[26]

Nothing was yet definitively decided. The passage of time since the wreck of the *Comet*, which one might have expected to lend greater clarity to the questions at hand, only complicated matters. Great Britain's continued divergence from its long history of slavery, capped off by the implementation of the Slavery Abolition Act, only widened the chasm between the Crown and the U.S. government. The geographic boundaries around the practice of slaveholding in the Atlantic world were shrinking just as the American commitment to the institution was growing stronger than ever. The "speedy adjustment" that U.S. diplomat Aaron Vail hoped for became an elusive dream.

With the Crown lawyers returning to their deliberations, armed with additional information, the wait continued for the owners and insurers of enslaved people seized from both the *Comet* and the *Encomium*. For them, daily life never stopped. Only a month after the wreck of the *Encomium*, Antonio Della Torre appeared on the verge of his next grand venture. On March 3, 1834, he posted a notice in the Charleston newspapers of his intent to close his establishment at 65 Broad Street and put his three-story brick house up for sale. It appeared that Della Torre, like so many thousands of other slave owners during the flush times, had succumbed to the siren song of the Old Southwest. By late 1834, he had acquired a Louisiana sugar plantation as part of a long-term investment strategy. For the time being, he was in no great rush to relocate, perhaps because he lacked the enslaved laborers necessary to work the property. He instead offered to rent it out to "a person who will place on the Estate from 40 to 60 good working Negroes" to cultivate it "for a term of five or ten years." Alternatively, with "30 to 35 working hands," the land could be converted "into a most desirable Rice Plantation." A year later, Della Torre may have located someone to rent his Louisiana sugar plantation. Fellow Catholic and business associate Dr. James C.W. McDonnald announced in early November 1835 his intention "to remove his hands to the West." He therefore put up for sale his sprawling 1,500-acre plantation located ten miles outside of Charleston, directing interested parties to apply to Antonio Della Torre.[27]

Della Torre remained in Charleston several more years engaged in the commission business. The Panic of 1837 may have further delayed Della Torre's plans to relocate to New Orleans, but by 1840, he had finally set up shop in the Crescent City at 100 Royal Street, and later at 55 Chartres Street, offering for sale "a splendid assortment of fancy articles." In 1850, the seventy-year-old Della Torre was back living in Charleston, recorded in the census as a sawmill operator and master of twenty-one enslaved people. Owning and trading in slaves had enabled him to achieve his American Dream by the time of his death in 1858. A devout Catholic, Della Torre was portrayed in obituaries in religious newspapers as far away as New York as a model Christian, with a "warm and benevolent heart . . . open alike to all" and sympathetic to the "poor and suffering." Whether he was as well disposed toward his enslaved people as the "helpless immigrants" he generously aided is unknown.[28]

Perhaps Della Torre's religious faith helped him accept trials in stride and endure the sufferings that visited him. When colonial authorities in Nassau seized and liberated the enslaved captives from the *Encomium* in February 1834, he lost half a dozen enslaved people, none of them insured. No records survive to document whatever attempts Della Torre may have made to secure compensation for the emancipated human cargo. The silence surrounding the Italian commission merchant, however, stands in stark contrast to the noisy, blusterous protests of *Encomium* passenger and similarly uninsured slave owner John Waddell.[29]

6

John Waddell, Slave Owner

Born in 1803 in coastal New Hanover County, North Carolina, John Waddell Jr. displayed his ambition early. At the age of twenty-one, as a merchant in Wilmington, he already received shipments of goods from faraway Boston, and by 1827, he entered the "Commission and Factorage business" with John R. Callender. The firm of Waddell & Callender sold a range of essential commodities to the people of Wilmington: salt, corn, molasses, sugar, rice, flour, whiskey, beef, pork, iron, whale oil, butter, soap, candles, tobacco, wine, paint, hay, and gunpowder. Counting among the North Carolina elite, Waddell and his wife, Anna Campbell, lived on his father's plantation in neighboring Brunswick County, surrounded in 1830 by the family's 124 enslaved people. That same year, Anna gave birth to the couple's son, John Marsden. Still in her twenties, Anna passed away in February 1831, leaving Waddell a widower with an infant son.[1]

The personal tragedy of his wife's death may have spurred Waddell to join the westward exodus of the flush times. In the autumn of 1833, Waddell ventured to the north-central Louisiana village of Natchitoches, a hub for gathering bales of cotton to float downriver to New Orleans. He purchased a tract of land near the Red River and also entered into an agreement with local plantation owner Sylvester Bossier "to raise a crop in common" in Natchitoches Parish. Bossier supplied the land; "Waddell was to furnish a certain number of Slaves" to work it. Waddell returned to North Carolina to gather a portion of his bondpeople, who would become part of a massive forced migration to the Old Southwest. Upholding his half of the arrangement with Bossier, Waddell, accompanied by his older brother, Haynes, boarded the *Encomium* in February 1834 with twenty-two enslaved people bound for Louisiana.[2]

Because of the wreck, the names of those individuals are known, unlike the identities of most held in bondage. Forced on board were fourteen enslaved men, all between seventeen and twenty-five years of age, at the peak of their physical strength. Waddell anticipated that the strong backs, arms, and legs of Ben, Crawford, Solomon, Jack, Joe, Hales, David, Bosseau, Ferdinand, Marcellus, John, Josh, Ned, and John would cultivate the soil of the Red River Valley. The Waddell brothers also deposited six young women, all eighteen to twenty-two, onto the *Encomium*: Hagar, Mary, Stella, Diana, Elsey, and Lucy. At least one of them was the mother to children Henry, five, and Jack, three. No doubt Waddell expected the other young women would become mothers soon, too, adding to his wealth in persons. Altogether, Waddell accounted for almost half the enslaved people on board the *Encomium*.[3]

When British colonial authorities in Nassau seized the enslaved cargo, Waddell had the most to lose. He therefore stood at the forefront of each and every objection to the confiscation and liberation of the captives. While still in Nassau on February 12, Waddell joined Capt. Paschal Sheffield and his crew in filing a protest with U.S. consul George Huyler. That marked the first of several careful, conscientious steps the North Carolina slave owner took to protect his economic interests in human capital.[4]

Ultimately nine of the twenty-two enslaved people he shipped on the *Encomium* voluntarily elected to return with him to the United States. Before he left Nassau, however, Waddell was foresighted enough to envision a possible collision with the U.S. law, effective January 1, 1808, against the importation of enslaved people from abroad. Although the captives had been his lawful property before the voyage, since they had landed in the Bahamas, they might be considered foreign imports. Taking no chances, Waddell solicited Lt. Gov. Blayney Townley Balfour "to get some legal papers . . . to prove that those who preferred returning with him were free" at the time they made their choice to return. Those documents, Waddell hoped, would prevent anyone from "his own Nation . . . from seizing him" on a charge of smuggling enslaved people into the country and, at the same time, protect him from authorities in the Bahamas from pursuing him and claiming that he was illegally carrying them out of the colony. Balfour obliged with certificates of manumission, signed by the governor, stating that those departing with Waddell were free residents acting of their own accord.[5]

According to Balfour, Waddell also "wished to have some regular indentures made binding the men to him to serve him"—a formal acknowledgment that the former captives agreed to re-enter slavery under his authority. This Balfour "declined to sanction, in any way." Waddell was displeased.[6]

Before embarking on the *Sarah Jane* for Key West, with the nine bondpeople returning with him to the United States, Waddell could not help but issue a parting shot concerning the thirteen others who remained free in Nassau. He told Lt. Gov. Balfour directly "that either 'Uncle Sam' or 'John Bull'"—the U.S. or the British government—"should pay him the price of his Slaves," for "he considered them to be well sold." Waddell thought himself plundered of a great treasure, money in human form, and his grudge ran deep.[7]

From Key West, Waddell journeyed to New Orleans, where he laid the groundwork for demanding compensation from his government for the enslaved people divested from him. For insured enslavers such as Amédée Gardanne or Robert Eagar, the Charleston Fire and Marine Insurance Company encouraged clients "to sue, labour, and travel for, in and about the defence, safeguard, and recovery of the said goods and merchandize" lost in a given calamity. Ideally, from their perspective, policyholders would take as many pains on the company's behalf as "if the property had not been insured" at all. For the uninsured, like Waddell, personal exertion assumed still greater import.[8]

Waddell undertook his quest for restitution with all due diligence. He affixed his name to the public complaint over British mistreatment published in the *New Orleans Bee* on March 4. A week later, he and fellow *Encomium* passengers Henry Reilley, Amédée Gardanne, and William Dalzell submitted documentation of their ordeal with New Orleans notary public Jules Mossy.[9]

On March 11, the same day he visited the notary, Waddell got all twenty-two enslaved people whom he had placed aboard the *Encomium* in Charleston appraised. This would have been a remarkable feat, given that he had no more than nine of the bondpeople with him. In seeking the appraisal, Waddell consulted Joseph Walker, Charles Mulholan, John Compton, Sostene A. Baillie, and Thomas O. Moore, all "gentlemen of high standing and respectability, and very competent Judges in matters of that kind." Whether at Waddell's specific request, or based on the markets the men knew best, the valuations were "fixed at Louisiana prices at the time of seizure." That worked to Waddell's benefit. With the insatiable demand for laboring bodies on the cotton frontier and Louisiana sugar plantations, the slave markets of the Old Southwest were heated, and individual bondpeople sold for sometimes hundreds of dollars more than they would back east. Seeking maximum indemnity, Waddell surely wanted his enslaved people priced most advantageously.[10]

The five local experts on slave prices in Louisiana came through for Waddell. They estimated eleven of the fourteen men at $850 each. At age seventeen, Ferdinand, the youngest, received the lowest valuation among the men, at $800. The most expensive were skilled bondmen Ned Gibbs, the blacksmith, and Marcellus Paine, the "first rate Carpenter," valued at $1,200 and $1,500, respectively. The Louisiana gentlemen appraised the men at a total of $12,850. The six bondwomen were assessed less generously, with half at $600 and half at $650. The same five experts callously declared five-year-old Henry worth $200, and three-year-old Jack $150. Altogether, the gentlemen determined that the North Carolina slave owner's human cargo was worth $16,950, or more than half a million dollars today.[11] Satisfied with that result, Waddell contacted Sylvester Bossier, either by letter or in person. With so many of his enslaved people stolen away to freedom by the British, Waddell could not meet his obligation to supply laborers on Bossier's property. At the North Carolina slave owner's behest, Bossier appeared before a Natchitoches Parish judge on March 24 and deposed that, "in consequence of this seizure, . . . Waddell has been unable to furnish the Slaves as agreed upon." Bossier further swore "that the loss thereby sustained by . . . Waddell will be, at least, . . . four thousand Dollars" worth of uncultivated crops.[12]

As Waddell gathered evidence in Louisiana, prominent citizens in Wilmington, North Carolina, convened a public meeting on Friday, March 28, "to take into consideration the gross insult offered to American citizens by certain officers of His Britannic Majesty, at Nassau." Col. Gabriel Holmes, the longtime sheriff of New Hanover County and a respected community leader, chaired the meeting. Wilmington's Alexander Anderson, a member of the board of directors of the U.S. branch bank in Fayetteville, was appointed meeting secretary. William B. Meares, a state senator who represented New Hanover in the North Carolina General Assembly, addressed the crowd. All three men were slave owners who may have called the town meeting of their own accord after reading newspaper accounts of British officials in the Bahamas stripping enslaved people from local merchant and friend John Waddell. Or Waddell himself may have sent a letter encouraging them to hold it. Either way, Waddell was well connected with the Wilmington elite, and they, like him, would not suffer in silence.[13]

In light of the wreck of the *Encomium*, the British confiscation of American slave owners' property, and colonial officials' appalling conduct, Meares submitted a preamble and a series of six resolutions for the assembly's consideration. The first two resolutions expressed "the strongest indignation at the insults and injuries . . . offered our Fellow Citizens" and condemned "the forcible seizure and detention of the property of" shipwrecked American citizens as "contrary to the rights of hospitality, and a palpable violation of the laws of civilized nations." The third resolution stated plainly that the people gathered in Wilmington "know no difference, nor will . . . recognise any distinction between property in *persons* (as known to our laws,) and property in *things*." The remaining resolutions looked toward the future. They encouraged the U.S. government "to take the most *prompt*, *decisive* and *efficient* measures to inquire into, *and to redress* this outrage on our citizens," for "we at all times, stand ready and willing, and pledge ourselves, to repel insult and aggressions on the persons or property of American citizens." The last resolution directed "that a copy of these resolutions be forwarded to the President of the United States, and to our Senators and Representatives in Congress." Attendees at the meeting "unanimously adopted" all resolutions and appointed Holmes, Anderson, and Meares responsible for submitting the proceedings to North Carolina's two U.S. senators, Bedford Brown and Willie P. Mangum; to each of the state's thirteen members of the U.S. House; and, most of all, to their presidential ally Andrew Jackson.[14]

When Gabriel Holmes submitted to Andrew Jackson the resolutions from the meeting in Wilmington, he was only adding to the correspondence the president was receiving about the *Encomium*. Recall that an anonymous white "gentleman" shipwrecked in the Bahamas, likely Waddell himself, wrote Jackson as well. Waddell had demonstrated his willingness to pursue recompense aggressively, and sending the president a message directly was in keeping with his character. The set of resolutions from Wilmington's concerned citizens could not have hurt Waddell's cause, and it was a simultaneous boon for Sheriff Gabriel Holmes, who reminded the president of his political activism and allegiance. Notoriously loyal to those loyal to him, the following month, Jackson rewarded Holmes with a patronage appointment, naming him inspector of the revenue for the port of Wilmington and surveyor for the district.[15]

Newspapers throughout the Southern Atlantic and in Northern cities such as New York reported on the Wilmington town meeting. Only once before had he "witnessed so large and respectable an assemblage," raved one correspondent. "Our Town Hall was literally crowded, and . . . the greatest unanimity prevailed." As word of the Wilmington resolutions spread, however, so did controversy over Capt. Paschal Sheffield and the precise character of events endured by the *Encomium* castaways.[16]

When the *New Orleans Bee* printed the white passengers' complaints about their treatment, the *Charleston Courier* suspected the account was exaggerated. An interview with Capt. Sheffield in early April confirmed the paper's skepticism. By 1834, Sheffield served as one of several captains piloting packet ships that regularly shuttled freight and passengers between Charleston and New Orleans. He sought to correct the record of the *Encomium*'s final voyage and, in the process, preserve his own reputation.[17]

Sheffield indicated several inaccuracies in the passengers' account. First, the captain denied that they were "prevented from landing at Nassau, longer than usual, under similar circumstances, where quarantine regulations are in force." As an experienced seafarer, Sheffield knew that pulling into port and disembarking were two distinct steps, depending upon the regulations in place at the port and upon shipboard conditions. Authorities often required passengers aboard vessels arriving from certain locales with known outbreaks of disease, or those on ships upon which sickness had broken out, to wait a period of time before entering the city. When health official Thomas Pindar appeared at the wreckers in Nassau to assess the physical condition of those on board, it was nothing out of the ordinary. If anything, Sheffield observed, the complaining passengers "were permitted to leave the vessel sooner than was expected, on account of their being in a distressed situation." The *Encomium*'s passengers had no cause for grievance on that score.[18]

Second, Sheffield dismissed the alleged rudeness of the British officials who engaged with the shipwreck survivors. According to the captain, the officers from the British warship *Pearl* treated the passengers "politely," and Lt. Gov. Balfour's threat to hang American slave owners only applied to "those who should attempt to force away the slaves, and did not apply to persons who wished to take slaves that were willing to go with their masters." Passengers who conveyed enslaved people out of Nassau harbor, including John Waddell and Capt. Sheffield himself, lived to tell the tale, their necks unharmed.[19]

Third, Sheffield defended the safety features of the *Encomium* itself. He refuted the passengers' characterization of the lifeboat as a small "jolly boat," insisting that it was "a first rate long boat" with greater capacity to convey shipwrecked passengers away from the sunken vessel.[20]

Sheffield's conversation with the *Courier* cast doubt on the *Encomium* passengers' version of events in Nassau. Some readers concluded that their "whole story of the outrages and barbarities committed by the British authorities" was "little better than a figment of the imagination." John Waddell was livid. The *Courier*'s story had impugned the passengers' words and reputations, a weighty matter in the honor culture of the Old South. Waddell responded to the insult with a letter to his hometown paper, the *People's Press and Wilmington Advertiser*.[21]

Waddell felt compelled to "contradict" Sheffield's statement as "an act of justice" to himself and his fellow passengers. He believed the *Courier* too eager to demonstrate its prediction that the passengers' account was exaggerated by giving credence to and amplifying the one dissenting view. To Waddell, it made far more sense to believe the other nine gentlemen who signed the letter to the *Bee*, five of whom "had no slaves on board" and had no other motive for speaking out than to expose the truth.[22]

That Sheffield had signed his name to the white passengers' litany of complaints that appeared in the *Bee* seemed to support Waddell's argument. In later speaking to the *Courier*, the captain explained that putting his name on that document was a mistake. One of the passengers had "presented [it] to him" while Sheffield was otherwise "engaged," and he, "not having time to read the whole paper," scribbled his name on it, even though it "was unquestionably written when under great excitement." Waddell was having none of it. Sheffield had also signed the protest before U.S. consul George Huyler in Nassau, "under the solemn obligations of an oath," and that statement was "substantially" similar.[23]

In the remainder of Waddell's letter to the editor, he rebutted Sheffield point by point on a host of issues. He insisted that the passengers' six-hour wait to land was out of the ordinary, especially for the "unfortunate sufferers from a shipwreck." Nor was their lengthy detention part of standard quarantine procedure, especially since the British warship *Pearl* had its guns trained on the castaways. Waddell acknowledged that Capt. Sheffield carried an enslaved man away from the Bahamas, back to the United States, unimpeded, but he also noted that this was the *Encomium*'s "cook, and . . . on the crew list." In contrast, the British seized thirteen of Waddell's enslaved laborers, and those who returned with him voluntarily were actually "cleared at the office of the customs as free persons and passengers on board the vessel" that took them to the United States. Finally, although an admittedly minor issue, Waddell disputed Sheffield's depiction of the vessel used in evacuating the sinking *Encomium* as "a first rate long boat." According to the disgruntled slave owner, "the long boat . . . was swept from the deck" during the disaster "and . . . never seen by the passengers."[24]

"Mr. Waddell appears to be quite out of humor with us," observed the *Courier* in its printed reply less than a week later. But the editor held firm. He found it difficult to grasp "that the public officers of a friendly Government, in a port which our vessels are daily visiting, and respecting whom we have never before heard a complaint, should have been so regardless of all the courtesies which characterize civilized men, as to . . . exhibit . . . their savage and unfeeling disposition towards a number of unoffending shipwrecked individuals, among whom were several ladies." Diplomatic, economic, and humanitarian reasons, bolstered by the expected gentlemanly conformity to gender conventions, all combined to strain the credibility of Waddell and the other complainants listed in the *Bee*. Capt. Sheffield, on the other hand, gave his account long "after the excitement," with the benefit of time to pause and reflect.[25]

Waddell soon gained an ally in fellow *Encomium* passenger Henry Reilley, who owned no enslaved people aboard the vessel. After reading Capt. Sheffield's report "with perfect astonishment," Reilley, still in New Orleans, fired off a letter for publication in the *Bee*. In it, he refuted the excuse that Sheffield had been too busy to read the contents of the protest he had signed, because, as Reilley explained, he himself had read the statement out loud to Sheffield "in Mrs. Fisher's Hotel, and he highly approved of it." According to Reilley, the only reason Sheffield had turned against the other signatories was that "we positively refused to give him a card of thanks for wrecking his vessel on a fine star lit night with a moderate six [k]not breeze."[26]

Reilley placed blame for the disaster squarely on Capt. Sheffield. As soon as he reached Fish Cay, Reilley openly declared his "firm impression" that "the Encomium was 'intentionally' wrecked," an assertion he stated he would be willing to repeat under oath in a court of law. In fact, he wanted to publicize his belief as soon as he arrived at New Orleans, but "my fellow passengers . . . dissuaded me from it, and thought it was better to get clear of Sheffield, as speedily as possible." Reilley instead resolved to contact the firm that insured the *Encomium*, the Neptune Insurance Company of New York, so that Sheffield "might not recover" the benefits due on the policy. The incensed Reilley, traumatized by the shipwreck, deemed the captain "a maniac," "unworthy and incompetent ever again to command even a common water tank."[27]

Reilley's seething hatred for the *Encomium*'s captain spilled out onto the pages of the *Bee*. He skewered Sheffield for his allegedly callous indifference to his passengers' welfare. While on Fish Cay, Sheffield reportedly divulged to slave owner Charles Allen "that he expected the vessel would have thumped to pieces." Allen asked if the captain thought they "would all have perished," to which the captain replied, if the *Encomium* had broken apart, "he with his crew intended taking to the boat," leaving the passengers "to shift for [them]selves." Later, "while the passengers were lamenting their deplorable condition, he [Sheffield] was as unconcerned about the past as a thoughtless infant," Reilley raged. Upon reaching New Orleans, "he refused to speak to any of us."[28]

Two fellow passengers, William D. Smith and Amédée Gardanne, signed off on the veracity of Reilley's remarks. They appended a statement noting how suspicious it seemed that Sheffield never refuted the original letter published in the *Bee* "while the rest of the passengers" were still in New Orleans. The captain was in town for "upwards of ten days" after the public statement appeared in print, giving him ample opportunity to respond in a timely manner. Instead, he waited for a month, voicing his thoughts in a newspaper almost eight hundred miles away. It smacked of cowardice, they implied. They shared Reilley's hope "that this case will be litigated," exposing Capt. Sheffield's "foul" deeds and "murky" heart. Some in the press looked forward to an investigation and, should the charges be proven, Sheffield's punishment. No master of a ship should ever "sacrifice or jeopardise the life of a number of fellow creatures, for the gratification of mercenary motives."[29]

In all likelihood, Sheffield's silence and withdrawal from his passengers while in New Orleans had more to do with embarrassment and shame at having lost his ship. The allegation that the captain intentionally wrecked the vessel to collect insurance money has little merit. In Nassau, Sheffield attributed the loss of the *Encomium* to a "strong south westerly current" flowing counter to the brig's course. In the treacherous shoals surrounding the Bahama Islands, the "adverse currents" were powerful enough to toss the vessel onto the reef from which it could not be dislodged. The relentless waves pounding it onto the rock left it a "total wreck," submerged by the beautiful but unforgiving Bahamian waters.[30]

Capt. Sheffield departed Charleston in early April for New York City. While there on May 1, New York's *Evening Star* republished the accounts from New Orleans besmirching his character. Sheffield and a friend immediately ventured to the newspaper office to declare the charges against him false. The next day, the *Evening Star* printed a story that exhibited full confidence in the mariner. "He is well known in this city by many of our most respectable merchants," it explained, "and a private enquiry is now being made which will ultimately exonerate him, and place the cause of the flagitious attack in its true light." The investigation concluded successfully for Capt. Sheffield, with no lasting harm to his reputation. Before the year was over, he again navigated the seas, piloting the brigs *Lawrence* from Charleston to New York City and *Warsaw* from Charleston to New Orleans. By 1860, the successful seafarer had amassed $12,000 in both real estate and personal property (the equivalent of about three-quarters of a million dollars today), a portion of it accrued from shipping property in people.[31]

The enslaved people seized from John Waddell in Nassau led to a corresponding decrease in his fortune. However, as news of the *Encomium* spread across the South in March and April 1834, one consistent feature of the reporting was the confidence, expressed by both the passengers and the Southern press, of the U.S. government's role to play in securing restitution for the slave owners victimized by British policy. "The passengers call loudly upon the government to resent the indignity and wrong which they have suffered," recorded the Fayetteville, North Carolina, *Observer*, an organ that often published news relevant to John Waddell and others in the vicinity of Wilmington. About one hundred miles northeast of Wilmington, the *Newbern Spectator* decried the "injustice and inhumanity" suffered by the crew and passengers of the *Encomium*, but it felt sure "that the United States Government will thoroughly investigate the matter and take the course which becomes it." The Charleston papers concurred. According to the *Courier*, the British officers behaved inappropriately. "The detention of the slaves was . . . unwarrantable," but the incident will "be properly examined" by the government.[32]

The *Courier*'s welcome embrace of federal assistance came as no surprise. Since the offending party was a foreign government, the U.S. government had the constitutional obligation to respond. States lacked the authority to conduct diplomacy abroad, a point that was in no way disputed. South Carolina had by 1834 acquired a reputation for hostility toward the national government, as a proponent of the states' rights doctrine under which individual states could declare null and void federal laws that they found intolerable, such as tariffs. Yet even the most ardent states' rights advocates voiced no objections when the weight of the federal government was used to buttress the institution of slavery. The *Courier* looked forward to the U.S. government's intervention in the case of the *Encomium*: "None are more anxious than ourselves that the persons and property of American citizens should be protected from any and every indignity or outrage that may be offered them, with the most scrupulous care." The U.S. government had a necessary role to play in bringing about a resolution to the slave owners' problems.[33]

The British government was already considering American claims for compensation throughout the summer and fall. But anxious slave owners like John Waddell heard nothing and were unaware of these deliberations. Growing impatient, he pursued some resolution to his grievance in two other ways.

Drawing on his, or possibly his father's, political experience as a one-term state lawmaker, Waddell submitted a petition to the North Carolina legislature in Raleigh. Edward B. Dudley, the newly elected representative for the town of Wilmington, presented the memorial on Monday, December 8. Signed by Waddell, it railed against "the treatment of himself and fellow passengers by the authorities of Nassau" while in the Bahamas and was referred to a committee for consideration.[34]

Waddell's petition chronicled the voyage of the *Encomium*, the indignities he and his fellow passengers believed they had suffered, and the seizure of the enslaved people he had transported. "Thus has your Memorialist been not only unfortunate in having been shipwrecked & delayed in his proposed settlement in Louisiana, but has been plundered of his property," moaned Waddell. He called upon "his native State to make common cause with her sisters of the South on this most delicate, but vital subject." More vessels carrying enslaved property, whether in company with migrating owners or through the domestic slave trade, would navigate the busy commercial waterway that separated the Bahamas from the southeastern United States. Inevitably, Waddell warned, some "are liable to be thrown by stress of weather" upon British colonial shores. He then spelled out the fear he assumed the masses of Southern slave masters shared. If the British government made it policy "to establish the freedom of our slaves" upon landing there, "it will be holding out a *premium to insurrection*" to the captives on board. Something, in short, must be done to protect Southern slave owners and domestic slave traders. Otherwise, enslaved people imprisoned on slave ships would rebel and head toward British territory.[35]

The North Carolina General Assembly understood that the federal division of powers placed diplomacy on behalf of "aggrieved" citizens in the hands of the U.S. government, but it saw fit to act on Waddell's concern for other states. North Carolina lawmakers shared Waddell's "anxiety" and recognized the dangers "if the Federal Government should permit so flagrant an outrage upon the peculiar rights of Southern citizens to pass unheeded." Both the memory of the 1831 Nat Turner revolt and the 1834 initiation of the gradual emancipation of enslaved people in the British West Indies, in close proximity to the U.S. southern coastline, made for perilous times for American shippers of captive laborers.[36]

If the South could not count upon "the imbecile or corrupt functionaries of a foreign power," such as British colonial officials in the Bahamas, it must rely on the U.S. government, even if that meant "the last resort of nations": war. According to the North Carolina General Assembly, "Peace obtained at the sacrifice of honor, or tame submission to injury, is never permanent, unless it terminates in entire subserviency to the nation perpetrating the wrong." Under those circumstances, North Carolina state legislators voiced their preference for war to peace. But that would not be necessary, they continued. All that was required was "prudent, yet firm and energetic conduct on the part of the General Government, in demanding indemnity to our citizens for injuries committed by the authorities of the British Crown, and the adoption of such measures as may tend to prevent a recurrence of such injuries."[37]

Moved to act by Waddell's petition, the North Carolina General Assembly passed four resolutions on January 3, 1835. It declared the detention of the shipwrecked slaves from the *Encomium* "a breach of the rites of hospitality, and an infraction of the laws of nations"; denied "any distinction in principle between property in persons . . . and property in things"; and expressed confidence in the U.S. government to take the necessary measures to right the injustice. Finally, it requested that Gov. David Swain transmit copies of the lawmakers' report and resolutions to each North Carolina congressman in Washington, DC, to every sitting state governor, and to President Andrew Jackson. For at least the third time, a direct appeal reached Jackson on behalf of the *Encomium*'s slave owners.[38]

Waddell could not have known the extensive diplomatic efforts already underway. As the law officers of the Crown continued their deliberations, American chargé d'affaires Aaron Vail arranged an interview with the Duke of Wellington on January 12 to once again press the urgency of the *Encomium* as well as the four-year-old wreck of the *Comet*. The duke had yet to receive the paperwork he had requested on the two cases but assured the U.S. diplomat that he would attend to them "without delay," adding that he would "accelerate . . . the final adjustment of the matter." Vail appreciated the "earnest tone" of the duke's "promises" and conveyed to Secretary of State John Forsyth his optimism "that the termination of this long-pending negotiation is not far remote."[39]

After speaking with Lord Aberdeen, the newly installed colonial secretary, the Duke of Wellington offered Vail further assurances later in January that a resolution was afoot. Yet two months later, the promises of a speedy settlement had yet to materialize. Vail hoped to arrange a meeting with the prime minister, Sir Robert Peel, and Lord Aberdeen to hold a "final discussion of the merits of the claim."[40]

Around the same time, John Waddell made preparations to complete his long-delayed relocation to Louisiana's Red River Valley. He sold his New Field Plantation in North Carolina before the end of 1834 and later settled at a plantation "on the Rigolette de Bondieu, ten miles below the town of Natchitoches." After more than four years as a widower, he had also remarried and established a household with the Virginia-born Lucia Chauncey Porter. She gave birth to a baby boy but, like John's first wife, passed away in her twenties while her son was still an infant.[41]

Despite the tragedies afflicting his personal life, Waddell eventually achieved the economic dreams that motivated his move to the Louisiana cotton frontier. Waddell's Natchitoches Parish plantation boasted one hundred captive laborers, almost equally divided by sex. In April 1846, enabled by the labor of his sizeable workforce, Waddell joined with William Protho to buy an additional tract of land from William M. Lambeth in what would become Winn Parish. In 1850, Waddell owned $10,000 in real estate, a figure that would double in the coming decade, despite auctioning off various tracts of land in Natchitoches and Winn parishes in 1858. On the cusp of the Civil War, a full accounting of Waddell's assets, human and otherwise, made him the equivalent of a modern-day millionaire.[42]

In the Old South, wealth marked a key ingredient for community esteem and social prominence. Waddell became a justice of the peace of

Natchitoches Parish in 1841. Five years later, he served as captain for a regiment of eighty Natchitoches volunteers deployed for action in the Mexican-American War, a conflict that promised to solidify and expand U.S. claims to territory friendly to slavery. In 1847, Waddell emerged as the Whig candidate for Congress from Louisiana's Fourth District, although he lost the race to the Democratic incumbent. Upon the death of the Whig Party in the mid-1850s, Waddell became active in the anti-immigrant American, or Know-Nothing, Party in Natchitoches. The leisure time that facilitated Waddell's civic-mindedness could be traced directly to the enslaved men and women who produced his wealth.[43]

Though largely silent, his captive laborers occasionally spoke through their actions. When they did, they condemned their owner's behavior. Before migrating to Louisiana in 1835, Waddell sold "a negro woman" named Luna ("Luner") to Robert Council of Bladen County, North Carolina. Luna was "about five feet high, with a small scar on her forehead," but Waddell likely left her behind because she was, for his purposes, old: "between thirty and thirty-five years of age." Owners most prized enslaved people in their later teens and twenties, with strong muscles and fertile wombs. Separated from loved ones, Luna fled her new owner, who suspected her "to be lurking about" Brunswick County, on the lands of John Waddell's brother Alfred, where she might reconnect with kin.[44]

Three of Waddell's enslaved people self-liberated within a year of their arrival in Louisiana. Bondman Dick ran away on April 15, 1836, and Watty and Jack followed suit two weeks later, although Waddell believed all three fugitives were together and in cahoots. His runaway advertisement listed the age, height, and complexion of each. Dick was twenty-five years old, five feet nine inches tall, "black, and a very likely boy." Watty was a decade older, five feet seven inches tall, and "very black." The youngest, Jack, was "about 20 years of age, a mustee, about five feet seven inches high." Jack shared the name but not the physical description of an enslaved adult shipped on the *Encomium*, so the fugitive was not one of the captives who voluntarily accompanied Waddell back to the United States. None of the three bondmen wanted to live in Louisiana. "These negroes having been recently brought from North Carolina, may attempt to return to that State by the way of Natchez or New Orleans," Waddell speculated. To make that long journey, he prognosticated, "they will probably attempt to secret themselves on board some steamboat, or make their escape in a canoe."[45]

If Waddell's dogged pursuit of recompense for his enslaved people liberated from the *Encomium* was any indication, he would track down Dick, Watty, and Jack with a relentlessness that would make escape from his clutches virtually impossible. For the individuals emancipated in the Bahamas but over whom Waddell claimed ownership, he required greater assistance. He and other individual slave owners like him viewed the national government as an auxiliary to and extension of their own mastery. They saw the U.S. government as a provider of essential economic services, no less than the companies that paid out on maritime insurance policies on enslaved cargoes, and they felt entitled to its protections. The clamor for action was about to grow even louder.

7

Emancipation from the *Enterprise*

George Hammett boarded the *Enterprise* against his will around January 22, 1835. The twenty-five-year-old, standing five foot seven inches tall, was enchained for the profit of another. His name headed a slave manifest that listed seventy-eight enslaved people bound for Charleston, South Carolina, from the port of Alexandria.[1]

Professional slave dealer Joseph W. Neal shipped Hammett and all but five of the captives put on the *Enterprise*. Based in Washington, DC, Neal began advertising as a human trafficker in the fall of 1831. That October, he expressed a desire "to purchase from fifty to sixty likely Negroes, of both sexes, families included." Neal promised "the highest price in cash" for Chesapeake bondpeople, whom he intended to transport and sell in the slave markets of the Deep South. Initially, Neal ran his operation out of Washington Robey's tavern "on Ninth Street, near the General Post Office."[2]

Roughly equidistant between the President's House and the U.S. Capitol, Robey's property lay just two blocks north of the Centre Market, where vendors peddled fresh produce to residents of the district. The stream of customers likely stopped by Robey's establishment to find camaraderie and drink, as well as to sell the proprietor enslaved people for Southern markets. Robey had dealt in slaves at the Ninth Street location since at least 1825, when he first issued a public call for "fifteen to twenty likely young NEGROES of both sexes, from ten to twenty-five years of age." While awaiting a sufficient lot of enslaved people to ship south, he imprisoned them in outbuildings situated on the property. Other slave dealers without a slave jail, including Joseph W. Neal, made use of Robey's incarceration facilities, for a fee.[3]

In the summer of 1832, Robey vacated his Ninth Street location and invited those wishing to sell enslaved people to call upon him either "in the rear of Gadsby's National Hotel" on Pennsylvania Avenue or at his new

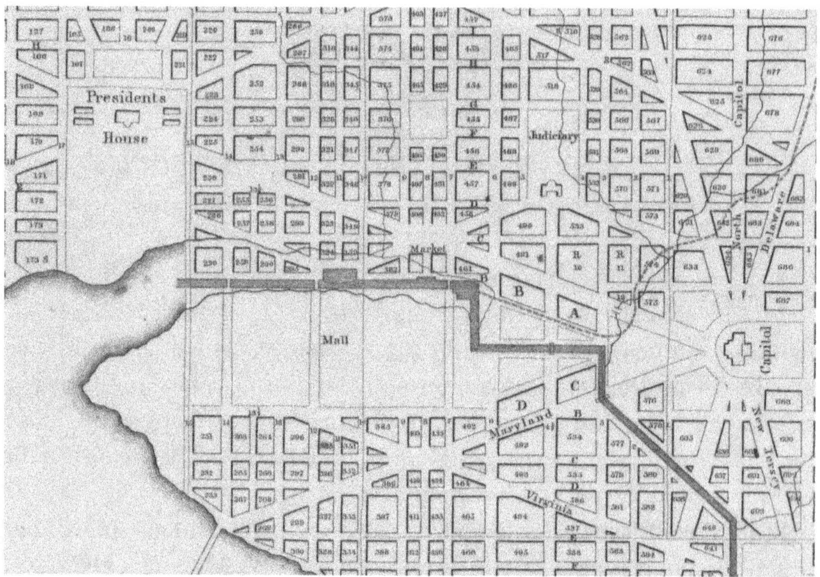

Map of Washington, DC, in 1840.

tavern, on the east side of Seventh Street, just south of the National Mall. His adjacent slave pen occupied the same block, bound by B Street to the north and, on the south, Maryland Avenue, which ran diagonally southwest from the halls of Congress to the Long Bridge over the Potomac.[4]

When British traveler E.S. Abdy visited Robey's Seventh Street pen in 1833, he described it as a "wretched hovel," "surrounded by a wooden paling fourteen or fifteen feet in height," a structure obviously erected to quell inmates' escape. Enslaved captives of "both sexes, and all ages," Abdy recorded, were exposed to scorching summer heat and brutal winter cold, with some reportedly having "actually frozen to death." Yet Abdy was denied admission to inspect the slave jail personally and forbidden the opportunity to cast his eyes upon the suffering inside. As a "colored" man who served as "the overseer of the pen" explained to another visitor eager to investigate the facility, "it was not customary to admit strangers."[5]

One need not gain access to the interior to divine the torment endured by the enslaved inmates on the other side of the wooden walls. The aural experience of Robey's slave pen alone generously hinted at the prisoners' mental and physical anguish. In 1834, a correspondent from *The Liberator*,

William Lloyd Garrison's Boston-based abolitionist newspaper, filed a report in which he explained that, from the street, he could plainly hear "the clanking of chains" pierce the air as well as "vulgar oath[s]" emanating from within. At the same time, these noises "strangely commingl[ed] with the sound of music and dancing" and sporadic, "discordant laugh[s]." It was a puzzling cacophony for the correspondent's ear to take in. He attributed the apparent "mirth" to the captives' respite from labor as they bided their time in Robey's pen. After all, he reasoned, "some had escaped a hard service" under a "severe" master and anticipated better treatment after their impending sales. The reporter also shared a widely held racial stereotype among nineteenth-century whites that Black people displayed a "natural fondness for music and social enjoyment." The sounds of "momentary pleasure" floating in the wind, however, disguised the overwhelming grief of agonizing separations from loved ones and the pain of tortuous imprisonment. Relying on fellow inmates for strength and support through song and dance marked one of the few coping mechanisms available to prisoners of the slave pen.[6]

Separated by only a narrow passageway from this nightmarish site of emotional and bodily pain stood Robey's relocated tavern. Joseph W. Neal and business partner Oliver Simpson adopted Robey's relocated establishment as the headquarters of their new slave-trading enterprise. In October 1832, the firm of Simpson & Neal advertised its desire to acquire "one hundred likely young negroes": male or female, alone or in families, "house servants, field hands, and mechanics of every description." It really did not matter, as long as they were young and healthy enough for the rigors of labor in the Deep South. Simpson & Neal advertised heavily in the Washington newspapers for seventeen months, through the end of February 1834.[7]

When Neal reappeared in the columns of the Washington dailies, in June, he could still be found at Robey's tavern on Seventh, but he styled his partnership Joseph W. Neal & Co. Vying for surplus Chesapeake slaves with the preeminent DC slave-trading firm of Franklin & Armfield and individual slave dealers such as James H. Birch, Neal pledged a willingness to "pay the highest prices in cash" for 150 or 200 "NEGROES," running the same notices from September 1834 to January 1835, right up to the day before the *Enterprise*'s departure. Despite the change in their firm's name, Neal's partner Oliver Simpson was still active in the business.

The slave house of Washington, DC, trader Joseph W. Neal.

After Neal marched their seventy-three captives out of Robey's pen, down Maryland Avenue, and across the Long Bridge over the Potomac to Alexandria for loading onto the *Enterprise*, he consigned the valuable cargo to Simpson, who awaited their arrival in Charleston.[8]

Those herded onto the *Enterprise* consisted of thirty-six male and forty-two female bondpersons. By complexion, thirty-four were judged "Black," thirty-five "Copper," and nine "Yellow." The shipment was distinguished by the youthful ages of those on board. Only twenty-three of the seventy-eight captives (29 percent) were eighteen or older. The remaining fifty-five were sixteen or younger, with thirty-one of them under ten. Betsey Groom, thirty-one, boarded the *Enterprise* with her four children: Easter, fourteen; Thomas, nine; Martha, four; and Louisa, two. Twenty-four-year-old Eliza Tinney was held captive with her five children, the oldest of whom was eight. At three weeks old, her infant son, Richard, was the youngest prisoner included in the shipment. Based on the surnames listed on the slave manifest, about half the children under ten undertook the voyage unaccompanied by any parent.[9]

Although not reported at the time, a majority of the human cargo deposited on the *Enterprise* had been kidnapped from slave owners in the Chesapeake and sold to Joseph W. Neal. Networks of villains in the antebellum decades conducted a thriving illicit trade in free Black people abducted and sold into slavery. Less common, though not unheard of, in the Southern states was the crime of slave stealing. In a society where the law prioritized masters' property rights, convictions for slave stealing carried stiff penalties, including death, in Maryland and other states. The theft of slaves in the commonwealth of Virginia brought a two- to ten-year prison sentence in the state penitentiary in Richmond. Despite the high stakes, the potential profits of kidnapping and reselling enslaved people made it worth the risk for a desperate or criminal few. Enslaved children readily enticed away or physically overpowered made the easiest targets. Selling them as one's own to a domestic slave trader then disposed of the evidence of the crime, as the slave dealer either marched them south in an overland coffle or stashed them aboard an outgoing merchant vessel. Neal may not have known or cared that all five of the Warfield youngsters on board the *Enterprise*, ranging in age from eight to fifteen, had been stolen from the same plantation. For the time being, Charles, Mary, Mahaley, Elizabeth Jane, and Mary Ann Warfield remained together, but they shared a hold in a slaving brig about to carry them to an unknown future.[10]

As required by law, shipper Joseph W. Neal swore before Alexandria port collector George Brent on January 22 that his enslaved cargo had not, to his knowledge, been illegally imported into the United States after the 1808 closure of the transatlantic slave trade, nor were any of the slaves entitled to their freedom. Thomas N. Davis, a slave trader from Loudoun County, Virginia, followed suit. Davis accounted for the balance of the enslaved people transported aboard the *Enterprise*. His five captives were thirty-five-year-old Phil Redout; the twenty-five-year-old "yellow" bondwoman Dinah Buckingham; and her three children: eight-year-old Emiline, six-year-old Jane, and a six-week-old girl. Capt. Elliot Smith, a thirty-three-year-old mariner from Maine, most recently at the helm of the *Leonidas*, affixed his signature to the manifest as well, affirming the legality of the *Enterprise*'s routine coastwise voyage to Charleston. Smith was a veteran sea captain, with ten years' experience.[11]

Built in Hallowell, Maine, in 1823 and based out of Boston (although registered in New York in late 1834), the brig *Enterprise* boasted a cargo volume of just under 128 tons. It was strictly a merchant ship, outfitted for trade and "mounted with no guns." When it departed Alexandria on

January 22, it carried "Bricks, Tobacco, [and] Garden seeds," in addition to the "78 Slaves," a six-man crew, two or "three passengers," and "thirty days' provisions on board"—more than enough to sustain them during the brief journey down the coast. The *Enterprise* cleared the Virginia capes on January 30 and entered the Atlantic Ocean.[12]

Adverse weather immediately frustrated Capt. Smith's progress at sea. Brutal cold gripped the entire East Coast in early 1835. In January, winter temperatures plummeted to sixteen degrees below zero in the District of Columbia. The intense cold disrupted travel, canceled worship services, and delayed meetings of bank stockholders. After the *Enterprise*'s departure from Alexandria, likely at least two powerful cold fronts overtook the vessel at sea. One of these reinforcing rounds of cold air produced snow flurries in Charleston and temperatures low enough to postpone commission merchant M.C. Mordecai's scheduled auction. Another front brought a "severe snow storm" to North Carolina and some of "the coldest weather ever known" to the region. The frigid pall blanketing the Tar Heel State marked the worst in memory, save for a few old-timers who recalled an even deeper and longer-lasting arctic blast during the Revolutionary War. The same system gave Charleston sleet before the mercury bottomed out overnight to eight above and struggled to reach thirteen before noon. "Though the sun shone brightly" in Charleston by Sunday, February 8, residents huddled inside their homes, sequestered for warmth: "the streets and the churches were almost deserted." Likewise, the city's harbor was not as busy as it should have been. Mysteriously, the *Enterprise* had yet to make its appearance in port. Oliver Simpson, ready to receive seventy-three of the seventy-eight captives aboard the brig, grew anxious.[13]

The wintry winds churned the sea and buffeted the vessel on the open ocean. It experienced, as the *Charleston Courier* later reported, not a single incident but rather "a succession of bad weather, which drove her off the coast." Repeated rounds of violent, "tempestuous weather" battered the *Enterprise*, and "head winds and gales" blew it well off the intended route to Charleston, "far to the Eastward of the gulf stream" and out into the Atlantic. The ship sprouted leaks and suffered damage to its "hull sails and rigging." Terrifying waves "washed overboard" part of its provisions. The situation grew increasingly dire. With the journey unexpectedly lengthened and food and water running short, on February 5, Capt. Smith made for "the nearest land"—the Bermuda Islands—to repair his

The road to Hamilton, Bermuda.

ship and restock his depleted supplies. The distressed vessel limped to the British colonial outpost of Port Hamilton on Wednesday, February 11. After twenty days at sea, the beleaguered *Enterprise* was hundreds of miles off course.[14]

About 770 nautical miles almost due west lay Charleston harbor, still in the clutches of an unprecedented freeze. The cold snap hit the enslaved people of the Carolinas hard. Owners were generally stingy in the disbursement of clothing, which was manufactured for warm weather wear. Bondpeople often supplemented their basic, meager wardrobes when they could, but the extreme temperatures of early 1835 brought inherent dangers. In January, two "negroes . . . were found frozen to death" in a boat on the Savannah River after spending the previous night "exposed to the inclemency of the weather" in South Carolina. In North Carolina, an unidentified ten-year-old "negro girl" sleeping next to a fire was "enveloped in flames" when a stray ember ignited her clothes during the night. Wrapping a carpet around her smothered the fire and spared her life, but she was left "badly burnt."[15]

The wintry weather of February 1835 would alter the fates of the captives aboard the *Enterprise* as well, but to their advantage. When Capt.

Many Black Bermudians made their living in the maritime trades.

Elliot Smith entered the harbor at Hamilton with his enslaved cargo, he encountered a society in flux. Slavery had existed on Bermuda for more than two centuries, yet the island colony's twenty-one square miles did not support the agricultural regimes traditionally associated with bondage elsewhere in the Atlantic world. Most enslaved people in Bermuda engaged in maritime pursuits or worked as skilled laborers. In either case, they enjoyed relative autonomy compared with their counterparts in Britain's sugar-producing colonies or in the United States. By 1834, its slave population of about 4,600 outnumbered the colony's 3,900 whites. Another 740 free Black people lived in Bermuda in 1834, a number that would grow after Parliament's Slavery Abolition Act went into effect on August 1. Many slave owners in Bermuda liberated their chattel right away, dispensing with the period of apprenticeship written into the law. The damaged *Enterprise* arrived in Hamilton a little more than six months after the process of emancipation had begun.[16]

Capt. Smith understood the risk of seizure by the British. Shippers who transported captives in the coastwise domestic slave trade could hardly have been unaware of the still-undecided cases of the *Comet* and *Encomium*, and the implementation of the abolition law only added to the danger. But the

The sea was central to Black life in Bermuda.

condition of his vessel and the diminished stores on board left the captain no real choice. On his arrival, customshouse officers discovered the enslaved cargo. Predictably, as Smith recounted, they "seized my vessel immediately on my arrival in this Port" because the *Enterprise* had "slaves on board" and confiscated the ship's papers. Yet "after a day or two," authorities redelivered the brig to Smith and told him "that they had nothing further to do with either the Vessel or [its] Cargo." They pledged to surrender the ship's papers, still on deposit in the customshouse, as soon as the *Enterprise* was fully provisioned, repaired, and able to proceed to Charleston.[17]

For the next week, Capt. Smith oversaw the replacement of his ship's exhausted supplies and "the repair of the sails" damaged by the relentless gales. During that time, he took precautions for the safekeeping of his valuable human cargo, anchoring the brig some three hundred yards offshore, away from land. The *Enterprise* "was not brought to the wharf," and "no one from the shore was allowed to communicate with the slaves."[18]

News of the enslaved people on the *Enterprise* spread through the colonial capital of Hamilton, reaching Sir Stephen Remnant Chapman, governor of Bermuda, and the Privy Council. At a meeting of the Privy Council on February 17, deliberations concluded with a resolution to empower the governor to adopt "some measure" that would enable the captives held aboard the *Enterprise* "to assert any right of freedom they might conceive themselves entitled to, if they were so disposed." But before any further steps were taken, the Privy Council sought "the opinion of the Attorney and Solicitor General." The law officers agreed. They believed the enslaved people on the *Enterprise* "should be made acquainted with the situation in which they stood, in a country where slavery had ceased to exist." Acting upon the law officers' advice and recommendation, the Privy Council directed the collector and comptroller of the customs in Bermuda not to authorize the *Enterprise* to resume its journey to Charleston, an order that contradicted customs agents' previous promise to Capt. Smith.[19]

The next day, February 18, Smith reported to the customshouse at about 2:00 p.m. Following a week's worth of work, the *Enterprise* was ready for departure, but the captain required clearance to leave port. To Smith's surprise, "the collector stated that he had received a verbal order from the council to detain the brig's papers until the governor's pleasure could be known" concerning the enslaved captives onboard. As a result, the collector explained, "he would not give up the papers that evening." Curiously, though, he offered to "report the vessel out the next morning, as early as the captain might choose to call for the papers." The importance of the delay would not become clear for a few more hours.[20]

With the essential documents withheld, Capt. Smith could not lawfully head out to sea. He threatened to leave anyway, but Bermudian customs agents summoned "a gunboat and Royal Navy officers to detain the ship." Furious, Smith filed a formal protest "against the collector and comptroller for the detention of his ship's papers" and vowed to "hold them responsible" for their actions. As he explained to the collector, he "feared the colored people of Hamilton would come on board his vessel at night and rescue the slaves."[21]

Although the collector tried to ease the captain's anxiety, Smith, in fact, had reason for concern. While the captain was seeking permission to depart, elsewhere on the island a benevolent organization of Black Bermudians gained an audience with Chief Justice Thomas Butterfield of the Bermuda Supreme Court. With the onset of emancipation in Bermuda, friendly societies sprouted for the purposes of Black self-help and mutual aid. Such associations were essential to combat the lack of governmental support for Bermudian freedpeople, as neither British nor Bermudian lawmakers embarked upon any strategy to aid the formerly enslaved or to develop any program to help them transition to freedom. To the contrary, the white minority in Bermuda took steps to maintain its political and economic power over a segregated society. In this racially oppressive climate, friendly societies harnessed the energy and resources of Bermuda's Black population to promote education, job opportunities, and racial uplift. Among their roles was tending to sick and dying members, offering financial support to those too ill or otherwise unable to work, and watching over widows and orphans. The valuable, empowering roles that friendly societies played in Black Bermudian life led to their proliferation after emancipation began in 1834.[22]

The president of the Young Men's Friendly Institution in Pembroke Parish, Richard Tucker, was a free Black man, property holder, and business owner. Tucker intervened on behalf of the *Enterprise*'s enslaved cargo. His friendly society indeed "threatened" Smith, as the shipper claimed, with the liberation of the hostages held on his brig in Hamilton's harbor, but the free Black Bermudians concocted a plan unlike the direct physical assault upon the ship that the captain envisioned. Instead, Tucker convinced the comptroller of the port of Hamilton not to surrender the ship's papers, as a way to buy time. During the hours he gained by delaying the *Enterprise*'s departure, Tucker spearheaded a legal action in Bermuda's Supreme Court, in which he appealed to Chief Justice Butterfield to consider the enslaved people's desire for freedom. The friendly society president applied for a writ of habeas corpus, which would compel Capt. Smith to produce his prisoners before the judge and allow them to state whether they would prefer to proceed to Charleston "and continue as Slaves, or remain here and be free." In a legal triumph, Tucker's friendly society secured the writ.[23]

At about 5:40 p.m., the local constable, writ in hand and probably accompanied by Tucker, boarded a boat to head out to the *Enterprise*, still anchored well offshore. In the presence of multiple witnesses, he personally served the writ to Capt. Smith, explaining to him that his captives would appear before the Supreme Court to express their preference for returning to slavery in the United States or remaining as free persons in Bermuda. Smith passed the writ to another "gentleman on the deck of the vessel, and asked him to read it." After the unnamed man did as instructed, he "observed that the document was not served in proper form" and attempted to hand it back to the constable. When the officer refused to take it, "it was dropped into the bottom of his boat" in an apparent gesture of contempt. The constable returned to shore to report the outcome of the encounter.[24]

Soon after, Smith ventured into Hamilton. A merchant in town who had served as a witness and had seen the unceremonious discarding of the writ advised the captain to track down the document. Smith first humbled himself to ask for it from the crew of the constable's boat, who refused to assist him. Their unwillingness to help forced the captain into the indignity of requesting the constable's aid directly. The officer presented Smith the writ for a second time, and the captain grudgingly appeared before the Supreme Court as required. There, he pleaded to defer compliance with the writ until the following morning. Perhaps Smith sought the delay to afford him the opportunity to sail out of the harbor that night clandestinely, under cover of darkness, in defiance of Bermudian officials. But Chief Justice Butterfield was unyielding. The enslaved captives would appear in his court that night. The judge gave further incentive for Smith to comply, sending a "file of black soldiers armed" to accompany him back to the vessel. Ironically, the soldiers probably belonged to one of the regiments the British Army created using the involuntary labor of kidnapped Africans whom they had rescued from the illegal transatlantic slave trade.[25]

Despite Capt. Smith's continued grumbling and protests, he obeyed the writ. He had little choice. Under the direction of the Black soldiers, "the whole of the Slaves" were "forcibly taken" from the *Enterprise*. The desperate captain convinced at least one person under his direction "to tamper" with the captives by bribing them. As they exited the brig, this crewman reportedly "promis[ed] them money if they would . . . say when questioned, they had rather proceed with the vessel." The situation must already have seemed confusing for the enslaved men, women, and children of the *Enterprise* by the time they landed on shore to the cacophonous cheers of an "immense" crowd "assembled to welcome" them. The boisterous throng followed the enslaved people as they were "marshalled into Court" at about 9:00 p.m.[26]

"The Court Room . . . filled almost to suffocation," reported one newspaper. The crowd supporting the captives included "people of color," such as Richard Tucker and other free Black members of Bermuda's friendly societies. Also in attendance were a number of individuals "who had but a short time since, been owners of Slaves" and "spoke with disgust and utter detestation of the Slavery System." The correspondent considered the presence of antislavery whites a positive indication of the "change . . . in the minds of the people of this Colony."[27]

The biracial cross-section of the Bermudian public that packed the courtroom witnessed a scene described by the *Bermuda Royal Gazette* as "most degrading and revolting to Christianity." The youth of the enslaved cargo made a deep impression upon the onlookers: "There were children without a single connexion with them, who had no doubt been torn from the very arms of their parents to gratify man, who is ever inventing means to gain filthy lucre; there were women too, with infants at the breast." The sight of "the poor and oppressed" captives was appalling.[28]

Chief Justice Thomas Butterfield beheld the assemblage of enslaved persons before him and informed them that, because they had "arrived in a Colony in which Slavery was abolished," freedom was theirs for the taking. It was up to them. "If they wished to remain in the colony," the judge explained, "they would be protected by the authorities," but they "must [also] obey the laws, and would be punished for any breach of them." According to one newspaper, a wave of "surprise and joy" rippled through the captives upon "hearing the change that awaited them," and they reportedly "expressed their gratitude in the most lively and peculiar manner."[29]

Butterfield then spoke to the captives one by one, "plainly, kindly, and very appropriately," beginning with twenty-five-year-old George Hammett. The chief justice summoned the captive to stand and face him. "Your name is *George Hammett*," Butterfield intoned.

> You came in the brig *Enterprise*, as a *Slave*, and it is my duty, to inform you (understanding that you were kept on board that vessel against your will), that in this country you are free,—free as any white person; and should it be your wish to remain here, instead of proceeding to the port whither you were bound, to be sold or held to service as a slave, you will be protected by the authorities here; and if you do decide to remain you will become as I have observed, a free person, and will be punished for any breach or breaking of the laws of this colony; while if you conduct yourself with propriety, soberness, honesty and industry, you will meet with encouragement from the whole community—do you therefore wish to remain and be a free person; or continue your voyage to the vessel[']s destined port, and be a Slave?

As Capt. Elliot Smith frowned and glared, Hammett's face filled with "joy and wonderment" as he cast aside the fear of his captor and declared publicly, "audibly and unhesitatingly" his preference for freedom in Bermuda.[30]

Butterfield addressed the other captives individually in like manner. Bermudian authorities took an especially gentle approach with "the poor little boys, some of whom were barely six years old" and who "said they had no relation whatever with them." The gut-wrenching and "melancholy scene" of young children stolen from their families mingled with the unfolding exuberance that accompanied the unanticipated escape from a lifetime of slavery. One by one, the chief justice progressed through the names on the slave manifest. Within about three hours, "the whole of the Slaves," except for one woman and her five children, opted for liberation in Bermuda.[31]

Twenty-five-year-old Matilda Ridgley elected to go back with Capt. Smith to the *Enterprise* and return to bondage in the American South, accompanied by her daughters Martha, ten; Helen, seven; Mahaley, five; Betsey, three; and Ann, five months old. Matilda's rationale is unclear. It might have seemed a daunting prospect to raise her large family alone in a foreign, unfamiliar land. Perhaps she, unlike the vast majority of enslaved people caught up in the domestic slave trade, knew her intended purchaser. That knowledge could have been a factor in convincing her that the certainty of bondage was preferable to the uncertainties of liberty. Maybe she had been assured that, if she remained enslaved, her family would remain together. The enslaved in the American South took extraordinary steps to preserve the integrity of their families; sometimes free Black people even voluntarily reentered slavery to keep family units intact. According to one account, Ridgley was among several *Enterprise* captives who had been born free, kidnapped, and sold into slavery. In Bermuda, she had the opportunity to reclaim her liberty, but the five daughters with her were not her only children. Others had been left behind in the slave states, and perhaps she refused freedom rather than abandon them to the torments of bondage without their mother. Under this scenario, if true, a combination of love and hope for reunion inspired her choice.[32]

Newspapers dropped a titillating clue hinting at a different supposed motivation for Matilda's decision. According to one report, she had allegedly "formed an intimacy with the cook of the *Enterprise*." Was this true, or mere salacious rumor that fed into stereotypes of Black female sexuality? Had Matilda, over the course of just three weeks at sea, forged such a relationship? And if so, had she parleyed that connection into a promise to purchase her and her daughters, to keep her family together? Or even a promise of liberation in the United States? Although cases did exist of bondwomen using their sexuality to improve their condition in bondage, enslaved female sexuality did not automatically translate into agency. To

Photograph, with her grandson, of Mary Warfield, one of the enslaved captives liberated from the *Enterprise* in 1835 when she was a young girl.

the contrary, at sea as well as on land, the sexual exploitation and rape of enslaved women proved vastly more common than their ability to manipulate men to their advantage.[33]

Ridgley and her children excepted, seventy-two of the *Enterprise*'s captives claimed their right to freedom in Chief Justice Butterfield's court on February 18. The judge left the freedpeople with "a parting admonition" that, though free, they would need to work. All were to locate "an industrious, sober, honest line of conduct, as by their good or evil course of life they must stand or fall." He encouraged the former slaves not to waste the freedom that "Divine Providence had . . . granted to them."[34]

After the chief justice's remarks, the court hearing drew to a close about midnight. At that late hour, Attorney General John Harvey Darrell called for a subscription to raise money to meet "the present emergencies" of the freedpeople until "they began to feel their way." He promptly collected $70 in donations from those present. Mayor William Cox made available "an unoccupied Store-Room in the town of Hamilton" as a temporary shelter for the liberated slaves. In less than a week, all of them obtained employment as domestic servants or were "taken under the protection" of Richard Tucker's friendly society, whose exertions in "rescu[ing] so many of their fellow beings from cruel thral[l]dom" Chief Justice Butterfield openly praised in court. Members of the friendly society welcomed the orphan children into their own homes. A local Black woman adopted nine-year-old Mary Warfield, one of the many young girls rescued from the *Enterprise*.[35]

A later report appearing only in the *Charleston Courier* stated that Capt. Elliot Smith "was . . . thrown into prison" in Hamilton for "several days." Although that publication neglected to explain the charge against him, the *Royal Gazette*'s account of the *Enterprise* observed that Smith's contempt for Bermudian law and his initial disdain for the writ of habeas corpus merited firm punishment. If true, the captain's incarceration may explain the delay before the *Enterprise* at last weighed anchor on March 1, leaving Bermuda with its cargo of bricks, tobacco, and seeds but only six of the original seventy-eight enslaved people who boarded in Alexandria. The vessel entered Charleston harbor two weeks later, on March 15, fifty-two days after departing the District of Columbia. As George Hammett and dozens of his shipmates adjusted to their newfound freedom in Bermuda, their emancipation generated fresh controversies within the United States—and new tensions between its slaveholders' government and that of Great Britain.[36]

2

Law, Diplomacy, and Politics

8

Britain's Decision

ANOTHER SEIZURE OF AMERICAN SLAVES, screamed the *New York Journal of Commerce* headline. First, the *Comet*, then the *Encomium*, now the *Enterprise*. The U.S. press was detecting a pattern.[1]

Yet press coverage also changed during the four years between these maritime incidents. Newspapers across the country had reported the loss of the enslaved cargo from the *Comet* in 1831 as a great national concern. By the spring of 1835, that was no longer the case. Stories about the *Enterprise* betrayed the growing sectional schism within the United States over the institution of slavery. Outrage over the enslaved people emancipated in Bermuda was confined almost exclusively to "the Southern country," where their liberation "created a strong sensation" and "caused no little excitement." Northern newspapers generally—abolitionist as well as mainstream publications—no longer shared the South's sentiments when a domestic slave trading voyage resulted in freedom rather than profit.[2]

On the domestic front, the rise of radical abolitionism in the early 1830s had caught Southern slave owners off guard. The inaugural issue of William Lloyd Garrison's newspaper, *The Liberator*, published in January 1831 was indicative of the growing urgency of the antislavery movement. Nat Turner's revolt, later that year, which distressed slave owners erroneously blamed on Garrison's newspaper, belied masters' claims of happy, loyal slaves. Widespread panic in the wake of the insurrection prompted Virginia lawmakers to consider a proposal to gradually emancipate the commonwealth's slaves. The plan never came to fruition, but the vote was closer than anyone could have predicted before the rebellion. Afterward, slave owners in the Old Dominion and across the American South more aggressively defended the institution from mounting attacks.

Internationally, the loss of enslaved people from the *Enterprise* marked the first such incident to occur in a British territory after Parliament's Slavery Abolition Act had gone into effect. "O! that other nations would follow the glorious example of the British people in doing away [with] the odious system of Slavery," declared the *Bermuda Royal Gazette*, "which . . . will in after ages be spoken of as one of the noblest acts a nation ever accomplished." Growing moral condemnations of slavery imposed new pressures on the human traffickers still operating in the Atlantic basin, and early reports out of Bermuda hinted that the British government would fully back Chief Justice Thomas Butterfield and the liberation of the *Enterprise* captives. The altered legal context within Britain's Atlantic realms alarmed those participating in the U.S. domestic slave trade, concerned that such liberations "will doubtless continue to be repeated as often as American slaves shall by accident or otherwise, be found in British ports."[3]

That reality contributed to the sectional polarization over the *Enterprise*. "Considerable indignation is manifested by some of the southern newspapers, at the recent decision in Bermuda," observed one publication. In Charleston, where Capt. Smith's vessel finally arrived on March 15, the *Courier* condemned the "unwarrantable conduct of the officers of the British Government, in interfering with . . . the property of American citizens." The captives aboard the *Enterprise* had done nothing more than claim the opportunity for freedom presented them, yet the Southern press faulted the British for "forcibly taking possession" of them as an act of "legalized robbery." The *Courier* characterized British behavior in Bermuda as "*piracy*, under cover of law."[4]

With few exceptions, the Northern press dismissed the allegations of piracy. "How strangely does slavery pervert all common ideas of justice and morality!" exclaimed the *New York Journal of Commerce*. "What was the *piracy* which is thus denounced? It was simply restoring to seventy-three of our fellow citizens the rights of which they were deprived by fraud or force." The true pirates, the same paper explained, were the slave traders and shippers who conveyed "innocent men, neither convicted, nor accused of crime, by violence, against their will, from their homes to a distant shore." In this light, the "*wrongs* and *insults*" to the South complained of by the *Charleston Courier* were better understood as "triumphs of christian benevolence and justice." As one New Hampshire publication assured its readers, "The *dealers* in flesh are not to be pitied. Great Britain has set a noble example."[5]

Some Northern voices disputed the Southern propensity to refer to the action in Bermuda as a "seizure" of enslaved people. That word struck them as too harsh and not an accurate reflection of the reality of what had happened. Judge Thomas Butterfield had performed his duty in giving the captives the ability to choose freedom, just as most of those aboard the *Comet* and *Encomium* had done before. British colonial officials enabled the prisoners to decide for themselves but did not forcibly emancipate anyone. Nevertheless, for owners with interests in the domestic slave trade, the purported plundering constituted a clear violation of sacrosanct property rights.[6]

Southern outrage produced isolated grumbles in 1835 calling for war with Great Britain. According to a small number of newspaper editors, the "high-handed proceeding" in Bermuda afforded a "legitimate ground" for conflict. The *Southern Christian Herald* predicted "the seizure . . . and liberation of slaves belonging to American citizens . . . [was] likely to produce some jarring between England and the United States." Some Northern papers likewise prophesied "that the next serious controversy with a foreign nation will grow out of southern slavery," a war waged "in defense of slavery." But the Northern press decried any foreign conflict on those grounds. As one newspaper in Pennsylvania inquired, "How would our government appear before the world, going to war with a christian nation in support of a sort of trade which itself" was a form of piracy?[7]

The sporadic chatter of armed struggle was hyperbole. "When war is talked of as a remedy for the Bermuda affair," explained the *Baltimore Gazette and Daily Advertiser*, "the language is altogether too strong." It and other more moderate publications accepted that "when vessels enter a foreign port, . . . the masters, the crews, and the passengers, become, for a time, subjects to the laws of [that] country," to which they must submit, regardless of whether those ships were "in distress." Northern papers agreed. "The moment" enslaved American captives "entered an English port," wrote the *New York Journal of Commerce*, "they became free by the law of England. No man in Bermuda had any authority to make them slaves again."[8]

Still, offended Southern slave-owning interests pleaded for the intervention of the highest authorities as a matter of national pride. The "high-handed insult to the Flag of the United States, calls for the action of our Government," asserted the *Charleston Courier*, "and we confidently trust that prompt measures will be taken to redress the wrongs, and avenge the insult which has been thus . . . offered to this country." The newspaper expected the U.S. government to make exertions on behalf of the slave owners who absorbed losses from the liberation of the *Enterprise*'s human cargo. In contrast, Northern papers declared that the federal government should do no more to aid the claimants "than it should to assist a highway robber in recovering his ill-gotten gains."[9]

But the U.S. government was a slaveholders' government. American diplomats had already exerted themselves for four years in an attempt to recover indemnity for those seized from the *Comet* in 1831. Barely a week before the *Enterprise* reached Bermuda, the law officers of the Crown were reconsidering whether the landing of the castaways from the shipwrecked *Comet* "was sufficient to deprive" the owners of captives aboard that vessel "of their claim to compensation." A trio of lawyers agreed on February 3 that it was not. Indemnification for the *Comet* remained on the table.[10]

The latest loss of an enslaved American cargo in a British Atlantic colony meant still more work for U.S. chargé d'affaires Aaron Vail. Secretary of State John Forsyth informed him in late March that it was "the wish of the President that the case" of the *Enterprise* "should be immediately brought to the attention of the British Government" and "that redress be claimed for this gross outrage upon the rights and interests of American citizens." He also instructed Vail to "make use of this occasion . . . to call the attention of his Majesty's Government to the unreasonable delay . . . in deciding upon the questions of a similar character" surrounding the *Comet* and the *Encomium*.[11]

Vail lodged a new complaint with Lord Palmerston over yet "another illegal seizure of slaves." "The case," he wrote, "though varying in some of its details from those of the brigs 'Comet' and 'Encomium,' . . . involves the same considerations, and, consequently, gives rise to a third claim of a precisely similar character." As in his previous protests, Vail stressed the legality of the voyage under U.S. law and that the *Enterprise* was only forced into a British port "by the act of God." Capt. Elliot Smith needed "a refuge from the tempest, [and] relief from starvation." The "code of humanity as well as the immutable laws of justice . . . secure to the distressed mariner" the "aid, protection, and hospitality" found in foreign ports, and even though Smith sought assistance in one of His Majesty's colonies, he took pains to avoid any violation of laws against the physical introduction of the enslaved onto British soil. Vail pointed out that it was not the captain but the "gratuitous and uncalled for interference . . . of the local authorities" in Hamilton who compelled the captives' landing on Bermuda. Forcing them off the vessel to declare them free marked, in Vail's words, "a flagrant violation of all the principles which regulate the intercourse and promote confidence among friendly nations." Unlike his previous letters to

Lord Palmerston, the American diplomat kept his missive about the *Enterprise* brief, "confident" in the "expectation of prompt reparation."[12]

As delicately as possible, Vail reminded Palmerston of the long delays in resolving the analogous cases of the *Comet* and the *Encomium*, despite "repeated and earnest appeals to . . . justice." Couched in the most diplomatic language he could muster, Vail expressed his gratitude for Palmerston's attention to the earlier pair of shipwrecks but conveyed President Jackson's growing impatience, alleging that "the delay has been protracted far beyond any period that could have been considered necessary for the most deliberate examination." Had Great Britain and the United States dealt successfully with the *Comet*, Vail scolded, similar subsequent problems could have been avoided, and the U.S. government "would have been spared the unpleasant duty of ordering . . . another fresh appeal to the justice of Great Britain." Vail shared his hope with Forsyth that his letter reinforced the U.S. government's adamant opposition to the seizure of enslaved American cargoes without using "language that could produce any thing like irritation."[13]

In the summer of 1835, the cases of the *Comet* and the *Encomium* languished, following the Board of Treasury's recommendation to the Crown lawyers to rethink their initial opinion in favor of restitution. The prospect for payments for the enslaved people emancipated from the *Enterprise* appeared even less likely, since the British emancipation act had already become law before that vessel ever reached Bermuda. In his appeals to Lord Palmerston, Vail focused not on the differences between the three cases but on their similarities. In each, Vail reminded him, "the actual landing of the slaves within the British jurisdiction had been the act of British authorities." The American captains of the vessels had objected to their enslaved cargoes stepping foot on British soil, and after they proved helpless to stop it, they filed protests with the proper officials. Slave owners could hardly find fault with any of the three ship masters.[14]

In an interview with Vail, Palmerston acknowledged the tardiness of the British response to the shipwrecks. To be sure, the "delicate nature" of the subject required careful deliberation, but as Palmerston admitted, the complexity of the matter had produced virtual paralysis. "The law officers of the Crown . . . had found the subject so full of difficulties and involving points of such moment," he said, "that they had almost shrunk from the task of arriving at definitive and binding conclusions upon them."[15]

Palmerston sought further guidance. In the autumn of 1835, he consulted Prime Minister William Lamb and Thomas Spring Rice, the former colonial secretary who had been named chancellor of the Exchequer the previous April. Their deliberations convinced the three of them that "the ordinary law authorities" were incapable of rendering a final decision. They therefore resolved "to refer the whole matter to the judicial committee of the Privy Council, in whom resides the highest legal power in the State." The Treasury advanced all pertinent documents related to the U.S. claims to compensation to the committee for examination.[16]

Palmerston did his best to allay Vail's concerns over the continued postponement of the reparation question. On one hand, with the Privy Council involved, any refusal to supply indemnification would be based on a legal justification that could not help but "satisfy" President Andrew Jackson and maintain "friendly" relations with the United States. On the other hand, should the Privy Council's opinion prove "favorable to the claimants," the application for restitution could be made "to Parliament by authority of the highest character." Palmerston verbally promised Vail the Privy Council's "prompt" attention to the claims.[17]

Nonetheless, another eight months elapsed with no further developments, except for the replacement of the U.S. chargé d'affaires in July 1836. During his four years in that diplomatic post, Aaron Vail had been singularly unsuccessful in pursuing compensation for the enslaved cargoes of the *Comet*, *Encomium*, and *Enterprise*. His successor, Andrew Stevenson, was a fifty-two-year-old native of Culpeper County, Virginia, who had served thirteen years in the U.S. House of Representatives, seven of them as Speaker. He was not only a loyal Jacksonian Democrat but also a slave owner himself. President Jackson calculated that sending a robustly proslavery Virginian to England would bring renewed energy to negotiations and yield the results that Vail had failed to produce.[18]

Secretary of State John Forsyth informed the new U.S. minister that "the most immediately pressing" issue for him was "the claim of certain American citizens against Great Britain for indemnification for a number of slaves, the cargoes of three vessels wrecked on British islands in the Atlantic." Supplying Stevenson all the correspondence that had accumulated on the matter over the past five years, Forsyth underscored "the President's anxious wish that no time should be lost, and no exertion spared on your part, to effect an early adjustment of this long-pending claim."[19]

Within two weeks of beginning his appointment, Stevenson sent Lord Palmerston "an earnest appeal for a speedy and final answer" from the British government. He opened with delicately worded complaints about the long delays, noting that some of the American owners and insurers had already written to him directly about their extended waits for restitution. Stevenson implied, in the coded language of diplomats, that the British government was procrastinating and, in so doing, jeopardizing "the friendly relations of the two countries."[20]

At least as thoroughly as Martin Van Buren and Aaron Vail had done before him, Andrew Stevenson renewed the United States' case for reparations from the *Comet*, *Encomium*, and *Enterprise*. The "principles and doctrines" at stake were so great, the British colonial authorities' actions so "alarming . . . to national sovereignty," American "sensibility," and slave owners' "rights of property," that he revisited each case, paying special attention to the *Enterprise*. Stevenson criticized Britain's reliance on the "West India emancipation act" of 1834 to justify the liberation of the enslaved people in Bermuda, since the United States, as an independent nation, had its own laws. Southern statutes, Stevenson indicated, in language that mirrored the resolutions passed at the Wilmington town meeting concerning the *Encomium*, made "no distinction in principle between property in persons and property in things." At the national level, too, Stevenson insisted, because the U.S. government regarded the enslaved "as property and not as persons," it compensated owners whose bondpeople were "killed in the service of the United States, even in a state of war." Unbeknownst to Lord Palmerston, this statement was false; the federal government had no history of reimbursing slaveholders for lost human chattel. Nevertheless, with righteous indignation, Stevenson informed Palmerston that "slaves shall be regarded as property in every nation whose municipal regulations sanction slavery" and that the United States, "as a sovereign and independent nation," would "not consent to surrender" the right to govern itself.[21]

Stevenson pressed the American cause on the basis of the law of nations: that set of rights and obligations owed by sovereign states to one another. "When or where has the doctrine ever been established, that slavery or the slave trade was prohibited or condemned by the law of nations?" he asked. He quoted several judges and eminent legal minds in both Europe and the United States who noted that British strictures against slavery or the slave trade could not apply to foreign nations. Under the law of nations, no government possessed the power to act as "'judge' of the government of another state or its internal conduct." Independent states set policy for themselves. It followed that neither slavery in the American South nor its domestic slave trade were "prohibited by the public law" of Britain but were, rather, "wholly untouched by it." As Stevenson explained, the international law of slavery undercut British colonial authorities' presumed right to liberate enslaved captives from American vessels.[22]

Already Britain exerted moral dominion over the ocean by using its navy to assume almost complete responsibility for policing the transatlantic slave trade, intercepting more than 95 percent of all slave ships discovered on the high seas. After decades of patrolling the Atlantic, it appeared to alarmed Southern slaveholders that the British government was prepared not merely to quell slave smuggling but to imbue its emancipation law with extraterritorial force. The U.S. minister reminded Lord Palmerston that the Slavery Abolition Act of 1834 applied only to British colonies and not to other nations.[23]

Stevenson pondered the calamitous consequences were "any one nation to extend its laws beyond its own territory and subjects, to those of other nations." A British violation of U.S. sovereignty in the cases of the three slave ships would "destroy" not only the coastwise domestic slave trade but also the "peaceful and friendly relations" between the two nations, upon which "the interests and happiness of both so especially depend." Great Britain would thus be unwise to support its colonial authorities in the three seizures of enslaved cargoes.[24]

After presenting his evidence, the U.S. minister reached his conclusion. If slavery was "not . . . prohibited by the law of nations, or the Government and laws of the United States, but protected by both," and if Great Britain had "no right to extend her laws beyond her territories" and could not impose "her act of West India emancipation" on others, British colonial authorities had made "unauthorized and illegal" seizures in the cases of the *Comet*, *Encomium*, and *Enterprise*. As such, "the indemnity asked of his Majesty's Government" was "both equitable and just." Stevenson confidently presumed an outcome favorable to American slave-owning interests. Once the diplomatic principles at issue were settled, he informed Lord Palmerston, "the character of the indemnity, and amount of compensation" can be determined. The two governments could then hammer out "satisfactory arrangements . . . for ascertaining the value of the slaves, and the injuries sustained."[25]

Secretary of State Forsyth thought Stevenson did an admirable job in representing U.S. claims to restitution. He took particular note of the fact that "two of the cases occurred before the [British] emancipation law was of force." Forsyth could not have known just how important that distinction would soon become.[26]

Minister Stevenson did not expect an immediate response to his letter to Lord Palmerston. Cabinet ministers were perpetually busy, and during the summer many prominent British officeholders left London until Parliament reconvened in the fall. As the months dragged on, however, Stevenson grew increasingly concerned. In November, he reassured Forsyth that he would "urge a decision" once the cabinet ministers returned to the city.[27]

Met with continued silence and "seeing no prospect of any thing being done," in mid-December Stevenson followed up with Lord Palmerston. He noted that the first U.S. claims to restitution for the *Comet* had been registered almost five years earlier and that Stevenson himself had yet to receive the courtesy of a reply to his letter from four months before. Hoping to maintain "amicable relations" between the United States and Great Britain, Stevenson renewed his plea for a "final and satisfactory" settlement.[28]

The U.S. minister had not yet been informed that there had been movement on the question of restitution. A month and a half earlier, on October 31, 1836, the King's advocate, attorney general, and solicitor general issued their final verdict on the three cases of shipwrecked slaves. "We have finally come to the conclusion," they wrote, "that the claims of the American Government" for indemnification are "not well founded with respect to the Enterprize [*sic*] but . . . [are] well founded with respect to the Comet and the Encomium."[29]

In finding just the first two voyages deserving of reimbursement, they clarified the rule that they followed: "The Slave owner is entitled to compensation where he has been lawfully in possession of the Slaves within the English Territory." Since slavery was still legal in British colonies during the seizures of the *Comet*'s and *Encomium*'s enslaved cargoes, the law officers of the Crown were willing to offer indemnity for them. However, with slavery ended in the British Atlantic and throughout most of the empire by the time the *Enterprise* ran low on supplies, "the moment the ship entered the port at Bermuda," the captives "were free" and "had acquired rights which the Court there were [*sic*] bound to recognize and protect." The British government was, in short, imposing its laws on foreigners who entered its colonial possessions.[30]

The Crown lawyers had reached a consensus to support restitution for U.S. slave owners and insurers as far back as April 1834, but what changed at the end of October 1836 was their rationale for doing so. "Our former opinion" in support of compensation, they explained, was that a ship "driven by stress of weather" was "not subject to our Municipal law" of slavery. That position "now appears to us to be erroneous from our having disregarded the distinction between Slaves and inanimate objects or irrational animals." The law officers of the Crown conceded that, in cases of commodities or livestock "driven by stress of weather into any foreign port," certainly "the owner would be aggrieved if he was to be deprived of what belonged to him by the Municipal Law of a State to which he had not voluntarily submitted." But enslaved people were another matter: they "as human beings are to be heard before their fate is decided." The paradox of claiming people as a form of property stood at the crux of the October 31 ruling. According to the Crown lawyers, enslaved people carried into a country where slavery is forbidden must be regarded as "aliens who have always been free." If the government handed them over, the alien "would be aggrieved and would be entitled to sue for damages."[31]

Because slavery still existed in the Bahamas in 1831 and early 1834, restitution was merited for owners of enslaved people on the *Comet* and *Encomium*. According to the Crown lawyers, "the slaves . . . were actually in the possession of the Owner within the English Territory and they were illegally seized by a functionary of the English Government. Had it not been for this voluntary Interference there can be little doubt that the slaves would have been reshipped . . . and would have reached their port of destination." The same set of legal experts insisted, however, that these two cases marked "the last of the sort" for which indemnification could be paid. With "slavery being now abolished throughout the British Empire there can be no well founded claim for compensation" for "slaves that may come under any circumstances into the colonies" in the future.[32]

The final determination by the King's advocate, attorney general, and solicitor general largely accepted the terms of the American argument first framed by Martin Van Buren in 1832. The Crown lawyers could have chosen to adopt a far more radical antislavery policy against granting any compensation whatsoever, as both William Rothery and Thomas Spring Rice preferred. Such a judgment would have been more consistent with Britain's contemporary abolitionist principles as well as with the spirit of the 1818 Robinson/Gifford letter and the decision by William Vesey Munnings that it inspired. The law officers of the Crown refrained from carrying the matter that far, however, likely with the diplomatic ramifications of their decision in mind. Meeting U.S. demands in two-thirds of the cases seemed a reasonable compromise.

Lord Palmerston did not alert Andrew Stevenson of the Crown lawyers' decision until January 7, 1837. The opening portion of his letter excused the long delay in his reply. Practically, the granting of restitution would require an appropriation of funds from Parliament, so the British government needed "fully to investigate the justice of [the] claim." Politically, too, "the great importance of the questions" at stake demanded "the fullest and most deliberate consideration." The Crown was obliged to settle "not merely . . . the existence or extent of a pecuniary liability" but important interpretations of the law. The "gravity" of these issues precluded "an earlier answer" to Stevenson's entreaties.[33]

Palmerston explained that "the rule by which these claims should be decided is, that those claimants must be considered entitled to compensation who were lawfully in possession of their slaves within the British territory, and who were disturbed in their legal possession of those slaves by functionaries of the British Government." On that basis, his government would indemnify the United States for losses sustained from both the *Comet* and the *Encomium*, but not from the *Enterprise*, which merited no compensation. Knowing the news would drop like a bombshell, Palmerston relayed the Crown lawyers' arguments in their own language as he justified Britain's decision to Minister Stevenson. "His Majesty's Government, therefore, consider the claim respecting the slaves of the '*Enterprise*' to be finally disposed of, by the principles thus laid down," Palmerston concluded, "and it follows, likewise, . . . that no claim of that kind can ever be entertained" again.[34]

Stevenson disguised his personal reaction to Palmerston's missive. An optimist might have been pleased to have secured a two-thirds victory for U.S. slaveholding interests, but slave owners never earned much of a reputation for moderation or compromise. Stevenson's reply on January 14 hinted at his displeasure. "What course the Government of the United States will feel itself justified in taking" he dared not predict, but he assumed with confidence that Britain's decision, "and the principles on which it is attempted to be justified, will be received with painful surprise and regret . . . , and the deepest sensibility by the whole Union." Lacking further instruction, Stevenson kept his remarks brief. He nevertheless commented on his disappointment "at the essential difference of opinion which is likely to arise between the two Governments." Their disagreements involved "matters of higher and deeper importance, connected with the national interest and institutions" of the United States, and they would be difficult to reconcile "with . . . friendly relations subsisting between the two countries." Forwarding a copy of Lord Palmerston's letter, Stevenson communicated the disconcerting news back home.[35]

9

The Law of Nations

On January 28, 1837, John C. Calhoun introduced a resolution in the U.S. Senate. The South Carolina senator, politically estranged from Andrew Jackson since 1830, requested that the president, soon to enter his last full month in office, "communicate to the Senate a copy of the correspondence with the Government of Great Britain, in relation to the outrage committed on our flag, and the rights of our citizens, by the authorities of Bermuda and New Providence, in seizing the slaves on board of the brigs Encomium and Enterprize." In late January, Calhoun did not yet know that a decision had been reached in London over the enslaved American cargoes liberated in British territories. He wanted answers, for, as the champion of the slaveholding interest shockingly declared in early February, slavery was in his mind not a "necessary evil" but a "positive good."[1]

Calhoun's resolution went before the Senate on February 7. To him, the *Encomium* and *Enterprise* represented, with no hyperbole, two "of the greatest outrages ever committed on the rights of individuals by a civilized Power." He knew that many of the enslaved people seized from the *Encomium* belonged to Wilmington-area slave owner John Waddell and that the North Carolina legislature had condemned Britain's "unwarrantable conduct" and "unanimously passed resolutions" demanding the U.S. government investigate. Calhoun also understood that "stormy weather" had forced the *Enterprise* to Bermuda, where the captives on board were set free. According to Calhoun, no foreign power could search either vessel. Both ships, in "sailing from one port of the United States to another," proceeded lawfully, and when they encountered "stress of weather," were entitled to enter "a foreign port" with their cargoes. Calhoun failed to comprehend how, over the past several years, "the slaves had not been restored, nor any compensation made to the owners." He intended his resolution to secure "information on the subject, . . . in order that justice might be done to our citizens." The Senate adopted Calhoun's request,

John C. Calhoun.

modifying it slightly to clarify that President Jackson need not comply if he "deem[ed] it incompatible with the public interests."[2]

Calhoun had grown up in the presence of the enslaved people owned by his father and had managed his widowed mother's plantation before accumulating chattel of his own. Early in his political career, as a member of the South Carolina legislature, his first assignment was as chairman of the Committee on Claims, which reviewed petitions by the state's citizens for damages or compensation. When slave owners sought payments for enslaved convicts executed by the state, their memorials went to him. Calhoun, in short, had an unwavering commitment to slavery and experience in aiding enslavers in distress.[3]

Although no friend of Calhoun, Jackson, too, was a slaveholder devoted to the institution of slavery. He complied with the Senate's request within a week, transmitting a report from Secretary of State John Forsyth, along with copies of State Department instructions to U.S. diplomats in England and the long train of correspondence between the two governments over the *Encomium* and *Enterprise* as well as the *Comet*. Calhoun had somehow overlooked the *Comet*, the oldest of the three cases, explaining to the Senate on March 2 that "he was not aware" of that ship when he first proposed his resolution. He added it to his list of grievances. "Our Executive has been" not "knocking" forcefully but "tapping gently at the door of the British Secretary, to obtain justice, without receiving an answer," Calhoun grumbled. U.S. diplomats "had written . . . more than enough," the senator continued. The three human cargoes in dispute collectively represented, in his mind, "the plainest case imaginable."[4]

Calhoun found no fault with his longtime political foe Martin Van Buren, who would take office as the eighth president in just two days. Van Buren's initial correspondence in 1832 concerning the *Comet* struck Calhoun as "a plain statement of the facts, . . . given in a very clear and satisfactory manner." In contrast, subsequent missives, written after protracted silences from the British government, smacked of weakness, inadequate in conveying "the outrage on the flag and honor of the Union."[5]

By March 1837, Calhoun still spoke the language of great principle, albeit with a more uniquely Southern twang. The rise of radical abolitionism in the early 1830s caught him and other Southern slave owners by surprise. In 1835, Northern forces hostile to slavery launched a mass mailing of pamphlets to the South. Proslavery actors destroyed the abolitionist propaganda rather than risk it falling into the hands of the enslaved and nurturing ideas dangerous to the racial status quo. Abolitionists followed up with a barrage of petitions to Congress, most of which requested the termination of slavery or the slave trade in the District of Columbia. Calhoun spearheaded the defense against slave owners' internal enemies from the North.[6]

With slavery already under heightened attack domestically, Calhoun demonstrated little patience with assaults upon slave owners' rights from overseas. During his early days in the House of Representatives, Calhoun had read widely in international law as the War of 1812 loomed. That conflict had been prompted, in part, by British violations of freedom of the seas and their impressment of American sailors into His Majesty's navy. Twenty-five years later, Calhoun deployed his accumulated knowledge to denounce the latest British outrages that led to the emancipation of enslaved Southerners. "No one in the least conversant with the laws of nations can doubt," Calhoun informed his senatorial colleagues in early March 1837, that the *Comet*, *Encomium*, and *Enterprise* "were . . . under the protection of our flag, while on their voyage . . . from one port of the Union to another." The situation was no different than "if they were in [an American] port, lying at the wharves, within our acknowledged jurisdiction." The rights of the U.S. "passengers and crews" were in no way diminished while upon the high seas, especially since shipwreck or "stress of weather," rather than any intentional act, had carried them "into the British dominions." Calhoun further insisted that the "misfortunes" that befell the three vessels lent the white people on board "the additional rights which the laws of humanity extend to the unfortunate in their situation, and which are regarded by all civilized nations as sacred." More to the point, by Calhoun's understanding of the law of nations, the municipal laws of a given land—the Bahamas or Bermuda, for example—could not divest American slave owners of their enslaved property transported on board the three vessels.[7]

Calhoun's conviction reflected a traditional understanding of the law of nations that was being transformed in the 1830s. In the eighteenth century, slavery was a common condition across many parts of the globe. It was not until 1772 that Great Britain began the process of slowly chipping away at slavery's normative character, in the famous *Somerset* case. James Somerset, a native African enslaved by a customs officer in Boston, was compelled by his owner to accompany him on a business trip to London, where Somerset sued for his freedom in the English courts. His argument was that in England, English law, which did not explicitly sanction slavery, took precedence over Massachusetts law, which did. Lord Mansfield, sitting as chief justice on the Court of King's Bench, ruled in Somerset's favor, declaring that slavery existed only where written into positive law. This municipal theory of slavery, or freedom principle, presumed individuals' freedom unless stated otherwise by statute. It became a feature of the common law in Great Britain as well as in the United States. On the American side of the Atlantic, the U.S. government did not positively recognize slavery despite the many protections the Constitution granted it; instead, states determined slave law. Yet in the arena of international law, nations had relied upon the principle of comity whenever different sets of laws clashed. For the sake of harmonious trade and commerce, they recognized foreigners' legal rights while in transit through jurisdictions with conflicting statutes. As far back as 1759, Lord Mansfield had observed that "the maritime law is not the law of a particular country, but the general law of nations." Adhering to the customs of the law of nations, Calhoun and the Southern shippers whose concerns he represented expected their right to enslaved property to remain unmolested in foreign ports. For that reason, the Southern press condemned each of the seizures of American slaves as a "DISGRACEFUL OUTRAGE" and "merciless violation of the laws of nations."[8]

Parliament's passage of the Slavery Abolition Act altered the dynamics of Anglo-American relations over slavery. The 1833 law extended the freedom principle, as outlined in the *Somerset* case, from the British Isles to the vast majority of the British Empire. British legislative action advanced the case for freedom as the natural condition of mankind, rendering slavery an increasingly anomalous and immoral institution in the Atlantic world and carrying implications for long-standing practices under the law of nations. After the implementation of the emancipation law in 1834, British legal authorities believed themselves justified in denying the comity that they had previously granted to American shippers of enslaved cargoes, as they better aligned the operation of the law of nations with the natural law. Using that logic, the Crown had agreed to pay compensation for the lost human cargoes of the *Comet* and *Encomium*, but not for those liberated from the *Enterprise*.[9]

Unaware of the British verdict in early March 1837, Calhoun could not comprehend the delay in bringing about a resolution to a problem first raised five years earlier. Great Britain "has not only withheld redress, but has not even deigned to answer the often-repeated application of our Government for redress," he groused before the Senate. He then gave voice to his greatest concern, speculating that the British government had perhaps reached the unfathomable conclusion "that there could not be property in persons." Calhoun shuddered to ponder it, but against a backdrop of rising abolitionist agitation domestically, the passage of Britain's Slavery Abolition Act furthered the anxieties of Southern slave owners already on edge. The British government, of course, had the right to adopt the freedom principle for itself, but the South Carolinian denied that its laws could encroach upon or apply to the United States or its citizens without presenting an "insulting" and "outrageous" affront to the law of nations. Moreover, considering that the British were once "the greatest slaveholder of any on earth," it would be the height of "folly and hypocrisy" for the Crown to condemn others for "what . . . they are more guilty [of] themselves," "if there be guilt" at all. Calhoun drew a parallel between the institution of Southern slavery and the dominion that Great Britain exercised over its colonial territories, a relationship that the British government was not surrendering. It also did not escape Calhoun's notice that slavery itself continued in portions of the British Empire. The inconsistency of condemning slavery in one part of the world while permitting it in another was obvious. For all of these reasons, the South Carolina senator concluded that any newfound British commitment to the freedom principle was "utterly indefensible."[10]

Calhoun warned that the very future of "peace and harmony" between the United States and Great Britain hinged upon the conditions of "perfect equality and a mutual respect for their respective institutions." To deny redress in the cases of the *Comet*, *Encomium*, and *Enterprise*, he cautioned, jeopardized "the friendly relations . . . between the two countries." As a senator from a slaveholding state, he pledged to work tirelessly to see his version of justice fulfilled.[11]

On March 5, three days after Calhoun's speech and one day into the Van Buren presidency, Secretary of State John Forsyth finally received U.S. minister Andrew Stevenson's January letter outlining British plans for compensation. Forsyth appreciated the Crown's "readiness . . . to render the justice which is due to the owners for the slaves cast away upon the British shores in the 'Comet' and 'Encomium,' and liberated by the colonial authorities." At the same time, "the rejection of the claim" from the *Enterprise* asserted principles the U.S. government found disturbing and "inconsistent with the respect due from all foreign powers to the institutions of a friendly nation."[12]

Explaining the denial of indemnity in the case of the *Enterprise*, Lord Palmerston pointed out the basic problem of claiming to hold property in persons. He insisted upon "a distinction between laws bearing upon the personal liberty of man, and laws bearing upon the property which man may claim in irrational animals or in inanimate things." When "stress of weather" drove animals or other nonhuman cargoes into foreign ports, "there would be but two parties interested in the transaction—the foreign owner and the local authority," Palmerston explained. The calculus changed when the cargo consisted of enslaved human beings. In that case, "there are three parties to the transaction: the owner of the cargo, the local authority, and the alleged slave," who also deserved a hearing and the possible benefits that "the law of the land may afford him." Should enslaved people arrive in a place like Bermuda, where the institution of slavery had been outlawed, they "can in no shape be restrained of their liberty by their former master," regardless of the circumstances that carried them there. The laws of the owners' home country held no sway whatsoever. Palmerston dismissed the prospect of compensating those owners for liberated bondpeople as "absurd."[13]

Palmerston then made plain the fundamental differences between his government's position and that of John C. Calhoun: their conflicting interpretations over the international law of slavery and the concomitant responsibilities under comity. Any "municipal law," like that adopted by Parliament in 1833, "which forbids slavery is no violation of the law of nations. It is, on the contrary, in strict harmony with the law of nature," Palmerston wrote. In contrast, Calhoun based his arguments on an older understanding of the law of nations, in an Atlantic world where slavery had been more widely accepted. In undertaking emancipation, Great Britain declared slavery an unnatural condition, which in turn redefined its obligations under international law. Comity ceased to function as had been customary when the cargo in question consisted of enslaved human property. "Therefore, when slaves are liberated, according to such municipal law, there is no wrong done," Palmerston announced, "and there can be no compensation granted."[14]

One newspaper from the slaveholding commonwealth of Virginia detected in the British foreign secretary's declaration evidence "of a dark fanaticism" hostile to slavery. The reaction from the U.S. government was no less palpable, yet more carefully measured. "It would be impossible to look back on the history of nations without feeling surprise at the positions laid down by Lord Palmerston," Secretary of State Forsyth marveled in a letter to Andrew Stevenson. Despite Great Britain's centuries of support and protection of the institution of slavery, which continued in specific corners of its empire, Palmerston believed his government's policy "in entire harmony with the law of nations."[15]

Forsyth spelled out the U.S. government's objections in his instructions to Stevenson. He opened by acknowledging that it would be no violation of the law of nations to apply municipal laws over foreigners if they entered a country voluntarily. But in the cases of the three American vessels, the enslaved cargoes landed on British soil involuntarily. No one with captives on either the *Comet*, the *Encomium*, or the *Enterprise* "could be deprived of their property by the operation of any municipal law" because they "never yielded submission" to that law. The American understanding of the law of nations maintained that owners must instead be treated according to the laws of their home country, where the "right of property" originated. Under the law of nations, "the municipal laws of an independent State" that authorized slavery were no less important than those of a state that abolished slavery. At the time slave owners on the *Enterprise* were forced to take refuge in Bermuda, they benefited from the right to own property in slaves, a right long "recognised by the law of nations." To deprive them of that right "by a municipal law to which they had never voluntarily submitted themselves" marked a "great injustice."[16]

Forsyth next took issue with Lord Palmerston's distinction between the ownership of property in persons versus in animals or things. For that to carry any weight, he explained, Great Britain would have needed to abolish "not merely . . . *slavery for life*" but slavery "*anywhere* or to *any extent*." Parliament's Slavery Abolition Act did not do that. Portions of the British Empire were excluded, and even where emancipation was effected, an obligatory term of apprenticeship continued to extract "the services of the slaves, for years to come, without the[ir] consent . . . and without remuneration." Moreover, the British government awarded compensation to slave owners based "on the previous right of property in the slaves for life." The British position struck Forsyth as nonsensical and disingenuous. The Crown's own abolition law recognized "a *temporary* right" to the work of the enslaved, even as it told the American owners of captives taken off the *Enterprise* that their bondpeople must be treated "as aliens who have, at all times, from their birth, been free." Although Britain was attempting to separate the labor of the slave from the personhood of the slave, Forsyth regarded such fine parsing as a distinction without a difference.[17]

He then rebutted Palmerston's claim that enslaved people represented a third party—in addition to the owner and the local authority—when a vessel in distress entered a foreign port. The captives aboard the *Enterprise* had not sought the aid of British officials; rather, "the intermeddling of the colonial authorities was unsolicited and officious." These "self-constituted judges" imposed as their "standard of justice the municipal law of England"—a law, Forsyth added, that the Crown "did not feel itself authorized to enact without the payment of money for the slaves . . . to the colonial owners." For the secretary of state, that fact alone afforded U.S. slave owners "a fair and sufficient ground for a claim to compensation."[18]

Forsyth discerned that Great Britain was tampering "with the unchanging laws of nations." To assert that a foreigner's right to enslaved property was protected one day and not the next was absurd, for as Forsyth declared, "the law of nations is the same." Yet, with passage of the Slavery Abolition Act, "Great Britain wrests slaves from their masters when driven into her ports by stress of weather, denies all compensation, and declares that no claim for slaves will be entertained, who come, under any circumstances, into British territory." The innovative British effort to use its municipal law of slavery to deprive the subjects of another country of their property rights was unprecedented and could not be taken lightly.[19]

According to Forsyth's report, newly inaugurated president Martin Van Buren was frustrated. Palmerston's forceful denial of claims for enslaved Americans reaching British dominions "under any circumstances" would invite the very bondpeople of the Eastern Seaboard forcibly relocated to the Old Southwest to flee their owners, with the aim of smuggling themselves onto a ship bound for a nearby British holding in the Atlantic. At the same time, the British proclamation encouraged abolitionists to abduct enslaved people "by fraud or force" for delivery to freedom in a British colony. Van Buren had spent much of his political career knitting together a coalition of Northern and Southern voters, and with the radical abolitionist movement slowly gaining strength throughout the 1830s, antislavery machinations in the British colonial Atlantic generated "a spirit hostile to the repose and security of the United States."[20]

The U.S. government could not accept a British policy founded upon principles so antithetical to the "interests and sensibilities" of Southern slaveholders and to the nation as a whole. Based on "recent experience," Forsyth explained, "the proximity" of the United States to Britain's Atlantic territories virtually guaranteed similar incidents in coming years, a likelihood that would poison Anglo-American relations. Hinting at the prospect of a third war between the countries since 1775, Forsyth suggested the negotiation of "some immediate conventional arrangement" to prevent similar clashes over enslaved American cargoes. In the meantime, he hoped that Andrew Stevenson might use the arguments contained in his letter to convince Lord Palmerston to abandon the grounds upon which the British government denied compensation in the case of the *Enterprise*.[21]

Having received Forsyth's instructions, Stevenson on May 12 transmitted to Palmerston an acknowledgment that claims would be paid to American owners and insurers of enslaved people liberated from the *Comet* and *Encomium*. Yet he also faithfully recapitulated the objections to the British position conveyed to him by the secretary of state in late March.[22]

Not until seven months later did Lord Palmerston write to say that he "regret[ted]" the U.S. reaction to Britain's decision, but he did not waver. The British government "is still of opinion that the claim in the case of the Enterprise is inadmissible," because U.S. objections were "founded upon the assumption that, by the law of nations, an independent State is not entitled to enact a law declaring that the condition of slavery shall under no circumstances be recognised within its own territories." The Crown "can never admit" to such a limitation.[23]

On this point, Palmerston took his cues from the Treasury's admiralty referee, William Rothery. The government had relied on Rothery's expertise to determine "whether Great Britain is by the Law of Nations bound to pay the value of Slaves owned by Foreigners" and "who, by the act of God[,] have been brought within her dominions." The British municipal law of slavery, extended to its colonies by the Slavery Abolition Act, maintained that enslaved people landing within the British dominion "had an indefeasible right to claim and enjoy their freedom." As Rothery reasoned, then, the central question could be distilled to this: Could "any Country . . . by the Law of Nations" be compelled "to Indemnify [a] loss sustained in conseq[uen]ce" of obeying its own municipal law? The entire argument of the U.S. government hinged on the supposition that it could, but Rothery located no legal precedent for such an argument. To the contrary, Rothery concluded, "nothing can be more directly in violation of the Law of Nations than for one state to require indemnity from another, on account of the operation of its own Municipal Laws." Each nation maintained "a perfect right to make such laws as it may think fit for the regulation of its own Dominions." Any exceptions must be noted by treaty.[24]

It fell to Palmerston to break the news to the U.S. minister. "The law of the mother country" applied equally to the colonies, he explained, and the British government could not offer compensation for the *Enterprise* slaves without admitting that its law violated the law of nations. Furthermore, granting indemnity in the case of the *Enterprise* would set a precedent for the reimbursement "for all slaves who, from time to time," entered British dominions and were liberated. Henceforth, Palmerston emphasized, the British government would continue to deny payment, regardless of the circumstances under which foreign slaving vessels fell under the Crown's jurisdiction. The owners of the *Enterprise*'s bondpeople indeed "suffered a loss," the foreign secretary admitted, "but it is a loss without a wrong." The enslaved Americans were "justly and of right entitled to their freedom upon arriving within British jurisdiction," so it was better for the owners to think of the incident "as if their property had been destroyed by shipwreck, or by any other accident."[25]

Palmerston conceded that the law of nations generally did decide legal questions like that involving the *Enterprise* according to the laws of the people on board foreign vessels rather than to the laws of England. But slavery, he insisted, marked a noteworthy exception because British law no longer recognized the right of property in persons. Other nations were free to perpetuate slavery and the domestic slave trade without violating the law of nations, but the British government had the equal right to make and enforce laws against the institution. The necessary outcome for U.S. slave owners was clear. As Palmerston put it, "the execution of a rightful law cannot be wrong; and where no wrong is done no compensation can be due." He closed his letter by repeating the identical British position from the preceding January: "there can be no well-founded claim on the part of any foreigner, in respect of slaves who, under any circumstances whatever, may come into the British colonies."[26]

Stevenson's reply was forceful. He wrote Palmerston on December 23 that Britain's unbending reassertion of principle could not "be admitted or acquiesced in" by the U.S. government. The slaveholder disputed Britain's insistence "that persons cannot be made subjects of property." Each state's municipal law "decide[d] the question for itself," and the law of nations had long recognized as much. "The right of one nation to decide for another what is property," Stevenson criticized, was a novel argument suddenly put forth by Great Britain, "obnoxious" to all precedent. The United States could not possibly yield this right to another nation. Stevenson had to tread carefully, however, since he was protesting the denial of the *Enterprise* claim at the same time that he assumed responsibility for negotiating successful settlements for the two vessels shipwrecked in the Bahamas. He had instructions from Secretary Forsyth "to accept the tender of satisfaction which has been made for those claims."[27]

The "gratifying news" of impending compensation for the *Comet* and *Encomium* met with jubilation in Wilmington, North Carolina. One of the resolutions the white community had developed at their public meeting declared that "*Southern people could recognize no difference between property in persons, and property in things*," a point later emphasized by both Forsyth and Stevenson in correspondence with Britain. Knowing this, Wilmington's citizens flattered themselves into thinking that their stated principle had informed U.S. negotiations. The local newspaper recognized state senator William B. Meares for "the bold and decided language" of the resolutions, which he steered into the hands of prominent politicians in Washington, DC.[28]

The white people of Wilmington also gave credit to another great advocate of slave owners. According to the local paper, "The Hon. John C. Calhoun . . . deserves the thanks of his Country, for the part he has sustained in the adjustment of this matter." Anglo-American diplomacy had already produced an agreement before Calhoun's widely publicized Senate resolution of late January. The timing of the news's arrival in the United States conveyed the mistaken impression that Calhoun had been responsible for the breakthrough in the long impasse and further enhanced his reputation as a proslavery leader. Despite that public misconception, Calhoun's thoughts on the law of nations presaged his later insistence upon slave owners' right to carry enslaved property unfettered into the western territories of the United States. Whether in international relations, in disputes surrounding domestic slave-trading vessels landing in British Atlantic colonies, or in congressional debates over slavery's extension into the territories, Calhoun consistently supported Southern slave owners and the expansive reach of their property rights.[29]

10

Compensation

All that remained for John Waddell and other owners of enslaved people taken from the *Comet* and *Encomium* to do was to fulfill the British government's request for "specific information as to the value of such . . . slaves on board." Once received, the Crown pledged to make "reasonable" restitution "for any injury the owners may be presumed to have sustained from the interference of the British functionaries in landing the slaves at the Bahamas." The State Department requested that American owners and insurers "furnish on oath, a list" of those seized and liberated, accompanied by "their ages, sexes, &c. &c.," for transmission to Andrew Stevenson in London. The assembled data would "serve as a basis upon which to fix the amount of indemnification justly due to the claimants." Predictably, the sums to "which the owners may be entitled to receive" for the lost "services of their slaves" emerged as a contentious issue. As Southern slaveholders and insurance companies pursued maximum payouts, the Crown studiously pored over the numbers to minimize its expenses. Regardless of their divergent agendas, however, all parties handled the valuation of the enslaved cargoes with the utmost seriousness and sobriety, a point that underscored both the significant pecuniary worth of property in slaves and the mutual desire of the British and the American governments to settle their dispute amicably.[1]

Soon after the wreck of the *Comet* in 1831, various estimates of the enslaved people's value appeared in Bahamian and U.S. newspapers. Members of the House of Assembly in Nassau expected some of the most expensive laborers to have brought "from 1000 to 1200 dollars each" in the New Orleans slave markets, "and a large proportion of the rest are prime young negroes, worth . . . about 800 dollars each." According to one calculation, "the average value of the slaves" from the *Comet* "may be fairly computed at about £200 sterling per head, or £33,000 sterling for the whole"—more than $160,000 in 1831, or almost

$5 million today. Lawmakers in the Bahamas fretted over predictions in the spring of 1831 that "the British nation will have to become the paymaster," for "the slaves in question [would] have been well sold." Tamping down the alarm over the damage to British coffers, U.S. minister Martin Van Buren had assured Lord Palmerston in early 1832 that the American claimants would "be content with a moderate valuation, much less than that put upon the slaves by the Legislative Assembly of New Providence." In March 1837, Secretary of State John Forsyth was finally able to instruct Stevenson to prepare himself for the process of calculating indemnities. With diligence and seriousness, the U.S. government embarked upon the task of running the numbers with all the commitment that the slaveholding interest expected.[2]

After Forsyth instructed claimants "to furnish the requisite evidence," lists of enslaved people and the financial losses incurred as a result of their seizure poured into the State Department for transmission to London. New Orleans insurers who had already paid out on the policies they issued accounted for the bulk of the claims. Of the 164 captives that set out from Alexandria aboard the *Comet*, 146 were insured. On May 16, 1837, John K. West, president of the Louisiana State Marine and Fire Insurance Company, certified three policies, numbered 6878 through 6880, made at the behest of slave trader Isaac Franklin, which covered a total of fifty-seven of them. The Mississippi Marine and Fire Insurance Company, led by its president Charles Harrod, supplied the names, ages, and sexes of forty slaves insured under policy number 2212, and Merchants Insurance Company president A. Dupuy did the same for forty-nine under his office's policy 778.[3]

The certificates offered by the company presidents listed neither the premiums paid for the policies nor, more significantly, the sums for which the slaves were insured, either individually or as a group. The insurers of the *Comet* prisoners were all located in New Orleans, the port of destination, and wrote their policies on enslaved cargoes sight unseen, based on the total value of the shipment as determined by the slave trader—as temporary owner of the captive—or other slaveholders and transmitted to a partner or agent in New Orleans. Owners wanted to insure their enslaved cargoes sufficiently against risk, but escalating premiums as the estimated value of a human cargo rose deterred attempts to overinsure against the unlikely odds of disaster on any given voyage. Moreover, any excess outlay for insurance cut into owners' bottom line or slave traders' ultimate profit. The marine insurance policies could theoretically have served as an accurate guide in determining the desired compensation from Great Britain, but those who took out policies generally insured the enslaved for less than their full market value.[4]

Complicating the valuation question, by May 1837 none of the three New Orleans insurance companies had apparently retained copies of the policies written on the *Comet*'s captives. They may have destroyed the contracts after paying the claims. Perhaps shoddy bookkeeping or filing practices explains their disappearance, or maybe an accident led to the loss of the records. For whatever reason, the insurance companies provided no solid, direct evidence of the amounts disbursed to policyholders. Without the paperwork necessary for supplying a precise dollar figure, they instead estimated the slaves' value by consulting a panel of seven respectable, knowledgeable Louisiana planters resident in the state in 1831, who agreed that, based on the descriptions they read of the captives aboard the *Comet*, the prisoners would have been worth an average of $600 each, "had they arrived at New Orleans" as scheduled. William Boswell, a Crescent City notary whose job routinely involved documenting slave bills of sale, attached his own certificate concurring in that assessment. At $600 apiece, the 146 insured slaves from the *Comet* were valued at $87,600.[5] That figure was less than the total amount claimed. The three insurance companies added $3,000 in expenses incurred by their agent, lawyer Nathan Morse, who had journeyed to Nassau and Washington, DC, and back to New Orleans. John Storr, the U.S. commercial agent in Nassau, filed for reimbursement with the secretary of state for another $519.47 in expenditures related to the *Comet*, which included paying the laborers who equipped Capt. Isaac Staples's intended replacement vessel and the constables who kept watch to prevent the captives from landing in Nassau. Storr also paid to charter the schooner that conveyed Staples to New Orleans to file his protest with a notary there. The cost of "procuring Documents" in May 1837 added another $50. The subtotal for the *Comet* came to $91,169.47, excluding the accumulating interest of 6 percent that the U.S. government claimed.[6]

John Waddell went to the greatest lengths to secure restitution. Uninsured, he had yet to receive payment for the thirteen enslaved people he was forced to leave behind in the Bahamas. In what was likely an act of fraud, Waddell supplied the U.S. government a valuation of all twenty-two of his bondpeople shipwrecked on the *Encomium*, even though nine journeyed with him back to the United States. Like the three New Orleans insurance companies, Waddell assessed his captive laborers informally, consulting local experts on slave prices. He took the additional step of obtaining vouchers from prominent citizens of Louisiana to validate their credentials. Five men—Joseph Walker, Charles Mulholan, John Compton, Sostene A. Baillie, and Thomas O. Moore—valued Waddell's "22 Negroes" at $16,950. Henry A. Bullard, a judge on the Louisiana Supreme Court, supplied a certificate acknowledging that he was "personally acquainted" with the assessors—all "Gentlemen of high standing and respectability, and very competent Judges in matters of that kind"—and vouched for their signatures as genuine. Associate Judge O.P. Jackson of the City Court of New Orleans verified another affidavit from an impartial observer who similarly deemed the valuation "in all respects reasonable and correct." Louisiana governor Edward D. White Sr. further certified that both Bullard and Jackson held the esteemed legal positions as shown on their statements. Waddell had useful friends in high places.[7]

In addition to Waddell's twenty-two captives, twenty-three other enslaved people reached Nassau after the wreck of the *Encomium*. In April 1837, Charleston slave traders Thomas N. Gadsden and Alexander McDonald drew upon their professional expertise to provide notarized assessments of the bondpeople's values had they arrived in New Orleans in 1834. Robert Eagar's seven bondpeople were valued at $6,150, Amédée Gardanne's six at $3,750. Whereas their losses had already been partially covered by policies with the Charleston Fire and Marine Insurance Company, the six enslaved people shipped by merchant Antonio Della Torre to Joseph A. Barelli, the one belonging to Capt. Noah B. Sisson, and the three owned by Charles Allen were uninsured. U.S. consul George Huyler, "personally present at the landing and examination of the 45 American Slaves" in Nassau, had deposed in February 1834 that they "were all in good health" and that, "as a body[,] he never saw a finer or better looking" group of bondpeople. The American legation anticipated a generous payout.[8]

In mid-May 1837, while slave owners and insurers from the *Comet* and *Encomium* were submitting evidence for reimbursement from the Crown, Andrew Stevenson alerted Lord Palmerston that he would soon "be ready to enter upon an adjustment" of American claims from the two vessels. Forsyth sent all of the evidence assembled by the State Department to his minister in London in early August. The *Encomium*'s claims totaled $34,575, a pittance compared with those from the more heavily populated *Comet*. By November 6, 1837, when Stevenson presented the American accounts to Palmerston, the 6 percent annual interest compounding on losses from the *Comet* added $35,536.41 to the tally for that ship. Altogether, the three New Orleans insurance companies claimed restitution for the *Comet* amounting to $126,705.88.[9]

Palmerston acknowledged receipt of the claims on November 23 and referred them to the lords of the Treasury for a decision. In late January 1838, the lords commissioners requested to view the documents in Stevenson's possession pertinent to the claims. Stevenson offered them the opportunity to review his thick bundle of supporting evidence—a plethora of slave manifests, valuations, certificates, and depositions. He gave ample assurances that all these documents would be freely "exhibited for inspection and examination."[10]

Palmerston relayed Stevenson's message to the lords of the Treasury and, after their review of the evidence, communicated their assessment to the U.S. minister in mid-September 1838. The Crown presented three objections to the American claims. First, the lords commissioners disputed the number of slaves for whom indemnity was due. Stevenson had based the U.S. figures on "the number embarked on board the vessels, and afterwards shipwrecked at the Bahamas." But, as Palmerston indicated, eleven captives from the *Comet* had escaped the wreckers by swimming to New Providence and had not, in fact, been seized by British colonial authorities. Therefore, the Crown could not be held responsible for paying for these fugitives. Palmerston furthermore counted eleven captives who "returned to America with the respective owners"—ten from the *Encomium* and, according to the British foreign minister, one from the *Comet* (although no other surviving records mention or identify any prisoner returning with Capt. Staples). "Owners can obviously have no claim on account of slaves" over which "they actually retained possession," Palmerston remarked. Based on the lords commissioners' examination of the data, a total of "22 slaves should be excluded from the number for which compensation is claimed." Subtract them, and the British government agreed to pay for 153 of the 165 captives from the *Comet*, and 35 of the 45 from the *Encomium*.[11]

In a second objection, the lords commissioners opposed reimbursing U.S. owners based on their enslaved property's "probable price" in New Orleans. To value the bondpeople as though they reached their port of destination took for granted that "they had arrived in due course, and in a healthy state," which meant maximum "anticipated profits" for "the adventurers." Even without the interference of British officers in Nassau, the inherent risks of sailing from Nassau to New Orleans may have prevented a safe or timely arrival. Therefore, it seemed more reasonable to the lords of the Treasury to calculate slave owners' losses based on "the value of the slaves at the places from which they were originally shipped." The domestic slave trade was only profitable for slave dealers because they could buy low in the East and sell at such a premium in the Old Southwest that sale prices offset the costs of feeding, temporarily housing, transporting, and prepping enslaved people for market. The lords commissioners proposed payment based on the cheaper side of the trade. To that end, Palmerston requested that Stevenson send him "information about the value of the slaves at their point of origin."[12]

Treasury officials' desire to spare the Crown's coffers, already devastated by millions of pounds by the compensated emancipation of enslaved people throughout Britain's Atlantic empire, produced a third point of contention: the interest the U.S. government was charging on the amounts due. The lords commissioners dismissed the need for interest payments on "the expenses incurred by the owners or their agents" in seeking "the recovery of the slaves"; however, they did acknowledge Britain's tardiness in agreeing to a settlement. Palmerston therefore shared his government's willingness "to pay the going rate of interest, backdated to January 7, 1837, "the date at which the claim for some compensation in respect to the slaves of the 'Comet' and 'Encomium' was first admitted." Coming six and three years, respectively, after the wrecks of the two vessels, the offer reflected Britain's desire not to pay more than the bare minimum.[13]

Stevenson greeted Britain's parsimoniousness with a mixture of "regret" and "surprise." That British Treasury officials never deputized anyone to examine the documentary evidence Stevenson had made available in February, despite specifically requesting to see it, bewildered him. He repeatedly encouraged chancellor of the Exchequer Thomas Spring Rice to order the papers that he had assembled studied. Had the Treasury followed through, Stevenson insisted, they could not have reached such faulty conclusions.[14]

In early December 1838, before Stevenson ever heard from his superiors up the diplomatic chain, the proslavery Virginian challenged the "correctness" and "justice of the principles assumed by the Lords

Commissioners . . . in relation to the number" and the "value of the slaves liberated," as well as "the period of time from which the interest ought to commence." Citing several contemporary sources, he corrected Palmerston's undercounting of the numbers: All 165 enslaved people from the *Comet*, including the eleven who had momentarily escaped, "were afterwards taken possession of" by British colonial authorities. They appeared at the Government House and were directed to the police office, "committed to the workhouse" in Nassau, "and finally liberated." As to the eleven said to have returned to the United States, Stevenson stated that "some doubts may be entertained." He requested further evidence that they had, in fact, rejoined their masters.[15]

Still "greater difficulty" attended the question of the geographic location upon which to affix the emancipated slaves' value. If anything, Stevenson assumed that assessments based on even New Orleans prices undervalued the captives' worth. Since the large slave-trading firm of Franklin & Armfield had already been reimbursed by insurance, the U.S. minister turned Palmerston's attention to the plight of individual slave owners seeking restitution. Alluding to John Waddell in particular, he noted that they were cotton and sugar planters, removing their slaves for the purpose of using their labor upon valuable estates in the fertile regions of the Mississippi. By the seizure and liberation of their slaves, not only were they deprived of the reasonable profits and fruits that they had a just right to expect from the labor of those slaves, but some of the owners were forced to incur very heavy pecuniary losses, in consequence of existing contracts that they had entered into, and that they were deprived of the means of fulfilling by the seizure and loss of their property. By Stevenson's reckoning, the "fair value" in New Orleans did not even approximate "the actual loss and injury which they sustained by the improper and illegal interference of the British authorities." The proposal to use New Orleans prices was, in his mind, already a compromise; however, he was willing to negotiate the point if it would lead to a suitable adjustment.[16]

On the final question, the date from which interest should accrue, Stevenson proved inflexible. He launched into an elaborate and at times condescending discourse on the legal principles surrounding the need for and purpose of paying interest, citing various precedents and several revered authorities at law. Quite simply, if restitution for physical property wrongfully withheld cannot be made, its monetary value, plus interest, served as a reasonable substitute. In the cases of the captives from the *Comet* and

Encomium, justice dictated that the interest accumulate "from the period of their seizure and detention" until the date the adjustment was finalized.[17]

In January 1839, Stevenson penned a follow-up message. After "the extraordinary delay" in achieving an adjustment of the American claims, pressure was building on him from President Van Buren and Secretary of State Forsyth to produce "a final settlement of the indemnification." He urged Lord Palmerston to present "the whole matter to . . . Parliament . . . to obtain the necessary appropriation for satisfying these claims." In a face-to-face meeting, Palmerston assured Stevenson "that he would immediately address an official note to the Treasury, and urge the settlement." Stevenson also gained an interview with Thomas Spring Rice, chancellor of the Exchequer, who explained that the Treasury official to whom he had assigned the indemnification paperwork—the elderly admiralty referee William Rothery—had been too "ill for some months . . . to discharge his public duties." The frustrating delay in receiving payment had nothing to do with any lack of effort on Stevenson's part.[18]

On February 1, 1839, just over two years since his first inquiry into the status of the American vessels, John C. Calhoun submitted a motion asking President Van Buren to inform the Senate whether compensation had yet been paid for the *Comet*, *Encomium*, or *Enterprise*. If not, he wanted to know the reasons why and requested "a copy of the correspondence between the two Governments."[19]

At the time of Calhoun's inquiry, the question of restitution had fallen to William Rothery. The lords commissioners had instructed him to begin an inspection and examination of Stevenson's documents the previous September, but because of his poor health, he did not go to the American legation to start that process until January 30. At that meeting, Rothery fixated on the value of the enslaved at the port of shipment, taking particular interest in the insurance policies on the human cargoes. Stevenson observed "that Owners do not generally insure, and that when they do, it is not to the full amount of their property." "That may be very true in some instances," Rothery countered, "but . . . it was not an uncommon thing for persons to insure to the full extent of the value, even including the profit of the voyage." Stevenson conceded the importance of securing copies of the policies and promised to look through his existing papers to see what he could find.[20]

Stevenson pressed for reimbursement for all 165 enslaved people from the *Comet*, including the baby born during the voyage, and almost all prisoners from the *Encomium*, but Rothery sidestepped the issue. He first needed to conduct a thorough, independent inspection of the evidence. Stevenson gave him copies of the papers he had assembled—one packet for each vessel—to take with him. The issue of compounding interest also remained troublesome. Nevertheless, after the initial conference with Rothery, Stevenson emphasized the progress they had made.[21]

By the time of their second interview, Rothery had reviewed Stevenson's papers. He discovered the two insurance policies issued by the Charleston Fire and Marine Insurance Company for human cargoes aboard the *Encomium*: $3,000 for Amédée Gardanne's six captives and $3,200 for Robert Eagar's seven. Rothery immediately calculated that those policies amounted to $500 and $457 per slave, respectively, or about $476 per slave overall. Were there any more insurance policies? he asked. Any from the *Comet*? So far, the Treasury official had encountered "no Evidence whatever . . . to shew the value of the Slaves in the Comet, at the Port of Shipment." He had viewed an affidavit from Noah B. Sisson stating that his thirty-five-year-old "mustee male slave" aboard the *Encomium* was worth $500, but he had seen nothing similar from the first of the shipwrecked vessels. Although Stevenson had not yet located the policies Rothery sought, he felt confident that, since those bondpeople had been shipped by a professional slave trader, "certainly the greater part of the Slaves in the Comet had been insured," which they were.[22]

The U.S. minister then began to "read a variety of Letters" to Rothery. One piece of correspondence from Nathan Morse, agent for the New Orleans insurers of the *Comet*'s human cargo, revealed a useful bit of information: 146 of the 164 original captives were insured for a total of $70,000. "I considered this to be important," commented Rothery, "as by dividing that sum by 146 it would give less than 480 Dollars for each Slave." Running the numbers in his head, the Treasury agent was forming a strong impression of the average valuation of the bondpeople for which restitution was due. He uttered not a word to Stevenson, however, for he "did not . . . think it prudent to make any observation . . . at the time." With the three New Orleans insurance companies currently claiming $600 per slave, Rothery may have silently wondered if they were attempting to swindle the British treasury and pad their own accounts.[23]

In the absence of the actual insurance policies on the enslaved aboard the *Comet*, Stevenson proposed taking advantage of the specialized knowledge of "two Gentlemen of the highest reputation," fortuitously visiting London at the time. One was Virgil Maxcy of Maryland, the U.S. chargé d'affaires to Belgium, close confidant of John C. Calhoun, and owner of about sixty enslaved people. Maxcy declared in a written statement that the average value of enslaved people in Alexandria in 1830 and 1831 "was not less than 600 Dollars each." The other reported expert on slave prices was Col. John Heth, "one of the largest Proprietors of Coal mines in Virginia." In 1821, he had inherited from his father the Black Heath coal pits, the largest such mining operation in the United States. During 1830 and 1831, Heth "purchased . . . 70 Slaves to stock his Estate" in Chesterfield County. "They averaged more than 700 Dollars each," Heth recalled. Among them "were a good many children," who at market cost less than young adults. In his estimation, "if 700 Dollars a head was allowed for the Slaves in the Comet, it would be extremely low."[24]

Stevenson was optimistic that the pair of appraisals by those familiar with slave prices at Chesapeake rates during the two years in question would satisfy Rothery. Should prices at the point of departure become the terms of their agreement, Stevenson wrote Secretary of State Forsyth, he entertained "strong hopes of adjusting the claims without additional evidence of the value of the slaves at the ports of embarkation." But Rothery did not consider these testimonials conclusive. Even "if they were put into a more formal shape" and properly notarized, he could not regard them as reliable, "for how could any person who had never seen any of these Slaves, give testimony as to the precise value of them[?]" Merchants anticipating indemnity from a foreign government would likely overestimate "the real value of the commodity," and none of the insurance companies, "even at New Orleans," claimed an average price for "the whole of these Slaves [at] more than 600 Dollars each."[25]

Rothery cautioned Stevenson against "overrating" the value of the enslaved cargoes. The losses resulted from "shipwreck, the act of God," near the Abaco Islands. "It might very fairly be argued," he posited, that if the British government was obligated "to indemnify, that the value of the Slaves at the Bahamas ought to be the criterion." Any assessment on that basis would be devastating for U.S. slave owners and insurers. With little use for plantation laborers, enslaved people in Nassau could be had for cheap, at "only . . . about 150 Dollars [for] each Slave." Stevenson courteously rejected such an absurd proposal, adding a pledge to procure formal affidavits from his informants, Maxcy and Heth, to lend them credibility.[26]

After a series of meetings in February, Stevenson backed off his insistence on $600 in compensation per slave and instead advanced a proposal whereby the British Treasury would reimburse $600 for each enslaved man, $500 for each enslaved woman, and $400 for each enslaved child aboard the *Comet* and *Encomium*. Rothery dutifully agreed to submit Stevenson's compensation plan to the lords commissioners, but he suspected even those valuations were high. By that time, Stevenson had secured certificates from the New Orleans companies confirming that 146 of the enslaved people aboard the *Comet* had been insured. Rothery was still not satisfied, however, because the certificates were not the policies themselves. It was essential that "they should be produced," he insisted. Without the policies, he could not know either the precise amounts of the insurance, the amounts the underwriters paid the affected owners, or the names of those owners. Until he saw the policies, Rothery doubted that the *Comet*'s human cargo would individually fetch $600 in New Orleans, as the insurers claimed. His preference was to repay whatever amount the insurance companies disbursed through their policies. None of the slave owners already compensated by the underwriters had filed any complaint indicating "that the amount which they had received from the Insurance Companies did not fully satisfy them," so the amounts reimbursed must have been sufficient. Stevenson initially believed this method of calculation would shortchange the slave owners for their losses, but Rothery saw the plan as a means to prevent the Queen's Treasury from shelling out a shilling more than necessary.[27]

The insurance policies also mattered because they served as a useful gauge for reimbursing uninsured slave owners among the claimants, such as the *Comet*'s Sylvester W. Mudd and Col. Charles P. Tutt. By 1839, both men were dead, but their widows still sought indemnity for their nine enslaved people apiece seized by the British. In the cases of both the Mudd and the Tutt estates, Rothery pointed out, "there are no Documents whatever . . . to establish the loss[es] . . . sustained"—nothing to indicate "the value of any of these Slaves at the places of shipment." Since "no proof had been offered, relative to the loss of the 18 Slaves uninsured," the Treasury agent suggested that the best approach would be to reimburse them at the same rate as the insured bondpeople. Stevenson concurred on this point.[28]

On February 21, Rothery returned to Stevenson all of the documents he had borrowed for examination. They conversed that day "for about two hours," during which time Rothery broached the touchy subject of the total number of emancipated slaves for whom restitution was due. He insisted upon deducting the 11 fugitives who jumped from the *Comet.* Rothery also observed that, based on the evidence he had seen from the *Encomium*, there existed no claim whatsoever on 3 of the 45 enslaved people aboard. Charles Allen's bondman Joe definitely accompanied his owner to New Orleans on the *Thurle*, so the Treasury official assumed that Allen's two other bondpeople, Billy and Peggy, accounted for the others upon whom no claim had been filed. Of the remaining 42 slaves, 22 were the property of John Waddell, but 9 of those, Rothery learned from the documents, "had accompanied their Owner . . . to Key West, . . . which reduced his claim for Indemnification to 13 Slaves." In attempting to gain payment for nine bondpeople still in his possession, Rothery observed, "Mr. Waddell has been guilty of fraud." The total number of bondpeople from the *Encomium* meriting compensation dwindled to 33.[29]

From the 165 captives aboard the *Comet* and the 45 aboard the *Encomium*, Stevenson only readily conceded to deduct the 3 without a claim. By the end of February, then, the question for him was the value attached to the remaining 207 liberated slaves. Had the captives reached New Orleans, market prices for some individuals were predicted to reach as high as $1,600, but Rothery thought those numbers "excessive" and denied the premise behind them. At an average New Orleans price of even $600 each, as the New Orleans insurers proposed, the 207 slaves were worth $124,200, or £24,840, in compensation. Stevenson's compromise proposal to appraise captives differently based on sex and age whittled that figure down to $111,000, or £22,200. Rothery's suggestion translated into still lower restitution. Using the insurance policy average payout of $476 as a guide for pricing the insured as well as the uninsured slaves would yield compensation in the amount of $98,500, or £19,700, and "very much simplify the mode of Indemnification." At Bahamas prices, an outcome totally unacceptable to American interests, the indemnity would total a paltry $31,000, or £6,200. None of these figures included interest. Rothery did not feel "authorized" to discuss interest but cautioned Stevenson that "it is impossible for him to expect more than 4 per Cent," only two-thirds of the 6 percent the U.S. minister believed fair. But at the moment, the interest was secondary to the principal, and Rothery was not yet prepared to admit restitution based on 207 captives. He still planned to fight to reduce that total by 20—the 9 who returned with Waddell to New Orleans and the 11 runaways.[30]

Coincidentally, as negotiations over the freed slaves dragged on, dozens of the captives liberated by British colonial authorities on New Providence took their final step on the path to a new life in the Bahamas. On February 27, "a special court" in Nassau "was held for the purpose of naturalizing" forty-three "of the *American negroes* and others . . . , doubtless a part of the *cargoes* of the Comet and the Encomium." Formerly property, bought and sold as commodities, the individuals, unidentified by name in the press, began the next chapter of their lives. The British government had enabled their escape from slavery into freedom, but they made the effort to complete the transition from free alien to British subject.[31]

In mid-March 1839, Rothery and Stevenson finished reviewing the assembled materials without reaching a clear agreement. Rothery filed a report with Chancellor Spring Rice. Stevenson did not see it but suspected "that it was favorable, both as to the character and sufficiency of the evidence." Although "the number and value of the slaves for whom compensation is to be made" remained in doubt, Spring Rice assured Stevenson in a face-to-face meeting "that, as soon as he had time to take up the report and examine it, he would be prepared to adjust with [Stevenson] the whole matter." After more than seven years spent attempting to secure restitution, a "final settlement" mutually agreeable to the U.S. claimants and the British government appeared on the horizon.[32]

Rothery met with Stevenson on March 23 to attempt to iron out the final number of enslaved people for whom compensation was due. The Treasury agent insisted "that no demand ought to be made for the value" of the infant born aboard the *Comet*, overlooked during previous negotiations. He repeated the British resolve not to pay for the nine bondpeople who returned with John Waddell. Stevenson did not possess original documents showing that that had happened but agreed to the reduction once Lord Palmerston submitted a copy of the relevant letter as proof. Rothery also made deductions for two captives who died, four or five others who reportedly "had fled from liberty . . . , with a view of returning to voluntary servitude, under their former masters," and the eleven fugitives from the *Comet*. These categories of deductions remained troublesome. Stevenson stated "that if the whole had died he should maintain his claim for every one that landed, and did not return with their Owners to America."

He could not speak to the few who supposedly returned to the United States, "for . . . he had nothing to shew they had so done." As to the eleven runaways, neither side was prepared to budge. According to Stevenson, "there was no reason why he should not be paid for them also," but Rothery explained that the British government would not "concede the point."[33]

In his final report to the lords commissioners of the Treasury, Rothery shared his impressions of how restitution should proceed. He recommended payment for 146 of the 165 enslaved people from the *Comet*, coincidentally the precise number of insured captives on board. He valued them at an average of nearly $480 apiece, resulting in a recommendation that the British government distribute $70,000, or £14,000, for the human merchandise from the *Comet*. The admiralty referee also advocated payment for 33 of the 45 bondpeople from the *Encomium*. Noah B. Sisson, owner of the lone bondman, Tay, should be paid $500, Tay's documented value at the port of departure. Based on the two known insurance policies on 13 of the *Encomium*'s captives, they and the uninsured slaves other than Tay should be reimbursed at just under $477 apiece, for a total of $15,762, or £3,152.8.-. Altogether, indemnification for the captives emancipated from the *Comet* and *Encomium* totaled $85,762, excluding interest and the American claims for expenses incurred in attempting to recover the liberated slaves. In offering per capita reimbursement rates well below what Stevenson had lobbied for, Rothery expressed a misplaced confidence that the U.S. minister would be amenable to the evaluative process he had devised.[34]

The lords commissioners of the Treasury adopted Rothery's report almost in its entirety. They agreed with the wisdom and fairness of determining compensation based on the insurance policies submitted as evidence. They deviated from Rothery's calculations on only one point. The lords commissioners assessed the *Encomium*'s human cargo at a marginally lower $15,739 (£3,147.16) by not allotting Capt. Sisson the recommended $500 for Tay. Instead, they valued each of the twenty uninsured bondpeople from the *Encomium* equally at $476.95, thereby saving the Treasury more than four and one-half pounds. The Treasury's stunning parsimoniousness likely stemmed from the general resentment at paying reparation for liberated American slaves while already expending millions of pounds in compensation to British slave owners. The lords commissioners allowed the additional payment of 4 percent interest on the amounts due the U.S. slave owners and insurers. The rate was 2 percent less than what Stevenson had agitated for, but as the U.S. minister desired, it accumulated "from the dates of the respective seizures by the officers of customs at the Bahamas" to the eventual date of payment.[35]

While the lords commissioners' proposed plan for restitution awaited review and approval by Lord Palmerston, Stevenson anxiously pressed the chancellor of the Exchequer and the lords of the Treasury for news, trying in vain to ascertain "the final decision" of the British government. At last, on May 2, Palmerston issued his decision, concurring with the commissioners' compensation scheme. In a letter to Stevenson, he shared the numbers and dollar values settled upon by the commissioners and pledged an additional sum of $1,900, or £400, to reimburse American slave owners for "the expenses incurred by them in procuring evidence" to back their claims. At the Treasury's urging, Palmerston emphasized "that the proposed payment" for the *Comet* and *Encomium* must "be considered final and conclusive" and that the British government would never again allow "any claim for compensation in respect to slaves thrown within British jurisdiction, after the period when slavery was abolished throughout the British dominions"—an obvious reference to the *Enterprise*.[36]

Despite the plan's deviations from his initial preferences, Stevenson welcomed news of the long-delayed settlement. He shared the "gratifying intelligence" of the adjustment with Secretary of State Forsyth in a note dated May 8. Altogether, compensation for the human cargoes from the *Comet* and *Encomium*, plus expenses and anticipated interest "from the time of seizure until the probable time of payment," would total about $115,000 (more than $3.3 million in the present day).[37]

Stevenson spent the greater portion of the letter reveling in self-congratulations. Because it had taken so long to gain reparation, fellow "southern statesmen" had criticized him, as they had Aaron Vail before him, for "supposed neglect, or inattention" to the matter, when in truth the Crown prolonged the repayment despite the diligence of American efforts. In the end, the average valuation agreed to, of nearly $500 per slave, dwarfed the $200 apiece wrested by treaty from Britain in 1818 for enslaved people lost in the War of 1812. "Having succeeded in obtaining a much larger average value than had ever been before allowed, together with interest upon the whole amount for the time of the seizure and loss," Stevenson boasted, "I deemed it best to interpose no obstacle to the terms finally offered, but to accept them, and close the negotiation." The U.S. minister's words conveyed the misleading impression that he controlled negotiations and dictated the final terms, disguising the disappointments, unheeded pleas, and delays he endured throughout the process. But Stevenson refused to let reality dampen his effusiveness. "Having accomplished this result, after great labor and difficulty on my part, and as a large portion of the slaves were women and children, some of them under five years of age," he continued, "I flatter myself that the adjustment, and the basis upon which it has been made, will prove alike satisfactory to the claimants and the Government," for it marked a great victory for slave owners and a government structured to protect their interests.[38]

The news traveled across the Atlantic by early June 1839. Many Southern newspapers shared Stevenson's reaction. John Waddell's hometown newspaper, the *People's Press and Wilmington Advertiser*, described the settlement as "a happy arrangement," applauding the U.S. minister's efforts during "a protracted and arduous negotiation." The North Carolina editor deemed the settlement important not only to "our citizens" in the "immediate neighborhood," where "a portion of these negroes were from" but also as "a matter of deeper interest to the country at large." The negotiation reportedly "establishe[d] a great and important *principle*," although what that was went unstated. If he believed the outcome validated the principle of property in man, or the belief that the British had no right to emancipate American slaves, he was wide of the mark.[39]

If anything, the principles affirmed by Lord Palmerston in his compensation message proved hostile to customary Southern practices. They precluded any hope for a similar remedy for owners of captives shipped aboard the *Enterprise* or any future domestic slave-trading vessel sunk or stranded in a British colony. Since the British government had announced its policy, irate Southern newspaper editors had railed against Palmerston and Britain's redefinition of the law of nations that denied compensation for the enslaved people freed in Bermuda. For American slave owners, the sudden innovation defied common sense. Why should masters "lose the protection of international law" because "Great Britain, the author of the Slave Trade, had[,] in a fit of humanity and morality," emancipated slaves in its Atlantic colonies? Other nations did not get "to determine the tenure by which we hold our property, [or] to determine what shall be or not, property in this country." According to the *Charleston Mercury*, "This matter can never be permitted to rest." One owner of enslaved captives aboard the *Enterprise* made sure of that.[40]

11

An Alarm of Fire

Oliver Simpson probably met the *Enterprise* at the docks after it entered Charleston harbor on March 15, 1835. The ship was weeks behind schedule; worse still for Simpson, its cargo was woefully incomplete. Only six of the seventy-three enslaved people consigned to him by his business associate, Joseph W. Neal, were present for him to retrieve. Matilda Ridgley had decided to return to the American South with her five daughters, but what became of them is not known. Perhaps Ridgley's purported lover, the unidentified cook from the *Enterprise*, did actually purchase them and spare them from the depths of slavery, but it's not likely. Probably, like so many others ensnared in the domestic slave trade, they ended up on the auction block for purchase by the highest bidder. Whereas Ridgley's story was lost after stepping off the *Enterprise*, her enslaver Oliver Simpson's personal quest for restitution proves easier to piece together.[1]

Born in Virginia in the mid-1780s, Simpson first appeared in federal census records in 1820 in Rockingham County, North Carolina, located adjacent to the border between the two states. Rockingham County occupied a rural rectangle in the tier of counties north of Greensboro, south of Martinsville, Virginia, and southwest of Danville. Although it held well more than eleven thousand residents, it averaged only about twenty people per square mile, most of whom made their living from farming. Master of nine enslaved people, including six toiling in agriculture, Oliver Simpson was better off than most. Over the next decades, slavery improved his financial fortunes. By 1830, in his mid-forties, he controlled the labor of twenty-eight captives. Two years later, he was dealing in slaves in the nation's capital as half the partnership of Simpson & Neal.[2]

By 1835, the year of the *Enterprise*'s unintended voyage to Bermuda, Simpson had looked southward to increase his wealth. While maintaining his property in North Carolina, he bought up tracts of land in the notoriously violent Edgefield District of South Carolina, across the Savannah

River from Augusta, Georgia. He established himself in the village of Hamburg, founded by German immigrant Henry Shultz in 1821. Shultz had been a prominent citizen, community developer, and banker in Augusta. The German's efforts secured the financing for a toll bridge that carried traffic over the Savannah River for much of the nineteenth century. Shultz parleyed the success of the span into a company that issued its own currency, but when the Panic of 1819 struck, he went bankrupt, and creditors seized the bridge to pay off his debts. Despondent, Shultz failed in a suicide attempt before resolving instead to exact revenge upon his enemies. He purchased land directly across the river, where he created a settlement designed to compete with Augusta, to spite the town that he thought spurned him.[3]

By the early 1830s, Hamburg had grown into a thriving inland port. From there, area planters shipped cotton downriver to Savannah. Starting in 1833, the South Carolina Railroad connected the town over land to Charleston. Plank roads teemed with farmers riding their wagons into town. What "but a few years since, was an unsightly marsh, sending forth its pestiferous exhalations," wrote the *Edgefield Advertiser*, "is now covered with stately buildings, and is the great emporium of trade, for a large section of South Carolina." Hamburg was a bustling, prosperous place, rife with opportunity for someone like Oliver Simpson.[4]

The slave trader immersed himself in the economic life of the Hamburg community. He became one of the town's leading landholders, with almost $11,000 invested in local real estate. He later opened a livery stable "in the rear of the Old American Hotel, . . . opposite the Rail Road depot," where customers could rent a horse for 50¢ per day or $10 per month. Later still, he partnered "in an apothecary shop or drug store . . . under the name of S. D. Clark & Co." These sorts of diversified business ventures were not unusual for slave traders. Nor was his first undertaking, as a commissioner for the Bank of Hamburg, along with town founder Henry Shultz and bank president Wyatt W. Stark. Slave traders frequently involved themselves in the banking enterprises that funneled them the cash necessary to purchase and resell unwanted or surplus slaves or those disposed of to alleviate owners' economic embarrassments.[5]

After the Supreme Court of Bermuda allowed prisoners from the *Enterprise* to choose freedom, one Northern newspaper expressed its wish that the U.S. government "no[t] interfere to aid [Oliver] Simpson" recover compensation. As a shrewd businessman, Simpson did not require governmental exertions or the conclusion of international negotiations. He had been smart enough to take out a pair of insurance policies on the human cargo he ultimately lost. The Charleston Fire and Marine Insurance Company and the Augusta Insurance and Banking Company each covered a portion of the prisoners. Simpson paid a $100 premium to underwriters in Charleston to issue a policy in the amount of $20,000 on thirty-eight captives. It covered twenty-six men for $14,450, individually ranging in value from the $300 Shade Reed, just seven years old, to the $1,000 George Hammett. The average male slave was insured for $555, an amount most closely matched by twelve-year-old Oscar Worthy, valued at $550. Simpson's policy also covered twelve female slaves for $5,550, ranging from eight-year-old Louisa Brooks, at $325, to sixteen-year-old Nancy Brown, at $600. At $450, twelve-year-old Elizabeth Jane Warfield, one of five enslaved "copper"-colored Warfield youngsters, all between the ages of eight and fifteen, best approximated the average value of $462.50 for the female captives on board the *Enterprise*.[6]

Less clear are the details of the policy with the Augusta Insurance and Banking Company, likely purchased from the company's Charleston agent William Patton. Compared with the policy with Charleston Fire and Marine, the one with the Augusta firm must have been for no more than half the amount of insurance. It protected against the loss of fewer enslaved people, collectively worth less at market.[7]

With policies in hand, Oliver Simpson filed claims with the two insurance companies to recover his losses from the *Enterprise*. Neither the Charleston Fire and Marine Insurance Company nor the Augusta Insurance and Banking Company, however, rewarded Simpson's business acumen and foresight by honoring the terms of their respective policies. Both firms denied his claims. Simpson waited, perhaps placing his faith in the ability of U.S. diplomats to secure indemnity from Britain for the *Enterprise*. When it became evident in early March 1837 that compensation for the liberated slaves from Capt. Smith's vessel was not going to materialize, Simpson sued his two insurers in court for "nonperformance of their promises." Specifically, he alleged that they violated "the clause of the policy against loss *by perils of the sea, and the arrest and detention of princes and people*." Given his specific circumstances as an insured policyholder, Simpson could pursue redress in courts of law where U.S. diplomacy had so far failed.[8]

The Court of Common Pleas for Charleston District heard Simpson's case against the Charleston Fire and Marine Insurance Company during the May 1837 term. South Carolina attorney and slave owner Henry Grimké, brother of famed abolitionist sisters Sarah and Angelina Grimké, defended the insurers. He argued that the unusual circumstances under which the *Enterprise*'s enslaved cargo was stripped from Simpson's possession did not fall under the covered terms of his policy. Simpson's attorneys contended that the events in Bermuda qualified "under the risks enumerated" therein against "arrests, restraints, and detainments of all kings, princes, or people, of what nation, condition, or quality soever." Judge John Belton O'Neall instructed the twelve jurors to think of Chief Justice Butterfield's discharge of the captives as if it had been "done by the king of Great Britain" himself, since "the government of Bermuda emanated from him, and was administered in his name, and by his authority." The jury convened for deliberations.[9]

A clear majority of the twelve jurors, all white men, appear to have owned enslaved people and were sympathetic to the plight of a fellow slave owner. On May 26, they awarded Simpson $18,985, plus interest dating back to 1835. Sources disagree whether the recovery of Matilda Ridgley and her five girls accounted for the discrepancy between the settlement and the $20,000 value of the policy. The enslaved mother and her children were not listed in the court papers among the thirty-eight insured by the Charleston Fire and Marine policy, meaning either that they had already been excluded from the record or that they were covered under a different policy. Interest in the amount of $2,685 and court costs of $126 brought the total sum owed by the insurance company to $21,796 (the equivalent of more than $600,000). "There will doubtless be an appeal," predicted the *Charleston Courier*.[10]

When reporting the verdict, the same newspaper mentioned that Simpson had a nearly identical case pending in Georgia against the Augusta Insurance and Banking Company, concerning "a policy . . . on another set of slaves belonging to the emancipated gang" from the *Enterprise*. That case went before the Richmond County Superior Court, under presiding judge John Shly, three weeks later. The end result was the same. Foreman John Garner announced that the jury found in favor of Simpson to the amount of $8,959.63, plus interest and costs of the suit.[11]

Simpson's days in court battling over the captives of the *Enterprise* were not over just yet. As the *Courier* anticipated, the Charleston Fire and Marine Insurance Company filed an appeal in the case. The company charged that the *Enterprise* "was not tight and staunch when the insurance was effected, or that she was too deeply laden, and therefore not seaworthy." Its "want of provisions" adequate for the journey, the alleged "ignorance and incapacity of the captain and mate," and the purported lack of "a skil[l]ful and competent crew" further invalidated the jury's verdict and demanded that it "be set aside." The insurer also charged that Judge O'Neall "erred in charging the jury" that the facts of the case "amounted to an 'arrest, restraint, or detainment, of any prince, potentate, or people.'" Crucial to the company's argument, "if there was no arrest or detainment, . . . the loss" must be classified as "an escape, which was an excepted peril" under Simpson's policy.[12]

Judge O'Neall—the same jurist from the case that appeared before the Court of Common Pleas—presided over the Court of Appeals in 1838. Based on the "abundant" evidence from the first trial, he quickly dismissed the contentions that the *Enterprise* was unseaworthy or sailed by an incompetent captain and crew. The only legal question concerned whether Chief Justice Butterfield's action in summoning the slaves to his court constituted "capture, seizure, or detention, by the officer or agent of some government." As O'Neall reasoned, "The master of a vessel was bound to yield obedience to the writ of *habeas corpus*." Anyone in a foreign country must "observe its laws, and yield to its legal and proper process." The liberation of the captives therefore seemed to O'Neall "an act done in a course of justice and by the judgment of a Court exercising a competent jurisdiction." Finding the "detention by judicial process . . . an enumerated risk" covered by Oliver Simpson's policy, O'Neall dismissed the Charleston Fire and Marine Insurance Company's appeal. Simpson received all he was legally owed by March 24, 1838. He alone accounted for more than half of the company's nearly $39,000 in payouts for marine losses in the first six months of 1838.[13]

Simpson received his money more than two years earlier than did any of the insurance companies or uninsured slave owners awaiting payment from the British government for losses aboard the *Comet* and *Encomium*. At the start of May 1839, Lord Palmerston announced his support for the settlement worked out by William Rothery and Andrew Stevenson over the two vessels. Eager to conclude the final adjustment of the claims, Stevenson urged Palmerston to push for "an immediate appropriation . . . from Parliament, to meet the amount which her Majesty's Government has admitted to be justly due." Although compensation was tantalizingly close, the process still required parliamentary approval. The lords commissioners of the Treasury prepared the written expenditure for Parliament to vote upon. Stevenson believed payment would "be made" eventually, but, at the same time, he expected "strong efforts . . . in the [House of] Commons to defeat any appropriation for these claims, arising out of the excited state of public feeling" in Britain "on all subjects connected with slavery."[14]

Stevenson probably expected the greatest resistance in Parliament from Dublin's member, the internationally known Irish abolitionist Daniel O'Connell. The year before, the two had sparred over newspaper reports that O'Connell, in a speech in Birmingham, England, called Stevenson, a slave-owning Virginian, "a slave-breeder; one of those beings who rear up slaves for the purpose of traffic." "Is it possible," O'Connell asked, "that America would send here a man" to serve as ambassador "who is a disgrace to human nature?" Stevenson took offense. Southern slave owners routinely denounced slave breeding even as most of them engaged in some variety of the practice to encourage the growth of their enslaved labor forces. In this instance, O'Connell was reportedly suggesting that the U.S. minister participated in the basest, most reprehensible form of breeding: intentionally forcing bondpeople's reproduction exclusively so that he could sell their offspring in the domestic slave trade. Stevenson therefore challenged O'Connell to a duel. The Irishman declined, stating that he had been misquoted in the paper. Stevenson accepted O'Connell's explanation as "a disavowal of the offensive expressions contained in . . . [the] speech" and declared himself "satisfied." It was enough to avert the duel, although O'Connell, not backing down, insisted in the press that his reply to Stevenson did not constitute an apology and that for him to think so "was either fancy or diplomacy." "I care not which," he added. The abolitionist then condemned the "detestable," "abominable," "hideous," and "revolting" custom of slave breeding that he noted was especially prevalent in Stevenson's native Virginia.[15]

Rather than O'Connell, abolitionist Stephen Lushington, longtime member of Parliament and, since 1838, privy councillor and judge of the High Court of Admiralty, emerged as the loudest voice at Westminster during the August 5 discussion of the reparation payment. The total indemnity for the enslaved people freed from the *Comet* and *Encomium* amounted to £23,500. Lushington believed the claim questionable and "entertained considerable doubt whether this sum was legally due." Nevertheless, he and fellow abolitionists took solace in that "this was the last claim of the kind which could possibly be brought forward." With the arrangement having already been concluded, Lushington "thought it would not be wise to object to the passing of the vote." Before concluding his remarks, however, he used the opportunity to share slave runaway advertisements from newspapers in the American South, to decry slavery as "a disgrace to any country calling itself civilized," and to credit "the northern states" for their "noblest exertions" trying "to rescue the American character from this foul blot."[16]

Daniel O'Connell agreed to follow Lushington's lead in not opposing the appropriation. Not one to shy from speaking out against injustice, he nevertheless rose to lambast the fledgling Republic of Texas and the "set of land pirates, who had established a government [there] on a principle in which slavery was an essential ingredient." The overwhelming majority of U.S. citizens who settled in Texas were, in fact, Southern slave owners in search of fresh cotton lands, and O'Connell opposed Britain recognizing Texas's independence "so long as slavery and land piracy was allowed to exist" and Texas continued its brisk slave trade with the United States.[17]

Chancellor of the Exchequer Thomas Spring Rice and Joseph Hume, one of Parliament's most frustratingly budget-conscious members, each spoke "a few words" as well. Finally, on August 5, 1839, the long sought-after restitution for the enslaved people liberated from the *Comet* and *Encomium* was approved. "The sum of £23,500 sterling was voted last night in the House of Commons," Andrew Stevenson beamed, "without a division, and after little debate." Compensation was imminent, more than eight and a half and five and a half years after the respective wrecks of the two vessels. It marked a hard-won triumph for slave-owner diplomacy.[18]

All Stevenson needed from Secretary of State Forsyth was instructions on how he preferred the indemnity should "be received and disposed of." "When payment is offered," Forsyth replied, Stevenson must deposit "the whole . . . with the bankers of the United States in London to the credit" of the U.S. State Department and "subject to the drafts of the Secretary of State." Upon the British government depositing the agreed-upon funds, Forsyth authorized Stevenson "to execute the proper acquittances."[19]

The task "of dividing the proceeds among the American claimants," though, devolved upon the secretary of state. Forsyth therefore asked Stevenson to transmit any evidence he had in his possession "regarding the individual ownership and title to the negroes in question . . . to aid the proper partition" of the British indemnity. Forsyth wanted to know in particular which "of the three slaves of the Comet's cargo" had died, "the names of the eleven who escaped from the same vessel," and the identities "of the five who returned to the United States," plus the names of all of their owners, for the terms of the adjustment specified that he withhold compensation for them from their former masters. Likewise, he requested the names of the enslaved people from the *Encomium* "who returned to the United States with their masters, and the names of their respective owners." Even with the funds from the Bank of England in hand, distributing them turned into more of a bureaucratic headache than Forsyth anticipated.[20]

No news of the final adjustment of claims for the *Comet* and *Encomium* appeared in the American press for the rest of 1839. The State Department may have kept it out of the headlines as Forsyth did the complicated work of calculating who was owed what. At the same time, the emerging saga of the *Amistad*, beginning in late August 1839, captured national attention. The previous month, illegally enslaved Mende captives stolen from Africa revolted aboard the schooner *Amistad* while en route to their Spanish buyers' sugar plantations in Cuba. Ignoring the rebels' demand to return to Africa, the owners deceived them, sailed north, and meandered for weeks off of the East Coast of the United States before being intercepted off Long Island, New York, on August 26 and taken into custody. The resulting legal battles over the Mende generated widespread curiosity, both in the United States and abroad. Amid the uproar, public attention to the status of reparation for the *Comet* and *Encomium* was diverted.[21]

The two wrecked slave ships returned to the spotlight in early 1840. On January 13, Sen. John C. Calhoun redirected congressional energies to the British "outrages" committed on U.S. vessels. He made a motion that President Martin Van Buren "communicate to the Senate, whether the Government of Great Britain has yet made compensation to our citizens in the case of the brigs Enterprise, Encomium, and Comet." The Senate agreed, and before the month was out, Van Buren submitted to the body a full report from Secretary of State John Forsyth. It explained that Britain had agreed to indemnify two of the three lost cargoes, listed the amounts for each, and outlined "the disposition ordered to be made of it."[22]

Although Southern members of Congress were gratified to learn that slave owners would be receiving £23,500 in compensation for the *Comet* and *Encomium*, their immediate concern was the conspicuous absence of an indemnity for the *Enterprise*. Proslavery congressman Robert Barnwell Rhett of South Carolina proposed a resolution that the Committee on Foreign Affairs conduct a full investigation into the case of the *Enterprise* and report back to the full House. In the Senate, Calhoun submitted a motion on March 4 consisting of three resolutions that sought to imprint his proslavery ideology on American foreign policy. Implicitly challenging Britain's attempted revision to the law of nations, they conveyed Calhoun's own understanding of the international law of slavery and his desire to extend Southern slave owner rights into the Atlantic basin. First, Calhoun declared his belief that "a ship or vessel on the high seas, in time of peace, engaged in a lawful voyage, is, according to the laws of nations, under the exclusive jurisdiction of the State to which her flag belongs." Second, if "stress of weather, or other unavoidable cause," forced that ship "into the port of a friendly power," it lost "none of the rights" it enjoyed "on the high seas." The people on board, "with their property, . . . would be placed under the protection which the laws of nations extend to the unfortunate under such circumstances." Third and most specifically, the *Enterprise* fell "within the principles embraced in the foregoing resolutions, and . . . the seizure and detention of the negroes on board by the local authority of the island [of Bermuda], was an act in violation of the laws of nations, and highly unjust to our own citizens to whom they belong." After being read, the resolutions were "ordered . . . printed."[23]

The Senate took up Calhoun's *Enterprise* resolutions on Friday, March 13. Defending them himself, the South Carolina senator commenced speaking before crowded galleries, the overflow of curious listeners spilling into the lobbies. He barely began when "an alarm of fire" sounded, clearing the Senate chamber. The rush to the exits interrupted the proceedings. A chimney had caught fire, and the flames "communicated to one of the domes, but it was soon extinguished," and "order was restored." Calhoun resumed his speech, offering the rapt throng what one correspondent described as "a strain of argument and eloquence seldom surpassed in this or any other country." In doing so, he blared his own metaphorical "alarm of fire" for Southern slaveholding interests.[24]

Calhoun summarized the three cases of the *Comet*, *Encomium*, and *Enterprise*. Despite the similar circumstances surrounding them, he complained, Britain granted indemnity in only the first two, making the excuse that it had abolished slavery prior to the 1835 landing of the *Enterprise*. Calhoun objected to the distinction. He admitted Britain's right to abolish slavery within its territorial possessions but not to liberate bondpeople who involuntary found themselves in British colonies. For the British to uphold the right to emancipate foreign slaves, they either had to make municipal laws "paramount" to the law of nations when "their provisions happen to come into conflict" or to reject "the right of man to hold property in man," neither of which Calhoun could accept. Surely Great Britain recognized that people could be property, he reasoned: England had long been "the greatest slave dealer on earth." Moreover, in portions of the British Empire, slavery continued to exist after the passage of the Slavery Abolition Act. In fact, Calhoun insisted, the English gentlemen incorporated into the East India Company exercised a "power . . . far more unlimited and despotic than that of any Southern planter over his slaves." The South Carolina senator concluded with an ominous warning. Although he wished to maintain peace between the United States and Great Britain, one "indispensable" precondition for peace was justice, and in the case of the *Enterprise*, "justice has been withheld on grounds utterly untenable." If Britain "persisted" in its current position, "that must strike a fatal blow at the peace of the two countries."[25]

Calhoun admitted his foremost concern for "a principle vital to us of the South"—that domestic slave-trading vessels be released with their valuable human cargoes when forced by inclement weather into foreign ports—yet also believed it "of deep interest to the rest of the Union." Through his rhetorical magic, wrote one correspondent, Calhoun's speech in the Senate chamber sounded like "a *national one*." His unique combination of recent history lesson, criticism of British hypocrisy, and appeals to American pride and honor attempted to transcend narrow sectional concerns and convince a broader coalition of senators to support his three resolutions. Several Northern newspaper correspondents raved over his performance. "Calhoun made a remarkably vigorous and impressive speech," wrote one. His "splendid and powerful argument" marked "one of the most conclusive and eloquent . . . ever delivered in the capitol."[26]

Following some brief remarks from Sen. Felix Grundy of Tennessee, Alabama senator William Rufus King made a motion to forward Calhoun's resolutions to the Committee on Foreign Affairs. Pennsylvania's James Buchanan chaired that committee, which made some minor revisions to the resolutions' wording. He showed the changes to Calhoun, who, "without hesitation, assented to them."[27]

The reading of the amended resolutions on April 15 elicited commentary from Sen. Henry Clay of Kentucky. He did not doubt "the general principles contained in the resolutions." His main inquiry for Calhoun was the purpose they served: "What good could result, what benefit was proposed, by their introduction[?]" Lord Palmerston's language clearly indicated that negotiations had concluded, so even though Clay intended to vote for the resolutions, he did not understand the "utility" of adopting them.[28]

Calhoun stressed the importance of the principle at stake, "especially to the portion of the Union he represented." The British refusal to release coastwise domestic slavers was a practical "question of no small magnitude": "the increased hazard from this new danger" threatened to "have the effect of closing the intercourse by sea between the Southern Atlantic ports and these of the Gulf, so far as our slave property is concerned." Denying compensation to slave owners, as in the case of the *Enterprise*, only "added [to] the injury done to our citizens."[29]

Turning Clay's concerns about "utility" on their head, Calhoun argued that the Senate needed to pass his resolutions precisely because Palmerston had ended negotiations. With "justice refused," congressional "silence would have been construed into an abandonment of the claim of our citizens, and an acquiescence in the dangerous principle on which it was rejected." In contrast, passing the resolutions "would keep alive the claim" and, "more important, rebut any inferred abandonment of the principle on which it rests." The stakes were high. "If we now yield"—Calhoun warned—"if the Senate should refuse to act on the resolutions, or vote them down, we surrender both right and principle." The vote, too, served as an important test amid growing abolitionist sentiment domestically. It would determine whether the Senate—in particular, his colleagues from the North—defended "the rights of the South to the great mass of its property" in slaves or sided with Great Britain in distinguishing between slavery "and every other description of property."[30]

Though ready to defend slavery, Clay doubted that Great Britain's refusal to pay indemnity for the *Enterprise* indicated any intention to "interrupt or interfere with [the U.S.] coasting trade" or "assail" the captives on board. For the time being, he minimized Calhoun's concerns and dismissed the implication that war with Britain would be an appropriate form of redress. Britain's action in liberating captives from the *Enterprise* did not present "such an open, undisguised attack upon us as to justify such a measure."[31]

Calhoun did not believe that the British would intentionally "seize [U.S.] vessels at sea" like pirates, "with the view of liberating slaves on board," or "plunder our coasting trade." But the net effect of Britain's refusal to provide compensation for a liberated shipment of enslaved captives was the same, interfering with "the intercourse by sea between one half of this

Union and the other" and the "most valuable portion of the property of the South." Calhoun's resolutions before the Senate, if passed, would register U.S. dissatisfaction with Britain's handling of these episodes.[32]

At that point, Augustus Seymour Porter of Michigan, a virtual unknown compared with senatorial giants Clay and Calhoun, entered into the discussion. No abolitionist, he recognized that the U.S. Constitution protected slavery as a domestic institution, but that did not mean it could be enforced outside "the limits of our own jurisdiction," such as in British ports. He feared putting the "national honor" of the United States on a collision course "with the local laws and jurisdiction of a foreign country," thereby provoking an "international controversy" or "national war." Questioning "the necessity and expediency" of the Senate dealing prematurely with "a subject of this magnitude and delicacy," Porter proposed setting aside Calhoun's resolutions. The roll call vote showed that Porter alone approved his motion.[33]

After a few additional observations from Sen. Thomas Hart Benton of Missouri, the Senate voted on Calhoun's resolutions. They passed on April 15, with thirty-three votes in favor and none opposed. The result was deceptive, however, for nineteen of the fifty-two senators abstained from the vote. Of the thirty-three who voted affirmatively, twenty-two represented slave-owning states. With the number of slave-owning and non-slave-owning states equal in 1840, at thirteen apiece, the popularity of Calhoun's *Enterprise* resolutions was magnified in those locations where some people held others as property.[34]

Despite later touting the technically "unanimous vote," Calhoun was disappointed in the result. "The immediate object I had for introducing these resolutions," he explained in his speech of March 13, was to take the temperature of the Senate on reparation for the *Enterprise*. He continued, "I wish to afford to our brethren in the other sections" of the country "an opportunity of exhibiting a proof of their attachment to the common interest, by sustaining a cause where we [of the South] are particularly concerned." Some Southern newspapers saw the two affirmative votes apiece from New Hampshire, Pennsylvania, Ohio, and Illinois and the single yeas from Maine, Rhode Island, and Michigan as evidence that the North would not "tamely submit to outrages perpetrated upon Southern property." Others interpreted the voting patterns differently. The vote did not demonstrate as strong of a united front against British interference with the domestic slave trade as Calhoun had hoped. Moreover, Calhoun saw in the results the dangers of party discipline and partisan loyalty to the South. Of the eleven Northern votes supporting the resolutions, only one was cast by a Whig: Sen. Nathan Dixon of Rhode Island. The rest of the Northern members of the Whig Party "turned their backs upon the resolutions and walked out of the Senate rather than vote for them." Democrats in the North and South alike supported Calhoun's measures, but antislavery sentiments among Northern Conscience Whigs prevented them from joining their Southern counterparts. The same sectional tension within the Whig Party on display during the vote on Calhoun's resolutions portended the Whigs' destruction in the 1850s.[35]

Calhoun's efforts to secure indemnity for the *Enterprise*'s liberated slaves continued, but Oliver Simpson no longer needed the assistance of his senator. After its failed appeal, the Charleston Fire and Marine Insurance Company paid Simpson in March 1838 the last monies owed him from his policies. The insurer, in turn, undertook to "prosecute, through the U.S. Government, their claims for indemnity against the British Government." Slavery was the lifeblood of the U.S. economy, and the insurers protected that investment in bound labor during the forced migrations of the domestic slave trade. When those journeys went awry, necessitating huge payouts to policyholders, insurance companies reflexively turned to the federal government as the insurers' insurer. Through the intercession of American ministers abroad, they hoped to secure restitution to keep their businesses solvent and successful. Their shared interest in slavery facilitated a mutually beneficial relationship.[36]

12

The Wreck of the *Hermosa*

After the rapid succession of incidents involving the *Comet*, *Encomium*, and *Enterprise* between 1831 and 1835, U.S. newspaper editors, politicians, and diplomats had warned of the danger of future shipwrecks of American slavers in the British Atlantic. Slavery was an emotionally charged topic, and losses of enslaved property roused the passions of their former owners and the slaveholding states generally. Some voices had already raised the specter of war should the Crown refuse to respect American property rights on the high seas. Surely a better solution could be had. By late 1837, President Martin Van Buren encouraged U.S. minister Andrew Stevenson "to enter upon the negotiation of a convention for regulating the disposition of slaves belonging to the United States" in the event that they inadvertently ended up in British Atlantic colonies. Van Buren hoped that such a treaty would extradite back to the United States Southern slaves shipwrecked or otherwise accidentally thrown upon British territory. The goal of developing an explicit arrangement was simple: "the prevention of the ill effects to be apprehended from future collisions" between the United States and Great Britain, over "a subject so liable to produce, in the people of the respective countries, a high degree of excitement and irritation." In its first thirty-eight years as a nation, the United States had fought two wars with Great Britain. Why risk a third when the two nations could negotiate an agreement in advance of the inevitable next incident?[1]

In April 1838, Stevenson proposed to Lord Palmerston that their two countries pursue a "conventional arrangement, providing for the disposition of all slaves belonging to the United States" who involuntarily came "within the British colonies" of the Atlantic. Even though the two nations did not agree on the fundamental principles surrounding the United States' coastwise domestic slave trade, Stevenson shared Van Buren's "earnest desire" to "adopt measures" designed to prevent "the evils that . . . arise from such difference in opinion." In making the proposition, Stevenson explained, the president hoped "to adjust this matter in the most amicable manner," finding "some ground of accommodation consistent with the true interests and honor of both factions."[2]

Palmerston presented the idea to unspecified officers of the Crown, but, as he reported back in May, "Her Majesty's Government do not, at present, see how any conventional arrangement could be formed for the purpose contemplated in Mr. Stevenson's note." Instead, he invited the U.S. minister "to give a more definite explanation of the nature of the proposal" the U.S. government had in mind. Until Stevenson could offer some concrete details, though, "it would be premature to pronounce any opinion."[3]

Secretary of State John Forsyth offered some specifics for Stevenson to pass along. Van Buren wanted an agreement that would "stipulate" Great Britain "refrain from forcing liberty upon American slaves . . . driven into her colonial ports." He believed that he could achieve this objective by restricting the operation of "existing British laws . . . to terra firma." As long as enslaved cargoes remained shipboard and did not physically land on British soil, they could be sent on their way to their intended destinations. "In cases of imperious necessity, however," Forsyth added, "the negroes might be placed in a fortification or other place under military command, for temporary safe keeping, until their owners could provide the means for their reshipment without unnecessary delay." If the United States could negotiate these terms, "the local authorities of the British islands near this continent would be prevented from improperly interfering with this species of American property when driven into [their] waters."[4]

The British government saw the terms Stevenson relayed in July as a nonstarter. In September, Palmerston explained that British law was "protective and not compulsory," predicated upon "the free exercise of . . . will." No "British law . . . forces a slave to quit a master with whom he is desirous of remaining." Enslaved persons reaching Britain's Atlantic colonies could remain with their owners, or not. The point was, they got to choose "and to emancipate" themselves if they wished. So far, history showed that such people almost always preferred freedom over slavery, which was "consistent with the known principles of human nature."[5]

Knowing all that, Palmerston continued, "it would be impossible to propose to Parliament a law for the purpose of taking away from American slaves, who have come within the British dominions, the right" to choose liberty. Any law that did so "would be so entirely at variance with every principle of the British constitution, that no Government could venture to propose it to Parliament, and no Parliament would agree to adopt it."[6]

The recommended confinement of British laws to the terra firma and exclusion of "the harbors of British colonial seaports" deviated from both English law and the law of nations. As Palmerston explained, "The law of nations draws no distinction between the land of a country and the waters within its jurisdiction." The American proposal marked an assault upon British territorial sovereignty.[7]

Her Majesty's government also rejected the imprisonment of enslaved Americans "for temporary safe custody under a military guard." The "insurmountable objections" to this proposal included the unwillingness of the government to employ its troops for that purpose and the British army's own repugnance toward that duty. The British military was already active in the suppression of the transatlantic slave trade and needed no added burdens.[8]

Finally, Palmerston explained that Britain did not want to set a precedent by making any deal that could be construed as proslavery. If it did, the government could not refuse similar agreements with other nations, such as France, Spain, Portugal, Denmark, or Sweden. Britain's "great aim" for many years had been "to put an end to the slave trade, and to set an example of the abolition of slavery." Any arrangement to the contrary would incorrectly suggest a reversal of course. Britain had proudly taken steps against slavery "unparalleled in the history of the world," Palmerston boasted, and the Crown was not about to undo them.[9]

The rejection of the U.S. proposal could not have been more thorough. Effectively, negotiations ended before they even began. Talks were actively underway over restitution for the *Comet* and *Encomium* in early November 1838 when Stevenson informed Secretary of State Forsyth that Britain would not be holding parallel negotiations to determine how to handle the possibility of another wrecked American slave ship on British colonial shores. As a result, the U.S. and British governments had no preemptive plan in place when the *Hermosa* sank on October 19, 1840.[10]

The *Hermosa* was a "fine coppered and copper fastened" schooner with a cargo capacity of just under 134 tons. In late September, it was docked along the James River in Richmond, Virginia. The firm of James Fisher & Son, merchants in the Virginia capital since at least 1836, advertised in a local newspaper welcoming the public to secure passage on its upcoming voyage. The *Hermosa* was prepared to load a variety of freight at Pickett's Wharf, but the preponderance of the *Hermosa*'s cargo would consist of enchained human beings.[11]

In 1840, Richmond was not yet the largest slave depot in the Chesapeake, but along with Baltimore, Washington, DC, and Alexandria, it served as an important centralized depository on the supply side for the Lower South's distant slave markets. Steamboats and sailing vessels plied the James River, while roads and railroads converged on the Virginia capital. Most fundamentally, the surplus slave population in the region gave a bevy of Richmond-based slave traders ample business. Rice Ballard, Bacon Tait, Silas Omohundro, and dozens more bought up bondpeople from surrounding areas and warehoused them in one of several Richmond slave jails prior to shipment to the Deep South.[12]

The responsibility of shipping the *Hermosa*'s cargo of tobacco and forty-eight bondpeople out of Richmond fell to its pilot, John S. Chattin. The thirty-year-old captain from New York was slated to deliver the captives aboard his vessel to the slave markets of New Orleans. After the Panic of 1837, a stubborn economic downturn still gripped the country in 1840. The auction blocks of the Crescent City no longer witnessed the same frenetic pace of sales or astronomical prices as in the flush times, but the slave markets still generated money for the taking.[13]

When Capt. Chattin pulled out of Pickett's Wharf and set a course down the James River on October 10, he carried enslaved people from three different owners. Landon C. Read sent a solitary forty-five-year-old bondman named Lewis Johnson to merchant and Virginia native James H. Dudley of New Orleans. Commission merchants and auctioneers Lancaster, Denby & Co. of Richmond consigned nine enslaved persons to well-established New Orleans cotton factors A. Ledoux & Co. All of these captives—Isaac, David, Tazewell, John, and Horace; Sarah Reilly, Lucy, Mariah, and Eliza—were young people between the ages of eleven and sixteen, facing a future, as far as they knew, of lifelong bondage in the Old Southwest.[14]

Newspaper reports misidentified the owner of the balance of the shipment as Richmond slave trader Robert Lumpkin. The remaining thirty-eight bondpeople actually belonged to another of the city's prominent slave dealers, Henry N. Templeman. A native Virginian, thirty-six-year-old Templeman in the late 1820s was a slave buyer on Maryland's Eastern Shore. By 1830 he kept the City Coffee House in Richmond, where he served oysters and other delicacies made-to-order and stocked his bar "with the best Liquors" and "Wines of every fashionable variety." After initially running his establishment as a solo operation, he partnered with Edward N. Allen, a move that perhaps liberated Templeman to devote more time to the slave-dealing business in which he had previously been employed.[15]

Templeman was buying enslaved people in Lancaster County, on Virginia's Northern Neck, in 1832. Two years later, he partnered with William H. Goodwin to buy the Richmond slave jail formerly operated by Rice Ballard, Franklin & Armfield's agent and slave buyer in the city. In September 1834, Goodwin and Templeman announced their readiness to receive "slaves for safe-keeping" at their facility on Valley (Seventeenth) Street, adjacent to Seabrook's tobacco warehouse. "The buildings are strong and airy," they boasted, "and consist of several apartments, (for males and females,) together with a comfortable Hospital." The site was "dry and healthy," with clean, potable water. In addition, the two partners offered Richmond masters concierge service, willing to pick up and convey "slaves, from any part of the city to our jail, free of charge." In 1840, Templeman also joined with R.H. Dickinson to run the Richmond auction house of Messrs. Templeman & Dickinson, which provided yet another valuable service in the process of buying and selling enslaved property.[16]

Aboard the *Hermosa*, Templeman's thirty-eight captives included twenty-one males, sixteen females, and an unspecified "child," likely an infant, traveling with her twenty-two-year-old mother, Malinda. In addition to the "child," Templeman's human cargo consisted of three ten-year-olds, eleven teens, twenty people in their twenties, and three in their thirties. At thirty-five, Edmond Parker was the oldest. Twenty-four of the prisoners were listed in the manifest as black, ten as brown, and four as yellow. One captive, Isabella Allen, had just "one eye," but as a young Black woman in her early twenties, her productive and reproductive potential in the Old Southwest offset her disability. Had she been totally blind, she likely would not have been snatched up in the interstate slave trade at all. Shipping the thirty-eight prisoners cost Templeman $625.[17]

Four and a half days' sailing past Cape Henry, Virginia, the *Hermosa* reached the archipelago of the Bahamas. Capt. Chattin soon learned firsthand the navigational dangers of the same stretch of ocean that had claimed the *Comet* and *Encomium*. On the night of October 19, the *Hermosa* "struck on a reef of rocks near the East end of the Island of Abaco," near Spanish Cay, and "bilged immediately." As Bahamian governor Sir Francis Cockburn told it, "every Soul would have perished but for the gallant exertions of the Boatmen" of Abaco, who rescued them "from a watery grave." A wrecker took the captain, crew, and enslaved passengers stranded on the reef and delivered them initially to Abaco. Capt. Chattin requested that they be taken to a U.S. port, but contrary to his preference, the wrecker instead conveyed them to the port of Nassau on the evening of October 22. The boatmen "saved a part of the Tobacco" as well, although "in a damaged state."[18]

Upon arriving at the colonial capital, Chattin never intended "to land the slaves from the wrecker, but . . . to keep them on Board & claim the protection of the government." With the salvage vessel safely anchored in the harbor, away from the wharves, the captain set out in a boat for Nassau to see consul John F. Bacon about securing a replacement ship to resume the journey to Louisiana. In Chattin's absence and against his wishes, British officers boarded the wrecker, "immediately seized" the captives from the *Hermosa*, stripped them from the captain's possession, and ordered them to shore, where uniformed soldiers armed with "muskets and bayonets" waited. Chattin filed a protest to register his displeasure. Gov. Cockburn denied having any role in the events that transpired, insisting that he sought to avoid undue trouble for himself or the Crown. Based on prior instructions from England, however, he permitted the captives to land on the island of New Providence. The soldiers marched the prisoners "before a magistrate at Nassau." Repeating a now-familiar process, officials asked the *Hermosa* survivors about their occupations and "whether they desired to remain on the island." With perhaps one exception, all accepted the freedom proffered them and were "set at liberty." As Capt. Chattin related the story, the magistrate also informed Henry N. Templeman that the slave trader would not "get the negroes Back & that John Bull would not pay further either." Another fortuitous shipwreck had liberated a cargo of Southern slaves.[19]

The most immediate problem for the freedpeople from the *Hermosa*, Gov. Cockburn explained, was that it was "nearly dark when they landed & too late for them to procure the means of lodging themselves." Cockburn did not want "to afford them the use of the government building . . . about a mile from Town," where illegal shipments of Africans captured by British squadrons on the open Atlantic were housed, "lest it should have the appearance of my taking any possession of them." In lieu of that, he allowed "some of them . . . to shelter" for the night—"as a matter of Charity"—"in the Building appropriated to the use of the Police." The emancipated captives remained under police custody until the next morning. Most then found work "in the service of the inhabitants" of Nassau. They were "portioned out among both the black and white citizens, there being a great rush for them." The freed adults from the *Hermosa* augmented the already expanded free labor force of the Bahamas, where the apprenticeship system for emancipated slaves ended in 1838, two years earlier than originally planned. "Those under age were bound out" until they reached maturity.[20]

The *Hermosa* brought the total number of enslaved people liberated from the four U.S. coastwise slaving vessels since 1831 to more than 300. Reflecting on the emancipations, one abolitionist chortled that "accident" had "transformed [chattels] . . . into men." Yet for the nearly 250 slaves emancipated in the Bahamas from the *Comet*, *Encomium*, and *Hermosa*, freedom did not often translate into prosperity. During his term as governor, from 1837 to 1844, Cockburn struggled with the challenge of growing numbers of destitute and impoverished former slaves on Nassau's streets. Some captives liberated from slave ships found work as domestics, fishermen, or subsistence farmers, but many were vulnerable to exploitation by Bahamian whites who took advantage of the oversupply of labor to extract long hours of work for low wages.[21]

While managing the influx of foreign slaves into his colony, Gov. Cockburn's thoughts also turned to the wreckers who rescued those aboard the *Hermosa*. "The master of the vessel who first saved & then brought them to Nassau has received no remuneration of any sort," he informed the Crown. He thought it unfair, for if the unnamed mariner had "employed his vessel in saving goods from the wreck, . . . he would have been entitled to a large Salvage" for his efforts. As it was, he prioritized the people, saving only a small quantity of tobacco in poor condition. "Tis a pity that such humane & praiseworthy conduct should entail a loss" to the altruistic seaman. Despite the governor's appeal, he learned in February 1841 "that there is no fund . . . from which remuneration could be granted to the Boatmen of Abaco for their laudable exertions in saving the slaves."[22]

Slave trader Henry N. Templeman expected a better outcome as he set out to recoup his losses. U.S. newspapers noted in the first stories they ran of the *Hermosa*'s sinking that "the entire cargo was insured." Templeman had paid a $173.12 premium to insure his thirty-eight prisoners for a total of $27,700, an average of almost $729 each. The New Orleans Insurance Company and the Louisiana State Marine and Fire Insurance Company of New Orleans each insured half the total amount, or $13,850 apiece. The policy specifically protected the slave trader against "the risk of seizure, capture, detention or hindrance by the British Government, its officers or agents."[23]

Since Templeman had lost the slaves "by perils insured against" in his policy, he filed a claim with his insurers on November 25, 1840. Upon the slave dealer "furnish[ing] . . . proper and reasonable preliminary proof of the loss," the New Orleans Insurance Company paid its half of the policy. Louisiana State Marine and Fire refused, however, and demanded a higher standard of evidence. "I am directed by the Board to inform you," insurance company president John K. West wrote Templeman on December 12, "that they are ready to pay said Loss when legal proof is exhibited of said slaves being lost by a peril insured against." In response, Templeman filed suit in the New Orleans Commercial Court to compel them to pay, "with interest and costs & for general relief."[24]

The Commercial Court received Templeman's complaint on December 23. The next day, the deputy sheriff served papers to John K. West. In early January 1841, Templeman tried to convince the court of the urgency of his case, particularly with respect to the testimony of John S. Chattin. The *Hermosa*'s captain, the slave trader explained, was "a seafaring man" with "no permanent residence . . . temporarily in New Orleans." His statement, which Templeman was confident would bolster his case, had to be secured before he departed the city "in a day or two."[25]

The Commercial Court scheduled Templeman's case against the insurer for Tuesday, February 2. The slave dealer's attorneys presented the *Hermosa*'s bill of lading, certified by a New Orleans notary public, and highlighted the testimony of Capt. Chattin, still in the city, who gave a detailed account of the events leading to the loss of the human cargo. Louisiana State Marine and Fire sent lawyer Charles M. Conrad to defend the insurance company. He denied their responsibility to pay on the claim, arguing that "the British . . . officers were only passive in relation to the . . . Slaves carried to Nassau by the wrecker" and that the case should therefore be dismissed.[26]

The court declared the evidence "conclusive" that authorities in the Bahamas had "made a seizure & took the control" of Templeman's enslaved property "& placed it beyond his control or power of recovery." The slave trader suffered a "total loss" and was entitled to receive full indemnity "under the written clause in the policy" protecting him against "loss occasioned by the capture or retention of the British Government, its officers, or agents." Simply put, ruled the Commercial Court, "there can be no Doubt of the plaintiff's right to recover." It awarded him the full $13,850 owed, plus 5 percent interest dating from December 23, 1840, "and Costs of [the] Suit." As with Oliver Simpson's two cases relating to losses from the *Enterprise*, another Southern court championed slaveholders' property rights against insurance companies reluctant to pay claims on their marine policies.[27]

"The political question" at the center of Templeman's suit, the New Orleans Commercial Court added, "must be settled between the Governments" of the United States and Great Britain. The remark captured the general thrust of the commentary in newspapers first announcing the wreck of the *Hermosa*. The American public had read the same basic story before and was familiar with the contours of the plot. The captives' "liberation" by British authorities "will . . . form another troublesome question for our minister at the Court of St. James to settle," predicted the *Richmond Compiler*. It "will be another knotty one for our Minister to England," concurred the *Baltimore Sun*. Presses across the United States expected the loss of the *Hermosa*'s captives to become the "subject of litigation between ours and the British government." The London papers, meanwhile, marveled at "the grasping rapacity of America."[28]

The *Hermosa*'s time in the headlines was brief, as yet another incident involving an American slaver soon overshadowed it. The brig *Creole* departed Richmond for New Orleans in late October 1841, with 135 enslaved captives on board. Like those on the *Comet*, *Encomium*, and *Hermosa*, the *Creole* slaves ended up in the Bahamas, but under much different circumstances. In this case, the enslaved people themselves determined their fate. On November 7, Madison Washington and eighteen fellow bondmen staged a shipboard revolt, successfully seizing control of the *Creole*. The rebels spared a sufficient crew to navigate the hijacked slaver to the insurgents' preferred destination. They knew their desired port. As two of them explained, "they did not want to go anywhere else but where Mr. Lumpkin's negroes went last year," referencing the *Hermosa* captives mistakenly identified as belonging to Richmond slave trader Robert Lumpkin. Gathered from around Virginia and then shipped out of the same Virginia port where Lumpkin operated, some of the *Creole* prisoners had either heard, overheard, or perhaps even read in the newspapers that at least the *Hermosa* slaves—and maybe those on the *Comet* and *Encomium* before them—had gone free in the Bahamas. The captives on the *Creole* took proactive steps to become the next enslaved American cargo liberated in the British colony.[29]

The rebels ordered the *Creole*'s crew to set course for Nassau. As the vessel neared the harbor on November 9, a Bahamian pilot boat approached. Unaware of the shipboard insurrection that had taken place but recognizing a slave ship when he saw one, one of the Black crewmen from the pilot boat boarded the *Creole* and informed the African Americans assembled on the deck that "he came out from Charleston, and . . . got free by coming out there in that way." Likely among those emancipated from the *Encomium*, the crewman's announcement elicited a wave of elation. Much relieved, the *Creole* captives broke out in laughter and celebration, kissing and embracing as brothers the Black crewmen of the pilot boat. British authorities granted immediate freedom to all but the mutinous bondmen delivered to Nassau. The rebels gained emancipation later, after approval by the government in London.[30]

Southern proslavery newspapers were quick to blame the *Creole* revolt on the dangerous precedents set by British authorities in the earlier cases of U.S. slave ships in distress. It was precisely as they had feared. According to the *Richmond Enquirer*, "It was predicted that the protection given to the slaves in the case of the Enterprise, 'would be the strongest inducement for flight or abduction of slaves by *fraud* or *force* from their masters.'" Consider the violence aboard the *Creole* a "prediction . . . fulfilled," urged the *Enquirer*. "By insurrection and murder," the rebellious slaves claimed a freedom "virtually promised them in advance." Slaveholders' security in the ownership of their human property had long served as the driving force in U.S. diplomacy with the Crown. "The slave mutineers," commented one Mobile, Alabama, newspaper, only added "to the important controversies already pending with Great Britain, in which her claims to liberate American slaves under her own municipal law, is involved."[31]

The slave-owning South's furor over British abolitionism once again spilled onto the floor of Congress, on December 22, 1841. While the dramatic uprising and violence aboard the *Creole* accounted for much of the uproar, the *Hermosa* contributed to it. The New Orleans Insurance Company, which had paid Henry N. Templeman its share of the losses the Richmond slave dealer sustained on that voyage, turned to freshman Louisiana senator Alexander Barrow in a petition seeking "redress" from the U.S. government. The memorial did not indicate the specific form that redress should take but expressed "confidence" in "the energy and unbending determination of government to protect the property of its citizens, and cause ample indemnity for the wrongs . . . inflicted." It also hoped that

Congress would "devise means to prevent in [the] future the recurrence of similar outrages." Because the British presumed to suppress the lawful coastwise slave trade "between the States," Barrow "was satisfied that this subject involved the question of peace or war between this country and Great Britain." The "flagrant character of this outrage" demanded that Congress act at once. Barrow moved to refer the insurer's memorial to the Senate Committee on Foreign Relations. John C. Calhoun seconded the motion.[32]

In Calhoun's estimation, the *Hermosa* and the "special case" of the *Creole* involved "the same principle." He also reminded the Senate of the unresolved case of the *Enterprise*. Great Britain's "dangerous innovation" in its interpretation of the law of nations attacked the "national rights and national honor" of the United States. Looking at the scope of British action "in the case of the slave vessels, . . . all must see the necessity of some prompt measures on the part of the Government," Calhoun stated. "It was time for the Southern portion of this country to understand whether they were to be protected in their property or not." He "trusted the Committee on Foreign Relations" to "give the subject . . . careful consideration."[33]

Requesting a reading of the insurance company memorial, Sen. William R. King of Alabama declared that it "ought to excite alarm" and spoke in favor of referring it to the committee as well. He recalled British resistance to paying indemnity for the *Enterprise* and Calhoun's resolutions justifying why compensation should be paid but observed that "the British Government had gone on, step by step, in refusing to be responsible for the acts of her citizens who had been engaged in capturing and liberating American property." Unless the Crown changed course, King predicted, and granted reparation for all the American slavers, "the time was not far off when the question of war must inevitably arise." By taking up the subject, the Committee on Foreign Relations would demonstrate to Great Britain "the determination of [the United States]. It was high time that the laws of nations should be enforced . . . , to show her how far the rights of property and our flag are to be respected."[34]

Most of King's senatorial colleagues did not share his dire outlook on the prospect of war. According to William C. Preston, a member of the Foreign Relations Committee, the British violation of the law of nations was so obvious that he doubted it "a cause for serious collision between the two countries." The South Carolina senator was hopeful that Great Britain's new Conservative government, under Prime Minister Sir Robert Peel, might reverse or modify "the decisions of the former British

Cabinet with regard to the seizure of the slaves." With the basic facts of the slave ships' cases not in dispute, Preston believed the two nations could reconcile their differences and "preserve amicable relations." He classified the possibility of conflict as "remote" but added that the United States "also required some new action in the way of diplomacy."[35]

Veteran senator William C. Rives of Virginia rose to "assert that a continuance of peace" with Great Britain "was imminently precarious" but agreed with Preston that a clash with that country was not "highly probable." Nevertheless, he recommended that the case of the *Hermosa* not "be agitated," opposing discussion of the New Orleans Insurance Company's petition as "incidental and premature." Rives regarded "the affair of the Creole" as distinct and "more grave and important" than that of the *Hermosa* but was willing to submit the memorial to the Foreign Relations Committee if that was the will of the Senate.[36]

Although the *Hermosa* and the *Creole* involved the same fundamental principle, Calhoun, too, ranked the *Creole* of greater importance, considering it an unparalleled outrage. At the same time, he "expressed his extreme regret" about the talk of war with Great Britain. He agreed with Rives in anticipating "little danger of immediate conflict" but noted that, if the two countries did come to blows, the cause would be the U.S. desire "to secure common respect."[37]

Sen. Barrow replied to his colleagues "with much energy." Although his fellow senators seemed to diminish the *Hermosa*'s importance relative to the *Creole*, the Louisiana senator wanted the *Hermosa* "acted upon on its own merits." "As the representative of the individuals who had addressed the memorial to Congress" from the insurance company, "he was not willing that they should submit to the injustice of a foreign power." An animated Barrow, "unwilling to wait another ten years of tardy and dilatory negotiation," declared it "high time" to act. "The people of the South," he stormed, would be "the last to submit to the precarious principles of international law, as explained by Great Britain," a nation that distinguished "between slaves" on the one hand and "goods, wares, and merchandise" on the other. To the Louisiana senator, there was no distinction: they were all equally things to buy, sell, and trade. But Great Britain, "because she has abolished slavery, . . . will not recognize the principles which Southern men assert." That infringement on slave-owner rights could not stand, for "property at the South was not now safe." As Barrow explained, "The transfer of slaves from one Southern State to another was an every day's occurrence."

So if "these contemptible British subjects at Nassau . . . seize, by force of arms, the slaves belonging to American citizens and liberat[e] them," there could be but one solution: "the South would be compelled to fit out" a fleet of cruisers "and destroy Nassau, and . . . the towns which trampled under foot the laws of nations and the rights of American citizens."[38]

Most senators believed Barrow too bellicose in his language. Rives reiterated Calhoun's point that the South Carolina senator's resolutions in the wake of the *Enterprise*'s unintended emergency stop in Bermuda made plain the U.S. government's position on British seizures of enslaved American cargoes. Still, a majority of senators were amenable to discussing the issue once again in light of the *Creole* revolt. Thus, on December 22, 1841, they referred the New Orleans Insurance Company's memorial to the Foreign Relations Committee.[39]

By that point, slave trader Henry N. Templeman had long received the last of the insurance policy claims owed him. The New Orleans Insurance Company had paid the slave trader without undue effort on his part soon after the October 1840 wreck of the *Hermosa*. The verdict of the New Orleans Commercial Court probably placed a check in Templeman's hands from the Louisiana State Marine and Fire Insurance Company in either February or March 1841. Nine or ten months later, as the New Orleans Insurance Company was pursuing reimbursement via Congress, Templeman continued to trade slaves, his pockets no lighter than before the *Hermosa*.

He went on to form a series of partnerships in the 1840s with other leading slave dealers in Richmond. A collaboration with Silas Omohundro ended in May 1845, but the dissolution of Omohundro & Templeman spawned the creation of Templeman & Ratcliffe. Templeman and William B. Ratcliffe peddled enslaved people and sold a variety of groceries and liquor in Richmond until March 1846. Templeman next joined with Hector Davis Jr. to trade slaves. When the partnership of Templeman & Davis ended in May 1847, Templeman continued to buy and sell bondpeople on his own. He also maintained "a safe and comfortable jail for their safe keeping, situated at the South corner of the Exchange Hotel." Templeman was still trading slaves in Richmond on the eve of the Civil War. When a census taker visited Richmond's third ward in 1860, the fifty-six-year-old Templeman did not hide his profession behind the euphemistic labels of merchant or gentleman. Without shame, he declared his occupation as "Negro Trader."[40]

13

Relief

By early 1840, Mary E. Mudd had long since lost her patience. Her late husband, Sylvester, had shipped nine enslaved people aboard the *Comet* in December 1830, without taking out insurance on them. Nearly nine years later, Great Britain agreed to grant restitution for captives freed from the brig, but she had not yet seen payment. In her fifties, Mrs. Mudd lived in the village of Opelousas, in St. Landry Parish, Louisiana, about sixty miles west of Baton Rouge. She presided as mistress over twelve enslaved people, equally divided by sex. In her mind, there should have been nine more, but they were living as freedpeople in the Bahamas. At least she could still get compensated a decent fraction of their monetary value. She consulted her well-connected senator to do her bidding.[1]

Alexandre Mouton, from a wealthy Acadian family, practiced law in Lafayette Parish in 1825 before serving in the state House of Representatives and being chosen to fill a seat in the U.S. Senate left vacant by a resignation. Probably in early 1840, Mary E. Mudd contacted him to seek information on the compensation due her. Mouton proved sympathetic. Though a woman unable to vote, Mrs. Mudd was his constituent, from a parish just north of his own. Perhaps Mouton had even been acquainted with her deceased husband and, as a personal kindness, took it upon himself to look after her interests. As the owner of a sugar plantation worked by dozens of enslaved people, he shared a common interest in slaveholding with Mrs. Mudd. Sen. Mouton reached out to Secretary of State John Forsyth to inquire on her behalf.[2]

Forsyth indeed had news to share. Restitution from Great Britain had finally arrived. After the moneychangers at the Bank of America deducted their fees, U.S. government coffers contained a grand total of $115,024.41 to distribute among the slave owners and insurers from the *Comet* and *Encomium*. In service to a proslavery government, Forsyth undertook his

Table 13.1. Compensation granted by Great Britain for the enslaved seized from the *Comet* and *Encomium*, 1840

	Amount (£) Britain paid government	Amount ($) Britain paid	Amount ($) received by the U.S.
Comet			
Indemnity + interest	19,382.17.2	94,354.52	93,899.18
Expenses	322.2.7½	1,617.48	1,608.99
Subtotal	19,704.19.9½	95,972	95,508.17
Encomium			
Indemnity + interest	3,960.14.3	19,288.67	19,187.45
Expenses	67.17.4½	330.52	328.79
Subtotal	4,028.11.7½	19,619.19	19,516.24
Total	23,733.11.5	115,591.19	115,024.41

Source: Indemnity for slaves per the *Comet* and *Encomium*, 27th Cong., 2d sess., House Doc. No. 242, p. 3. The original source incorrectly places the total British payment at £23,743.11.5, or $115,631.19. A minor error of addition accounts for the $40 difference between the figures in the source and those presented here. The overall exchange rate was roughly $4.87 per British pound.

duty with meticulousness to ensure that the accurate amount of the indemnity made it into affected slaveholders' pockets.[3]

In his reply of April 20, Forsyth spelled out the results of almost a decade of Anglo-American diplomacy for Mary Mudd. He lacked sufficient information to distribute all of the funds advanced from the Crown in one fell swoop, but to avoid further delays, he issued an initial disbursement. From the *Comet*, Britain denied compensation for eighteen captives: the eleven enslaved people who fled to Nassau; the five—never identified by name or by owner in surviving records—who allegedly returned to the United States; and the two who died, one of whom was Charles P. Tutt's bondman Dennis Young. Based on the available evidence, it appeared to Forsyth that none of the nine Mudd bondpeople had escaped to shore in the Bahamas or proceeded to New Orleans. The only outstanding question was whether one of them counted among the dead. "If it should be ascertained that the other slave who died was not the property of Mr. Mudd," Forsyth explained to Sen. Mouton, his widow "would be entitled to receive 9-146ths" of the $93,899.13 allowed for compensation and interest in the case of the *Comet*,

Table 13.2. Distribution of the British indemnity for the enslaved seized from the *Comet*, 1840

	No. slaves claimed	Amount ($) for slaves	Amount ($) for expenses	Amount ($) reimbursed
Mary E. Mudd	9	5,788.30	99.19	5,145.15
Col. Charles P. Tutt	9	5,788.30	99.19	5,145.15
Mississippi Marine and Fire Insurance Co.	40	22,554.15	386.47	22,940.62
Merchants Insurance Co.	49	27,628.81	473.42	28,102.23
Louisiana State Marine and Fire Insurance Co.	57	32,139.62	550.72	32,690.34
	164	93,899.18	1,608.99	94,023.49

Source: Indemnity for slaves per the *Comet* and *Encomium*, 27th Cong., 2d sess., House Doc. No. 242, p. 3.

or $5,788.30. "But," Forsyth continued, "as it is not certain to whom that [deceased] slave belonged, I have been obliged to retain" one-ninth of the total owed her. Deducting that $643.15, the secretary of state submitted a payment to Mary Mudd in the amount of $5,145.15. Forsyth enclosed in his letter "a check on the Bank of America, New York," with the acknowledgment that further apportionment could yet be made. For reasons not made clear, Mrs. Mudd was denied the expenses due her, at least for the time being.[4]

The same day that Forsyth responded to Mary Mudd, he alerted the three New Orleans companies that had insured the human cargo aboard the *Comet*—all of whom had paid on the policies they issued—of his initial distribution of the British indemnity. The total amount of compensation and interest for just the *Comet* amounted to £19,382.17.2. Forsyth held in reserve an 18/146ths portion of that total, or £2,389.13.4, for the Mudd and Tutt slaves, pending the identification of the owners of the enslaved people who escaped, returned to the United States, or died. To the balance of £16,993.3.10, Forsyth added £291.3.7½ in reimbursement for expenses incurred in Nassau by insurance company agent Nathan Morse. That left a total of £17,284.7.5½ for Forsyth to distribute in the correct proportions to the three New Orleans insurance companies. The secretary of state wrote checks on Bank of America that he mailed to the individual company presidents.[5]

Forsyth confessed his difficulties in distributing the entirety of the funds from the *Comet* given the lack of information at his disposal. The process of disbursing the indemnity to its recipients could not be completed until he determined precisely whose enslaved people had escaped to Nassau prior to the British seizure, which ones had proceeded to the United States, and which one, other than Col. Tutt's bondman, had died. If that data could not be obtained, Forsyth observed, "It appears to me that the only mode by which a final distribution can be made will be to make the loss" of those slaves "an average one" among all owners of captives aboard the *Comet*, unless "the parties interested were to come to an agreement" that "would expedite the distribution and final payment." In the meantime, thousands of dollars allotted to the *Comet*'s slave owners remained in U.S. government hands.[6]

Indemnity for the captives taken from the *Encomium* required disbursement as well. Forsyth forwarded payments to Italian merchant Antonio Della Torre's partner, Joseph A. Barelli, mariner Noah B. Sisson, and, to cover its payouts to policyholders Amédée Gardanne and Robert Eagar, the Charleston Fire and Marine Insurance Company. John Waddell received a check for only the thirteen enslaved people taken from his possession, despite his fraudulently claiming nine others who accompanied him back to the United States. Altogether, Forsyth distributed $19,187.45 to slave owners and insurers associated with the *Encomium*. He authorized payment for none of their expenses, however, pending proof that they spent money in Nassau in support of their claims.[7]

The settlement between Great Britain and the United States disallowed Charles Allen's claim to compensation for all three enslaved people he placed aboard the *Encomium*. The Missouri slave owner submitted a complaint with his state's senior U.S. senator, Thomas Hart Benton, who explained to his Senate colleagues that Allen "was returning" home "from a Southern State with a few valuable family slaves," when they "were taken from him by the authorities at Nassau." The British consul had mistakenly "stated that the slaves departed" with Allen for the United States, Benton related, so while "the owners of the other slaves have been compensated," Allen, despite making "due proof of the loss of his slaves by the act of the British authorities[,] . . . has been notified that he will receive no compensation." Surviving records indicate that Allen's bondman

Table 13.3. Distribution of the British indemnity for the enslaved seized from the *Encomium*, 1840

	No. slaves claimed	Amount ($) for slaves	Amount ($) for expenses	Amount ($) reim-bursed
Noah B. Sisson	1	581.44	9.98	581.44
Joseph A. Barelli	6	3,488.62	59.79	3,488.62
Charleston Fire and Marine Insurance Company	13	7,558.69½	129.51	7,558.69
John Waddell	13	7,558.69½	129.51	7,558.69
	33	19,187.45	328.79	19,187.44

Source: Indemnity for slaves per the *Comet* and *Encomium*, 27th Cong., 2d sess., House Doc. No. 242, p. 3.

Joe did, in fact, return to Missouri with him. If correct, the slave owner should have received compensation for his two other bondpeople—Billy and Peggy—under the terms of the U.S. arrangement with the Crown.[8]

Benton raised the perceived injustice suffered by Charles Allen on April 15, during the Senate's debate over John C. Calhoun's three amended resolutions concerning the law of nations and the *Enterprise*. For Benton, the cruel denial of Allen's claim proved why it was imperative to vote in favor of the resolutions: "the principle avowed by the British Government," by which it upheld the right to free enslaved Southerners, must be rejected. Otherwise, he warned, "the certificate of a [British] consul, given in a case where he can hardly know any thing[,] . . . deprive[s] an American citizen of his property." Such "conduct of the British Government . . . was unjustifiable" and should be formally called out.[9]

Allen excepted, the distribution of indemnities went more smoothly in the case of the *Encomium* than in the *Comet*. That the *Encomium* bore only about one-quarter of the number of captives reduced the confusion surrounding the allotment of funds. As a consequence of Secretary of State Forsyth's initial round of disbursements in 1840, the U.S. government transferred more than $107,484 of the $115,024.41 worth of British indemnities into the pockets of Southern slaveholders and insurance companies. An undistributed balance of some $7,540 continued to accumulate interest while its proper recipients could be determined.[10]

The work of gaining restitution, first launched by Martin Van Buren more than eight years earlier, in February 1832, had finally borne tangible fruits for the owners. The distribution of the indemnity to his fellow slaveholders marked the crowning achievement in Andrew Stevenson's career as U.S. minister to Great Britain. Still, when a new presidential administration removed him in October 1841, the cases of the *Enterprise* and *Hermosa* remained unresolved.[11]

Unlike the man whom he replaced as ambassador to the United Kingdom, Edward Everett was a Northerner. He had previously represented his home state of Massachusetts in the U.S. House and served as that commonwealth's governor. Not rabidly proslavery like his predecessor from Virginia, Everett had early in his career nevertheless acknowledged, to his own political detriment, that the Bible implored servants to obey their masters. Upon taking his new post, he found himself representing slave owners' interests. On May 3, 1842, Everett wrote George Hamilton-Gordon, the Earl of Aberdeen, who had replaced Lord Palmerston as the new British secretary of state for foreign affairs the previous September. He reminded Lord Aberdeen of the *Hermosa* and the *Creole* and the need "for a just indemnification," despite the Crown lawyers' determination in late 1836 that no further compensation would be forthcoming in future cases of enslaved American cargoes lost in British Atlantic possessions.[12]

Everett reiterated the U.S. government position, that it "can not admit that the vessels of a friendly power, driven by stress of weather, or by mutiny, into her Majesty's ports, can, in consequence of a change in the municipal law of England, be rightfully deprived of any aid and assistance to which they are entitled by the law and comity of nations." He added a new twist to previous arguments as well. "British civil and military authorities" could not "forcibly interfere to liberate" enslaved cargoes "without violently infringing [upon] that authority of the captain of the vessel over the ship's company." In other words, he summarized, "if the law of England converts slaves into passengers," it "exempt[s] them from one kind of control" no longer recognized in the British Atlantic—slavery—but "subjects them to another" kind that was: the captain's.[13]

Everett also pointed out the inconsistency of the British policy denying payment to affected U.S. shippers. Under the terms of the British Slavery Abolition Act, British slave owners "divest[ed] . . . of their property" received compensation for their liberated labor forces. The law declared it "just and expedient that a reasonable compensation should be made to the persons hitherto entitled to the services of such slaves, for the loss which they will incur by being deprived of their right to such services." Surely, Everett assumed, if "it would have been unjust to liberate the slaves of her Majesty's subjects without compensating the master, . . . much more would it be unjust toward the citizens of a friendly and foreign State."[14]

Lord Aberdeen deflected Everett's concerns. He argued that, in the case of the *Hermosa*, "the vessel in which the negroes entered Nassau"—the wrecker—"was not an American, but a British vessel." As such, the magistrate in the case dealt with it "strictly according to British law." With slavery abolished for years in the British Atlantic, it was the official's responsibility to assess if "any illegal constraint was put upon the liberties or inclinations of those . . . rescued" and "to see their freedom vindicated." Emancipating the enslaved cargo therefore represented no "violent infringement of the authority of the American captain." Aberdeen dismissed Everett's argument about the justice of compensation for American slave owners as well, referring him to the correspondence between Andrew Stevenson and Lord Palmerston in 1837 over the *Enterprise*. He warned the minister not to expect any deviation from its previous position, regardless of the circumstances that landed U.S. slaves on British colonial soil.[15]

At least three other points of contention strained Anglo-American relations as Lord Aberdeen and Edward Everett settled into their new governmental roles. The longest-standing problem concerned the African slave trade, outlawed by Britain and the United States in 1807 and 1808, respectively. Both nations condemned the illegal traffic in the 1814 Treaty of Ghent, but the British navy almost exclusively carried the burden of patrolling the Atlantic. Meanwhile, slave smugglers, to increase their odds of success, fraudulently flew the U.S. flag, knowing the government's hostility to Britain searching vessels flying the Stars and Stripes. A second source of friction between the two countries dated to the 1837 *Caroline* affair. Canadians in favor of independence from Britain allied with hundreds of sympathetic U.S. citizens. British forces set fire to the *Caroline*, an American vessel hired to aid the insurgents, and sent it hurtling, ablaze, over Niagara Falls. In 1840, U.S. officials arrested Alexander McLeod, a deputy sheriff from Canada, on American soil for his role in the *Caroline* affair and refused British demands for his return, sparking years of mutual outrage on both sides of the Atlantic. Finally, disagreements over the U.S.-Canadian border—most immediately, the Maine boundary—in 1838 and 1839 led to a clash dubbed the Aroostook War. The accumulating incidents, combined with the uncompensated losses of American enslaved cargoes from the *Enterprise*, *Hermosa*, and *Creole*, heightened Anglo-American tensions. One member of Congress despaired of being able to "rest on a peaceful security."[16]

The Webster-Ashburton Treaty, signed in Washington, DC, in August 1842, resolved many of the immediate sources of conflict between the two countries and tamped down rumblings of war. New Englander Daniel Webster, who had replaced Georgia's John Forsyth as U.S. secretary of state, negotiated its terms with his friend Alexander Baring, the first Lord Ashburton, an active partner in the powerful Baring Brothers merchant house of London. Together, they hashed out an agreement whereby the United States agreed to aid British squadrons patrolling the Atlantic against the illegal slave trade from Africa. The two countries also settled the boundary between the United States and Canada and set the terms under which accused criminals captured in the other's territory were eligible for extradition. The treaty, however, bypassed the matter of restitution for the captives liberated from the *Enterprise*, *Hermosa*, and *Creole* or the larger maritime legal principles at stake. Webster pursued the issues raised by the domestic slavers, and as much as Lord Ashburton may have been willing to discuss them, the Crown had not authorized him to deal with such matters. Ashburton later confessed during a meeting with New York abolitionist Lewis Tappan that the British government would never have ratified the treaty had it included a provision earmarking compensation for lost cargoes of enslaved Americans. The most the United States could coax out of the British envoy was an ambiguous and unofficial indication that colonial authorities would be more mindful of U.S. shipping interests in the future and eschew "officious interference."[17]

The Senate took up the Webster-Ashburton Treaty for possible ratification in mid-August. Multiple issues surfaced during the ensuing debates, but in weighing the advantages and disadvantages of the agreement, the absence of a formal provision dealing with the *Enterprise*, *Hermosa*, and *Creole* figured prominently. One of the senators who spoke was Charles M. Conrad of Louisiana. In April 1842, fourteen months after representing the Louisiana State Marine and Fire Insurance Company in its bid to avoid paying on slave trader Henry N. Templeman's policy on the *Hermosa*'s enslaved cargo, Conrad occupied the Senate seat vacated by Mary E. Mudd's lawyer, Alexandre Mouton. On Thursday, August 18, Conrad submitted a resolution requesting that President John Tyler furnish all paperwork housed in the State Department related to the loss of enslaved people from the *Hermosa*. The Senate approved Conrad's motion by unanimous consent, and securing the president's prompt approval, Webster had the original copies delivered the same day.[18]

Conrad did not intend to participate in the debate over the treaty, but after resolving to vote against it, he determined to elaborate. "My objections to it . . . are not so much on account of what it does, as of what it does not contain," Conrad explained. He had mistakenly assumed that Lord Ashburton was empowered to settle all divisive questions generating tension with Great Britain, but the issue of compensation for the most recent three of the five shiploads of liberated slaves "was left precisely where it stood before the arrival of the British ambassador." In Conrad's estimation, unless redress for the *Enterprise* was made, war would ensue. But then came the "outrage" involving the schooner *Hermosa*, "precisely similar in character to the one complained of." The *Hermosa*'s human cargo, like so many others, was headed to Conrad's state of Louisiana when "set at liberty" by "some petty magistrate." Before Great Britain responded to the latest U.S. appeal for indemnity, the slave revolt erupted aboard the *Creole*. That case, the Louisiana senator admitted, differed because "it occurred on the high seas, and was effected by the slaves themselves." Nevertheless, the Bahamian government sheltered the rebels. Conrad could imagine no issue between the United States and Great Britain "more important, or more urgent in its character, than that growing out of these repeated outrages" involving "national honor, national interests, national safety even."[19]

Conrad discerned the pressure of British abolitionism at work. He produced a letter in which Lord Ashburton confessed to Webster, "There are certain great principles too deeply rooted in the consciences and sympathies of the people of Great Britain for any minister to be able to overlook; *and any engagement I might make in opposition to them would be instantly disavowed.*" This was the same letter in which the British envoy offered ambiguous assurances to U.S. shippers going forward. Conrad insisted that any "pledge for the future" be explicitly "inserted in the treaty" for it to have real meaning. The "principles involved"—"the inviolability of our flag, and the right to regulate our domestic institutions as we see fit"—were too great to abandon to Britain's "insidious policy" of abolition, "which is treason and madness with us."[20]

Conrad also reviewed Lord Aberdeen's response to Edward Everett in May 1842, in which he stated that the British government "*would not, henceforward, entertain the question of compensation for slaves . . . under any circumstances whatever.*" The conclusion seemed unequivocal, the senator explained: "not even when the vessels containing them are driven there by tempest, like the Enterprise; by shipwreck, like the Hermosa; or by mutiny and murder, like the Creole." Conrad condemned such an "inhuman doctrine" that "imposes a penalty on misfortune, and holds out a premium to insurrection and murder." The Louisiana senator strongly believed that the U.S. government should have made the settlement of the *Enterprise*, *Hermosa*, and *Creole* cases a condition for further negotiations on other topics.[21]

Conrad dismissed the notion that his inflexible position risked war with Britain. The British, he assumed, "Would never go to war for the sake of maintaining a principle which is only important to her as a means of annoying us." Yet even if they did, Conrad concluded, "I would prefer to encounter war . . . than to purchase an ignomin[i]ous peace by the surrender of a principle." He was not willing to vote for the Webster-Ashburton Treaty "as the price of peace" because he did not believe that any peace established by the treaty would prove lasting until Britain acknowledged U.S. rights to enslaved property as outlined in Calhoun's resolutions. If anything, Conrad predicted, the ratification of the existing treaty would "only increase the insolence of Great Britain, and encourage the repetition of outrages like those of the Hermosa and the Creole."[22]

Like Conrad, Thomas Hart Benton of Missouri also took a strong stand in opposition to the Webster-Ashburton Treaty. Both senators had aided their constituents in the ongoing matters involving the slave ships interfered with by British authorities. Benton understood the increasingly important place of "western states" like his to an expanding South. "The liberation of slaves from wrecked vessels" in the Bahamas, Benton warned, tampered with the western slave states' "line of communication with the Atlantic States, with the high seas, and with the whole world. They cannot tolerate the insecurity of that passage." Benton took seriously his responsibility to protect coastwise domestic slave trading routes.[23]

In a long speech delivered on August 18, Benton complained that the five U.S. slavers were not received with hospitality in Britain's Atlantic colonies or "allowed to depart with all convenient despatch, . . . with all her contents of persons and property" as required by the law of nations. "We cannot tolerate the spoil and pillage of our own citizens, within sight of our own coasts," Benton declared. Worse still, in the most recent three instances, "neither compensation to the owners, whose property has been taken; nor apology to the Government, whose flag has been insulted; nor security for the future, by giving up the practice," had been granted.[24]

The safety of U.S. shipping demanded guarantees through treaty provision. Yet despite the gross offense Britain had shown the United States on multiple occasions, Lord Ashburton claimed an inability "*to enter into a stipulation by treaty for the prevention of such occurrences hereafter.*" Benton was incredulous: "The special mission, which came to settle everything, and to establish peace, will not settle this thing." Instead, Ashburton stated that he would recommend instructions be given to British colonial authorities "to regulate their conduct in conformity with the rights of citizens of the United States." To Benton, this weak promise of "politeness" offered a poor substitute for a treaty provision. He pronounced Lord Ashburton's pledge a "solemn bamboozlement" and an American capitulation to the British.[25]

The Webster-Ashburton Treaty dealt a blow not just to Southern slaveholding interests but to the Senate as a whole. According to Benton, "the honor of the Senate as a body, and the honor of the greater part of the Senators now present individually," was invested in the five U.S. slave ships stripped of their human cargoes. The Senate had stated its position clearly when it passed John C. Calhoun's resolutions of 1840 "unanimously." "I cannot vote for the ratification of a treaty which refuses the slightest notice of these outrages," he declared.[26]

Mid-speech, Benton took his opposition one step further. He offered an amendment to the treaty designed to "vindicate the rights of our vessels, under the law of nations, as resolved by the Senate." Benton's proposed addition held "that a vessel of the United States, engaged in a lawful voyage, and driven by tempest, or carried by violence, or forced by necessity, into a British West India port, during peace with Great Britain, shall be received with the hospitality due to misfortune, and be allowed to depart with all convenient despatch, and with all her contents of persons and property." The Senate rejected the suggested provision.[27]

In the Webster-Ashburton Treaty as presented to the upper chamber, Benton saw evidence of an aggrieved South under siege, victim of an Atlantic "abolition crusade against slavery" that "tends to excite insurrection and servile war in our country." Besides overlooking the safety of coastwise domestic slave traders, the treaty also did not obligate Canada to return fugitive slaves to the United States, despite other provisions dealing with extradition. Benton concluded that the document, "made for the Northern States," left the South friendless and "alone." The Southern states, "with the sympathies of half the Union and all the world against her, must now expect greater outrages than ever, in all that relates to her slave property." The protection of slaving vessels, an issue "affecting so many States, and so pregnant of war, deserved to be settled." Because the treaty "shirk[ed]" the question, Benton felt "bound to oppose it."[28]

The South's contingent in the Senate did not align itself in a unified bloc against the treaty, however. John C. Calhoun lent his prominent voice in its support. If any senator had the right to feel shortchanged by the treaty, it would have been Calhoun. He prided himself on his role in securing the partial compensation already recovered from Great Britain. He boasted that he had "revived" American claims when they "lay dead and buried among the archives of the State Department" and, after the loss of the *Enterprise*'s captives, "moved resolutions affirming the principles of the law of nations" that gained the unanimous approval of the Senate. Yet Calhoun did not feel slighted by the treaty. Unlike Benton, he placed greater faith in the informal assurances from Lord Ashburton that the British government would respect the international law of slavery and that the instructions it issued to its colonial authorities would eliminate "officious interference" with U.S. shipping in the future. On balance, the treaty marked a step in the direction of peace between the United States and Great Britain and served to reduce "the hazard of collision between the countries." For that reason, Calhoun could overlook its imperfections and cast a vote in its favor.[29]

Most senators agreed with their South Carolina colleague. According to one, Ashburton's "declarations and engagements, in their spirit and obvious import, go far towards giving us the practical security we have so long sought," even without "the *formality* of a treaty stipulation." On August 20, the Senate ratified the Webster-Ashburton Treaty, without amendment, by a resounding vote of 39 to 9, the largest margin in favor of a treaty in U.S. history at that time.[30]

Across the Atlantic, in 1843, the Webster-Ashburton Treaty passed the House of Lords unanimously and the House of Commons by a vote of 238 to 96. As in the United States, a vocal contingent of British politicians opposed it. They contended that Lord Ashburton had surrendered too much. Addressing the House of Commons, Lord Palmerston described the negotiations as "ill conducted and unskillfully concluded," the treaty's "terms . . . needlessly disadvantageous" to the Crown. Its British critics were perturbed that Ashburton's informal pledge to respect U.S. shipping contravened English law and undermined the firmly established British policy that denied compensation for captives liberated from U.S. slaving vessels. Ashburton's comments, Palmerston alleged, would embolden U.S. slave owners, further encourage them to feel entitled to reparation, and complicate Britain's "efforts . . . to abolish slavery." Lord Campbell agreed that Daniel Webster demonstrated "far more ability" than his British counterpart, who "no doubt was not aware of the concessions he was making, or of the principles by which he ought to have been guided."[31]

British abolitionists closely followed the messages their envoy sent. The U.S. pressure for concessions pointedly tested the British commitment to the principles recently enshrined into law during their great national reckoning with slavery. In the United States, abolitionists took keen notice of those voyages as well.

14

Opposition

On March 10, 1842, Rep. Joshua R. Giddings of Ohio called the attention of the U.S. House to a lone item in a general appropriations bill. Giddings had spotted some $30 in miscellaneous charges from the State Department to advertise "compensation for slaves." Curious about the expense, he inquired about it at the State Department. The congressman learned that the "sums of money had been paid to printers for publishing advertisements" "giving notice to owners of slaves on board the Comet and Encomium that the compensation for them had been received from the British Government." Although Giddings would have been aware for years of the planned distribution of British indemnities, using U.S. taxpayer money to advertise them was, he asserted, "unconstitutional." He managed to transform a minor, mundane business matter into an unlikely centerpiece of abolitionist political agitation.[1]

Joshua Giddings overcame his humble origins to become the premier attorney in Ohio's Western Reserve. An experience of religious conversion in 1837 infused him with the moral imperative to improve society, and the New Englanders who had relocated to Giddings's corner of the state made the region fertile ground for abolitionism. When Giddings was elected to Congress in 1838, he was primed to fight the evil of Southern slavery.[2]

Abolitionists before Giddings had latched on to the shipwrecks and seized human cargoes of the 1830s to condemn the peculiar institution. New York abolitionist and judge William Jay, son of the first chief justice of the U.S. Supreme Court, invoked the cases of the *Comet*, *Encomium*, and *Enterprise* in his sprawling book *A View of the Action of the Federal Government, in Behalf of Slavery*. Jay recounted all three incidents, each of which "roused the ready zeal of the Federal Government" to defend the rights of owners engaged in the domestic slave trade. "American diplomacy must be made subservient to the interests of the slaveholders," Jay criticized, "and republican ambassadors must bear to foreign courts the wailings of our Government for the escape of human property."[3]

Northern newspapers widely excerpted Jay's work when it went into its second edition in 1839. "We earnestly recommend this book," read one review, for it showed how "the Federal Government . . . has, in various ways, concerned itself with slavery . . . at the instigation of slave owners—that it has negotiated about it—obtained compensation for slaves—and, in the case of Great Britain, even hinted that war itself might be resorted to" should timely restitution not be made. The government in Washington kept "sending despatches to their agents in England, urging them to obtain payment from Great Britain for these cargoes of human flesh," and the agents were not "remiss or reluctant in fulfilling their instructions."[4]

In the summer of 1839, news of the indemnities granted for the *Comet* and *Encomium* fueled renewed outrage in the abolitionist press. "The South have gained a great point in favor of slavery," conceded the *Cincinnati Gazette*, and the beneficiaries were slave traders. Comparing the domestic and international slave trades, the paper found the horrors—the family separations, the transport to unfamiliar "lands, to burning suns, consuming labor, destroying hunger, [and] the lacerations of the whip"—identical. Yet whereas U.S. participation in the transatlantic slave trade was illegal and, as of 1820, a form of piracy subject to the death penalty, "the domestic slave trader is taken under the special protection of the Government of the United States!!" With that legal distinction in place, the process for slave dealers to follow was simple: after their human cargoes were liberated, "the slave trader came to Congress and Congress instructed the executive. And thus the power of the United States Government is put in requisition for the slave trader's benefit!"[5]

In March 1842, when Joshua Giddings challenged the $30 expenditure, he delivered a series of incendiary abolitionist speeches in the House chamber. On March 7, he presented a petition in favor of the dissolution of the Union. About eighty of his constituents from abolitionist-heavy Ashtabula County, Ohio, recommended an "amicable division" between the free and slave states. The House voted not to receive the memorial by a vote of 24 to 116. Even if it had been received, under the terms of the "gag rule," the House automatically tabled any petition dealing with slavery rather than reading, discussing, or printing it.[6]

Three days later, Giddings declared his objection to the $30 appropriation for advertising. The "notice to claimants for slaves which were on board the brigs Comet and Encomium," he explained, was paid for by "taking funds of the General Government, collected by taxation from the people of the U.S., and appropriating them to the support of slavery," which Giddings considered unconstitutional. He insisted that the government could not lawfully direct its monies "in any way to aid in the recapture of fugitive slaves." His assertion seemed at odds with the *Prigg v. Pennsylvania* decision rendered just days earlier, in which the Supreme Court made the apprehension of fugitives a federal responsibility. Nevertheless, Giddings declared that, to prove his point, "he was going to show the circumstances and conditions of the several States where the Constitution was adopted, and to give his views on the subject of Abolition generally." Southern members of the House groaned. After Giddings's nearly four years in Congress, the last thing slave state representatives wanted to hear was another of his long-winded diatribes against slavery. Giddings and the crafty John Quincy Adams of Massachusetts had made a mockery of the gag rule in their attempts to overturn it, and the Ohio abolitionist was stirring up trouble once again.[7]

Immediately after Giddings announced the $30 advertising expense unconstitutional, he "was repeatedly interrupted by calls of order," beginning with Rep. Philip Triplett of Kentucky, because "it was asserted that he was about to make an abolition speech." Chairing the proceedings, George Briggs of Massachusetts had to quell the confusion. He "decided that the gentleman [Giddings] was in order. He was objecting to an appropriation on the ground that the Department of State might apply it in a certain way." Giddings denied any intention "to excite an angry debate," but "his constituents had a right to know in what way their money was applied." When he began to review his understanding of the formation of the U.S. government, the framing of the Constitution, and the various states' "feelings and opinions" on slavery, however, Briggs "called him to order for irrelevancy."[8]

According to several accounts of the proceedings, a confused din erupted as multiple congressmen argued whether Giddings should be allowed to proceed or should be shut down. Amid the uproar, one newspaper correspondent confessed that he "could not distinctly hear all" that was said. When Briggs restored order in the chamber, Giddings resumed. To "take the funds of the nation [to] aid in the recapture of slaves, who had escaped from a slave State, was unconstitutional," he repeated, "and was never contemplated by those who framed the Constitution." At this, Richard Habersham of Georgia called Giddings to order, but again, the chair stated that the Ohio abolitionist was still within his right to speak. Rep. Triplett disagreed, and Hopkins Turney of Tennessee appealed Briggs's decision, arguing that Giddings had taken advantage of the opportunity to "discuss the question of slavery, which was not before the House."[9]

At last, the vote was taken on the appeal. The chair's decision to allow Giddings to speak was sustained by a margin of 75 to 42, but together those votes did not constitute a quorum. Giddings ploughed ahead, contending that "the Federal Government [lacked] the right to tax the free States for the purpose of aiding slavery at the South," but Briggs called him to order for not having the authority to make "an argument of this nature." Between the vehement opposition from several Southern congressmen and the chair's narrowly defined limits of debate, Giddings's "attempt at an Abolition speech was unsuccessful and he took his seat."[10]

The chaos that Giddings unleashed in the House chamber ended after Rep. Robert Caruthers of Tennessee made a motion to strike from the appropriations bill the entire clause that would pay the contingent expenses of the State Department. Caruthers's proposal passed, 87 to 54, and after an adventurous several hours, the House adjourned. The State Department lost $25,000 over Giddings's desire to save $30 out of principle.[11]

Giddings was not through incurring the wrath of his colleagues from the slave states. Less than two weeks later, on March 21, he presented a series of resolutions concerning the slave ship *Creole*. Penned for him by fellow abolitionist Theodore Dwight Weld, the nine resolutions served as a counterpoint to John C. Calhoun's three proslavery resolutions of March 4, 1840, inspired by the *Enterprise*. The Giddings resolutions challenged Calhoun's understanding of the law of nations and the extent of slave-owner rights on the Atlantic.[12]

Giddings maintained that slavery violated "the natural rights of man" and "can exist only by force of positive municipal law." As such, it could legally exist only in "the territorial jurisdiction of the power creating it." Therefore, whenever "a ship . . . leaves the waters and territory of such State and enters upon the high seas, the persons on board cease to be subject to the slave laws" of that state. They instead "resum[e] their natural rights of personal liberty," and "all attempts to regain possession of, or re-enslave" them "are unauthorized by the Constitution or laws of the United States, and . . . incompatible with our national honor." Furthermore, Giddings concluded, "All attempts to exert our national influence in favor of the coastwise slave trade," or the "'commerce in human beings,' are subversive of the rights and injurious to the feelings and the interests of the free States; are unauthorized by the Constitution and prejudicial to our national character." A motion to lay the resolutions on the table, or ignore them, failed by a vote of 52 to 125.[13]

While several congressmen asked to be excused from a final vote on the resolutions, Rep. Millard Fillmore inquired whether it would be in order to ask Giddings to withdraw the resolutions. Shouts of "No, no!!" echoed in the House chamber, as proslavery forces were salivating at the prospect of embarrassing their Ohio nemesis. When pressed by the Speaker either to withdraw the resolutions or to move forward with a vote, Giddings chose the former.[14]

At that point, Rep. John Minor Botts of Virginia offered a resolution of censure against his colleague from Ohio. With Anglo-American relations strained and negotiations that would lead to the Webster-Ashburton Treaty already underway, Botts claimed that Giddings's resolutions unnecessarily "create[d] excitement, dissatisfaction, and division among the people of the United States" and seemingly gave license to the "mutiny and murder" aboard the *Creole* "in terms shocking to all sense of law, order, and humanity." Giddings's conduct was, according to Southern congressmen, "altogether unwarranted and unwarrantable, and deserving [of] the severe condemnation of the people of this country" and of the House itself. By this point, it was so late that the House adjourned.[15]

When it reconvened the next day, the House again took up the resolution of censure. Giddings had asked for a postponement of the proceedings so that he might prepare his defense, and while the speaker was inclined to grant it, on appeal the House voted down that possibility. As one abolitionist newspaper summarized, "Fresh altercation[s] now arose, numerous questions of order were raised, and great confusion prevailed." When final votes were cast, the House adopted the resolution of censure 125 to 69. A separate vote on its preamble carried by a margin of 119 to 66. "As soon as the vote was announced," recounted the pages of *The Liberator* in admiration, "Giddings, with great calmness, gathered up his documents and papers, shook hands with Mr. Adams and other members, took his leave of the House, and the next morning sent in a letter containing his resignation as a member."[16]

Giddings's censure did not mandate resignation, but becoming the martyr served the congressman's political interests by incensing fellow abolitionists. According to one Massachusetts newspaper, his censure "awakened a deep feeling of indignation" over his "unjust and outrageous" treatment in the House. Giddings possessed the "perfect constitutional right" to offer his resolutions, and what transpired signified a dangerous censoring of Northern views. "Are we to be forever subject to the tyranny of slavery?" asked the *Salem Register*. "Are we to be governed by slavery, become involved in disputes with foreign governments for slavery, fight for slavery, [have] the mouths of our Representatives be muzzled by slaveholders, and they themselves unjustly expelled from the National Legislature, by the despotic influence of slavery?" A Washington correspondent from the *Boston Courier* agreed that the North could no longer endure "the dark designs of slavery" enacted by "an intolerant and overbearing majority."[17]

With Giddings in exile from the House, he was no longer present in early May 1842 when Secretary of State Daniel Webster sent House Ways and Means Committee chairman Millard Fillmore "an account of indemnities received from the British Government, for slaves per the Comet and Encomium." An enclosed statement showed that, as of March 11, 1841, a balance of $7,695.28 remained in the U.S. Treasury from the British indemnity payment. That tally included $7,540.07 in undistributed funds, plus another $155.21 in interest earned through March 10. The remaining monies belonged "to several individuals or companies" but, either because some had not yet applied for their share or because of an ongoing dispute over the proper division of expenses, "a final distribution . . . was not made." One of the parties owed money was "now urging his claim," Webster explained, with others expected to follow suit.[18]

Since Forsyth had deposited the balance in the Treasury, it could not lawfully "be withdrawn without an act of appropriation" from the House of Representatives. Webster urged the passage of an act to liberate those funds for disbursement to those legally entitled to it. In June, Rep. Fillmore announced House bill number 483 to distribute the outstanding balance.[19]

Late in the year, action moved to the Senate. On December 13, North Carolina's William Alexander Graham introduced Senate bill 11 for the relief of claimants from the *Comet* and *Encomium*. After passing through the Committee on Foreign Relations without amendment, it was taken up by the Committee of the Whole on January 6. John C. Calhoun was perplexed, thinking that the reparation payments had already been made. He and another senator inquired into its rationale, which Graham explained to their satisfaction. The Senate bill then finally passed.[20]

Washington newspaper correspondent David L. Child, the abolitionist husband of Lydia Maria Child, who would publish successful fugitive Harriet Jacobs's *Incidents in the Life of a Slave Girl*, commented on the lack of drama in the Senate when dealing with the "bill to distribute the residue of money given by the British government for American slaves lost from on board the Comet and Encomium. No opposition was made to it," he noted, "and no discussion had." The story proved markedly different in the House of Representatives, where "a bill for the same purpose has been on the calendar for some weeks."[21]

The main obstacle to its passage was the newly re-elected Joshua Giddings. The censured representative had gone back home to Ohio, but his constituents regarded him as an abolitionist hero, and during the special election held to fill his position, they promptly restored him to his congressional seat with 95 percent of the vote. In May 1842, he returned to Washington. For slave state members of the House, his absence had been regrettably brief.[22]

The relief bill from the Senate reached the House on January 10, 1843, but as David L.Child reported days earlier, "Mr. Giddings objects to its passing without discussion." Child explained that the Ohio abolitionist believed "Congress has no right, under the Constitution, to negotiate indemnities for slaves lost in the slave-trade, or to receive or pay monies on account of such, or to pass any regulation on the subject." Rep. Fillmore wanted Giddings to "withdraw his objection," but Giddings refused, leading Child to assume that Congress "may . . . expect a discussion on the subject." On January 12, the bill "was read a first and second time, and laid upon the Speaker's table." Two days later, it went before the Committee of the Whole.[23]

On February 3, the Committee of the Whole returned the bill for the relief of the claimants from the *Comet* and *Encomium*, with one amendment. The committee resolved that the bill be retitled "An act for the relief of William Selden, Treasurer of the United States." The revision, by specifically naming the individual empowered to collect and distribute the remaining indemnity monies, was intended to facilitate the last stages of that process. The House passed the bill, which moved to the Senate for discussion on February 10. The precise amendments the upper chamber made are not clearly documented in congressional records, but the bill returned to the House in an altered condition.[24]

On February 13, the House convened to consider the Senate version. North Carolina's Edward Stanly opened by observing that the bill required no tax upon the American people but merely directed that British monies already present in the U.S. Treasury be sent to those entitled to it. He moved to vote on the bill, but Giddings asked him to withdraw the motion, promising to renew it later. Stanly recognized that this would invite further discussion from the Ohio abolitionist. Politicians dreading a prolonged and inflammatory speech called out, "Hold on to it, Stanly," and "Don't let the old abolitionist waste the time of the House." After Stanly declined, Giddings again "appealed to the gentleman from North Carolina, as a man of *honor*, to withdraw the motion." By invoking the social ethic associated with the South, the Northerner's remark elicited "great noise and confusion" in the House. "God forbid, sir," Stanly replied, "that I should live to see the day when that gentleman shall be a judge of what is honorable." Giddings made several additional procedural attempts to obstruct or prevent the vote but was unsuccessful. Finally, the House passed the Senate bill in identical form.[25]

Unable to stop the bill from passing, Giddings revealed a crafty maneuver—what he called a "legislative stratagem"—that obligated the House to hear his abolitionist voice. "Is it in order, sir," he asked Speaker of the House John White, "to move a reconsideration of the vote just taken?" Under the rules, only representatives who voted with the majority could do so. Knowing the measure would pass with or without his vote, the Ohio congressman cleverly had voted in favor of a bill he opposed just to have the ability to speak on it after its passage. With the House Speaker's consent, Giddings "moved a reconsideration of the vote" so that he might offer "some observations . . . in opposition to the bill," or, as one detractor put it, "for the purpose of inflicting upon the House an abolition speech."[26]

Giddings knew he could do nothing to prevent the bill's implementation, but he did hope to "absolv[e]" himself from complicity with it. In encouraging the domestic slave trade, he believed the bill unconstitutional. As far as he was concerned, the British indemnity payment had been deposited in the Treasury "without authority of law, and could be safely withdrawn without any action of Congress." The bill just passed wasn't necessary because the treasurer did not need permission to dispose of the funds. The House had "never consented to act as trustee of these slave dealers" and "outlaws" in the first place, and Giddings refused to be implicated "in this crime of making merchandise of mankind."

Congress could not sanction the principle that federal protection of the domestic slave trader extended beyond the jurisdiction of the slave states and out into the Atlantic.[27]

Another of the abolitionist's leading objections was moral. Giddings explained that the bill promoted the nefarious interests of those "who deal in human flesh." He reminded his colleagues that slave traders regularly drove coffles aboard slave ships "lying at yonders [*sic*] wharf, in plain view of the windows in front of our Hall." Despite that offensive sight, the "American Congress sat gravely legislating for the benefit of 'slave-breeders' and 'slave-dealers,' . . . hucksterers in human flesh." It was shameful "and derogatory to the character of the United States."[28]

Giddings also protested the underlying legal principles embraced by the legislation. As he had insisted in his *Creole* resolutions, when slave ships "carried their cargo . . . beyond the jurisdiction of any slave state," the captives aboard "became *free in law*," a position Northern abolitionists held in common with the British government. When the prisoners landed on British soil, they each "had a legal and moral right" to seek their "own happiness." When the British colonial government refused to do slave owners' bidding, Giddings chortled, the enslavers "stood in mute astonishment, contemplating the immense loss they had sustained in this *locomotive property*."[29]

Desperate, "these dealers in the bones and sinews of their fellow-men" turned to the U.S. government. Slave owner and former president Andrew Jackson had "sympathized" with the request and "consented to act as the agent of these speculators, to use our national influence to sustain this traffic in the bodies of native-born Americans." Giddings condemned Jackson's "support of this piracy" as an unconstitutional "prostitution of our national character and influence," one that set the U.S. government on a course to war, "to enforce the demands of the slave dealers on board the Enterprise, the Hemora [*Hermosa*], and the Creole, . . . at the expense of [American] blood and treasure."[30]

Giddings unloaded a series of other criticisms and grievances during his time on the floor. He criticized U.S. minister Andrew Stevenson and others for their disingenuous arguments as "*agents for . . . slave merchants*." The Ohio congressman reserved special scorn for Secretary of State Martin Van Buren as a Northern man with Southern principles for his role as "assistant broker in this slave dealing concern," prioritizing reparation for lost slaves over other important issues, such as the boundary line with Canada.

Giddings revisited the episode from the previous year when he was censured by his colleagues and then restored to office by "the people" of his district. The Ohio abolitionist also marveled at the acquiescence of Northern colleagues like Caleb Cushing of Massachusetts and their willingness to help pass the present bill "*without* deliberation." "What power has thus miraculously silenced the voice of northern freedom and northern honor?" he asked.[31]

As Giddings's allotted time drew to a close, he dwelled on the "inconsistencies, absurdities, and contradictions" embedded in the law to distribute the last of the indemnity money. How, for example, could Congress pass a bill for the relief of slave traders when, in 1820, the transatlantic slave trade has been branded a form of piracy punishable by death? How could title to an enslaved person be proven when "the only title" that ever accomplished the denial of freedom was "*brute force*"? If the law directed the treasurer to disburse the sums the respective owners were entitled to receive, Giddings asked, "How will you estimate the value of a *man*?" For all of these reasons, Congress could not be made "*trustee* of these slave breeders" and "slave mongers."[32]

Giddings's "spirited abolition speech" against the bill elicited the sharp reactions he expected. Newspaper correspondents reported multiple interruptions. Giddings's words at times produced such "great noise and excitement" that "scarce a word could be heard." One unidentified congressman seated nearby implored, "Sit down, Giddings, for God's sake; you'll do no good by this violence." Another hissed under his breath, "The d-d old abolition scoundrel! he's been kicked out once, and we'll kick him out again." The House Speaker recognized Giddings's right to "exhaust his hour," however, which Giddings gladly did.[33]

During Giddings's speech, Louisiana representative John Bennett Dawson had glared "fiercely" at the abolitionist. A planter in his mid-forties, Dawson had dueled with a sword and regularly sat on the House floor armed with a pistol and bowie knife. In 1842, he had threatened to slash a colleague's throat "from ear to ear." At the conclusion of Giddings's remarks, Dawson ambled to the center of the House. In passing down the aisle while returning to his seat, he approached the Ohio congressmen from behind "and provokingly nudged him under the fifth rib." The shove to his back took Giddings by surprise. At six feet two inches tall and in excess of two hundred pounds, Giddings dwarfed Dawson, "a thin,

Joshua R. Giddings.

weakly man" who "weigh[ed] about half as much." The Ohioan turned and called out to Dawson, who had kept walking.[34]

The Louisiana representative looked back. "Well, sir."

"Did you mean that unkindly?" Giddings inquired.

"I did, sir, I did."

"As a wanton insult?"

"Yes, sir, I did—I did!"[35]

To Dawson, fanatical abolitionists like Giddings deserved disrespectful treatment. Slave state congressmen repeatedly tried to provoke their most reviled abolitionist adversary into violent confrontations during his twenty-year career in the House. Whereas they settled scores in duels with those who occupied the same social station as them, Southern elites like Dawson were not beneath beating, horsewhipping, caning, or pushing in the back someone they did not respect or judge their equal. Aware of how Southern honor functioned, Giddings never took the bait. "Well, we of the North, have a way to answer those insults, by appealing to public sentiment," he replied. The remark defused the immediate tension and denied the Louisiana politician's attempted performance of Southern honor.[36]

"You can have what remedy you please," Dawson sneered before whirling around and heading to the lobby. According to eyewitnesses, Dawson passed slowly through the aisle, the whole time "grasping in his bosom the handle of a bowie knife." Whether in public or in private, Giddings never appeared shaken by the threat of violence from his proslavery congressional colleagues. After the episode, wrote one correspondent, "Giddings took his seat, pocketing the affront" and taking as little offense as possible, "though it hurt his feelings."[37]

If the expiration of Giddings's time invited the encounter with Dawson, it also signaled the beginning of a lively series of official exchanges on the House floor. Called out by name during Giddings's remarks, Caleb Cushing disputed Giddings's contentions, arguing that voting for the bill neither violated the Constitution nor indicated "servility" to the South. What else could the United States do? If it failed to dispose of the money as intended, "it would amount to a fraud or embezzlement." The only other alternative was to "throw this money back to the British Government." Looking at all of the options, Cushing determined that it was the U.S. government's "duty to pay it over to those entitled to it."[38]

Tennessee representative Thomas Dickens Arnold hoped to avoid further discussion, so he moved to reject Giddings's question of reconsideration. Conflicting cries of "Good, Arnold," and "No, no" erupted. Rep. Stanly of North Carolina counted among the few who encouraged Arnold to withdraw the motion so that he might say a few words, but Arnold refused, "observing that, if he should do so, a long-continuing debate would be the consequence. There were twenty members ready to occupy the floor." John Quincy Adams piped up, "I am one of the twenty, sir; I strongly desire to speak." Several representatives ended up talking, struggling to be heard amid the "great noise and excitement" roiling the House.[39]

When the yeas and nays were ordered, the House voted by a healthy margin of 140 to 38 to set aside Giddings's motion to reconsider. The debate was over. The House's concurrence with the Senate bill stood. Maine congressman Elisha H. Allen sided with the majority to end the discussion. "We performed our duty as desired," Allen explained without regret. The bill did not involve "any principle either directly, or indirectly—but the principle of common honesty, to pay the money to whom it belonged."[40]

The day's drama was not yet over. With the motion to reconsider voted down, Giddings returned to the subject of Rep. Dawson's intentional, disrespectful bump. Dawson was no longer present when the Ohio congressman recapped the earlier incident and inquired "whether a member was free to insult another for remarks made in the House, in the exercise of his privileges as a member and a freeman." "I feel no personal anxiety about it," Giddings clarified, "but I wish to know if members are to be intimidated from expressing their honest sentiments on this floor. I fear not for my personal safety. I only ask the House to protect its own dignity." David L. Child reported that a "profound stillness" filled the chamber. The House Speaker had not been aware of the confrontation. "I presume it was very slight," he stated, "or I should certainly have prevented it."[41]

When Giddings took his seat, "great confusion" set in as House members clamored "to obtain the floor." While Rep. William B. Calhoun of Massachusetts urged consultation of the parliamentary manual to better understand members' rights and personal privileges, several pleaded with Giddings to "let the matter drop."[42]

Henry A. Wise, a representative from Virginia, proposed a theory. In his ardently proslavery version of events, the "kind and courteous" Dawson was passing up the narrow aisle of the House chamber when, as was common, he gave Giddings "the gentlest push imaginable" to shunt him aside so that he might skirt by. Under the scenario Wise outlined, the physical contact was innocuous and "not intended . . . as an affront." Besides, he added, "The affair was so slight that we who sat close by, even, did not see it." Among the few congressional eyewitnesses, one stated that Dawson "was in the best possible humor" at the time "and . . . intended no insult." "Oh yes, certainly," agreed other representatives eager to avoid raising the "exciting subject" of abolition. With so few days remaining in the present session of Congress, plus Dawson's absence, far better that "the matter might be passed over and forgotten." "*I presume*," quipped John Quincy Adams, in reference to Dawson's history of inflammatory speech, "*it was not a threat*" to "*cut the throat of the gentleman from ear to ear*"? Giddings answered that Dawson "said . . . he meant to insult me by it." Rep. Wise defended his slaveholding colleague, noting that the problem arose only after Giddings "called him back" to the scene of the slight, egging him on.[43]

With that, the Speaker wrangled the House to order, and "here the matter dropped." Nevertheless, the abolitionist press seized upon Dawson's menacing encounter with Giddings. *The Liberator* shared the awful lesson:

"that assaulting . . . members with the avowed purpose of insulting them for daring to speak in defence of the rights of freemen . . . is sanctioned by the House."[44]

The bill to distribute the last of the indemnity monies received from the British government reached the desk of President John Tyler on February 17, 1843, and was signed into law the next day. The government would soon send out the remaining funds for slave owners from the *Comet* and *Encomium*. Missouri's Charles Allen still hoped to partake of that relief. To date, a bureaucratic snafu had denied him compensation for Billy and Peggy. In January 1844, Allen's congressman, Gustavus Bower, presented a petition seeking restitution. It was referred to the Committee of Claims, but there the evidentiary trail vanishes. Another of the slave owners still awaiting compensation was Col. Charles P. Tutt's widow, Ann.[45]

15

The Trials of Widowhood

When British indemnities first arrived in the spring of 1840, Secretary of State John Forsyth prepared to distribute $5,788.30 for the nine enslaved people seized in the Bahamas from Col. Charles P. Tutt nine years earlier. At the time the Tutts' enslaved property was confiscated from the *Comet*, the bondwoman Milly and Richard (Dick) Douglass were both fifty years old. Dick's wife, Hannah, was ten years his junior. Their children Eliza, Martha, Robert, James, and Lydia ranged in age from three to twelve. All had spent almost a decade in freedom, the youngest probably having no recollections whatsoever of life in slavery. Because the eldest of the Tutt family captives, Dennis Young, passed away soon after the castaways' rescue and transport into Nassau, Forsyth deducted one-ninth of the funds initially set aside for Tutt. But Forsyth did not promptly issue a check to the Tutt household, as he had for Mary E. Mudd. The secretary of state continued to withhold the Tutts' $5,145.15, where it made up more than two-thirds of all the indemnity monies held in reserve during the disbursement process. The funds accumulated interest, but they did not get into Tutt family hands. The problem was an intrafamily squabble that kept Forsyth from knowing precisely who should receive the check for restitution. The conflict stemmed from questions related to widow Ann Tutt's hereditary claim to the indemnity, Southern gender conventions, and the legal ownership of the nine enslaved people bound for Pensacola who were deposited onto the *Comet*.[1]

Pensacola had once been part of the Spanish Empire, but the Adams-Onís Treaty ceded Florida to the United States in 1819. Five years later, Congress determined to establish a navy yard along the Gulf Coast. The barrier island of Santa Rosa sheltered Pensacola Bay from the Gulf of Mexico. Pensacola's strategic location and the depth of its harbor made it the logical choice for a military installation. Construction on the navy yard began in 1826, with the help of hired enslaved laborers. The next year, plans also took shape for the construction of Fort Pickens on the western tip of Santa Rosa Island, to protect the entrance to the harbor and the navy yard. Enslaved people likewise built Fort Pickens, starting in 1829 and completing their work in 1834. By the time Col. Charles P. Tutt was appointed agent and assigned to the new navy yard in April 1830, the seaport of Pensacola was a military outpost where most of "the respectable inhabitants" were those with commissions or serving in other governmental positions.[2]

Born sometime between 1780 and 1790, Charles Pendleton Tutt was a native of Loudoun County, Virginia. A veteran of the War of 1812, he served as quartermaster for the Fifty-Seventh Regiment of the Virginia militia. In early 1830, he was living in Leesburg, in Loudoun County, with his wife, Ann Mason Chichester Tutt, along with their four daughters, between ten and nineteen years old. They also held legal ownership over ten enslaved people when Tutt was summoned to Pensacola to become one of only eleven Navy agents employed by the U.S. government. By January 1831, Ann rejoined him, to her annoyance without the family servants who were to follow on the *Comet*. Ann's unhappiness in West Florida could only have increased upon the death of her husband in the fall of 1832. She was pregnant. A month later, in early November, she gave birth to a baby boy while still in Florida. She named him in honor of her deceased spouse.[3]

Ann Mason Chichester was born about 1790, like her future husband in Loudoun County. When she married Charles P. Tutt in 1806, at about the age of sixteen, her prosperous, slave-owning father gave the couple some enslaved people as a wedding gift. No marriage settlement that would have preserved the property Ann brought to the union in her name was signed prior to the wedding day. Such agreements were almost unheard of in advance of first marriages. Whatever property Ann Chichester carried into her marriage immediately transferred to the control of her new husband upon the exchange of vows under the law of coverture. With respect to enslaved property, men often served as women's proxies at slave markets and at slave auctions and in the administration of discipline. In practice, husbands did not direct the day-to-day management of the enslaved independent from the influence of their wives. White women, whose cruelty could at times equal if not exceed that of their husbands, were especially involved in giving orders to the house servants who performed domestic duties. Like white women from slave-owning families across the South, Ann M. Tutt was familiar with the governance of bondpeople and over the course of her lifetime grew accustomed to reaping the benefits of slavery.[4]

Still, she could not escape the legal impediments unique to her sex. During her husband's lifetime, Ann endured the frustration of watching Charles put up for sale enslaved people he came to own only through marriage to her. Widowhood technically removed Ann from her state of coverture and made her legally independent, yet she also learned the harsh lesson that slaveholding widows never enjoyed the same degree of mastery over enslaved property exercised by Southern white men. She was legally entitled to a minimum of one-third of her deceased husband's estate as her dower right, but she would spend years fighting to recover what she saw as her due. Slave-owning widows in the nineteenth century were routinely denied power as executors of their husbands' wills and were forced to rely increasingly on the discretion of Southern courts of law. Like others facing the challenges of widowhood, Ann experienced difficulties with the executors chosen to settle her deceased husband's affairs.[5]

In 1830, Col. Tutt, already stationed at the Pensacola Navy Yard, authorized a pair of trustees named Fayette Ball and Samuel Dawson to sell nine enslaved people—Dennis, Dick, James, Robert, Milly, Hannah, Lydia, Martha, and Eliza—at public auction back home in Loudoun County. Tutt had acquired each of these bondpeople, directly or indirectly, through his marriage to Ann. Dennis, Milly, Dick, and Hannah were old enough to have been bestowed upon the newlyweds by her father. Lydia, James, Robert, Martha, and Eliza were Dick and Hannah's children. All of them ended up on the auction block in November 1830 because, as Ann intimated, "her husband . . . was much embarrassed in his circumstances." Col. Tutt's finances were indeed in disarray. He owed debts to the Bank of the Valley in Leesburg, dating back to 1823. He was also in arrears with a long list of individuals, including members of his extended family, such as his brother-in-law George M. Chichester. Altogether, his debts of several thousand dollars compelled him to sell the nine "slaves for the benefit of his creditors." They functioned as a human form of ready capital.[6]

Ann was "anxious" and "distressed" at the prospect of losing the enslaved property that she had contributed to their union. "They were family servants," she explained. She invested "great store on this account, besides . . . their other qualities." Therefore, prior to the slave sale in November, Ann enlisted the assistance of her brother George, who agreed to attend the auction as her agent and purchase the nine Chichester family slaves on Ann's behalf "to be held separately" by her, "apart from the property of her . . . husband," and for her "sole benefit." Other men present at the sale deferred to George's familial interest in the lot of nine enslaved people, leaving him "the highest and only bidder." He procured the bondpeople for a combined sum of $950, a low purchase price because everyone present understood that Ann wanted to buy them and respectfully offered no competing bids. As Ann told the story, despite her husband's financial difficulties, she possessed the "separate means and thrift, to pay for them" with her own funds. The source of this money she allegedly controlled independently of Col. Tutt is not clear.[7]

Ann planned to reunite with her husband in Pensacola, but she did not wish to move without the "comfort and convenience" afforded by the Chichester family bondpeople. Shortly before she left for Florida, Ann paid to have George transport all nine enslaved laborers from Alexandria. "I sent the negros to Alexandria" twice, he wrote her in late December, but both times he was unable to secure them passage. Chichester therefore consulted slave traders Franklin & Armfield, who "appointed a day for them to be sent back." Following their instructions, he conveyed the bondpeople to Alexandria a third time, placing them aboard the *Comet* for a voyage to New Orleans. From there, they would be shipped to West Florida. "I suppose," he mistakenly assumed on December 28, 1830, they "are at, or near, New Orleans." He did not anticipate a shipwreck and the British seizure and liberation of the *Comet* captives spoiling his plans. In contrast, Col. Tutt imagined the possible dangers. In a letter from late January 1831, before he became aware of the *Comet* disaster, he reprimanded his brother-in-law for not sending "a bill of lading, for the negroes and furniture in order that I might have them insured. I feel some apprehension about them[,] for if they are lost it will be a serious loss."[8]

Ann finally received word of the *Comet*'s sinking in the Bahamas. No less invested in slavery than her husband, either she or Col. Tutt (Ann's accounts differ on this point) "employed the services of an agent at great expence" to journey to Nassau, retrieve the bondpeople, and charter a boat to deliver them to Pensacola. In this effort, the Tutts joined with the Louisiana State Marine and Fire Insurance Company, the Mississippi Marine and Fire Insurance Company, and the Merchants Insurance Company to hire lawyer Nathan Morse to represent their shared interest in the *Comet* castaways. When Morse failed to gain the captives' release, the Tutts again contributed to the attorney's expenses incurred in traveling to Washington to press the claim against the British government. Altogether, they contributed $600 toward Morse's mission to recover the liberated slaves or their value.[9]

The year after the *Comet* wreck, death took Charles Tutt. Three years later, in 1835, George Chichester died as well. His passing proved even more devastating than that of Col. Tutt's to Ann's chances of gaining compensation for the enslaved people freed in the Bahamas. According to Ann, George paid neither to purchase nor to transport the family's servants out of his funds, nor did he participate in "the prosecution of the . . . claim" against the British government. From winning the bid at the 1830 Loudoun County slave auction until his death, he "never in any manner . . . interfered" with "the said negroes, and never put forward any claim concerning them." Unfortunately for Ann, neither had he taken the necessary steps by 1835 to affirm his widowed sister's legal right of ownership over the enslaved people in question. Her brother, Ann ruefully acknowledged, "departed this life without having executed the necessary conveyance" of the legal title to her. It was a serious oversight with dire ramifications for Ann Tutt.[10]

During her widowhood, Tutt labored strenuously to defend her interests in the enslaved property liberated by British officials. Many widows struggled in the absence of their husbands as they dealt with various financial, legal, and familial difficulties thrust upon them during emotionally trying times, but Tutt handled her affairs with aplomb. Neither naïve, nor helpless, nor paralyzed with fear or doubt, she submitted her claim with the U.S. government for indemnity and remuneration.[11]

When news arrived from across the Atlantic in March 1837 that the British government agreed to reimburse Southern slave owners whose human merchandise aboard the *Comet* and *Encomium* had been freed, Tutt should have felt a combination of relief and elation. The Chichester family slaves would not be returned, but at least she would be buffered from the financial blow of losing the nine enslaved people. Her brother's negligence in his dealings on her behalf tempered her reaction, however. Despite George M. Chichester having during his lifetime "disclaimed all and [any] interest and admitted the full title" of his sister to the nine bondpeople on the *Comet*, the executors and trustees of his estate—friends and Loudoun County slave owners Robert Gilmore Bowie and William T.T. Mason—viewed the matter differently. Only after it became clear that the

British government would pay for the liberated slaves, and impending compensation was dangled in front of them, did Bowie and Mason claim that Chichester was the bondpeople's true owner. They based their contention on the fact that Chichester was the original purchaser of the nine bondpeople at the 1830 slave sale. For that reason alone, they alleged that his estate was owed the British indemnity.[12]

Ann Tutt fought back against the "pretended claim" of her brother's executors. After they challenged her claim to ownership, she composed a memorial to Secretary of State John Forsyth in 1840 requesting $5,152.98 from the indemnity monies received from the British government. She explained that Chichester purchased the nine bondpeople her husband put up for sale "for the sole benefit of herself and children" and that she alone had borne "the trouble and expense of prosecuting the claim." Why would she have done so if her brother or his estate possessed legitimate ownership rights?[13]

In another savvy move, she "procured various affidavits" supporting her petition. She gathered statements from no fewer than seven individuals, including the auctioneer from sale day in Loudoun County, who shared the impression that Chichester purchased "the negroes . . . for the exclusive benefit of his sister Mrs. Ann M. Tutt and her children."[14] The most detailed of the depositions she enclosed was a written oath given by her son-in-law, Prof. Charles Bonnycastle. After the wreck of the *Comet*, he spoke to Chichester "with some warmth" in defense of his mother-in-law, scolding Chichester for taking so "little care . . . to secure Mrs. Tutt, from injury." Any responsible party would have insured the enslaved people in advance of the voyage, Bonnycastle insisted. Chichester's response proved telling. "It was no business of his," he replied. "He had no interest in said slaves; direct or indirect, present or prospective." He had done everything he had—purchasing the enslaved people at auction and then depositing them aboard the *Comet*—"altogether on account of, and for the interests of Mrs. A. M. Tutt," and she had never instructed him to apply for insurance. Defending himself, Chichester declared "that he ought not to be blamed for the loss of property belonging to Mrs. Tutt" and that she should be grateful "for the trouble he had taken." Bonnycastle's statement clearly revealed a brother who had done the bare minimum for his sister and then divorced himself from her affairs.[15]

As the State Department faced two competing claims to the indemnity for one specific lot of captives from the *Comet*, bureaucratic paralysis set in. With the ownership of the slaves in doubt, the courts would have to determine the rightful recipient of the reimbursement monies. For widows like Ann Tutt, resort to the courts to protect their rights and resolve property disputes was nothing new. In Tutt's native Virginia, the law of the commonwealth granted widows relatively little control over enslaved property, and women whose husbands predeceased them received only a life interest in, rather than absolute rights over, dower slaves. Slaveholding widows often relied on appeals to Southern courts to gain approval to transfer or sell enslaved property or even to secure their dower share of their husbands' estate in the first place.[16]

Tutt presented her case before the Circuit Court of the District of Columbia for the County of Washington in January 1844. She sought an injunction that would prevent her brother's executors, Robert Gilmore Bowie and William T.T. Mason, from disturbing her title to the nine bondpeople liberated from the *Comet*, which in turn would permit her to receive the full indemnity she insisted she was lawfully due. All of the evidence originally sent to Secretary of State Forsyth was presented again in court.[17]

Bowie and Mason agreed in many of the particulars of the case as outlined by Tutt. They concurred that Fayette Ball and Samuel Dawson had sold the nine enslaved people at public auction as the property of Charles P. Tutt, that George M. Chichester had "purchased the said negroes," and that Ann had had them transported from Alexandria on the *Comet*. Where they deviated from her version of events was in denying that her brother bought the bondpeople "for her to be held separately by her apart from the property of her . . . husband," who was still living at the time of sale. According to them, Chichester had not "acted solely as the agent" of his sister; rather, they argued, he purchased the slaves at auction for himself.[18]

Bowie and Mason presented evidence to "establish their right to indemnity" from the government. Chronicling Charles P. Tutt's long history of indebtedness, they pointed out that Chichester and Mason had served as Tutt's sureties throughout most of the 1820s. In 1823, Col. Tutt had empowered the two, in a deed of trust, to sell "a family of negroes, together with other property," to "indemnify" themselves and hold themselves "harmless" in their shared role as his trustees. Chichester and Mason, however, realized that they might need "to purchase a part or all of the property conveyed in trust" to prevent Tutt from permanently losing it in a sale outside the family. Because they could not legally buy Tutt's property in their designated roles as trustees, in 1828, they secured a decree in chancery court by which Ball and Dawson substituted for them as Tutt's sureties. An audit of Chichester's accounts conducted by the commissioner of court revealed that Col. Tutt owed his brother-in-law in excess of $6,000. After Chichester's death in 1835, his executors pursued this money owed his estate, prompting their claim upon the nine emancipated slaves from the *Comet*. Bowie and Mason dismissed Ann Tutt's claim for restitution from the British government as "wholly untenable and unjust" because the Chichester estate must first be indemnified for the funds expended by Chichester in his former capacity as trustee. Already in November 1839, the total owed by the Tutt estate had ballooned to more than $7,700 in principal and interest, and it would be another five years before the case went before the Circuit Court of the District of Columbia for resolution.[19]

The executors' most compelling evidence in their favor came from the correspondence of the Tutt family. Writing from Pensacola in late January 1831, Ann informed her brother of Col. Tutt's preference that Chichester had "convey[ed] the negroes and articles purchased for me to Maj[r] Thomas Wright," serving in West Florida, "in trust for me with power to sell them. Then if it is necessary they can be sold without any difficulty." The next sentence proved the most devastating to Tutt's case. "Situated as they are we are obliged to keep them," she explained to her brother, "and in case of your death your executor would at once take possession of them, as they are your property." The same letter indicated that Chichester fronted the money to purchase the nine bondpeople at auction. Ann Tutt intended to pay her brother for them, but she had not yet done so. "You may rest assured I will remit to you the amount as soon as I possibly can," she explained. "Mr. Tutt will not have any money until the last of March, or early in April, when you will receive a part, and the ballance [*sic*] as soon after as practicable." Ann's later recounting of events to Secretary of State Forsyth declared her the purchaser of the enslaved people out of her own funds, which may have eventually been true but was not at the time of sale.[20]

One other letter cast serious doubt on Ann's ownership claims. On September 7, 1831, Col. Tutt wrote to George Chichester that he had "abandoned" hope of recovering "the negroes" from the *Comet* and was "prosecuting a claim upon the British Government for their value." The Navy agent was optimistic. "I have now an agent in Washington prosecuting," as he put it, "*my claim as consignee of the Slaves*." He explained to his brother-in-law, to whom he owed formidable sums, that any "*proceeds*" acquired in restitution from Britain, "*Shall be settled on your Sister*"—his wife, Ann Tutt—"*upon the same terms that the slaves were to have been, with power to her to apply the same, as she may think proper to the payment of my debts.*" Bowie and Mason saw this missive as proof that Chichester had not purchased the nine bondpeople for his sister; rather, Col. Tutt intended that the nine bondpeople be used to expunge a fraction of his own indebtedness and "discharge" himself "from liability." He would clamber out of debt on the backs of the human assets his wife brought to their marriage.[21]

The task of weighing the assembled evidence fell to the court, presided over by Chief Judge William Cranch. "The principal question in this case is," the court clarified at the outset, "whether Mr. Chichester purchased the negroes, with an agreement and understanding on his part that they should become her [Ann Tutt's] sole and separate property, upon payment of the $950 which he bid for them, and for which he purchased them." From the beginning of their opinion, Cranch and his two assistant judges, Buckner Thruston and James Morsell, detected a high probability that Chichester wanted his sister to "have some interest in the negroes, either absolute or contingent." The concerned brother may have intended for Ann to own them outright despite Col. Tutt's indebtedness to him, but the court could not know for certain.[22]

Turning first to the evidence provided by Ann Tutt, the court seemed unimpressed. According to the judges, "that the slaves were her property before her marriage" had no bearing on the case. It meant only that she "might have a stronger desire to retain them than if they were strangers" and that her brother "might be willing to gratify his sister in her wish." That "Mrs. Tutt paid for the transportation of the slaves," or that she pledged to repay Chichester the $950, demonstrated "an interest in the slaves" without clarifying whether her interest was absolute or contingent on the discharge of Col. Tutt's indebtedness to her brother.[23]

Several individuals deposed on Ann's behalf affirmed that Chichester "disclaimed all interest" in the enslaved people and "took no part in the prosecution of the claim for indemnity." The court swiftly set aside Chichester's apparent indifference, explaining that "the consignee of a cargo"—in this case, Col. Tutt—was the "*prima facie* . . . owner," with the responsibility to pursue redress. Chichester's seeming inaction did not indicate disinterest on his part, since he seemed more a "mortgagee, rather than [an] absolute owner." Judge Cranch outlined the likeliest scenario, as far as the court could discern. "It seems from the evidence," Cranch explained, "that Mr. Tutt & Mr. Chichester hoped and expected that Mr. Tutt's property, exclusive of the negroes[,] would enable him to pay his debts, or at least the debt due by him to Mr. Chichester, and the debts for which he (Mr. Chichester) was liable." If that were true—and it was not, since Col. Tutt's indebtedness proved too large—Chichester's "interest in the slaves would cease," and ownership would devolve upon Ann Tutt. Mrs. Tutt, in other words, held a "contingent interest" in the enslaved people. According to the District Court, Chichester "believed, no doubt, that the interest of Mrs. Tutt in the slaves was sufficient to induce her & her husband to prosecute the claim with zeal without his personal interference." His "acquiescence in their proceedings," therefore, "cannot be considered as an abandonment of his interest in the slaves."[24]

In addition, the District Court placed little stock in the affidavits that Ann Tutt collected as evidence. Much of the testimony recounted events and conversations that took place at least nine years earlier and could not be accepted as fully reliable. Moreover, with only one exception, no cross-examination was made. Some who gave affidavits, including Charles Bonnycastle, were kin to Ann "and liable to the natural Bias growing out of that relation." The court concluded that the testimony did "not furnish satisfactory evidence" that Chichester "intended to transfer these slaves absolutely to Mrs. Tutt as her sole and separate property." Nor did anything in the affidavits preclude the possibility that Chichester held legal title to the nine enslaved people and retained a lien upon them as security should Charles Tutt's estate "be insufficient to discharge the debts . . . for which Mr. Chichester was liable on account of Mr. Tutt." In the meantime, out of brotherly affection for his sister, he could let Ann enjoy "the use of her family servants, until it should be necessary to resort to them for the payment of her husband's debts."[25]

The District Court placed significant weight on the Tutt family's correspondence. Ann's letter to her brother George, in which she conveyed Col. Tutt's desire for the authority to sell the bondpeople and expressed her husband's fear of losing possession of them in the event of Chichester's death, was damning. She admitted that legal title to the enslaved property rested with her brother, while her husband acknowledged that the primary use for the nine bondpeople was "the payment of my debt."[26]

Although "Mrs. Tutt . . . asks that the legal title to the slaves or their proceeds" be removed from Chichester's executors and "vested in her," the court concluded that she was not entitled to lawful ownership over them.

The law of equity demanded that Col. Tutt's debts due to the estate of Ann's deceased brother take priority over her claim as a widow. At the same time, Judge Cranch held that Ann deserved compensation for the expenses she and her husband incurred in prosecuting their claim for indemnity against the British government, plus "a reasonable allowance . . . on the amount recovered." He ordered a government auditor to determine the correct amount.[27]

Auditor Joseph Forrest examined Ann Tutt's claims. He disallowed all of her expenditures related to the transportation of the enslaved people because that money was paid "not . . . in prosecuting a claim for their recovery, but rather to place the property in Jeopardy" by transporting them coastwise. Forrest accepted as valid $1,100 in Tutt family expenses related to the hiring of agent Nathan Morse and "the charter of a vessel" to retrieve the enslaved people from the Bahamas, despite Ann providing "no voucher, or positive proof" of them. As the auditor reasoned, "Mrs. Tutt considered at the time that she was sole owner of the property," so she did not think it "important or necessary" to ask for receipts, and those who might give her one in 1844 "have now been dead many years." Forrest authorized an additional $561 in interest on the $1,100, along with one-sixth of the $6,042.70 deposited in the U.S. Treasury as "compensation for active agency" in attempting to recover enslaved people liberated by British authorities. In late November 1844, Forrest calculated that Ann was "justly entitled" to a check for $2,668.12 in compensation. Reviewing his decision on January 4, 1845, the District Court made one adjustment. Rather than allowing the widow one-sixth of the $6,042.70, for unspecified reasons it allotted her one-tenth of the fund. The change reduced her payment to $2,265.27.[28]

The District Court denied Ann the ownership rights she tenaciously pursued in her dispute with her brother's executors. The compensation awarded her tallied less than half of the more than $5,000 she originally sought from Secretary of State Forsyth—far from a desirable outcome. Yet financial disappointment was not out of the ordinary for her. Ann had married a man who demonstrated consistent difficulty in managing his household economy, and she made sacrifices on account of his failures. When she joined her husband in Pensacola, she stated plainly, "The object of my coming here was not pleasure, but to save money which I shall do in every way I possibly can." The loss of Dennis, Milly, Dick, Hannah, Lydia, James, Robert, Martha, and Eliza in the Bahamas only added to Ann's woes. George Chichester felt immense "distress" in the spring of 1831 pondering "the privation she w[oul]d experience in her new home, with limited means," having lost "some negroes" to emancipation in Nassau. Writing from Pensacola, Ann agreed that "living here is certainly a great sacrifice."[29]

After Col. Tutt "died insolvent," Ann, in her forties, never remarried. She left the Florida Territory she found so unimpressive and returned initially to family in the commonwealth of Virginia. By 1860, she was living with her daughter Virginia and son-in-law, Philip Pendleton, in Allegany County, Maryland. In 1870, Ann, then in her eighties, owned $12,000 in personal estate (more than one-quarter of a million dollars today), a healthy sum during the post–Civil War years, when some ex–slave owners confronted financial ruin. Economically, she had long since recovered from the temporary damage sustained in 1831 by the loss of the Tutts' bondpeople. Though denied the full indemnity she sought, Ann successfully navigated the political and legal landscape to claim a share of the British reparation payment. For Ann M. Tutt, the wreck of the *Comet* caused both personal inconvenience and some degree of financial loss, the latter minimized somewhat through the intervention of the U.S. government.[30]

16

Unsettled Claims

In 1844, the same year that Ann M. Tutt's case appeared before the Circuit Court of the District of Columbia, other owners of enslaved property taken from U.S. domestic slave ships were still agitating for payment. Missouri's Charles Allen had yet to receive a solitary shilling in compensation for the loss of his pair of bondpeople, Billy and Peggy, from the *Encomium* in 1834, despite British willingness to pay it. Still seeking restitution, Allen petitioned Congressman Gustavus Bower for "compensation for the loss of two slaves liberated by the British authorities at Nassau." The memorial was referred to the Committee of Claims before the evidentiary trail chronicling Allen's quest for reimbursement ran cold. If other similar cases serve as any indication, Congress avoided expending the U.S. government's own monies in restitution for bondpeople liberated from American slave ships, despite the vessels' nagging reappearance in many political debates of the 1840s and early 1850s.[1]

South Carolina planter John Strohecker filed a well-documented complaint concerning the enslaved cargo from the still-uncompensated *Enterprise*. In 1835, Strohecker neither shipped nor was scheduled to receive the *Enterprise*'s captives. Instead, his interest in the case derived from his association with the Charleston Fire and Marine Insurance Company, the firm required by lawsuit in 1837 to pay almost $22,000 on its policy issued to slave trader Oliver Simpson. Strohecker and other prominent South Carolina slave owners were leading investors in the insurance company, and because of a combination of national economic downturn and imprudent management Charleston Fire and Marine had fallen on hard times. It had overextended itself, pledging to insure far more assets than it had the capital to cover. Then, in late April 1838, only a month after the company had paid for Oliver Simpson's human merchandise taken from the *Enterprise*, a fire raged uncontrolled through Charleston. The conflagration consumed as much as one-third of the city, causing more than

$3 million in property losses, about half of which was covered by insurance. The blaze accounted for more than $200,000 in fire losses alone for Charleston Fire and Marine. Confronted with such widespread devastation, the company could afford to pay only 75¢ on the dollar on its policies without depleting its monetary reserves.[2]

With the insurer confronting extreme financial hardship, Strohecker's name appeared atop an undated petition to the president and members of the South Carolina state senate seeking relief for the "Fire and Marine Insurance Company and the loss of property on board the Schooner Enterprize, caused by British interference." The memorial explained the "pecuniary loss" suffered by Charleston Fire and Marine and its "inability . . . to pay the full amount of their policies of insurance" in the wake of the "disasterous [*sic*] fire" that swept through the city. The implication was that the insurer could have honored its full policy obligations had the fire not been preceded by "the loss of seventy or Eighty negro slaves" from the *Enterprise.* Strohecker claimed that the maritime fiasco alone cost Charleston Fire and Marine $35,530 in insured losses and interest, a figure substantially higher than the amount documented in other sources. Hoping to capitalize on state senators' sense of patriarchal duty to protect the weak and vulnerable, Strohecker asserted that "many of those, who are interested in the claim, are Widows and orphans, who feel the loss [of the enslaved people freed in Bermuda] very severely." In truth, the enslaved cargo was consigned to a slave trader in Charleston from another slave trader in Washington. On behalf of both these alleged "widows and orphans" and his colleagues affiliated with the Charleston Fire and Marine Insurance Company, Strohecker pleaded for remuneration for the losses incurred, since "no satisfaction has been made" by the British government. The petition found its way to the South Carolina Senate's Committee on Federal Relations, which, in December 1844, reported back unfavorably. The house concurred in the finding.[3]

The South Carolina state legislature's refusal to aid Strohecker and the ailing Charleston Fire and Marine Insurance Company was almost certainly due to its unwillingness to pay from its own coffers. Like so many others before him who had suffered financially because of British emancipations of enslaved American cargoes, Strohecker and those he represented turned instead to the U.S. government in anticipation of federal aid. In December 1844, he submitted a petition to South Carolina Democrat Isaac Holmes in the House of Representatives, asking "to repay moneys paid by the Fire and Marine Insurance Company of Charleston, upon the loss of the brig Enterprise." South Carolina's Daniel Huger presented an identical or nearly identical petition in the U.S. Senate on January 7, 1845. The respective memorials were directed to the House Committee on Foreign Affairs and the Senate Committee on Foreign Relations.[4]

Neither house of Congress embraced Strohecker's cause. Great Britain had authorized no restitution for the *Enterprise*, so no monies earmarked for those affected by the liberation of the captives in Bermuda sat in the U.S. Treasury waiting for disbursement. The U.S. government energetically pursued reparation from the Crown and devoted untold man-hours to their distribution, but it drew the line at expending U.S. funds where diplomacy had failed.[5]

Strohecker and his associates at the Charleston Fire and Marine Insurance Company lobbied relentlessly for redress. In January 1846, they petitioned Rep. Holmes and Sen. John C. Calhoun, "praying for indemnity" for their losses. Again, the Committees on Foreign Affairs and on Foreign Relations withheld their endorsement of the request. Holmes's resubmission of the memorial in January 1848 fared no better.[6]

Strohecker was still agitating for compensation on behalf of the Charleston Fire and Marine Insurance Company for the *Enterprise*'s liberated cargo in May 1850 when he passed away suddenly at the age of forty-five. He died intestate, leaving his widow, Henrietta, administratrix of an estate that included nineteen enslaved persons, ranging in age from one to sixty and valued at just over $8,400. A panel of three commissioners distributed the bondpeople among the heirs, which included Henrietta and her seven children. Each Strohecker child, from three-year-old George to married daughter Margaret, received at least one enslaved person, usually worth a total of between $500 and $600, from the estate. Although the Stroheckers rejected a proposal "to sell a Negro" for cash to more equitably "arrange the balances," they blatantly disregarded blood connections among the enslaved and broke up Black families in the process of distributing enslaved property to the heirs. Henrietta Strohecker took on the burden of care for the "old and infirm negro" Nelly, worth a token $5.[7]

Whatever difficulties tending to Nelly would entail, the ongoing matter of compensation for the *Enterprise*'s captives did not trouble Henrietta's mind. Her husband had fought to gain restitution for an insurance company, not for his or his family's enslaved laborers. Henrietta's status as a slaveholder was secure for the foreseeable future, despite the calls for indemnification for the *Enterprise*, *Hermosa*, or *Creole* going unheeded.

Congress demonstrated a clear reluctance to use U.S. tax money to reimburse owners from the affected vessels, but the slave ships whose human cargoes were seized by the British constantly reappeared in the major political debates of the 1840s and early 1850s. In the mid-1840s, for example, the "outrage of the Comet, Encomium, Enterprise, and Hermosa cases" surfaced during discussions over the annexation of the independent, slaveholding Republic of Texas into the United States.[8]

Great Britain weighed heavily in calculations over the proper course of U.S. action in Texas. Having embarked upon its own process of emancipation in 1834, the British government's opposition to slave owning had delayed its recognition of the Republic of Texas, independent since 1836, until 1840. Even then, Her Majesty's government hoped to effect the extermination of slavery there or, failing that, to support a sovereign state that served as an economic counterweight to the American South.[9]

Many Southern whites gave voice to their anxieties over British influence in the Republic of Texas. The creation of lucrative commercial alliances between Britain and Texas fostered competition in the British cotton market. Texas's emergence as a possible primary supplier to British textile mills could adversely affect U.S. cotton producers from the Carolinas to Louisiana. Moreover, the economic impact would ripple outward to affect nonagricultural sectors of the economy and other parts of the United States. A bustling trade between Great Britain and Texas, it was feared, would promote an influx of rival British industrial goods into Texas and the United States, a development detrimental to domestic manufacturing in the North.[10]

More alarmingly still for Southern slave owners, the specter of British abolitionism loomed over the vast expanse of Texas's territory. Were Britain somehow to eradicate slavery in Texas and convert the republic to free labor, Texas would become a haven for fugitive American slaves in the Old Southwest. Even more important, the domestic market in enslaved people from the established slaveholding states to the east would be diminished. With the westward expansion of slavery held in check by a free Texas, bondpeople would become an economic "burden" to their owners rather than a source of profit. Proslavery observers feared that that prospect—made imaginable by the lurking British presence in Texas—jeopardized the future of slavery itself in the Southern states. "British interference in the institution of slavery amongst us is at this time most to be apprehended," declared Col. W.R. Hill, a Mississippi lawyer who had migrated from South Carolina in search of greater opportunity. "The cases of the Comet, Encomium, Enterprise, and Creole, furnish conclusive evidence of the unwillingness of the British government to recognize our title to this species of property." Southern trepidations about the nagging British influence over the fate of American slavery spurred Sen. John C. Calhoun and other like-minded politicians to aggressively pursue the annexation of Texas. If Texas was the next target of British abolitionism, only the republic's absorption into the United States could protect slavery there and permit the institution's further expansion.[11]

Texas's admission into the Union in late December 1845 ultimately secured additional territory for Southern slaveholders, but the extension of slavery into the West continued to dominate the political discourse throughout the decade and beyond. The leading political parties clashed over the issue during the presidential election of 1848. The Democrats nominated Lewis Cass of Michigan for president on a platform of popular (or squatter) sovereignty, the principle that allowed the voters of a territory to determine the fate of slavery there. The Whig Party advanced the ticket of slave-owning Mexican-American War veteran Gen. Zachary Taylor and running mate Millard Fillmore of New York. The Whigs were less forthcoming than the Democrats in their stance on slavery in the territories and evaded the question as much as possible. A new, third party took shape for the 1848 presidential contest as well. The Free Soil Party nominated New Yorker and former Democratic president Martin Van Buren.[12]

Two of the principal figures involved in the presidential election of 1848 came under scrutiny for their actions during the disputes with Great Britain over the shipwrecked and distressed slaving vessels from years before. Van Buren heading the Free Soil Party struck some contemporaries as an unusual choice. In the preceding two presidential elections, abolitionists had nominated their own candidate, ex-slaveholder James G. Birney. Supporting the still-unpopular abolitionist cause, Birney suffered a pair of crushing defeats in 1840 and 1844. In 1848, the Free Soil candidate Van Buren advocated for only the restriction of slavery to where it already existed rather than for outright abolition. Nevertheless, abolitionists such as Rep. Joshua Giddings of Ohio threw their support behind Van Buren.

Giddings's endorsement of Van Buren seemed puzzling to some. They recalled Giddings's past criticisms of Van Buren as "agent" and "*assistant broker*" for "slave dealers." At President Andrew Jackson's direction, in February 1832 Van Buren had ably laid out the initial case for reparation for enslaved people seized from the *Comet.* Despite his Yankee origins, Van Buren had proven himself a Northern man with "southern principles," earning him the derisive nickname "doughface," so popular in the late antebellum era. Giddings had once denounced Van Buren's "servility" to slaveholding interests during the latter's brief tenure as secretary of state and later as president, labeling it "an enduring memento of the degeneracy of the age." One Connecticut newspaper doubted the former president could be trusted as the standard-bearer for a party opposed to slavery's expansion. "We are not among those who are disposed to give Mr. Van Buren any credit for the opinions he now professes to entertain on the subject of restricting slavery," wrote the *Hartford Courant.* "If any thing was to be gained, he would, in all probability, be as ready to truckle to the South now, as in former years."[13]

The slaving voyages gone awry also dogged the campaign of Whig vice-presidential candidate Millard Fillmore. The Whigs had put forward a sectionally balanced ticket that included a Southern presidential and a Northern vice-presidential candidate, designed to appeal to a nationwide electorate of voting-age white men. For many Southern voters, Zachary Taylor's ownership of a sprawling plantation in Louisiana offered some assurance about his trustworthiness on the slavery question, but his running mate's soundness was more in doubt. The month before the election, the *Richmond Enquirer,* the leading Democratic newspaper in Virginia, shared its suspicion that Fillmore felt "sympathy with the infamous [abolitionist] Giddings."[14]

The *Enquirer* traced its allegations to 1842. That March, Giddings had introduced but then withdrawn his *Creole* resolutions. Rep. John Minor Botts of Virginia, who had brought the resolution of censure against Giddings, noticed on April 22 that the House clerk had entered into the record a petition placed on his table by Whig representative Patrick G. Goode from Ohio. In the memorial, Giddings's constituents from Ashtabula County condoned their representative's behavior and objected to his censure. Botts considered the resolutions offensive and insulting to the House and moved to strike them from the *House Journal.* When a motion was made to lay the matter on the table, Fillmore voted with the minority to set it aside, an incriminating sign for the *Enquirer* that the New York representative supported Giddings. On the motion to strike out mention of the Ohio resolutions from the record, Fillmore voted no. It passed anyway, but the vote again implied, as the *Enquirer* interpreted it, that "*Millard Fillmore* stood shoulder to shoulder with Giddings." He not only labored "to shield him from the just indignation of the South" but also "voted to *censure that very South* which had *dared* to rebuke an abolition incendiary."[15]

Other voices in the Southern press placed greater faith in Fillmore's soundness on the slave question. "Abolitionism was not, to our knowledge, imputed to Mr. Fillmore until he was put up as a candidate for the Vice Presidency," observed the *Wilmington (NC) Chronicle*. Speaker of the House John White, from slaveholding Kentucky, had appointed Fillmore chair of the powerful House Ways and Means Committee in 1841. "Is it at all probable . . . that a Southern man, a Slaveholder, would of his own volition, place a man whom he knew to be an abolitionist . . . in a position so responsible, so vastly important to the interests of the whole country?" asked the *Chronicle* rhetorically. As chair, Fillmore not only reported the bill to provide the last of the indemnity monies to owners of enslaved people liberated from the *Comet* and the *Encomium* but also voted in favor of it, setting himself apart from congressional abolitionists. The slaveholders of coastal North Carolina appreciated Fillmore's efforts. They well remembered that more than twenty of the captives seized from the *Encomium* belonged to one of their own, slave owner John Waddell, "removing from the neighborhood of Wilmington to Louisiana." Whether for good or ill, political figures' actions during the push for restitution from Great Britain followed them throughout their careers.[16]

The U.S. slave ships deprived of their human cargoes contributed to the political schism between Democrats John C. Calhoun of South Carolina and Thomas Hart Benton of Missouri as well. The rift between the senators dated back decades. During the presidency of Andrew Jackson, they clashed over political patronage, monetary policy, and the Senate's censure of Jackson for withdrawing federal funds to state "pet banks." They disagreed, too, over the future of slavery in the western territories of Oregon, California, and New Mexico. A unionist, Benton opposed slavery's expansion, despite representing Missouri slaveholders and owning enslaved people himself. His position put him at odds with Calhoun, the era's leading defender of slaveholders' right to carry their enslaved property wherever they wished.[17]

Benton elevated the pair's simmering hostility in a blistering speech delivered in Jefferson City, Missouri, on May 26, 1849. He excoriated Calhoun's rabidly proslavery positions as both self-serving and dangerous to the integrity of the Union. Among the criticisms Benton heaped upon Calhoun, he accused the South Carolina senator of having "abandoned the south" for the sake of boosting his presidential aspirations. According to Benton, Calhoun's choices "left me and a few others alone, by the side of the ill-fated owners of the Comet, Encomium, Creole, Enterprise, and others." Although the allegation was vague, the public understood Benton as denouncing Calhoun's support for the Webster-Ashburton Treaty of 1842, which had failed to grapple directly with the issue of U.S. domestic slavers in distress on the high seas.[18]

Recall that Benton voted against the treaty because it offered "no indemnity or redress of any kind" for the enslaved property aboard the *Enterprise*, *Hermosa*, or *Creole*, nor any "atonement to our insulted sovereignty." Failing to address those cases seemed to Benton "an invitation to the commission of new [outrages]." Already in 1842 he claimed that "the sympathies of half the Union and all the world" were arrayed against the South and "her slave property." It was inexcusable for a true Southerner to support a treaty that left the region's slave owners unreimbursed and still vulnerable to violation.[19]

Calhoun issued a reply on July 5 that deftly repelled Benton's attack on him. He not only admitted voting for the treaty but also boasted that, in doing so, he "rendered . . . [a] great and permanent service to the country" because the agreement averted a possible war with Great Britain. Calhoun acknowledged that "the treaty contained no stipulation in favor of the owners of the vessels" or any provisions "to prevent similar outrages," but Lord Ashburton did make an informal pledge outside the treaty to avoid "officious interference with American vessels driven by accident or violence into their ports." That commitment to execute British colonial laws "with careful attention" to Southern slaveholding interests promised to "maintain good neighborhood" in the Atlantic.[20]

Calhoun also pointed out that he had already persuaded the Senate to adopt his three resolutions in 1840 "to perpetuate our claim of right" to indemnity for the uncompensated losses from the *Enterprise*, *Hermosa*, and *Creole*. As he saw it, his efforts worked to assert principles that the "feeble and tame negotiation" that had secured restitution only for the *Comet* and the *Encomium* had not. The Van Buren administration "shamefully" acquiesced to the British position, but Calhoun refused to follow suit. Benton voted in favor of the three resolutions but "never uttered a word in their support," Calhoun observed.[21]

Benton's attempt to smear Calhoun over the Webster-Ashburton Treaty backfired. Editorials to the Democratic *Richmond Enquirer* and other Southern newspapers detected contradiction, inconsistency, and duplicity in the Missouri senator's Jefferson City speech. Benton insisted that U.S. slaveholders maintained their right to enslaved property "upon the high seas" and "even within the dominions of a foreign power" but declared that "Congress has the power to legislate upon slavery in [the] territories, and permit or prohibit its existence." Benton's preference for restricting slavery from the territories, wrote one anonymous editorialist, "is directly at war with the position which he maintained in the cases of 'the Comet, Encomium, Creole, Enterprise and others.'" Yet it was consistent with Benton's assertion "that slavery is local in its character, . . . enacted by law," and unable to extend "an inch beyond the limits of the State that enacted it."[22]

Calhoun disagreed. He saw "no distinction" between enslaved property and any other form of property and denied that Congress held the constitutional authority to limit slavery's expansion. He appeared to many Southern whites the truer defender of slave-owner rights. In contrast, Benton emerged in the proslavery press as a "traitor" to Southern principles, uniting with Northerners "in their schemes to exclude" slaveholders from the territories. A moderate Unionist in a radicalizing South, Benton had grown out of touch with his constituents and had become vulnerable to charges of the "dangerous heresy" of Free Soilism "and treachery to the South." Missouri slave owners forced a resolution through the state legislature requiring their senators to follow Calhoun's political lead, and lawmakers in Jefferson City opted not to return Benton to the Senate for a sixth term.[23]

More than any slave-state politician, Northern abolitionists kept the memory of the *Comet*, *Encomium*, *Enterprise*, and *Hermosa* alive in the years after Britain made restitution for the enslaved people liberated from two of the slave ships. Rep. Joshua Giddings of Ohio made the voyages a recurring theme as he railed against slavery in speeches both inside the House chamber and in other venues across the Northern states. Additional appeals to Congress for reimbursement for enslaved people stripped from their owners within U.S. territorial boundaries lent ample opportunity for Giddings to revisit the cases of the distressed vessels.[24]

In the late 1840s, a case brought by the heirs of Antonio Pacheco consumed hours of debate in the U.S. House. Its origins dated to 1835. During the Second Seminole War, the U.S. Army hired an enslaved man in Florida named Lewis, the property of the Pacheco family, "as an interpreter or guide" for troops under the command of Maj. Francis L. Dade. Lewis possessed "remarkable intelligence," with an ability to speak four languages, including Seminole. He was accompanying Dade's forces on a march from Fort Brooke to augment U.S. numbers at Fort King when Seminoles ambushed them, leaving few alive. Lewis survived the massacre and was either captured by his attackers, with whom he could converse, or took the opportunity to flee to them. He lived with the Indigenous Floridians for a year and a half, until Chief Jumper, who claimed Lewis as a spoil of battle and his slave, surrendered to Gen. Thomas Jesup in 1837.[25]

As soon as the Pacheco family learned of Lewis's reappearance, they demanded that U.S. officers return their hired slave to them. Gen. Jesup refused. He claimed that Lewis was "a dangerous man" and suspected that he had secretly allied with the Natives, betrayed Dade's forces, and then spent his time with the Seminoles participating "in their depredations against the white people" living in Florida's "frontier settlements." According to Jesup's conjectures, the enslaved Lewis, "with a knowledge of the wrongs which he and his people had suffered at the hands of those who claimed them as *property*, . . . must have thirsted for vengeance." He therefore allegedly fraternized with the "enemy," "murdered the people of Florida, and destroyed their property." Jesup stated that he would have preferred to have hanged the Pachecos' bondman, but he did not have the time. Still, he was convinced that Lewis posed a genuine threat to U.S. military forces. "The negro was an intriguing, treacherous, dangerous person," Jesup insisted: "a bad subject, an ugly fellow, a troublesome neighbor, [and] a plotting rogue" who could easily "be employed against our troops." To prevent him from causing further problems, the general ordered the "extraordinary" captive "to be removed" with the Seminoles "to the land reserved for them in the West." Jesup deemed the expulsion of Lewis from Florida to Indian Territory a "public good."[26]

Antonio Pacheco's heirs spent the decade of the 1840s seeking indemnity from the U.S. government for the loss of the multilingual enslaved man. They claimed that Jesup had acted irresponsibly and unlawfully in banishing their property to the West, so restitution was merited. Their repeated efforts made little headway until late 1848 and early 1849, when the House of Representatives approved a $1,000 payment to the Pacheco family.[27]

Joshua Giddings voted against the indemnity for Lewis, and the House debate over Pacheco's claim afforded him the opportunity to catalog the

U.S. government's long history of not compensating slaveholders for their losses. In the late 1820s, the House debated a pair of cases dating back to the War of 1812. Francis Larche sought reimbursement for a cart, horse, and an enslaved man named Antoine, all impressed into service by the U.S. government. The cart was destroyed, the horse died, and Antoine "was killed at the battle of New Orleans." Congress paid Larche for the cart and horse but not for the bondman. In a similar case, Marigny D'Auterive claimed compensation "for a negro man who was pressed into the public service in 1812, at New Orleans." Though not killed, the bondman was wounded and incurred medical bills for his master, who was denied the man's labor for a time. The Committee on Claims, which included three members from slaveholding states, unanimously rejected D'Auterive's petition, stating that the enslaved were not property and therefore not eligible for restitution payments. The House also rejected another bill in 1843, for approximately ninety enslaved people taken by Andrew Jackson in West Florida in 1814 against their owners' consent. The operating principle, as Giddings discerned it, was clear: that "there was no property in slaves."[28]

The rule did not always hold, though. In April 1842, the House of Representatives "slipped through" $21,604 in compensation "for the benefit of James C. Watson, of Georgia." Watson had paid "certain Creek warriors for slaves captured by them in the service of the United States." Gen. Jesup had made an agreement with his Indigenous, Muscogee allies to pay a bounty for Black people taken in war who had been held by "the Seminole Indians in Florida." The large sum handed over to Watson represented the Georgian's actual purchase costs, plus interest and "expenses incurred by him in endeavoring to obtain possession of said slaves." It took a clever maneuver to make compensation possible. Petitions requesting compensation for the enslaved were steered to the Committee on Claims, which Joshua Giddings chaired in early 1842. Knowing that committee's history of hostility to such memorials, supporters of Watson's claim managed to transfer his case to the Committee on Indian Affairs, circumventing the Ohio abolitionist's guaranteed objection.[29]

After being bypassed in the Watson case, Giddings was censured in March 1842, prompting his resignation from Congress and his replacement on the Committee on Claims. Within a matter of days, that same committee gave a favorable early report on the case of the Pachecos' enslaved man Lewis. Years later, long after Giddings's return to the House, the Ohio congressman still argued during the debate over the Pacheco family's claim for indemnification that "slaves had never been recognized as property, and never paid for as such by Congress, except in one solitary case"—that of James C. Watson.[30]

The *Comet* and the *Encomium* did not enter into Giddings's calculations. In those instances, restitution to slave traders and slave owners derived from "moneys that did not belong to [the United States]," he explained. "These cases were not to take the treasure of the people of the free States to pay for slaves." The funds that were distributed came from the British Crown. The U.S. Treasury merely held it in trust for those to whom it was owed. Indemnification for enslaved people seized from the *Comet* and *Encomium* therefore set no binding precedent.[31]

By the time the House debated compensation for Lewis in 1848 and 1849, the nation's politics had grown more sectionally polarized. Nearly two decades earlier, Northern and Southern members of the Committee on Claims could agree that Marigny D'Auterive did not deserve payment because the government only provided reimbursement for lost or damaged property, a designation that excluded the enslaved. The five slaveholding congressmen who composed the majority on the Committee on Military Affairs in the late 1840s took the opposite view. They saw Lewis as property and believed the U.S. government obligated to reimburse his owner's heirs. Giddings and the other Northern members of the committee maintained that they remained faithful to precedent in treating the enslaved interpreter and guide as a person for whom no money was owed. Giddings's historical arguments notwithstanding, the bill passed the House and moved on to the Senate, where it stalled out and failed to gain approval.[32]

While the owners of Lewis as well as the owners of the enslaved people liberated from the *Enterprise*, *Hermosa*, and *Creole* went uncompensated, they probably read about another high-profile case in which an enslaver did receive payment, albeit not from Congress. In the autumn of 1852, Jonathan and Juliet Lemmon departed Bath County, Virginia, with their seven children on a journey to a new home in Texas. Eight captive laborers joined them in a compulsory migration: two women in their early twenties, a young man of sixteen or seventeen, and five younger children, none of them named in news reports. Unwilling to wait several weeks for a vessel to carry the group directly to New Orleans, the Lemmons and all those under their charge instead booked passage on the steamer *City of Richmond*, bound for New York City. Once in the harbor, Jonathan Lemmon went ashore and arranged for transport to New Orleans. The steamer *Memphis* would ship out the following morning.[33]

Lemmon did not anticipate the trouble he encountered conveying his enslaved property through the Northern port. When he returned to the *City of Richmond* to transfer his family and the eight bondpeople in a horse-drawn carriage to the *Memphis*, the hack drivers carried them, over the Lemmons' protests, to a house on Carlisle Street, dropped everyone off, and sped away. Abandoned in an unfamiliar city, they spent the night there and missed the outbound steamer the next morning. Worse still for Jonathan and Juliet, New York City abolitionists, armed with a writ of habeas corpus, seized the enslaved people to carry before Judge Elijah Payne of the New York Superior Court in an attempt to gain their freedom. The Lemmons had fallen victim to either an elaborate abolitionist scheme or last-minute abolitionist interference in their plan to resume their travels.[34]

The wresting away of the bondpeople by the abolitionists devastated Jonathan and Juliet Lemmon financially. In his early forties, Jonathan had owned less than $1,000 worth of real estate in Bath County, where he was surrounded by neighbors who were much better off. Newspaper reports used visual cues to judge the couple and commented on their apparent lack of wealth, despite owning bondpeople. Jonathan's "dress and appearance bespeak him to be a man who has been and still is struggling with poverty," wrote one paper. "Mr. Lemmon, when informed of the possible if not probable loss of his slaves, cried like a child." He was unable to accept the prospect of "utter destitution which their being set at liberty must bring."[35]

Compared with her husband, Juliet Lemmon bore "in her dress the same marks of comparative poverty"; however, her manners were in "every way lady-like," and only a lack of "fashionable attire" prevented her from being "considered a splendid woman." The press correctly detected that Juliet had brought the bondpeople to the marriage, as an inheritance from her well-to-do father. When the enslaved people entered Judge Payne's courtroom, she made a heartfelt, personal appeal to them, begging that they remember how well she believed she had treated them. "One of the colored women was so affected by the address of her mistress," newspapers reported, "that the tears rolled down her cheeks, and the other colored woman commenced making a reply" until an abolitionist instructed her "to make no answer."[36]

In November 1852, Judge Payne handed down a ruling greeted by Southern slaveholders as an outrageous violation of their constitutional rights. He ordered that the Lemmons' enslaved people be discharged. Following the precedent set by the English *Somerset* decision of 1772, Payne observed that slavery could exist only by force of local law. Slavery had been abolished in New York since 1827, and since "by law of nature no one can have property in slaves, no one has a right to take slaves through a country where slavery does not exist." If the Lemmons had wished to transport their captives, Payne explained, they should have avoided passing through a free state. Moreover, since their bondpeople were not runaways seeking freedom, the court was not obligated to enforce the provisions of the latest Fugitive Slave Act, passed in 1850. The bondpeople were now free.[37]

The *New York Journal of Commerce*, the voice of the business community, betrayed alarm at the possibility of lost shipping traffic should enslaved people not be allowed to pass through the city's port unmolested while in transit south. The newspaper called upon the New York state legislature to compensate the Lemmons for the property "stripped" and "robbed" from them, valued at $5,000 for the eight captives. Until that money could be appropriated, the paper urged a voluntary subscription for the same amount to indemnify the Virginia slave owners. Support for the idea was widespread. Pledges poured into the fund from New York City merchants and other "responsible citizens," including the Lemmons' attorney, Henry D. Lapaugh, and Judge Payne himself. Soon, contributions of "*Lemmon aid*," as one newspaper dubbed it, exceeded the $5,000 goal. Restored the full value of the enslaved property taken from his family and spared from economic catastrophe, Jonathan Lemmon guaranteed to free the bondpeople should legal appeals later reverse Judge Payne's decision and determine that they should have remained in the Lemmons' possession. To formally manumit them at once, however, would end the appeals process and prevent the rendering of a final verdict on the principles of the case. Regardless of the ultimate outcome, by Christmas 1852, the Lemmons' former slaves were living in freedom in Canada.[38]

Of greater interest to many white observers in the North as well as in the South was the fact of Lemmon receiving payment. "A CITIZEN OF PENNSYLVANIA" praised "the noble and generous conduct of those patriotic citizens of New York" whose donations compensated the Lemmons the value of their enslaved people. Importantly, the U.S. Congress had "nothing to do with" supplying them restitution, he added, "but Congress must inevitably know of the judicial decision under which the wrong was inflicted." The anonymous Pennsylvanian argued that it was ultimately Congress's duty to award indemnities as "atonement for such a high-handed judicial outrage upon all the solemn guarantees and compromises of the constitution and the Union": "it should be for Congress to wipe it out."[39]

The Pennsylvania citizen then turned to the history of U.S. slave ships wrecked in Great Britain's "West India islands." In each instance, enslaved people "were being conveyed . . . by their owners from one port in the United States to another." After British authorities confiscated the captives aboard the *Comet* and *Encomium*, the Crown paid compensation. The examples struck the Pennsylvanian as "appropriate" and relevant to cases like the Lemmons': "Shall our own great nation be less just to her own citizens than a foreign nation?" he asked. He ended with a resounding call that "Congress hasten to reimburse the citizen whose property has been torn from him in violation of the constitution and laws of the United States, no matter whether by national or State authority."[40]

In March 1850, Jonathan and Juliet Lemmon's senator, Virginia's R.M.T. Hunter, took stock of the slaving vessels "unavoidably forced into the British islands, where the negroes were liberated." When the British refused compensation in the cases of the *Enterprise* and *Hermosa* and "did not admit the right of property in slaves" after abolition in the West Indies, Hunter alleged that the Crown "indirectly held out a strong temptation to negroes carried along our coast to rise upon the crew." The mutiny aboard the *Creole* illustrated the danger. John C. Calhoun's Senate resolutions asserted that ownership rights to the enslaved "followed the flag" onto the ocean, yet the Webster-Ashburton Treaty offered no formal promise to indemnify slave owners or to preserve the sanctity of U.S. slave shipping; rather, it gave "a mere assurance from Lord Ashburton that he would recommend the authorities in the British West India islands not to repeat the offense." The lack of similar incidents after 1841 was notable, Hunter observed, "but whether this proceeded from the want of opportunity or the want of disposition, I know not." Regardless, he concluded, "wrongs are unredressed."[41]

The damage had already been done. Enslaved people, particularly along the coastal South, understood that nearby British colonies held forth the inducement of freedom. Not one but multiple voyages of the coastwise domestic slave trade had exposed the possibility. The lure of the islands tempted a few enslaved laborers to concoct plans to somehow make their way to the Bahamas. During his residence in the Florida Territory from 1836 to 1842, Capt. Jonathan Walker of Massachusetts hired seven enslaved men to work for him. He treated them as he would white laborers in the

North, earning "the confidence and good will of the slaves." When Walker visited Pensacola again in June 1844, the bondmen asked their former employer to conduct them by water to Nassau. Walker assented, but his vessel was intercepted in July. He was jailed in Key West, remanded to prison in Pensacola, and tried and convicted of the crime of slave stealing. For his offense, Walker stood in the pillory for an hour, had the palm of his right hand branded with an "s.s.," and spent nearly a year in jail, until friends paid his fines and court costs. The seven unidentified bondmen's dreams of liberty in the Bahamas were dashed.[42]

With news reports like these, combined with the regular resurfacing of the American slave ships robbed of their human cargoes in the political discussions of the era, the issue of compensation never strayed from the public's attention. But with Congress hesitant to use public funds, any payments for enslaved people aboard the *Enterprise*, *Hermosa*, or *Creole* would require further diplomatic efforts.

Conclusion

By 1853, several insurers remained unreimbursed for payouts issued to policyholders for enslaved cargoes freed by British colonial authorities. The Charleston Fire and Marine Insurance Company and the Augusta Insurance and Banking Company still agitated for payments from the *Enterprise*'s voyage of 1835, and the New Orleans Insurance Company and the Louisiana State Marine and Fire Insurance Company awaited compensation for enslaved people liberated from the 1840 shipwreck of the *Hermosa*. Further outstanding claims derived from the 1841 slave revolt aboard the *Creole*.[1]

These calls for monetary relief joined a host of additional U.S. claims against Great Britain for assorted other alleged injustices, some more valid than others. The preponderance of the forty American complaints related to various maritime disputes. In turn, the Crown registered almost twice the number of protests against the United States. Altogether, more than one hundred points of contention, some of them simmering for decades and collectively totaling in excess of $1 million, set the two countries at loggerheads.[2]

The accumulated incidents reached a critical mass by 1853. On February 8, both nations agreed to a commission tasked with the adjustment of all unsettled disputes dating back to their signing of the Treaty of Ghent in December 1814. "It was an excellent idea," wrote the *New York Tribune*, "both as regards the friendly relations of the two countries and the interests of the individuals concerned, to bring all these controversies to a final settlement, and thus to remove what in case of future collisions might . . . inflame angry feelings between the two nations." Whatever the outcome of the upcoming deliberations, all decisions would be binding. Dealing with specific incidents rather than broad principles, the commission would not settle the issue of whether the United States or Great Britain maintained the correct interpretation of the law of nations. On that score, the two countries agreed to disagree.[3]

Each side appointed an agent to submit claims on behalf of his respective government. Gen. John A. Thomas of New York advanced the U.S. claims for redress; James Hannen, a London-born judge, presented those for the British. A pair of commissioners—fifty-two-year-old judge Nathaniel G. Upham for the United States and up-and-coming lawyer Edmund Hornby for Great Britain—examined each case and hashed out resolutions to those disagreements. The two commissioners first met in London on September 15, 1853, to begin their work on a full slate of contentious topics.[4]

Over the course of their negotiations, they dismissed many of the 115 disputes presented to them as outside their purview. Other issues Upham and Hornby assessed as so thorny that it would be impossible for them to agree on a decision. In mid-October, they invited former diplomat and U.S. president Martin Van Buren to serve as an impartial "umpire" to arbitrate the most difficult cases. Though flattered by the offer, Van Buren had retired from public affairs and declined the opportunity.[5]

Upham and Hornby then identified Joshua Bates as a perfect candidate. Although an American by birth, the Massachusetts native had pursued a career in London as a merchant, banker, and senior partner in Baring Brothers & Company, the world's greatest financial house. Familiar with business in both the United States and Great Britain and well respected on both sides of the Atlantic, Bates also appeared safe on the slavery issue. Although several of his nieces in New England, most notably Maria Weston Chapman, were active in U.S. abolitionist circles, Bates himself had "negotiated a loan to provide funds to compensate slave owners in the British West Indies" upon emancipation in that portion of the empire. His British employer boasted a fortune derived in no small measure from the slave trade, and the London banking firm continued to underwrite and profit from the expansion of the United States' slave-based economy. No one could accuse Bates of sharing in his extended family's abolitionism or could dispute his unparalleled knowledge and expertise in international finance. "Mr. Bates, of London, was selected as umpire," stated one report to the U.S. Senate, noting that "his labors [were] arduous, and his responsibility great."[6]

The U.S. agent, Gen. John A. Thomas, submitted dozens of American claims on March 14, 1854, including those for the *Enterprise*, *Hermosa*, and

Creole. A hearing on the *Enterprise* and *Hermosa* began on May 23 and lasted into the following day. Thomas made the case that Great Britain's violation of the law of nations entitled the United States to damages, while agent James Hannen explained the British denial of the claims. On May 24, the *Enterprise*'s "case was submitted for the decision of the commissioners." One additional day of discussion on the *Hermosa* took place on May 26. Gen. Thomas submitted additional paperwork in both cases nearly a month later, by which time the evidence on the *Creole* had also been heard. On September 26, commissioners Upham and Hornby concluded that they could not agree on any of the three claims and ordered them "committed to the decision of the umpire."[7]

Joshua Bates heard the cases on Thursday, October 19, and Saturday, October 21. The central question at stake concerned which country maintained legal jurisdiction over distressed slave ships forced into the Atlantic ports of another nation. Because the *Enterprise*, *Hermosa*, and *Creole* cases all "involve[d] substantially the same principles, and were embraced in one argument by counsel, and submitted together," for simplicity's sake the U.S. and British commissioners "drew up their opinions in full" regarding just the *Enterprise*, for presentation to the umpire, "without . . . further expression of their opinions" in the other two incidents.[8]

Commissioner Upham pressed the American claim by laying out the basic premises that all nations were equal with one another, that they must make their own laws "without the interference of any other power," and that they all enjoyed "the free right to navigate the ocean." Upham then employed John C. Calhoun's principles as outlined in his Senate resolutions from 1840 as the foundation for U.S. calls for compensation. Any "vessel on the high seas, in time of peace, engaged in a lawful voyage," remained, by the law of nations, "under the exclusive jurisdiction of the State" under whose flag it sailed, and if it was "forced, by stress of weather or other unavoidable circumstance, into the port of a friendly power," the rights of that state over the vessel, cargo, or the "personal relations of those on board" were in no way diminished. Under this reading of international law, Great Britain's abolition of slavery in the West Indies exerted no bearing on the status of the captives onboard U.S. slave ships.[9]

Upham elaborated on the framework he outlined in a succinct statement before the umpire. He acknowledged that if the U.S. vessels had entered British ports voluntarily, the Crown's refusal to pay would have made sense. As it was, Britain's failure to provide compensation was based on a change in British law. Upham questioned whether the Slavery Abolition Act of 1833 truly changed the lived reality for its enslaved subjects in the West Indies. As far as Upham could discern, the prolonged system of apprenticeship originally imposed by the law closely resembled slavery in its character; apprentices could still be bought and sold or used to pay off debts. Moreover, Upham indicated, the emancipation law granted compensation to British slave owners, which suggested that U.S. enslavers and insurers similarly deprived of their property should also be reimbursed. The British government had in fact admitted "the high injustice of seizing all property" from foreign vessels forced into its colonial ports, "except property in slaves." That the Crown had granted reparation in the cases of the *Comet* and *Encomium* seemed to Upham to validate the U.S. position. He conceded that the institution of slavery in the United States may be of "doubtful morality or justice," but it was nevertheless lawful.[10]

British commissioner Edmund Hornby opened his arguments by agreeing with the general principle that vessels like the *Enterprise*, "driven by stress of weather into a foreign port," were not subject to "the application of . . . local laws" since they did not arrive voluntarily. But he soon began to parse the law more closely: "While the vessel is . . . free from the operation of the local laws, it by no means follows that it is entitled to absolute exemption from the local jurisdiction." Passengers, for instance, were not free to commit crimes in foreign lands. They would appear in court to answer for alleged offenses because, as Hornby contended, "within the territories of a country the local tribunals are paramount, and have the right . . . to inquire into the legality" of acts committed within their jurisdiction. The law of nations, as Hornby explained it, bestowed "immunity from the operation of the local laws for some purposes, but not for all."[11]

The British commissioner outlined an interpretation of comity at variance with that of the United States. According to Hornby, laws did not automatically have force outside the country in which they were passed. Another nation might allow those laws to function within its territory, but not necessarily. Sovereign nations were free to judge foreign statutes for themselves and were not obligated to respect them within their territorial holdings. "No nation," Hornby declared, "can be called upon . . . to permit the operation of foreign laws within its territory when those laws are contrary to its interests or its moral sentiments."[12]

More than any other issue, slavery exposed the stark difference between British and U.S. understandings of international law. By virtue of the

Enterprise's unexpected detour to Bermuda, Hornby explained, the "operation of natural law and of English law" had granted the enslaved cargo "a character denied it by American law." British law did not recognize "that slaves are property in the ordinary sense of the word," and as Hornby told it, no "rule of international law" or principles of comity could compel the Crown to respect "the relation of master and slave" authorized by a foreign government. The logic of the British position demanded the rejection of slave-owner claims for indemnity.[13]

The final determination rested with umpire Joshua Bates. On December 23, just over two months after Upham and Hornby argued the case of the *Enterprise*, and presumably after intensive study of relevant records, Bates shared his decision. In passing judgment, he noted that the brig was participating in a domestic slave trading voyage legal under U.S. law, that it was in "distress," and that Capt. Elliot Smith had studiously avoided landing the enslaved merchandise or otherwise violating British municipal laws. In a comment that must have given a glimmer of hope to his abolitionist nieces, the umpire observed "that slavery is contrary to the principles of justice and humanity." But he immediately pivoted, pointing out that any country could establish slavery by law and that slavery persisted within portions of the British Empire. "It could not, then, be contrary to the law of nations," Bates concluded, "and the *Enterprize* was as much entitled to protection as though her cargo consisted of any other description of property."[14]

Finding the colonial authorities of Bermuda in violation of international law as well as the "laws of hospitality" through which vessels in distress could enter friendly ports, the umpire issued a verdict welcomed by U.S. insurers. Bates awarded the Charleston Fire and Marine Insurance Company $33,000 and the Augusta Insurance and Banking Company $16,000 to reimburse them for the losses they suffered, for a combined total of $49,000 (almost $1.6 million today). The umpire directed the Crown to pay by January 15, 1855, nearly twenty years to the day since George Hammett and seventy-seven other enslaved captives boarded Capt. Smith's ship.[15]

Bates did not issue his ruling on the *Hermosa* until Thursday, January 11, 1855. After the wreck of that schooner in the Bahamas, Richmond slave trader Henry N. Templeman had collected on policies underwritten by the New Orleans Insurance Company and the Louisiana State Marine and Fire Insurance Company. Both businesses hoped for an outcome from the umpire as favorable to them as the one the *Enterprise* insurers had received. Judging the circumstances leading to the loss of the enslaved cargo from the *Hermosa* virtually identical, Bates granted each of the *Hermosa*'s New Orleans–based insurers $8,000 in compensation. Given that the individual insurance policies were valued at $13,850, the two company presidents were surely disappointed with the result, even though it helped them recover some monies long since lost. Bates's decision on the *Hermosa* was stingier because the umpire made "allowance . . . for a reasonable salvage to the wreckers" who saved the passengers, crew, and cargo. As with the *Enterprise* verdict, Bates imposed the same January 15 deadline for the British government to pay, giving the Crown just four days to comply.[16]

Of the three U.S. claims for enslaved cargoes liberated from domestic slave ships, Bates issued his most generous judgment in the case of the *Creole*. On January 9, he awarded a total of $110,330 to the owners of the mutinous captives inspired by the *Hermosa* to emancipate themselves. Having sided with the American claimants in all three cases of the U.S. domestic slavers, the umpire from the House of Baring emerged as a champion of Southern slaveholding interests. "The arbitrator" took "the general ground . . . that a vessel navigating the ocean carries her own laws with her, so far as relates to the persons and property on board," reported the *New York Tribune*. "On the whole, Mr. Umpire Bates has done very well by the slaveholders and slave-traders."[17]

Bates's responsibilities drew to a close as the Claims Commission concluded its labors on January 15. Altogether, after sixteen months of negotiations, some $600,000, or about $22 million today, exchanged hands between the U.S. and British governments, with a majority of those monies awarded to American claimants. More than half the funds involved in these transactions stemmed from cases originating in either the unlawful international slave trade or the coastwise domestic slave trade still legal by U.S. statute. Owners and insurers of human merchandise aboard the *Enterprise*, *Hermosa*, and *Creole* collected a total of $175,330, well over one-quarter of all funds transferred between the two countries as a result of the deliberations. All adjustments made by the Claims Commission were final.[18]

Newspapers across the United States printed the outcomes of the commission's efforts in late January and early February 1855. Most offered straightforward, objective reporting of cases and amounts awarded to various claimants. In Southern port cities, more editorializing accompanied publication of the results. Pleased with the $49,000 allotted the insurers for the lost cargo aboard the *Enterprise*, the *Charleston (SC) Courier* declared, "We sincerely congratulate all concerned upon the result, as it is a tardy recognition of a great principle, of international law, which the British Government have long violated with impunity." Newspapers in Richmond, port of departure for the *Hermosa* and *Creole* voyages, concurred. "The judgement of the commission is a just one, and in an international point of view highly important and gratifying." Although in actuality, Great Britain did not concede any principle of international law, with remuneration for lost slaves secured after delays of as long as twenty years, the Southern press could still trumpet a practical final triumph of slaveholding diplomacy and the coastwise domestic slave trade's dominion over Atlantic waters.[19]

William Lloyd Garrison, publisher of the abolitionist newspaper *The Liberator*, pronounced compensation to slave owners an absurd, "highly reprehensible" act as early as the 1830s. At a national antislavery convention held in Philadelphia in 1833, he declared, "If compensation is to be given at all, it should be given to the outraged and guiltless slaves, and not to those who have plundered and abused them." His disgust was equally evident in 1837, when the first news of British willingness to pay restitution for the *Comet* and *Encomium* reached U.S. shores.[20]

Garrison discerned an important lesson from the impending payments for the slave ships' living cargoes: that slavery was not merely a Southern institution but a national one. The passage of several gradual emancipation laws by state legislatures in the North meant that only around 1,100 of the nation's 2.5 million enslaved people in 1840 still resided in Northern states. Practically all of the enslaved toiled in the South. Nevertheless, Garrison recognized the entire nation's complicity in their suffering. As the initial pursuit of reparation for captives taken off the slave ships revealed to the exasperated abolitionist, "the *American government* has been endeavoring . . . to obtain their market value in silver, for the benefit of southern planters!" It was rightfully a source of shame, he declared, and worthy of "shouts of derision at such a spectacle."[21]

Garrison had a point. Throughout the dramas of the *Comet*, *Encomium*, *Enterprise*, *Hermosa*, and *Creole*, the default position of the U.S. government privileged slavery over freedom, enslavers over the enslaved. The collective force and tireless efforts of the diplomatic corps served the Southern slaveholding interest. Northern-born government agents such as Martin Van

Buren did their occupational duty by participating in the process of securing recompense. Well before he ran as a Free Soil candidate for president, Van Buren spent years stitching together a national Democratic Party coalition that crossed the dividing lines of slaveholding and section. His diplomatic efforts with the Crown reflected a similar willingness to sacrifice for politics' sake the antislavery principles he later more fully embraced. As secretary of state, New Englander Daniel Webster, too, felt obligated to press the cause of the United States' domestic slave trade, to embrace John C. Calhoun's *Enterprise* resolutions, and to pursue compensation. "It was a great victory for the Slave Power," abolitionist Joshua Giddings later remarked. The Ohio congressman consistently condemned the involvement of "the people of the free States in the expense, disgrace, and crimes of the slave-trade" and the use of "our national influence to support" it.[22]

Giddings, who immersed himself as much as anyone in the history of the slave ships whose cargoes were liberated in the British Atlantic, blamed Andrew Jackson first and foremost for the U.S. government's misguided actions. For more than a decade, Giddings, both in the House chamber and outside of it, excoriated the former president. Beginning with the *Comet*, he recounted the same basic version of events and riled up audiences in a talk that by 1858 evolved into his American Piracy speech. After the seizures of the enslaved cargoes, "these slaveholders, these dealers in the bodies of women, these traffickers in children called upon—whom?" Giddings egged on crowds. President Jackson! "The slave merchants," the abolitionist continued, "demanded that the character and influence of the nation should be prostituted to aid them in obtaining a compensation for their loss from the government of England," and Jackson did not hesitate to issue the orders they craved. The slave traders, "chagrined and mortified" at the loss of their human merchandise, found "Executive favor" in "the President, himself a slaveholder, involved in all the moral turpitude of these hucksterers in our common humanity," who "at once espoused their cause" and "demand[ed] compensation from the people of England for permitting their African brethren . . . to enjoy their God given prerogatives."[23]

The Ohio abolitionist reserved further venom for slave-owning U.S. minister Andrew Stevenson, whom he charged with lying and deceit in his negotiations with England. Stevenson had denied any "distinction in principle between property in persons and property in things" in his talks with Lord Palmerston and had communicated to Great Britain that, historically, the U.S. government had compensated slave owners for losses of the enslaved because they were "regarded as property, and not as persons." Giddings's deep dives into decades of congressional records had proven Stevenson's assertions "deceptive and fraudulent," and he invited his critics to fact-check him. "The money thus extorted by fraud and misrepresentation," Giddings declared, "disgraced the government" of the United States. Only through Stevenson's "flagrant falsehood" did the U.S. Treasury obtain reparation and, Giddings added facetiously, "render American piracy honorable." The arresting disjuncture of the Claims Commission granting compensation to slave owners prompted him to wonder aloud how the umpire could have granted "full indemnity to these men, so richly deserving the gallows."[24]

With the exception of Giddings's repeated retellings, the stories of the *Comet*, *Encomium*, *Enterprise*, and *Hermosa* largely disappeared from public discussion in the years immediately before the Civil War. One reason was that none of the four voyages contributed directly or indirectly to the onset of armed conflict. They did, however, offer a noteworthy point of comparison as the United States grappled with the fate of slavery in its own western territories. Through his *Enterprise* resolutions of 1840, John C. Calhoun had taken the lead in championing the idea that slaveholders' property rights accompanied them out onto the open ocean and when forced involuntarily into foreign ports. He asserted the same essential position domestically. According to Calhoun's interpretation of the Constitution, Congress was prevented from lawfully restricting slavery from U.S. territories. The South Carolina senator argued that any attempt to prohibit slave owners from migrating to a western territory with their bondpeople in tow violated the Fifth Amendment's due process clause. His position marked yet another statement of the extraterritoriality of slave owners' rights to enslaved property. Seven years after the senator's death, the U.S. Supreme Court validated Calhoun's view in its infamous *Dred Scott v. Sandford* decision.

The consistency of Calhoun's unwavering commitment to slaveholding interests across different contexts earned him Southern slave owners' undying admiration. Ten years after Calhoun's death, a clear majority of Southern voters in the presidential election of 1860 looked for someone with similarly unblemished proslavery credentials. Few had such confidence in the candidacy of Democrat Stephen Douglas of Illinois. One of four candidates running for the nation's highest office, Douglas had long promoted the principle of popular sovereignty—or "squatter sovereignty," as it was sometimes dubbed—as the preferred solution for dealing with slavery in the territories. Douglas kept the decision to allow or disallow slavery in the territories out of Congress's hands and instead invested it in the voters of the territory itself, insisting that slavery could only exist where authorized by law.[25]

The mass of proslavery voters in the South rejected Douglas and refused "to swallow his doctrine." The case of the *Enterprise* offered a parallel case from the high seas that informed their judgment because it "show[ed] what the great men of the past generation thought about this matter." The slave owners affected by the loss of enslaved people emancipated in Bermuda in 1835 had "applied to the British Government for remuneration" but were refused on grounds suspiciously similar to Douglas's principle of popular sovereignty—"that slavery was the creature of local law." With "no local law in Bermuda Island authorizing or protecting slavery," the captives aboard the *Enterprise* went free. "What becomes now of Squatter Sovereignty?" mocked Douglas's Southern detractors. They dismissed Douglas's position as "heresy . . . in direct contradiction to the true Democratic doctrine," enunciated years earlier by Calhoun, "that the Federal Government was formed . . . for the protection of our property of all sorts." Their preferred candidate was the sitting vice president and reliably proslavery candidate John C. Breckinridge of Kentucky.[26]

A second reason for the retreat of the *Comet*, *Encomium*, *Enterprise*, and *Hermosa* from the pre–Civil War headlines was that all four cases were decided in the South's favor. None of the voyages merited further complaint. That fact, however, did not stop proslavery writer, minister, and college president Augustus B. Longstreet from mentioning the *Enterprise* in an editorial he penned in December 1860 promoting Southern secession. "The southern States should leave the Union," Longstreet declared, "because it costs them infinitely more than it is worth." The Union "has been but a torment and bloodsucker for forty years," with "nothing . . . to endear it to the people of the South." Longstreet grumbled about the seemingly annual stories of Southern "tourist[s] in the northern States," whose enslaved people were seized "and set free." Inexplicably, he also groused about the liberation of enslaved people from the *Enterprise*, even though he admitted in his letter that the U.S. government demanded and received "reparation . . . for the injury done to the owner."[27]

Five days after the publication of Longstreet's letter, South Carolina became the first state to exit the Union. The timing was purely coincidental. What secession and the Longstreet letter had in common, though, was an unwarranted sense of persecution and shared Southern white grievance. If slave owners occasionally lost enslaved people to freedom in the North, as Longstreet emphasized, the Fugitive Slave Act of 1850 assured that federal commissioners remanded hundreds of alleged fugitives to the South in the decade before the Civil War. On the subject of slave owners' property rights aboard domestic slave-trading vessels like the *Enterprise*, Longstreet could assert no legitimate complaint at all. For decades, concluding with the Claims Commission's rulings in 1854 and 1855, the federal government had undertaken extensive international efforts to, in Joshua Giddings's words, "compensate the oppressor."[28]

The owners of captives aboard the *Comet*, *Encomium*, *Enterprise*, *Hermosa*, and *Creole* were neither the first nor the last oppressors in the United States paid restitution for the loss of enslaved property. Southern colonial and almost all later slave-state governments paid compensation to owners of enslaved people executed or sold and transported outside of the United States as punishment for a crime. They either allotted the affected masters a certain percentage of the enslaved criminal's value, set a maximum dollar amount for reimbursement, or calculated a value based on a theoretical purchaser's knowledge of the commission of the crime, which would have diminished the guilty party's market price. After 1793, Georgia stood alone among Southern slave states in refusing to compensate owners of enslaved people convicted of capital crimes, preferring state-sanctioned lashings to executions that would require restitution.[29]

Despite a long pattern of reluctance to do so with its own funds, the U.S. government, too, paid slaveholders deprived of their chattel. Perhaps with some irony, the election of Abraham Lincoln in 1860 without any electoral support from the South and the subsequent defection of the eleven states that formed the Confederacy paved the way for compensation. In 1862, the U.S. government expended its own treasure—not funds received from the British Crown—to reimburse a small subset of slaveholders. Lincoln had long entertained various schemes of compensated emancipation for American slave owners and was able to implement one such program. On April 12, 1862, Congress—absent members from the Confederate states—passed a bill, signed by Lincoln four days later, that freed "all persons held to service or labor within the District of Columbia by reason of African descent." The measure also appropriated $1 million to reimburse DC slave owners for the loss of their bondpeople. Enslavers needed only to pledge loyalty to the United States and submit a written petition for compensation. A panel of three commissioners, aided by Baltimore slave trader Bernard M. Campbell, evaluated the claims and distributed the funds to more than 3,100 slave owners, at an average of $300 per bondperson.[30]

With the Confederate loss in the Civil War and the final eradication of slavery by constitutional amendment in 1865, no other Southern masters shared in DC slaveholders' good fortune to collect a check in exchange for the liberation of their enslaved property. The failure to compensate the masses of slave owners, in fact, spoke to the radicalism of the process of emancipation in the United States compared with other slave societies in the Americas, where compensated emancipation was the norm. The U.S. government paying slave owners for liberated slaves in the District more closely conformed to the example set by several European imperial powers of the nineteenth century. To comply with the terms of its Slavery Abolition Act of 1833, Great Britain allotted enslavers in its empire a total of £20 million in compensation for some 800,000 liberated bondpeople. More than 80 percent of the indemnities went to enslavers in the British West Indies and Caribbean. The Bahamas and Bermuda combined consumed more than £178,000 in restitution funds. Some 47,000 owners received reimbursement for the loss of their enslaved merchandise, with the largest payments going to the wealthiest masters who boasted the greatest numbers of captive laborers.[31] To help finance the massive outlays to slave owners, the British government in 1835 secured a loan of £15 million from bankers, financiers, and brothers-in-law Nathan Mayer Rothschild and Moses Montefiore. None of this enormous sum ever made it into the hands of the formerly enslaved. Meanwhile, the loan accumulated interest for the next 180 years, with the British government finally paying it off in 2015.[32]

A similar story unfolded in Haiti, the first independent Black republic founded in the Western Hemisphere. The events leading to the creation of Haiti began in 1791 with a successful slave revolt in the French colony of Saint-Domingue. France refused to recognize Haiti's official declaration of independence in 1804. Two decades later, France belatedly acknowledged Haiti's sovereign status in exchange for 150 million francs in restitution, paid to more than 7,900 French slave owners and their descendants for the loss of their human property. Payments to France began in 1825 and ended 122 years later, in 1947. French banks profited from the compounding interest on the loans granted Haiti to meet the financial obligations thrust upon it, which trapped Haiti in a state of artificially induced poverty.[33]

Compensated emancipation figured prominently in the demise of slavery in most quarters of the Western Hemisphere. Several European colonizing powers and independent nations in the Americas offered indemnities for the benefit of slave owners deprived of their property in persons. The awards granted Southern slaveholders and insurance companies for lost human cargoes aboard the *Comet*, *Encomium*, *Enterprise*, *Hermosa*, and *Creole* resulted from isolated incidents, disconnected from broader liberation movements. Nevertheless, they were consistent with a pattern common during much of the nineteenth century: governments went to great lengths to reimburse those affected by emancipation, but the beneficiaries were the former slave owners, not the formerly enslaved.[34]

Epilogue

In 1988, Congress issued a formal apology for the U.S. government's internment of Japanese Americans during World War II and offered $20,000 in restitution to each of the roughly sixty thousand living individuals who had been imprisoned in the camps. The direct payments authorized for victims of Japanese American internment sparked hopes for the redress of other historic wrongs.[1]

The following year, U.S. representative John Conyers Jr., a Democrat from Michigan and the congressional voice for the National Coalition of Blacks for Reparations in America (N'COBRA), introduced House Resolution 40, a bill that proposed the creation of a federal commission to investigate the lingering legacies of slavery and to recommend "appropriate remedies" moving forward. Conyers reintroduced the bill each legislative session until his retirement in 2017. In all those years, his modest proposal suggesting merely to study the possibility of reparations—not to implement a concrete set of programs or actions—never made it out of committee to the House floor for a vote.[2]

The numerical designation of Conyer's bill, HR 40, hearkened back to the Civil War–era promise of "40 acres and a mule" for the formerly enslaved. The waning months of the Civil War had raised the prospect that freedpeople would be granted at least a tiny fraction of what they were owed for their years of toil under the slave owner's lash. Gen. William Tecumseh Sherman issued Special Field Order No. 15 in January 1865, which distributed confiscated and abandoned lands in coastal South Carolina, Georgia, and Florida in forty-acre tracts to freedpeople. Sherman later added a mule to the bargain. His actions were motivated less by racial progressivism and more by a desire to relieve himself of the logistical burdens of tending to the thousands of Black refugees who had flocked to his army for protection, but the result was the same. Sherman set a precedent by which the formerly enslaved might reasonably expect the U.S. government to offer restitution to help with the economic transition to their newfound freedom.[3]

Redefined, "reparations" in the United States in 1865 referred to indemnification not for slave owners but for former slaves, in recognition of the hardships they endured. The term "reparations" has assumed multiple different meanings over time. Often employed to describe payments owed by one nation to another for damage inflicted in the context of war, reparations also refers to "amends . . . made to nonstate groups and individuals" as redress for past wrongs, injuries, or injustices. Today, as one scholar has observed, the term "reparations" is "used almost synonymously with compensation"—some form of financial award intended to make things right. In the twenty-first-century United States, "reparations" most commonly surfaces in discussions of what may be owed African Americans for the country's long history of slavery and centuries of racial oppression.[4]

The possibility of reparations immediately after the Civil War, in the form of "forty acres and a mule," met with a swift demise. After President Abraham Lincoln's assassination, his successor, Andrew Johnson, rescinded Sherman's order, terminating the model for reparations that the general had established. In a victory for ex–slave owners' property rights, Johnson restored Southern whites' former lands to them. The last generation of white Southerners guilty of slave owning escaped the direct financial responsibility of aiding the last generation of Black Southerners formally held in bondage, despite the available collective resources of the former and the abject desperation of the latter. With the failure of "forty acres and a mule" and the inability to pass or implement any other reparations program during the fraught years of Reconstruction, the prospect of a systemic solution for the recompense of freedpeople grew increasingly bleak. The Civil War ushered in nominal freedom, but reparations for the formerly enslaved were extremely rare, the product of either onetime masters' personal acts of restitution or lawsuits filed in court by freedpeople.[5]

The quest for reparations did not end with the failures of the Reconstruction era. In 1890, Rep. William Connell of Nebraska proposed HR 11119 to create a pension fund for the formerly enslaved, modeled on a federal program that benefited Union veterans from the Civil War. More than anyone, Callie House, a Black woman born into slavery in Tennessee, led the charge for reparations for freedpeople in the late nineteenth and early twentieth centuries. She eventually rose to lead the National Ex-Slave Mutual Relief, Bounty and Pension Association (MRB&PA). In 1915, the organization filed a class action lawsuit in federal court for reparations amounting to $68 million—the total amount of taxes collected between 1862 and 1868 on cotton, cultivated by Black labor. The suit failed. House was arrested in 1916, following years of dogged harassment by federal investigators, who alleged mail fraud against the MRB&PA. Her conviction and imprisonment dealt a severe blow to the reparations movement.[6]

Still, the drive for reparations continued during the twentieth century. Although not a primary thrust of the Black civil rights movement, reparations occasionally entered the conversation. In 1969, activist James Forman presented the Black Manifesto to the Black Economic Development Conference held in Detroit, Michigan. The manifesto called upon white Christian churches and Jewish synagogues in the United States to pay $500 million in reparations to atone for their complicity with slavery. Religious groups across the country roundly rejected the demand.[7]

When John Conyers introduced HR 40 in 1989, a lack of interest, if not outright hostility, toward reparations remained widespread, although several developments, especially within the last decade, have since chipped away at resistance to the idea. Journalist, author, and social commentator Ta-Nehisi Coates published a moving and influential essay in *The Atlantic* in 2014 that deepened the conversation about reparations by tying together the history of the four million emancipated slaves to a long legacy of Black land loss, discriminatory housing policies, residential segregation, racial terrorism, and violence. The long "plunder" of Black wealth that began during slavery did not end with slavery's demise. Rather, it extended past abolition to affect Black people's access to education, employment, housing, and health care down to the present.[8]

While Coates advanced a more comprehensive argument explaining the need for reparations, the United States has confronted an unprecedented reckoning with its history of slavery and its lingering effects in the twenty-first century. Beginning in 2013, the Black Lives Matter movement—galvanized by the murders of Trayvon Martin, Michael Brown, Eric Garner, Breonna Taylor, George Floyd, and hundreds of other Black victims—carried calls for racial justice into the mainstream across the nation and beyond.[9]

In an era of heightened racial awareness, as Confederate statues have been toppled and monuments removed, talk of reparations has revived. Several contenders for the Democratic presidential nomination in 2020 voiced a willingness to explore the possibility of reparations. One, New Jersey senator Cory Booker, introduced a bill in April 2019 calling upon the U.S. Senate to form a commission to study the issue. Rep. Sheila Jackson Lee, a Texas Democrat, sponsored similar legislation in the House, picking up John Conyers's mantle in promoting HR 40. In June 2019, the House Judiciary Subcommittee on the Constitution, Civil Rights and Civil Liberties held the first hearings on Conyers's resolution since 2007. In April 2021, thirty-two years after Conyers unveiled HR 40, members of the House Judiciary Committee voted, for the first time, to send it out of committee, for a possible floor vote by the full House. Although more than 170 representatives cosponsored Rep. Lee's bill to create a commission to study slavery's lasting impacts and possible remedies to the resulting inequalities, layers of challenges, most notably partisan ones, stand in the way of implementation.[10]

Where the federal government has fallen short, other institutions, such as colleges, churches, cities, and states, have recently taken steps in the direction of redress. A wave of universities, including Georgetown, Harvard, Yale, Brown, and the University of Virginia, has acknowledged its indebtedness to slavery. The Jesuit Conference of Canada and the United States has pledged $100 million "in reparation to descendants of Black people it enslaved and sold," with a goal of still more ambitious sums.[11] Evanston, Illinois, and Asheville, North Carolina, are two municipalities enacting programs designed to correct historic wrongs suffered by their Black populations.[12] At the state level, California has established a task force to investigate possible methods of redress for Black residents. In Florida, lawmakers approved compensation to the survivors of the 1923 Rosewood massacre and their descendants, although the measure gave direct payments to a total of just nine people.[13]

To date, the U.S. government that readily fought to secure payments for its slaveholding citizens prior to emancipation has proven ineffective in producing a program of recompense for freedpeople or their descendants. The vast majority of whites quickly dismiss the notion of reparations for Black Americans as unworkable, unfair, or both. Mountains of polling data show opposition to reparations among two-thirds of the general public. Although 73 percent of Black Americans favored them in one 2019 Gallup poll, whites overwhelmingly rejected them. The increased recognition of racial inequalities has not translated into a desire among white people to grant economic recompense to make amends for historic injustices. The 29 percent of all Americans who endorsed reparations in 2019 marked a doubling of support since 2002, but Black respondents were largely responsible for the growing interest.[14]

Any future nationwide reparations proposal would be subject to intense scrutiny. Who would be eligible for benefits under the program? How would recipients be identified and located? What form would reparations take? What would such programs cost? How would they be funded?[15]

These practical questions presented no particular problem in the nineteenth-century reparation cases from the slave ships *Comet*, *Encomium*, *Enterprise*, *Hermosa*, and *Creole*. The recipients were discrete sets of white slave owners, slave traders, or insurance companies, small in number, who filed for a monetary indemnity paid for by the British Treasury. The compensated emancipation of the enslaved in Civil War–era District of Columbia was in some ways more complicated. Although the claimants were from a restricted geographic area, their numbers were larger, and their petitions each required careful evaluation. Moreover, in this instance, the U.S. government made payments out of its own coffers, proving on a relatively small scale just how prohibitively costly compensated emancipation could be in a land of nearly four million enslaved people.[16]

A lasting consequence of centuries of enslavement of Africans and their descendants has been what Ta-Nehisi Coates called the "theft" of Black labor, wealth, and resources for the enrichment of their enslavers. All that was stolen from Black people accumulated in the hands of white people, who reaped the profits of compounding interest over time. The resulting racial wealth gap between Black and white Americans, statistically documented to be greater now than ever, represents, in historian and activist Ibram X. Kendi's words, the "economic death" of Black America. Coates and Kendi agree that the racial wealth gap cannot be closed without a meaningful program of reparations.[17]

Critics of reparations contend that the proper time to have implemented reparations was immediately after the Civil War, when those guilty of owning enslaved people could bear the burden of repaying their debt to them. There may be some truth to their point. Reparations have been customarily granted to those who suffered directly, as in the case of Japanese American internment. Having failed to do that, however, the question arises: When does it become too late to remedy an error? Is it ever too late to apologize and make amends? Do modern-day discussions of reparations reopen old wounds, as opponents charge, or were those wounds never actually closed?[18]

With increasing calls to compensate the descendants of the formerly enslaved for the ongoing effects of the historical wrongs their ancestors suffered, any plan to correct long-standing racial injustices and discrimination through economic remuneration requires a full accounting of the history of reparation/s. Recovering the histories of the *Comet*, *Encomium*, *Enterprise*, and *Hermosa* and what happened in their wake magnifies the insults inflicted under slavery. It is an uncomfortable truth that, more often than not, in the United States and elsewhere in the Atlantic world, enslavers, not the enslaved, reaped the financial rewards of compensation. What we do with that knowledge is our choice to make.[19]

Acknowledgments

The sole name on the cover of this book belies the collaborative effort that it truly was. Many librarians and archivists helped me along the way, and I am pleased to acknowledge them here. My quest for government documents and court records involved Keith Mitchell and the staff at the National Archives of the United Kingdom; Patrice Williams, Tomoko Smith, and the staff at the Bahamas National Archives in Nassau; and the staffs at the South Carolina Department of Archives and History in Columbia and the New Orleans Public Library. Theresa Hefner-Babb and Tom Rohrig successfully tracked down the congressional records I needed.

Throughout most of my research, I managed to stay half a step ahead of disaster. I completed research in England in February 2019, in the Bahamas that April, and in South Carolina and New Orleans that summer, all funded by a Distinguished Faculty Fellowship from Lamar University. After that, depleted funds and the onset of a global pandemic rendered travel impossible and unsafe. Several archivists rescued this project from stagnation. Damani Davis and Adebo Adetona at the National Archives in Washington, DC; Vann Evans at the North Carolina Department of Archives and History in Raleigh; Steve Tuttle at the South Carolina Department of Archives and History in Columbia; Edward Blessing at the University of South Carolina's South Caroliniana Library; Kayla Burnett at the Georgia State Archives in Morrow; Elizabeth Walter at the Bermuda Archives; and Ellen Hollis at the Bermuda National Library all came through in the clutch to maintain forward momentum. All mailed or emailed information I needed, for which I am indescribably grateful. Thanks, too, to attorney Ben Adamson and registrar Jane Downing of the National Museum of Bermuda for kindly assisting me in tracking down photographs in the late stages of preparation, and to David Worsham of Lamar University for his capable scanning.

Throughout my work on this project, many friends and colleagues offered useful advice or recommendations for readings more in their fields of expertise than in mine. Bruce Baker, John Davies, Cassandre Durso, Brendan Gillis, Randal Hall, Sheri Huerta, Cindy Kierner, and David Silkenat all fall into this camp. Bob Elder, a true gentleman and scholar, generously shared a copy of his biography of John C. Calhoun before it was publicly available. The LU history department brown bag group, consisting of Jimmy Bryan, Brendan Gillis, Tina Kibbe, Mark Mengerink, and Yasuko Sato, was the first to read and comment on a preliminary article-length version of what eventually morphed into this book. Bob Elder, Brendan Gillis, Peter Kolchin, and Susan Ferber deserve thanks for reading the full draft manuscript, guiding my revisions, and sparing me mistakes and miscues along the way. Their efforts are doubly appreciated since I was unable to participate in the usual conference circuit during the creation of this book. I did, however, have the opportunity to speak at the Greater Gulf Symposium held by the Center for History and Culture of Southeast Texas and the Upper Gulf Coast. Those remarks are printed in the *Texas Gulf Historical and Biographical Record* and appear in altered form here with permission. LU history department student worker Elton Truss helped me with various tasks around the office.

I owe a huge debt of gratitude to my agent Deirdre Mullane at Mullane Literary Associates for helping me craft the book proposal and for her tireless efforts to find the manuscript a happy home. Thanks, too, for the generous endorsements of Bob Elder and Caleb McDaniel. Editor Marc Favreau and the entire team at The New Press are wonderful people, true professionals, and my personal heroes. I also appreciate the anonymous readers whose comments guided my revisions.

The creation of this manuscript occurred amid terrible tragedy and death. Category 5 Hurricane Dorian devastated the Abaco Islands in the Bahamas—the general vicinity of three shipwrecks discussed in these pages—in September 2019, five months after my visit. Several dozen people perished, with others still unaccounted for years later. I was transcribing the photographed notes from my travels overseas during the spring 2020 semester when the arrival of the COVID-19 pandemic waylaid us all. By the time I finished the first chapter, coronavirus deaths were just topping one hundred thousand, unemployment had reached 40 million, and protests sparked by George Floyd's murder swept the country.

Almost all the writing took place during this period of national stress and dread.

Amid so much turmoil, my regular process of plugging away daily at the laptop surrendered to alternating bouts of productivity and inertia. I am thankful for the reduction to my course load in the spring 2021 semester and the semester-long Faculty Development Leave from Lamar University that fall, which relieved me of all teaching duties, enabled me to finish writing, and gave me time to revise as the Delta variant of the coronavirus spiked in my corner of the country.

I could not have made it through those difficult times without the support of the household that has long been my entire world, just more literally so during the pandemic: my wife, Sharon, and son, Gabe. They, as a teacher and a student, understand better than most the professional world of education and all the pressures that that entails. Yet I dedicate this book to the memories of three family members who are no longer here to see it to completion. Chris Forret, my first cousin, first friend, and classmate from kindergarten through our bachelor's degrees, left this world far too soon in 2019. Four months after losing him, my mom, Velma Forret, passed after five years' suffering the heartbreaking cruelties of old age. Had she been born in a different era, she might have been a history professor herself. She made many sacrifices for my sake, always prioritizing my education and supporting my academic endeavors and passion for history. I wish the realities of academia had allowed me to have been nearer to her, particularly during her last years. Finally, April 2021 brought the death of my father-in-law, Jim Hord. A longtime attorney in Charlotte, North Carolina, he opened his home to me decades ago as a research base while working on my dissertation. He enjoyed reading history books, especially in his semi-retirement, and I regret not getting his assessment of this one.

Appendix A: List of Captives Aboard the *Comet*

Name	Sex	Age	Height (Feet/ Inches)	Complexion	Shipper	Consignee
1. Sandy Bivan/Bivans/ Bevans	M	25	6 0¼	Black	Franklin & Armfield	Isaac Franklin
2. Henson Davis	M	20	5 5¼	Black	"	"
3. David Davis	M	19	5 5¼	Black	"	"
4. Charles Schaler/ Shalor/Skaler	M	15	4 9	Black	"	"
5. Joshua Jackson	M	14	4 7¾	Black	"	"
6. Joseph Davis	M	14	4 6¾	Black	"	"
7. Carter Brent	M	14	4 6	Black	"	"
8. Horace Davis	M	11	4 3¼	Black	"	"
9. Stephen Mashett/ Maskett/Musbett	M	25	6	Black	"	"
10. Perry Frisby	M	19	5 11¾	Black	"	"
11. William Duval/ Dewall	M	19	5 11	Black	"	"
12. John Brown	M	20	5 8¼	Black	"	"
13. Abraham/Abram Carter/Cantor	M	25	5 8½	Black	"	"
14. Josiah Hendsley/ Hendsly	M	25	5 10½	Black	"	"
15. Anthony Singleton	M	25	5 7½	Black	"	"
16. Nelson Simon/Lemon	M	19	5 6½	Black	"	"
17. Henry Fletcher	M	24	5 2	Black	"	"
18. Washington Banks	M	19	5 5¾	Black	"	"

(Continued)

Name	Sex	Age	Height (Feet/ Inches)	Complexion	Shipper	Consignee
19. William Wilson	M	20	5 7	Black	"	"
20. John Lewell/Serrell/ Jewell	M	19	5 7	Black	"	"
21. David/Daniel Jones	M	19	5 7½	Black	"	"
22. Cletus Williams/ Wilkinson	M	26	5 8½	Brown	"	"
23. Joseph Parker	M	19	5 6¼	Black	"	"
24. James Ross	M	19	5 6½	Black	"	"
25. Washington Brown/ Bowler/Bowser	M	25	5 5¼	Black	"	"
26. Seaman/Simon Beal	M	18	5 7	Yellow	"	"
27. Leander Naylor/Nailor	M	28	5 1½	Black	"	"
28. Moses Walker	M	21	5 5	Black	"	"
29. Adam Lee	M	26	5 5½	Black	"	"
30. Ezekiel Green	M	21	5 11½	Black	"	"
31. Henson Thomas	M	19	5 9	Black	"	"
32. Isaac Herrington	M	19	5 7¼	Black	"	"
33. William Brown	M	19	5 8	Black	"	"
34. Frederick Brent	M	14/16	4 7	Black	"	"
35. Henry Brooks	M	15	4 9½	Brown	"	"
36. Rosetta Bunchey/ Brumbles/Bumby/ Banks	F	16	5 6¼	Black	"	"
37. Celia Diggs	F	17	5 4	Black	"	"
38. Mary Jackson	F	15	5 3	Black	"	"
39. Judy McConky	F	14	5 2½	Black	"	"
40. Judy/Julia Frisby	F	16	5 1	Black	"	"
41. Fanny Ball/Brew	F	17	4 11½	Black	"	"
42. Susan Thomas	F	20	5 5¼	Yellow	"	"
43. Amy Diggs/Mary Briggs	F	20	4 11¼	Black	"	"
44. Aranna/Ananna/ Anana/Mary Ann Magruder/Macgruder/ McGrandry	F	17	5 4½	Black	"	"
45. Jane Byrd	F	25	5 2½	Black	"	"

Name	Sex	Age	Height (Feet/ Inches)	Complexion	Shipper	Consignee
46. Matilda White	F	11	4 6	Black	"	"
47. Rachael/Rachel Tippett	F	16	5 0½	Brown	"	"
48. Patsy/Patty Brown	F	11	4 8¾	Black	"	"
49. Hannah Linggums/ Linggams/Songens	F	16	4 10¼	Black	"	"
50. Letty Jordan	F	16	4 11¼	Black	"	"
51. Lydia Dawson/ Daughton	F	16	4 11	Black	"	"
52. Kitty Garner/Gaines/ Gaynor	F	16	5 0½	Black	"	"
53. Toby/Terris Winebury	F	22	5 5½	Black	"	"
54. Benson/Reason/ Roberson (child)	M	1		Brown	"	"
55. Winny McPherson	F	15	4 11½	Black	"	"
56. Polly McPherson	F	14/15	4 11¼	Black	"	"
57. Letty Holmes	F	16	4 11	Black	"	"
58. Mary Curtis/Curtain	F	14	4 9	Yellow	"	"
59. Jane Watkins	F	16	5	Black	"	"
60. Maria Gunnan/ Gurnan/Maree L. Gummans	F	23	5 0½	Black	"	"
61. Lucinda Miles/Myles/ Myers	F	18	5 4	Black	"	"
62. Elizabeth Noble/ Nobles	F	18	5 7½	Black	"	"
63. Lucinda Smith	F	20	5 5½	Black	"	"
64. Chloe Ann Gardner/ Garner	F	18	5 1	Black	"	"
65. Eliza Gibson	F	17	5 7	Black	"	"
66. Matilda Gant/Grant	F	17	5 5½	Black	"	"
67. Charlotte Carter/ Garland	F	15	4 11½	Black	"	"
68. Eliza Ann Jewell/ Sewell/Serrill	F	15	5 1	Black	"	"

(Continued)

Name	Sex	Age	Height (Feet/ Inches)	Complexion	Shipper	Consignee
69. Lucinda Morris/ Minks	F	17	5 4	Brown	"	"
70. Ann Burgess	F	17	5 2½	Black	"	"
71. Rachel/Rachael Carter/Canter/Conter/ Curten	F	17	5 3¼	Black	"	"
72. Hester Ann Mitchell	F	17	5 2½	Black	"	"
73. Mary Ann Barnet/ Barnes/Barny	F	18	4 11¼	Black	"	"
74. Olivia McKee	F	13	4 9½	Black	"	"
75. Sarah Milburn/ Milburne/Wilburn	F	20	5 5¼	Black	"	"
76. Peter Thomas	M	30	5 7½	Yellow	"	"
77. Frank Barnes/Barny	M	20	5 5¾	Brown	"	H.W. Barstow
78. Jack Dade	M	22	5 7¾	Brown	"	"
79. John Lee	M	19	5 5½	Black	"	"
80. Christian Green	M	26	5 7¾	Black	"	"
81. Peter (child)	M	5	3 7	Black	"	"
82. Ann (child)	F	1		Black	"	"
83. Cecelia [Thomas]	F	20	5 1½	Brown	"	"
84. Susan [Brown] (+ newborn)	F	19	5 4	Yellow	"	"
85. Richard Douglass	M	50	5 4½	Black	"	Charles P. Tutt
86. Dennis Young	M	60	5 11¼	Black	"	"
87. Milly	F	50	4 7	Black	"	"
88. Hannah Douglass	F	40	5 5½	Black	"	"
89. James Douglass	M	9	3 11	Black	"	"
90. Robert Douglass	M	8	3 9¼	Black	"	"
91. Lydia Douglass	F	12	4 9½	Black	"	"
92. Martha Douglass	F	5	3 3	Black	"	"
93. Eliza Douglass	F	3	3	Brown	"	"
94. Nelson Brent	M	24	5 3	Black	"	Isaac Franklin

Name	Sex	Age	Height (Feet/ Inches)	Complexion	Shipper	Consignee
95. Nathan Whiting	M	21	5 5	Black	"	"
96. Eveline Smith	F	18	5 2½	Brown	"	"
97. Sarah (her daughter)	F	4 mos.		Brown	"	"
98. Caroline/Carolina Dandridge	F	50	5	Brown	"	"
99. Edmund/Edmond/ Edward [Henry]	M	22	5 8¼	Black	"	John Woolfolk
100. George [Thompson]	M	16	5 5¼	Black	"	"
101. Philip/Phillip [Sly]	M	15	4 7¾	Yellow	"	"
102. Jack [Saunders]	M	23	5 8¼	Black	"	"
103. Lewis or Henry Moore	M	19	5 9	Brown	"	"
104. Polly [Davis]	F	13	4 10	Brown	"	"
105. Liza/Lizer	F	19	5 6	Black	"	"
106. Letty [Price]	F	24	5 1¾	Black	"	"
107. Ann [Morris]	F	14	5 2½	Brown	"	"
108. Matilda [Wyly]	F	11	4 7	Black	"	"
109. Gusty [Hinson]	F	14	4 9	Black	"	"
110. Elijah Wheeler	M	28	5 10¾	Black	"	Ira Bowman
111. Adam Davis	M	27	5 5¼	Black	"	"
112. Moses Mitchell	M	20	5 3½	Black	"	"
113. James Bailey	M	13	4 6¼	Black	"	"
114. Dick Bailey	M	11	4 1½	Black	"	"
115. Lawson/Lawrence Bailey	M	9	3 11¼	Black	"	"
116. William Johnson/ Johnston	M	8	3 10¼	Mulatto	"	"
117. Hamilton Bailey	M	7	3 6¼	Black	"	"
118. Mary/Merry Coleman	F	18	5 7½	Black	"	"
119. Betsy/Betsey Weaver	F	21	5 6¼	Black	"	"
120. Malinda Claxton/ Clarkston	F	15	4 8	Black	"	"

(Continued)

Name	Sex	Age	Height (Feet/ Inches)	Complexion	Shipper	Consignee
121. Charlotte Bofres/ Baggert/Boggey/ Baggins	F	12	4 3	Black	"	"
122. Maria/Mariah Cooper	F	13	4 10¾	Black	"	"
123. Matilda Rollins/ Robins	F	15	5 5	Black	"	"
124. Lavinia Bailey	F	13	5 3¼	Black	"	"
125. Matilda Bailey	F	6	3 5	Black	"	"
126. Toby Vincent	M	25/31	5 5	Black	Thomas W. Overley	John Woolfolk
127. James Spence/ Spencer	M	20/31	5 5	Black	"	"
128. Major White	M	20	5 9	Black	"	"
129. James/Samuel Dixon	M	28	5 9	Black	"	"
130. Kit Griffin	M	27	5 8	Black	"	"
131. Mark Wilkins	M	25	5 2	Black	"	"
132. Robert Kitchins/ Tethers/Pitchin/ Pitchins	M	20	5 2	Black	"	"
133. Virgil Highland	M	20	5 8	Mulatto	"	"
134. Job/Joseph Mitchell	M	19	5 8½	Mulatto	"	"
135. Garrison Graham	M	20	5 10	Mulatto	"	"
136. Charles Jones	M	25	5 8	Mulatto	"	"
137. Arthur Spady/Speady	M	21	6 2½	Black	"	"
138. Jacob Gunter/Ganter	M	20/28	5 7	Black	"	"
139. George Mapp	M	17	5 5	Black	"	"
140. Luke Mapp	M	35	5 6½	Black	"	"
141. Charles Robbins	M	18	5 3	Black	"	"
142. Anderson/Andrew Thomas	M	21	5 5	Black	"	"
143. Phil Tilman/ Tilghman	M	22	5 5½	Black	"	"
144. Summerset Nutter/ Nester Summersett/ Sumnest Rutter/ Somaset Nutter	M	22	5 7	Black	"	"

Name	Sex	Age	Height (Feet/ Inches)	Complexion	Shipper	Consignee
145. Adam Bishop	M	11/12	4 5	Black	"	"
146. Peggy Irvin/Irvine	F	16	5 5	Black	"	"
147. Mary E. Irvin/Irvine (infant)	F			Mulatto	"	"
148. Hester/Easter/Esther Hayman/Haymen/ Flayman	F	17	5 4	Mulatto	"	"
149. Jane Lowe	F	16	5 5½	Mulatto	"	"
150. Milky Bell	F	18	5	Black	"	"
151. Rose Bell	F	16	5 1	Black	"	"
152. Candis/Candy Elgy	F	25	5 6¼	Brown	"	"
153. Charles (her son)	M	5	3 7	Brown	"	"
154. Charlotte/Charlet Marshall	F	15	4 11¼	Brown	"	"
155. Jane Marshall	F	13	4 10½	Brown	"	"
156. Nicy Mapp	F	20	5	Mulatto	"	"
157. James/Sam Mapp (her son)	M	2	2	Mulatto	"	"
158. Anna/Celia Merick/ Miseck/Mizeck	F	18	5 4	Black	"	"
159. Anetta Dingle	F	11/12	4 5	Black	"	"
160. Catherine/ Catharine Mapp	F	26	5 2	Black	"	"
161. Joe Mapp (her son)	M	5	3 5	Black	"	"
162. Nathan Mapp (her son)	M	2½/3	2	Black	"	"
163. Bennett Mapp	M	17	5	Mulatto	"	"
164. Daniel [Brown]	M	14	4	Mulatto	"	"

Sources: Manifest of the *Comet*, December 17, 1830, pp. 187–91, CO 23/92 Secretary of State Correspondence, NAUK; Manifest of the *Comet*, December 17, 1830, T 1/3556 Treasury Long Papers, bundle 133, part 2, NAUK; Appraisement of slaves aboard the *Comet*, February 25, 1831, in William Melbourne Fox, *qui tam* vs. certain negroes or persons of colour, Instance Court of Vice Admiralty (1831), folios 83–85, reel 43, CO 23/84, BNAN; Statement of 49 Slaves Insured in the Merchants Insurance Office, New Orleans, T 1/3556; Mississippi Marine & Fire Ins. Co. Statement, T 1/3556, NAUK; Statement of 36 Slaves insured in the Louisiana State Marine Office, New Orleans. Also of 5 Slaves insured in said Office, and also of 16 Do. Do., T 1/3556, NAUK. In the table, last names showing in brackets appeared matched with their respective first names only in the appraisement of February 25, 1831. In all other sources, only a first name was given.

Appendix B:
List of Captives Aboard the *Encomium*

Name	Sex	Age	Height (Feet/ Inches)	Complexion	Shipper	Value
1. Billy	M				Charles Allen	
2. Joe	M				"	
3. Peggy	F				"	
4. Prince	M	45	5 2	Black	Robert Eagar	$1,600
5. Jim	M	30	5 6	Mulatto	"	$1,200
6. Kelly	M	35	5 4	Black	"	$600
7. Tom Elmey	M	25	5 5	Black	"	$900
8. Emily	F	40	5 4	Black	"	$500
9. Grace	F	40	5 5	Black	"	$500
10. Tom	M	28	6 2	Black	"	$850
11. Luke	M	52	5	Black	Amédée Gardanne Jr.	$500
[illegible] Sampson	M	22	5 6	Black	"	$900
[illegible]	M	29	6	Black	"	$850
[illegible]	F	21	5	Black	"	$700
[illegible]	[illegible]	39	5	Black	"	$500
[illegible]	[illegible]	[illegible]	[illegible]	Brown	"	$300
[illegible]	[illegible]	[illegible]	[illegible]	Black	Antonio Della Torre	$1,000
[illegible]	[illegible]	[illegible]	[illegible]	[illegible]	"	$850
[illegible]	[illegible]	[illegible]	[illegible]	[illegible]	"	$1,000
[illegible]	[illegible]	[illegible]	[illegible]	[illegible]	"	$1,000
[illegible]	[illegible]	[illegible]	[illegible]	[illegible]ack	"	$700

(Continued)

Name	Sex	Age	Height (Feet/ Inches)	Complexion	Shipper	Value
22. Georgiana	F	18	5 4	Black	"	$800
23. Tay	M	35	5 5	Mustee	Noah B. Sisson	$500
24. Ben	M	22	5 6/5 10	Black	John Waddell	$850
25. Crawford	M	20/24	6	Black	"	$850
26. Solomon	M	20	5 10	Mulatto/ Mustee	"	$850
27. Jack	M	23	5 10	Black	"	$850
28. Joe	M	20	5 10	Black	"	$850
29. Hale	M	20	5 10	Mustee	"	$850
30. David	M	25	5 9	Black	"	$850
31. Bosseau	M	25	5 9	Black	"	$850
32. Ferdinand	M	17	5 8	Black	"	$800
33. Marcellus	M	25	5 8/5 10	Black/ Mustee	"	$1,500
34. John	M	20	6	Black	"	$850
35. Josh	M	18	5 10	Black	"	$850
36. Ned	M	25	5 10	Black	"	$1,200
37. John	M	20	5 9/5 10	Black	"	$850
38. Hagar	F	18	5 4	Black	"	$650
39. Mary	F	22	5 6	Black	"	$650
40. Stella	F	21/22	5 4	Black	"	$650
41. Diana	F	18/20	5 4	Black	"	$600
42. Elsey	F	20	5 3/5 4	Black	"	$600
43. Lucy	F	20	5 4	Black	"	$600
44. Jack (child)	M	3		Black	"	$150
45. Henry (child)	M	5		Black	"	$200

Sources: I was unable to locate the unified outward manifest from Charleston for the *Encomiu*
final voyage; however, a series of manifests divided by shipper, insurance policies, deposit
valuations, and correspondence is available in T 1/3556 Treasury Long Papers, bundle 133,
and 2, NAUK. Using that material, I constructed the table above. Some of the sourc
include William Rothery to T.F. Baring, February 23, 1839; Manifest of Slaves be
Robert Eagar, April 6, 1837; Manifest of Slaves belonging to Amédée Gardanne
1837; Manifests of Slaves belonging to Antonio Della Torre, April 20, 1837; Ma
November 9, 1837; Deposition of Noah B. Sisson, May 15, 1837; Manifest of 2
by John Waddell, February 1, 1834; and Valuation of the 22 Negroes shipped
March 11, 1834.

Appendix C: List of Captives Aboard the *Enterprise*

Name	Sex	Age	Height (Feet/ Inches)	Complexion	Shipper	Consignee	Value
1. George Hammett	M	25	5 7	Black	Joseph W. Neal	Oliver Simpson	$1,000
2. Charles Dorsey	M	19	5 4½	Black	"	"	$750
3. Abram Stewart	M	21	5 5	Copper	"	"	$750
4. Daniel Jackson	M	30	5 3½	Copper	"	"	$650
5. Henry Hall	M	18	5 7¾	Yellow	"	"	$750
6. Charles Mahoney	M	24	5 3½	Yellow	"	"	$700
7. Thomas Wood	M	23	5 7¼	Black	"	"	$750
8. William Chase	M	16	5 ½	Black	"	"	$575
9. George Briscoe	M	13	4 7	Black	"	"	$550
10. Samuel James	M	12	4 4¾	Copper	"	"	$550
11. Hamilton Caintee	M	14	4 11	Black	"	"	$550
12. Lloyd Anderson	M	12	4 6	Copper	"	"	$525
13. Stephen Holliday	M	9	4 1	Copper	"	"	$475
14. John Woodly	M	7	3 8	Black	"	"	$325
15. Charles R. Warfield	M	8	4 ¼	Copper	"	"	$450
16. Charles Tolson	M	7	3 9	Black	"	"	$350

(Continued)

Name	Sex	Age	Height (Feet/ Inches)	Complexion	Shipper	Consignee	Value
17. Ned Tolson	M	6	3 7¾	Black	"	"	$325
18. Peter Thrift	M	10	4 2½	Black	"	"	$525
19. Abram Carter	M	14	4 8	Black	"	"	$550
20. John Ruffin	M	14	4 6½	Black	"	"	$575
21. Calbert King	M	9	4 1	Yellow	"	"	$400
22. Ben Thomas	M	12	4 4¼	Black	"	"	$525
23. George Washington	M	10	4 ½	Copper	"	"	$500
24. Henson Johnson	M	10	4 1	Black	"	"	$500
25. Shade Reed	M	7	3 7¾	Black	"	"	$300
26. Oscar Worthy	M	12	4 6	Copper	"	"	$550
27. Maria Lancaster	F	19	5 ½	Black	"	"	$500
28. Louisa Brooks	F	8	3 9¼	Black	"	"	$325
29. Lucy Johnson	F	23	5 2¼	Copper	"	"	$500
30. Julia Reeder	F	24	5 3	Black	"	"	$525
31. Charlotte Dent	F	20	5 3	Copper	"	"	$575
32. Nancy Brown	F	16	5 6¼	Black	"	"	$600
33. Maria Brown	F	10	4 3¼	Black	"	"	$375
34. Mary Ann Warfield	F	15	4 11½	Copper	"	"	$525
35. Elizabeth Jane Warfield	F	12	4 6¾	Copper	"	"	$450
36. Mahaley Warfield	F	11	4 4¾	Copper	"	"	$425
37. Mary Warfield	F	9	4 ¼	Copper	"	"	$375
38. Dafney Gray	F	20	5	Black	"	"	$375
39. Isaac Gray (child)	M	6 months		Black	"	"	

Name	Sex	Age	Height (Feet/ Inches)	Complexion	Shipper	Consignee	Value
40. Ana Maria Fendall	F	18	5 5	Black	"	"	
41. Sarah Burch	F	12	4 4¼	Black	"	"	
42. Mary Dobbins	F	10	4 2½	Copper	"	"	
43. Harriet Fisher	F	9	4 ¼	Copper	"	"	
44. Elizabeth Butler	F	20	4 10¾	Copper	"	"	
45. Harriet Ann (child)	F	2		Yellow	"	"	
46. Mahaley Ann Powel	F	13	4 8	Copper	"	"	
47. Eliza Tinney	F	24	5 4½	Copper	"	"	
48. Phil Tinney	M	8	3 10	Copper	"	"	
49. John Tinney	M	7	3 9	Copper	"	"	
50. Mary Tinney	F	4	3 5¼	Copper	"	"	
51. Rachael Tinney	F	2		Copper	"	"	
52. Richard Tinney	M	3 weeks		Copper	"	"	
53. Betsy Smith	F	15	4 10½	Copper	"	"	
54. Easter Lyles	F	25	4 10½	Copper	"	"	
55. John Lyles	M	8	3 9½	Copper	"	"	
56. Henrietta Lyles	F	3	2 10½	Copper	"	"	
57. Matilda Ridgley	F	25	5 1½	Copper	"	"	
58. Martha Ridgley	F	10	4 3½	Copper	"	"	
59. Helen Ridgley	F	7	3 9½	Copper	"	"	
60. Mahaley Ridgley	F	5	3 4½	Copper	"	"	

(Continued)

Name	Sex	Age	Height (Feet/ Inches)	Complexion	Shipper	Consignee	Value
61. Betsey Ridgley	F	3	3 ¼	Copper	"	"	
62. Ann Ridgley	F	5 months		Copper	"	"	
63. Betsey Groom	F	31	5 2	Black	"	"	
64. Easter Groom	F	14	4 7¼	Black	"	"	
65. Thomas Groom	M	9	3 10¼	Black	"	"	
66. Martha Leon Groom	F	4	2 11	Black	"	"	
67. Louisa Groom	F	2	2 4¼	Copper	"	"	
68. Salisbury	M	6	3 7	Black	"	"	
69. Susan Wilson	F	5	3 6¼	Black	"	"	
70. Sarah Brent	F	14	4 7½	Black	"	"	
71. Spencer	M	22	5 7	Yellow	"	"	
72. Mason	M	19	5 4¼	Black	"	"	
73. Parker	M	20	5 8¼	Copper	"	"	
74. Phil Redout	M	35	5 8½	Black	Thomas N. Davis	Thomas N. Godider	
75. Dinah Buckingham	F	25	5 ½	Yellow	"	"	
76. her infant	F	6 weeks		Yellow	"	"	
77. Emiline Buckingham	F	8	4	Yellow	"	"	
78. Jane Buckingham	F	6	3 7½	Yellow	"	"	

Sources: Manifest of the *Enterprise*, January 22, 1835, unpaginated, T 1/3556 Treasury Long Papers, bundle 133, part 2, NAUK; *Oliver Simpson v. Charleston Fire and Marine Insurance Co.*, Judgment Roll, Charleston District (L10018), June 10, 1837, Item 109A, SCDAH.

Appendix D:
List of Captives Aboard the *Hermosa*

Name	Sex	Age	Height (Feet/ Inches)	Complexion	Shipper	Consignee
1. Sarah Reilly	F	16			Lancaster, Denby & Co.	A. Ladeux & Co.
2. Lucy	F	13			"	"
3. Mariah	F	13			"	"
4. Eliza	F	12			"	"
5. Horace	M	11			"	"
6. John	M	12			"	"
7. Tazewell	M	13			"	"
8. Isaac	M	15			"	"
9. David	M	13			"	"
10. Charles Smith	M	19	5 10½	Black	H.N. Templeman	H.N. Templeman
11. Fountain Alvis	M	24	6	Brown	"	"
12. James/John Douglas	M	25	5 8	Brown	"	"
13. James Morris	M	26	5 6	Black	"	"
14. Daniel Holmes/ Harris	M	26	5 6	Black	"	"
15. Madison Edwards	M	22	5 6	Brown	"	"
16. Samuel Johnson/ Johnston	M	19	5 5½	Black	"	"
17. Ben Jackson/ Johnston	M	23	5 5½	Black	"	"
18. Essex West	M	21	5 6	Black	"	"
19. Edmond Page	M	25	5 6½	Black	"	"

(Continued)

Name	Sex	Age	Height (Feet/ Inches)	Complexion	Shipper	Consignee
20. Frank Dickenson	M	17	5 3	Black	"	"
21. Joshua Brown	M	17	5 2	Black	"	"
22. Reuben Francis	M	16	5	Black	"	"
23. William Lewis	M	15	5 ½	Brown	"	"
24. Henry Lacy	M	17	5 4½	Yellow	"	"
25. Tom Jones	M	30	5 6	Brown	"	"
26. William Robertson/ Robinson	M	23	5 6	Brown	"	"
27. Tom Young	M	25	5 6	Black	"	"
28. William Nelson	M	25	5 5	Black	"	"
29. Betsy Green	F	30	5 5½	Black	"	"
30. Jane Williams	F	22/27	5 7	Brown	"	"
31. Ann Morris	F	27	5 2½	Brown	"	"
32. Isabella Allen	F	21/22	5 ½	Black	"	"
33. Harriet Young	F	16	5 1	Black	"	"
34. Louisa Goode	F	15	5 ½	Black	"	"
35. Mary Henderson	F	17	5 2	Yellow	"	"
36. Rachael Bowyer/ Bony	F	16	5	Black	"	"
37. Lucy Rawlins	F	27	5 4	Black	"	"
38. Priscilla Ellen	F	20	5 3	Brown	"	"
39. Malinda Gibbs	F	25	5 3	Black	"	"
40. Louisa Gibbs	F	10	4 7	Yellow	"	"
41. Dicey Lumpkin	F	10	4 2	Black	"	"
42. Frances Tomblin	F	10	4 1	Black	"	"
43. Edmond Parker	M	35	5 7	Black	"	"
44. Malinda	F	22	5 2	Black	"	"
45. Malinda's child					"	"
46. William Smith	M	22	5 6	Yellow	"	"
47. Winny Smith	F	27	5 6	Brown	"	"
48. Lewis Johnson	M	45			L.C. Read	James H. Dudley

Sources: Manifest of the *Hermosa*, October 10, 1840, reel 59, folios 363–67, CO 23/107, BNAN; bill of lading, in *H. N. Templeman v. Louisiana State Marine & Fire Insurance Company*, case #3261, December 24, 1840, p. 15, New Orleans Commercial Court, NOPL.

Notes

Introduction

1. David W. Blight, ed., *Narrative of the Life of Frederick Douglass, an American Slave, Written by Himself* (New York: Bedford Books of St. Martin's Press, 1993), 114n60; John Ernest, ed., *Narrative of the Life of Henry Box Brown Written by Himself* (Chapel Hill: University of North Carolina Press, 2008); William Craft, *Running a Thousand Miles for Freedom; or, the Escape of William and Ellen Craft from Slavery* (London: William Tweedie, 1860); J. Brent Morris, *Dismal Freedom: A History of the Maroons of the Great Dismal Swamp* (Chapel Hill: University of North Carolina Press, 2022); John Hope Franklin and Loren Schweninger, *Runaway Slaves: Rebels on the Plantation* (New York: Oxford University Press, 1999); Timothy P. Walker, ed., *Sailing to Freedom: Maritime Dimensions of the Underground Railroad* (Amherst: University of Massachusetts Press, 2021); Alice L. Baumgartner, *South to Freedom: Runaway Slaves to Mexico and the Road to the Civil War* (New York: Basic Books, 2020).

2. James D. Rice, "Early American Environmental Histories," *William and Mary Quarterly* 3d ser., 75, no. 3 (July 2018): 406 (first quotation), 407 (second quotation), 419. Important environmental histories of the South include Albert E. Cowdrey, *This Land, This South: An Environmental History*, rev. ed. (Lexington: University Press of Kentucky, 1996); Mart A. Stewart, *"What Nature Suffers to Groe": Life, Labor, and Landscape on the Georgia Coast, 1680–1920* (Athens: University of Georgia Press, 1996); Mikko Saikku, *This Delta, This Land: An Environmental History of the Yazoo-Mississippi Floodplain* (Athens: University of Georgia Press, 2005); Lynn A. Nelson, *Pharsalia: An Environmental Biography of a Southern Plantation, 1780–1880* (Athens: University of Georgia Press, 2007); and Drew A. Swanson, *Remaking Wormsloe Plantation: The Environmental History of a Lowcountry Landscape* (Athens: University of Georgia Press, 2012). Environmental histories of the Atlantic world with relevance for this book include Matthew Mulcahy, *Hurricanes and Society in the British Greater Caribbean, 1624–1783* (Baltimore: Johns Hopkins University Press, 2006); Sherry Johnson, *Climate and Catastrophe in Cuba and the Atlantic World in the Age of Revolution* (Chapel Hill: University of North Carolina Press, 2011); and Stuart B. Schwartz, *Sea of Storms: A History of Hurricanes in the Greater Caribbean from Columbus to Katrina* (Princeton: Princeton University Press, 2015).

3. On the Middle Passage generally, see, for example, Marcus Rediker, *The Slave Ship: A Human History* (New York: Viking, 2007); Stephanie E. Smallwood, *Saltwater Slavery: A Middle Passage from Africa to American Diaspora* (Cambridge: Harvard University Press, 2007); Sowande' M. Mustakeem, *Slavery at Sea: Terror, Sex, and Sickness in the Middle Passage* (Urbana: University of Illinois Press, 2016). For studies focusing on particular ships, see Robert Harms, *The* Diligent*: A Voyage Through the Worlds of the Slave Trade* (New York: Basic Books, 2002); Sean M. Kelley, *The Voyage of the Slave Ship* Hare*: A Journey into Captivity from Sierra Leone to South Carolina* (Chapel Hill: University of North Carolina Press, 2016); Jonathan M. Bright, *Dark Places of the Earth: The Voyage of the Slave Ship* Antelope (New York: Liveright, 2015); Marcus Rediker, *The Amistad Rebellion: An Atlantic Odyssey of Slavery and Freedom* (New York: Viking, 2012); Sylviane A. Diouf, *Dreams of Africa in Alabama: The Slave Ship* Clotilda *and the Story of the Last Africans Brought to America* (New York: Oxford University Press, 2007); and Zora Neale Hurston, *Barracoon: The Story of the Last "Black Cargo,"* ed. Deborah G. Plant, with a foreword by Alice Walker (New York: Amistad, 2018). On a smuggler, see Jim Jordan, *The Slave-Trader's Letter-Book: Charles Lamar, the* Wanderer, *and Other Tales of the African Slave Trade* (Athens: University of Georgia Press, 2018). One recent work that examines efforts to squash that illegal trade into the United States is John Harris, *The Last Slave Ships: New York and the End of the Middle Passage* (New Haven: Yale University Press, 2020).

On the U.S. domestic slave trade, see Michael Tadman, *Speculators and Slaves: Masters, Traders, and Slaves in the Old South* (Madison: University of Wisconsin Press, 1989); Walter Johnson, *Soul by Soul: Life Inside the Antebellum Slave Market* (Cambridge: Harvard University Press, 1999); Robert H. Gudmestad, *A Troublesome Commerce: The Transformation of the Interstate Slave Trade* (Baton Rouge: Louisiana State University Press, 2003); Steven Deyle, *Carry Me Back: The Domestic Slave Trade in American Life* (New York: Oxford University Press, 2005); Walter Johnson, ed., *The Chattel Principle: Internal Slave Trades in the Americas* (New Haven: Yale University Press, 2006); Calvin Schermerhorn, *The Business of Slavery and the Rise of American Capitalism, 1815–1860* (New Haven: Yale University Press, 2015); Daina Ramey Berry, *The Price for Their Pound of Flesh: The Value of the Enslaved, from Womb to Grave, in the Building of a Nation* (Boston: Beacon, 2017); Alexandra J. Finley, *An Intimate Economy: Enslaved Women, Work, and America's Domestic Slave Trade* (Chapel Hill: University of North Carolina Press, 2020); and Joshua D. Rothman, *The Ledger and the Chain: How Domestic Slave Traders Shaped America* (New York: Basic Books, 2021).

For specific maritime incidents related to the coastwise slave trade, see Josephine F. Pacheco, *The* Pearl*: A Failed Slave Escape on the Potomac* (Chapel Hill: University of North Carolina Press, 2005); Mary Kay Ricks, *Escape on the* Pearl (New York: HarperCollins, 2007); Phillip Troutman, "Grapevine in the Slave Market: African American Geopolitical Literacy and the 1841 *Creole* Revolt," in *The Chattel Principle: Internal Slave Trades in the Americas*, ed. Walter Johnson (New Haven: Yale University Press,

2004), 203–33; Anita Rupprecht, "'All We Have Done, We Have Done for Freedom': The Creole Slave-Ship Revolt (1841) and the Revolutionary Atlantic," *International Review of Social History* 58 (2013): 253–77; Arthur T. Downey, *The* Creole *Affair: The Slave Rebellion That Led the U.S. and Great Britain to the Brink of War* (Lanham, MD: Rowman and Littlefield, 2014); Jeffrey R. Kerr-Ritchie, *Rebellious Passage: The* Creole *Revolt and America's Coastal Slave Trade* (New York: Cambridge University Press, 2019); and Jeff Forret, *Williams' Gang: A Notorious Slave Trader and His Cargo of Black Convicts* (New York: Cambridge University Press, 2020). Shipboard uprisings aboard the domestic slavers *Decatur* in 1826 and *Lafayette* in 1829 require further in-depth study. In the first, enslaved captives mutinied and tossed the captain and his mate overboard; in the latter, the attack upon the captain was suppressed.

Although the *Comet*, *Encomium*, *Enterprise*, and *Hermosa* were never forgotten (a term that gets overused by historians), scholars have never paid them much attention, and some of the published information about their voyages is incorrect. After the Civil War, onetime abolitionists remembered the slave ships studied here in such works as Henry Wilson, *History of the Rise and Fall of the Slave Power in America*, vol. 1, 3rd ed. (Boston: James R. Osgood, 1875), 439–43. In the following decades, they were mentioned in John Bassett Moore, *History and Digest of the International Arbitrations to Which the United States Has Been a Party*, vol. 1 (Washington, DC: Government Printing Office, 1898), 408–12, 419; Guy Carleton Lee, ed., *The History of North America*, vol. 13, *The Growth of the Nation, 1837 to 1860*, by Enoch Walter Sikes and William Morse Keener (Philadelphia: George Barrie's Sons, 1905), 69–70; Edwin Wiley, ed., *Lectures on the Growth and Development of the United States* (Washington, DC: American Educational Alliance, 1915), 452; and Carter G. Woodson, *The Negro in Our History* (Washington, DC: Associated Publishers, 1922), 208. More recently, one or more of the vessels earned brief mention by scholars, including Sandra Riley, *Homeward Bound: A History of the Bahama Islands to 1850 with a Definitive Study of Abaco in the American Loyalist Plantation Period* (Miami: Island Research, 1983), 211–13, 224–25; Don E. Fehrenbacher, *The Slaveholding Republic: An Account of the United States Government's Relations to Slavery*, ed. Ward M. McAfee (New York: Oxford University Press, 2001), 104–11; Edward Bartlett Rugemer, *The Problem of Emancipation: The Caribbean Roots of the American Civil War* (Baton Rouge: Louisiana State University Press, 2008), 197–204; Walter Johnson, "White Lies: Human Property and Domestic Slavery Aboard the Slave Ship *Creole*," *Atlantic Studies* 5, no. 2 (2008): 238, 241, 254; Gerald Horne, *Negro Comrades of the Crown: African Americans and the British Empire Fight the U.S. Before Emancipation* (New York: New York University Press, 2012), 99–101, 103, 107–10; R.J.M. Blackett, *Making Freedom: The Underground Railroad and the Politics of Slavery* (Chapel Hill: University of North Carolina Press, 2013), 22; Downey, Creole *Affair*, 13, 62–65, 79, 144, 145; Boyd Childress, "*Hermosa* Case (1840)," in *Encyclopedia of Emancipation and Abolition in the Transatlantic World*, vols. 1–3, ed. Junius Rodriguez (New York: Routledge, 2015), 296; Kerr-Ritchie,

Rebellious Passage, 66–76; Manisha Sinha, *The Slave's Cause: A History of Abolition* (New Haven: Yale University Press, 2016), 411, 413–15; Rothman, *The Ledger and the Chain*, 129, 159–61; and Elena K. Abbott, *Beacons of Liberty: International Free Soil and the Fight for Racial Justice in Antebellum America* (New York: Cambridge University Press, 2021), 161–63.

4. Sir J. Carmichael-Smyth to Lord Viscount Goderich, March 5, 1831, folio 60, reel 43, CO 23/84, BNAN; *Morning Post* (London), March 5, 1841.

5. Christopher Leslie Brown, *Moral Capital: Foundations of British Abolitionism* (Chapel Hill: University of North Carolina Press, 2006); Claudius K. Fergus, *Revolutionary Emancipation: Slavery and Abolitionism in the British West Indies* (Baton Rouge: Louisiana State University Press, 2013); Eric Williams, *Capitalism and Slavery*, 3rd ed. (1944; Chapel Hill: University of North Carolina Press, 2021).

6. *New York Journal of Commerce*, March 17, 1835 (first quotation); *Anti-Slavery Bugle* (Lisbon, Ohio), August 14, 1858 (second quotation). On the massive migration to the Lower Mississippi River Valley and the "flush times," see Joshua D. Rothman, *Flush Times and Fever Dreams: A Story of Capitalism and Slavery in the Age of Jackson* (Athens: University of Georgia Press, 2012); Walter Johnson, *River of Dark Dreams: Slavery and Empire in the Cotton Kingdom* (Cambridge: Belknap Press of Harvard University Press, 2013); Edward E. Baptist, *The Half Has Never Been Told: Slavery and the Making of American Capitalism* (New York: Basic Books, 2014).

7. Aaron Vail to Lord Palmerston, May 11, 1835, *Register of Debates*, 25th Cong., 1st sess., Appendix, p. 265.

8. For courtroom battles inspired by transatlantic slavers, see, among other works, Bright, *Dark Places of the Earth*; and Rediker, *Amistad Rebellion*.

9. On the connections between slavery and capitalism in the U.S. South, see Rothman, *Flush Times and Fever Dreams*; Johnson, *River of Dark Dreams*; Baptist, *Half Has Never Been Told*; Sven Beckert, *Empire of Cotton: A Global History* (New York: Vintage, 2015); Schermerhorn, *Business of Slavery*; Sven Beckert and Seth Rockman, eds., *Slavery's Capitalism* (Philadelphia: University of Pennsylvania Press, 2016); Berry, *Price for Their Pound of Flesh*; and Finley, *Intimate Economy*.

On insuring the enslaved, see Sharon Ann Murphy, "Securing Human Property: Slavery, Life Insurance, and Industrialization in the Upper South," *Journal of the Early Republic* 25 (Winter 2005): 615–52; Sharon Ann Murphy, *Investing in Life: Insurance in Antebellum America* (Baltimore: Johns Hopkins University Press, 2010), chap. 7; and Karen Kotzuk Ryder, "'Permanent Property': Slave Life Insurance in the Antebellum Southern United States" (PhD diss., University of Delaware, 2012). The most famous case involving the insurance of enslaved captives aboard a ship was that of the *Zong*. In 1781, fearing essential supplies were running low, the captain threw one-third of a shipment of Africans overboard during a transatlantic crossing. See James Walvin, *The* Zong*: A Massacre, the Law and the End of Slavery* (New Haven: Yale University Press, 2011).

10. This book offers a detailed case study of the argument presented in Matthew Karp, *This Vast Southern Empire: Slaveholders at the Helm of American Foreign Policy* (Cambridge: Harvard University Press, 2016). Karp deals with the vessels discussed here on pp. 17–19.

11. *Western Reserve Chronicle*, reprinted in *Huron Reflector* (Norwalk, Ohio), June 27, 1843.

12. John Fabian Witt, *Lincoln's Code: The Laws of War in American History* (New York: Free Press, 2012), 75–77 (quotations on p. 76).

13. Carla Ferstman, "Reparations," Oxford Bibliographies, www.oxfordbibliographies.com/view/document/obo-9780199796953/obo-9780199796953-0003.xml; Silvia Borelli, "State Responsibility," Oxford Bibliographies, www.oxfordbibliographies.com/view/document/obo-9780199796953/obo-9780199796953-0031.xml; John Torpey, *Making Whole What Has Been Smashed: On Reparation Politics* (Cambridge: Harvard University Press, 2006), 45 (quotations); Ana Lucia Araujo, *Reparations for Slavery and the Slave Trade: A Transnational and Comparative History* (New York: Bloomsbury, 2017), 2.

14. Araujo, *Reparations for Slavery*, 6, draws a distinction between payments to slave owners, which she calls "financial compensation," and "reparations," defined as payments for past wrongs for slavery or the slave trade. I will use "reparation" (singular) for the slave owners because, in the context of international relations, diplomats used the word at the time.

1. The Wreck of the *Comet*

1. The 1820 census lists an Isaac Staples living in Portland, Cumberland County, Maine, engaged in commerce. His household included, presumably, a wife of roughly his same age and two children under ten. The 1830 census shows apparently the same Isaac Staples living in Gardiner, Maine, in Kennebec County, in a household that had expanded from four to six with the addition of two more children. I believe this Isaac Staples the master of the *Comet* because a pair of slave manifests from 1829 identify the "Brig Comet of Gardiner" as going from Alexandria, DC, to New Orleans. Shipbuilding was an important industry in the community of Gardiner in the early nineteenth century, so the *Comet* may well have been built there. It makes sense that a local man such as Isaac Staples would have become its captain. Manuscript Census Returns, Fourth Census of the United States, 1820, Portland, Cumberland County, Maine, NAMS M-33, reel 33, p. 255; Manuscript Census Returns, Fifth Census of the United States, 1830, Gardiner, Kennebec County, Maine, NAMS M-19, reel 48, p. 258; Inward Slave Manifest, New Orleans, February 27, 1829 (*Comet*), NARA M1895, reel 6, image 168; Inward Slave Manifest, New Orleans, December 6, 1829 (*Comet*), NARA M1895, reel 6, image 455.

2. *United States Gazette* (Philadelphia), October 17, 1828; *Charleston (SC) Daily Courier*, December 27, 1828.

3. Manifest of the *Comet*, December 17, 1830, pp. 187–91, CO 23/92, NAUK; Isaac Staples and Stephen Foxwell, Public Act of Protest, New Orleans, filed with notary public Carlile Pollock, February 14, 1831, p. 164, CO 23/92 Secretary of State Correspondence, NAUK (first through fourth quotations); *National Gazette* (Philadelphia), January 6, 1831; *Edenton (NC) Gazette*, March 16, 1831 (fifth quotation).

4. Staples and Foxwell, Public Act of Protest, p. 164 (quotations); *Edenton (NC) Gazette*, March 16, 1831; Jeffrey R. Kerr-Ritchie, *Rebellious Passage: The* Creole *Revolt and America's Coastal Slave Trade* (New York: Cambridge University Press, 2019), 163.

5. William Melbourne Fox, *qui tam* against certain Negroes or persons of color, Instance Court of Vice Admiralty (1831), p. 86, TS 25/2047 Treasury Solicitor and HM Procurator General: Law Officers' and Counsel's Opinions, NAUK (first quotation); Manuscript Census Returns, Seventh Census of the United States, 1850, St. Mary's County, Maryland, NAMS M-432, reel 296, p. 278A; Staples and Foxwell, Public Act of Protest, pp. 164 (second quotation), 165 (third quotation); *Edenton Gazette*, March 16, 1831; Manifest of the *Comet*, December 17, 1830. In the original documents, Cay is variously spelled as Quay or Key.

6. *Charleston (SC) Daily Courier*, February 3, 1830; *Charleston (SC) Daily Courier*, April 26, 1830; *Evening Post* (New York), June 7, 1830; *Charleston (SC) Mercury*, June 30, 1830; Edward Ingersoll, comp., *A Digest of the Laws of the United States of America, from March 4th, 1789, to May 15th, 1820* (Philadelphia: James Maxwell, 1821), 799–800; *Commercial Bulletin, Price-Current and Shipping List* (New Orleans), November 6, 1830.

7. Walter Johnson, *River of Dark Dreams: Slavery and Empire in the Cotton Kingdom* (Cambridge: Belknap Press of Harvard University Press, 2013); Edward E. Baptist, *The Half Has Never Been Told: Slavery and the Making of American Capitalism* (New York: Basic Books, 2014); Calvin Schermerhorn, *The Business of Slavery and the Rise of American Capitalism, 1815–1860* (New Haven: Yale University Press, 2015); Jeff Forret, *Williams' Gang: A Notorious Slave Trader and His Cargo of Black Convicts* (New York: Cambridge University Press, 2020).

8. Manifest of the *Comet*, December 17, 1830; Ralph Clayton, *Cash for Blood: The Baltimore to New Orleans Domestic Slave Trade* (Westminster, MD: Heritage Books, 2007), 125; Forret, *Williams' Gang*, 79–80, 366–68 (appendix B); Clearance of the Brig *Comet*, December 17, 1830, T 1/3556 Treasury Long Papers, bundle 133, part 2, NAUK.

9. Fox, *qui tam*, p. 86; Manifest of the *Comet*, December 17, 1830 (quotation); William Rothery to J. Stewart, May 30, 1834, p. 370, CO 23/92, NAUK.

10. Manifest of the *Comet*, December 17, 1830 (quotations); Forret, *Williams' Gang*, 4, 36, 39. For a full history of Franklin & Armfield, see Joshua D. Rothman, *The Ledger and the Chain: How Domestic Slave Traders Shaped America* (New York: Basic Books, 2021).

11. Johnson, *River of Dark Dreams*, 2; Baptist, *Half Has Never Been Told*, xxiii, 2–3.

12. Clearance of the Brig *Comet*, December 17, 1830; Staples and Foxwell, Public Act of Protest, p. 165 (first quotation); Fox, *qui tam*, p. 87 (second quotation).

13. Michael Craton and Gail Saunders, *Islanders in the Stream: A History of the Bahamian People*, vol. 1 (Athens: University of Georgia Press, 1999), 86–87; Anita Rupprecht, "'All We Have Done, We Have Done for Freedom': The *Creole* Slave-Ship Revolt (1841) and the Revolutionary Atlantic," *International Review of Social History* 58 (2013): 170; William Rothery to J. Stewart, May 30, 1834, pp. 370 (first through third quotations), 371 (fourth and fifth quotations); *Edenton (NC) Gazette*, March 16, 1831.

14. *Edenton (NC) Gazette*, March 16, 1831 (first and second quotations); Robert Duncome examination of Summerset Nutter, January 13, 1831, p. 184, CO 23/92, NAUK; Robert Duncome examination of Nelson Lemon, January 15, 1831, p. 182, CO 23/92, NAUK; William Rothery to J. Stewart, p. 371 (third quotation); Fox, *qui tam*, p. 87 (fourth quotation); Staples and Foxwell, Public Act of Protest, p. 165; John Storr to Martin Van Buren, January 17, 1831, p. 178, CO 23/92, NAUK (fifth quotation).

15. www.measuringworth.com; Staples and Foxwell, Public Act of Protest, p. 165 (quotations); William Rothery to J. Stewart, pp. 371–72; *Edenton (NC) Gazette*, March 16, 1831; Fox, *qui tam*, p. 88.

16. Michael Craton, "We Shall Not Be Moved: Pompey's Slave Revolt in Exuma Island, Bahamas, 1830," *New West Indian Guide* 57, no. 1/2 (1983): 20; Michael Craton, "The Ambivalences of Independency: The Transition Out of Slavery in the Bahamas, c. 1800–1850," in *West Indies Accounts: Essays on the History of the British Caribbean and the Atlantic Economy in Honour of Richard Sheridan*, ed. Roderick A. McDonald (Kingston, Jamaica: University of the West Indies Press, 1996), 278, 284–86; Craton and Saunders, *Islanders in the Stream*, vol. 1, 289, 277. The slave population of New Providence stood at 2,250 right before abolition went into effect in 1834. See Kerr-Ritchie, *Rebellious Passage*, 161. Kerr-Ritchie also notes that the Royal Navy landed six thousand Africans rescued from the transatlantic slave trade in the Bahamas between 1811 and 1841. See p. 145.

17. Craton and Saunders, *Islanders in the Stream*, vol. 1, 214; *Niles National Register* (St. Louis), March 15, 1828; Martin Van Buren to Edward Livingston, February 28, 1832, pp. 99, 117, CO 23/92, NAUK; John Storr to Martin Van Buren, January 17, 1831, p. 178 (first quotation); Staples and Foxwell, Public Act of Protest, pp. 165 (second quotation), 166 (third quotation); *Edenton (NC) Gazette*, March 16, 1831.

18. John Storr to Martin Van Buren, p. 179 (quotation); Staples and Foxwell, Public Act of Protest, p. 166; Isaac Staples, Protest at Nassau, January 20, 1831, p. 171, CO 23/92, NAUK; *Charleston (SC) Courier*, February 2, 1831; *City Gazette* (Charleston, SC), February 3, 1831; *Savannah Georgian*, January 31, 1831, reprinted in *Evening Post*

(New York), February 11, 1831; William Rothery to the Right Honble the Lords &c, August 5 1831, p. 131, TS 25/2047, NAUK (second quotation).

19. Staples, Protest at Nassau, p. 171; Manifest of the *Comet*, December 17, 1830; Robert Duncome examination of Nelson Lemon, January 15, 1831, pp. 182 (first quotation), 182–83 (second quotation).

20. *Charleston (SC) Courier*, February 2, 1831 (quotation); Petition, House of Assembly to James Carmichael-Smyth, p. 93, TS 25/2047, NAUK; House of Assembly, Committee Report, 1831, p. 126, CO 23/92, NAUK; the Department of Archives, Commonwealth of the Bahamas, www.bahamasnationalarchives.bs/assets/smyth.pdf.

21. Petition, House of Assembly to James Carmichael-Smyth, January 14, 1831, folio 31, reel 43, CO 23/84, BNAN (quotations); *Charleston (SC) Courier*, February 2, 1831.

22. Petition, House of Assembly to James Carmichael-Smyth, folio 31 (first through fourth and seventh through twelfth quotations); Petition, House of Assembly to James Carmichael-Smyth, p. 90 (fifth and sixth quotations); *Charleston (SC) Courier*, February 2, 1831.

23. Petition, House of Assembly to James Carmichael-Smyth, folio 31. On colonial officials taking the initiative to compensate for lags in transoceanic communication in the Spanish colonial context, see John Leddy Phelan, "Authority and Flexibility in the Spanish Imperial Bureaucracy," *Administrative Science Quarterly* 5 (June 1960): 47–65.

24. Reply, James Carmichael-Smyth, January 14, 1831, folio 31, reel 43, CO 23/84, BNAN (quotations); *Charleston (SC) Courier*, February 2, 1831.

25. John Storr to Martin Van Buren, p. 179; Staples, Protest at Nassau, p. 171; Staples and Foxwell, Public Act of Protest, p. 166 (quotations); Martin Van Buren to Edward Livingston, p. 100; William Rothery to J. Stewart, p. 372.

26. Edward Livingston to Martin Van Buren, December 5, 1831, *Register of Debates*, 25th Cong., 1st sess., Appendix, p. 251; Padraic X. Scanlan, *Freedom's Debtors: British Antislavery in Sierra Leone in the Age of Revolution* (New Haven: Yale University Press, 2017), 98, 101; *Edenton (NC) Gazette*, March 16, 1831 (quotations); *Charleston (SC) Courier*, February 2, 1831. Staples registered another protest in Nassau on Thursday, January 20, 1831, before notary public George Campbell Anderson. That paperwork was later included in files notarized by Carlile Pollock in New Orleans on February 26. See Staples, Protest at Nassau, p. 170.

27. Manifest of the *Comet*, December 17, 1830.

28. Appraisement of slaves aboard the *Comet*, February 25, 1831, folios 83–84, reel 43, CO 23/84, BNAN; Manifest of the *Comet*, December 17, 1830. A Louisiana law of 1829 prevented the selling of children under the age of ten away from their mothers.

29. Report from the Collector and Comptroller of Customs in the Bahamas to the Board of Customs in London, January 20, 1831, pp. 123–24, TS 25/2047, NAUK; Manifest of the *Comet*, December 17, 1830; Robert Duncome examination of Summerset Nutter, January 13, 1831, p. 184; Robert Duncome examination of Nelson

Lemon, January 15, 1831, p. 183 (first quotation); *Edenton (NC) Gazette*, March 16, 1831; Nathan Morse to Edward Livingston, n.d., p. 122, CO 23/92, NAUK, p. 122; Sir J. Carmichael-Smyth to the Lord Viscount Goderich, January 31, 1831, folio 29, reel 43, CO 23/84, BNAN (second and third quotations).

30. Report from the Collector and Comptroller of Customs in the Bahamas to the Board of Customs in London, January 20, 1831, p. 122.

31. Report from the Collector and Comptroller of Customs in the Bahamas to the Board of Customs in London, January 20, 1831, p. 122 (first, second, and fourth through eighth quotations); House of Assembly, Committee Report, 1831, p. 130 (third quotation).

32. Report from the Collector and Comptroller of Customs in the Bahamas to the Board of Customs in London, January 20, 1831, p. 123 (quotations); *Charleston (SC) Daily Courier*, April 18, 1818; Sir J. Carmichael-Smyth to Lord Viscount Goderich, March 5, 1831, folio 60, reel 43, CO 23/84, BNAN; David Eltis, "The Traffic in Slaves Between the British West Indian Colonies, 1807–1833," *Economic History Review* 25, no. 1 (February 1972): 55. According to Carmichael-Smyth, the enslaved cargo was placed aboard an American vessel in Nassau before proceeding on its journey. See Sir J. Carmichael-Smyth to Lord Viscount Goderich, March 5, 1831, folio 61. In 1818, Thomas B. Wylly's father, William, served as attorney general when the 101 U.S. slaves were wrecked and sent on their way to New Orleans.

33. House of Assembly, Committee Report, 1831, p. 127; *Edenton (NC) Gazette*, March 16, 1831 (quotations).

34. House of Assembly, Committee Report, 1831, p. 130.

35. House of Assembly, Committee Report, 1831, p. 131.

36. House of Assembly, Committee Report, 1831, p. 131.

37. House of Assembly, Committee Report, 1831, pp. 131–32 (first quotation); Sir J. Carmichael-Smyth to the Lord Viscount Goderich, January 31, 1831, folio 28, 29 (second quotation); Report from the Collector and Comptroller of Customs in the Bahamas to the Board of Customs in London, January 20, 1831, p. 122 (third quotation).

38. *Pawtucket (RI) Chronicle and Manufacturers' and Artizans' Advocate*, February 25, 1831; *Savannah Georgian*, January 31, 1831, reprinted in *Evening Post* (New York), February 11, 1831; *Charleston (SC) Courier*, February 2, 1831; *City Gazette* (Charleston, SC), February 3, 1831 (quotation); *The Liberator* (Boston), February 19, 1831; *The Liberator* (Boston), April 9, 1831.

39. Sir J. Carmichael-Smyth to the Lord Viscount Goderich, January 31, 1831, folio 28 (first quotation); Staples and Foxwell, Public Act of Protest, pp. 166 (second through sixth quotations), 166–67 (seventh quotation); *Alexandria (DC) Gazette*, February 26, 1831. Despite the debacle with the *Comet*, Isaac Staples retained the confidence of Franklin & Armfield and went on to pilot their slave ship *Tribune*. See Schermerhorn, *Business of Slavery*, 146–47.

40. Staples and Foxwell, Public Act of Protest, pp. 167 (first and second quotations), 168 (third quotation).

41. *City Gazette* (Charleston, SC), February 28, 1831; Decree of William Vesey Munnings, p. 132, CO 23/92, NAUK; Fox, *qui tam*, pp. 89 (quotations), 90.

42. A. Vail to Lord Palmerston, September 20, 1834, *Register of Debates*, 25th Cong., 1st sess., Appendix, p. 262; William Rothery to ?, May 30, 1834, p. 376, CO 23/92, NAUK; Christ. Robinson and R. Gifford to Earl Bathurst, August 27, 1818, pp. 149 (first quotation), 151 (second through fourth quotations), 152 (fifth through eighth quotations), CO 23/92, NAUK; Earl Bathurst to William Vesey Munnings, September 15, 1818, pp. 144–46, CO 23/92, NAUK (ninth quotation, 145).

43. Edward Livingston to Martin Van Buren, December 5, 1831, *Register of Debates*, 25th Cong., 1st sess., Appendix, p. 251; *Fox, Searcher & qui tam vs. certain Negroes & Persons of Colour* (1831), folio 70, reel 43, CO 23/84, BNAN (quotations).

44. *Fox, Searcher & qui tam vs. certain Negroes & Persons of Colour*, folios 70–71 (first quotation), 70 (second quotation), 71 (third quotation).

45. *City Gazette* (Charleston, SC), February 28, 1831; *Charleston (SC) Courier*, February 28, 1831; *Evening Post* (New York), March 24, 1831 (first and second quotations); *The Liberator* (Boston), April 9, 1831 (third quotation); *Genius of Universal Emancipation* (Baltimore), reprinted in *Christian Register* (Boston), June 4, 1831 (fourth and fifth quotations).

2. Insuring Human Merchandise

1. Ann M. Tutt to Mason Chichester, January 29, 1831, RSPP, Petition 20484401, Series II, Part B, Reel 15, Washington, DC (quotations); Manuscript Census Returns, Fifth Census of the United States, 1830, Leesburg Township, Loudoun County, Virginia, NAMS M-19, reel 193, p. 38; *Index to the Compiled Military Service Records for the Volunteer Soldiers Who Served During the War of 1812*, NARA, M-602, reel 213; *U.S. Navy and Marine Corps Directory, 1831*; *Navy Register: Officers of the U.S. Navy and Marine, 1832*; Manifest of the *Comet*, December 17, 1830, pp. 187–91, CO 23/92 Secretary of State Correspondence, NAUK; Ellen Samuels, "'A Compilation of Complaints': Untangling Disability, Race, and Gender in William and Ellen Craft's *Running a Thousand Miles for Freedom*," *MELUS* 31, no. 3 (Fall 2006): 16.

2. *Genius of Universal Emancipation*, reprinted in *Christian Register* (Boston), June 4, 1831 (first and second quotations); Report from the Collector and Comptroller of Customs in the Bahamas to the Board of Customs in London, January 20, 1831, p. 123, TS 25/2047 Treasury Solicitor and HM Procurator General: Law Officers' and Counsel's Opinions, NAUK (third through fifth quotations).

3. Sharon Ann Murphy, "Securing Human Property: Slavery, Life Insurance, and Industrialization in the Upper South," *Journal of the Early Republic* 25 (Winter 2005): 649–50; Christopher Kingston, "Marine Insurance in Britain and America, 1720–1844:

A Comparative Institutional Analysis," *Journal of Economic History* 67 (June 2007): 380–81, 383; Todd L. Savitt, "Slave Life Insurance in Virginia and North Carolina," *Journal of Southern History* 43 (November 1977): 584–85, 591; Karen Ryder, "'To Realize Money Facilities': Slave Life Insurance, the Slave Trade, and Credit in the Old South," in *New Directions in Slavery Studies: Commodification, Community, and Comparison*, ed. Jeff Forret and Christine E. Sears (Baton Rouge: Louisiana State University Press, 2015), 54–56; Karen Kotzuk Ryder, "'Permanent Property': Slave Life Insurance in the Antebellum Southern United States" (PhD diss., University of Delaware, 2012), 2, 5, 27, 29; Rachel L. Swarns, "Insurance Policies on Slaves: New York Life's Complicated Past," *New York Times*, December 18, 2016.

4. Kingston, "Marine Insurance," 382, 392, 396; Ryder, "Permanent Property," 61, ix, 2; Cheryl Rhan-Hsin Chen and Gary Simon, "Actuarial Issues in Insurance on Slaves in the United States South," *Journal of African American History* 89 (Autumn 2004): 349. On the development of incorporated marine insurance companies in the American South, see A. Glenn Crothers, "Commercial Risk and Capital Formation in Early America: Virginia Merchants and the Rise of American Marine Insurance, 1750–1815," *Business History Review* 78 (Winter 2004): 607–33.

5. Royal Commission on Fugitive Slaves, *Report of the Commissioners. Minutes of the Evidence. And Appendix, with General Index, of Minutes of Evidence and Appendix* (London: George Edward Eyre and William Spottiswoode, 1876), 231; *Royal Gazette* (Nassau), March 9, 1831, quoted on p. 136, CO 23/92, NAUK; Lord Palmerston to Andrew Stevenson, May 2, 1839, 26th Cong., 1st sess., Sen. Doc. No. 119, p. 7; William Melbourne Fox, *qui tam* against certain Negroes or persons of color, Instance Court of Vice Admiralty (1831), p. 88, TS 25/2047, NAUK (quotation); Joshua D. Rothman, *The Ledger and the Chain: How Domestic Slave Traders Shaped America* (New York: Basic Books, 2021), 159, 161. Rothman notes that two of the insurers, combined, paid Franklin & Armfield $37,555, but the third insurer's payments may have upped that total. In 1831, the respective capitalizations for the Louisiana State Marine and Fire Insurance Company, the Mississippi Marine and Fire Insurance Company, and the Merchants Insurance Company of New Orleans were $400,000, $300,000, and $1 million. See *Beer's Louisiana and Mississippi Almanac, for the Year 1831* (Natchez, MS: F. Beaumont, n.d.), n.p.

6. *Royal Gazette* (Nassau), p. 136 (quotations); Martin Van Buren to Edward Livingston, February 25, 1832, *Register of Debates*, 25th Cong., 1st sess., Appendix, p. 254; www.measuringworth.com.

7. *Royal Gazette* (Nassau), p. 136; *Commercial Bulletin, Price-Current and Shipping List* (New Orleans), January 22, 1831; Van Buren to Livingston, February 25, 1832, p. 154 (quotations).

8. J. Walker and W. Webb to William Martin and T.B. Wylly, February 17, 1831, folios 72, 73 (quotations), reel 43, CO 23/84, BNAN. Walker and Webb expressed

concerns about their own legal liability should they prevent these various arrangements for removal.

9. Appraisement of slaves, February 25, 1831, folios 83–85, reel 43, CO23/84, BNAN.

10. Howard Johnson, *The Bahamas from Slavery to Servitude, 1783–1933* (Gainesville: University Press of Florida, 1996), 10, 32–33; Michael Craton, "The Ambivalences of Independency: The Transition Out of Slavery in the Bahamas, c. 1800–1850," in *West Indies Accounts: Essays on the History of the British Caribbean and the Atlantic Economy in Honour of Richard Sheridan*, ed. Roderick A. McDonald (Kingston, Jamaica: University of the West Indies Press, 1996), 278, 283; John Storr to Martin Van Buren, January 17, 1831, p. 180, CO 23/92, NAUK (quotations).

11. Appraisement of slaves, February 25, 1831, folios 83–85, reel 43, CO23/84, BNAN.

12. Report from the Collector and Comptroller of Customs in the Bahamas to the Board of Customs in London, January 20, 1831, p. 124, TS 25/2047, NAUK.

13. Sir J. Carmichael-Smyth to Lord Viscount Goderich, March 5, 1831, folios 63, (first quotation), 56 (second, third, and fifth quotations), 57 (fourth quotation), 56–57 (sixth quotation), reel 43, CO 23/84, BNAN.

14. Sir J. Carmichael-Smyth to Lord Viscount Goderich, March 5, 1831, folios 57 (first through third quotations), 62, 58 (fourth quotation), 60–63.

15. Sir J. Carmichael-Smyth to Lord Viscount Goderich, March 5, 1831, folios 57 (first quotation), 59; T.B. Wylly to James Carmichael-Smyth, folio 76 (second quotation), reel 43, CO 23/84, BNAN; William Martin to James Carmichael-Smyth, February 18, 1831, folio 75, reel 43, CO 23/84, BNAN.

16. Sir J. Carmichael-Smyth to Lord Viscount Goderich, March 5, 1831, folio 59, reel 43, CO 23/84, BNAN.

17. *Royal Gazette* (Nassau), p. 134 (quotations); Manifest of the *Comet*.

18. *Royal Gazette* (Nassau), p. 134, 135 (quotations); J.C. Smyth to Lord Goderich, March 19, 1831, p. 95, CO 23/92, NAUK.

19. Letter of Nathan Morse, n.d., p. 135, CO 23/92, NAUK (first, second, fifth, and sixth quotations); *Evening Post* (New York), March 24, 1831 (third and fourth quotations). See also *The Liberator* (Boston), April 9, 1831.

20. Letter of Nathan Morse, pp. 135 (first through third quotations), 136 (fourth through sixth quotations); Manifest of the *Comet*, December 17, 1830, T 1/3556 Treasury Long Papers, bundle 133, part 2, NAUK; Craton, "Ambivalences of Independency," 287, 286, 290; Nathan Morse to Sir James Carmichael Smyth, August 6, 1831, p. 155, CO 23/92, NAUK; Sir J.C. Smyth to Lord Goderich, February 5, 1832, p. 96, CO 23/92, NAUK (seventh and eighth quotations). Other mentions of the enslaved people from the *Comet* who returned to servitude in the United States may be found in Royal Commission on Fugitive Slaves, *Report of the Commissioners*, 231; Lord Palmerston to Andrew Stevenson, May 2, 1839, 26th Cong., 1st sess., Sen. Doc.

No. 119, p. 7; and Andrew Stevenson to John Forsyth, May 8, 1839, 26th Cong., 1st sess., Sen. Doc. No. 119, p. 6.

21. *Fox, Searcher & qui tam vs. certain Negroes & Persons of Colour,* folio 71 (first quotation); William Rothery to [the Lords Treasury?], June 14, 1832, Secretary of State Correspondence (loose papers), Gov. 15/1 1832–1921, BNAN (second quotation); J. Stewart to [Lord Howick?], August 2, 1832, Secretary of State Correspondence (loose papers), Gov. 15/1 1832–1921, BNAN (third quotation); Lord Goderich to James Carmichael-Smyth, folios 65 (fourth quotation), 66 (fifth and sixth quotations), reel 43, CO 23/84, BNAN.

22. Lord Goderich to James Carmichael-Smyth, 68 (first through third quotations); Lord Howick to J. Stewart, May 26, 1831, p. 129, TS 25/2047, NAUK (fourth through seventh quotations).

23. Lord Goderich to James Carmichael-Smyth, folio 66.

24. History of Parliament Trust, www.historyofparliamentonline.org/volume/1820-1832/member/grey-henry-1802-1894; Lord Goderich to James Carmichael-Smyth, folio 67, reel 43, CO 23/84, BNAN (quotations).

25. Lord Howick to J. Stewart, May 26, 1831, pp. 125 (first and fifth quotations), 126 (second through fourth quotations).

26. Lord Howick to J. Stewart, May 26, 1831, p. 128 (first, fourth, and fifth quotations), 127 (second quotation), 127–28 (third quotation).

27. William Rothery to the Right Honble the Lords &c, August 5 1831, pp. 132 (first and second quotations), 134 (third through fifth quotations), TS 25/2047, NAUK. See also Mr. Stewart to Lord Howick, August 30, 1831, p. 95, CO 23/92, NAUK; and CO 23/92, BNAK, p. 95: Lord Goderich to Sir J.C. Smyth, September 21, 1831, p. 95, CO 23/92, NAUK.

28. Nathan Morse to Sir James Carmichael Smyth, August 6, 1831, pp. 152 (first quotation), 153, (second quotation), 153–54 (third quotation), 154 (fourth and fifth quotations), CO 23/92, NAUK; J. Carmichael Smyth to Nathan Morse, August 6, 1831, pp. 155–56 (sixth quotation 156), CO 23/92, NAUK; Van Buren to Livingston, February 25, 1832, p. 254.

29. Nathan Morse to George Campbell Anderson, August 5, 1831, pp. 136 (first and second quotations), 137 (third through seventh quotations), CO 23/92, NAUK.

30. George Campbell Anderson to Nathan Morse, August 9, 1831, pp. 138, 139 (first and second quotations), 140–41 (third quotation), CO 23/92, NAUK.

31. George Campbell Anderson to Nathan Morse, August 9, 1831, pp. 141, 142, 143 (first and second quotations), 144 (third quotation).

32. *Bahama Argus*, reprinted in *Evening Post* (New York), October 5, 1831.

33. *Jamaica Courant* (Kingston), August 26, 1831, reprinted in *Alexandria (DC) Gazette*, October 7, 1831.

34. Storr to Van Buren, January 17, 1831, pp. 179–80 (quotation); *Alexandria Gazette*, October 7, 1831.

35. Letter of Nathan Morse, pp. 159 (first through third quotations), 160, CO 23/92, NAUK; *Jamaica Courant* (Kingston), August 26, 1831, reprinted in *Alexandria Gazette*, October 7, 1831 (fourth and fifth quotations).

36. *Alexandria Gazette*, October 7, 1831 (first and second quotations); *Jamaica Courant* (Kingston), August 26, 1831, reprinted in *Alexandria Gazette*, October 7, 1831 (third quotation).

37. Nathan Morse to Edward Livingston, n.d., p. 114, CO 23/92, NAUK (first and second quotations); William Rothery to T.F. Baring, March 23, 1839, T 1/3556, NAUK (third and fourth quotations).

38. Nathan Morse to Edward Livingston, October 7, 1831, pp. 174–75, CO 23/92, NAUK; Andrew Stevenson to John Forsyth, May 8, 1839, 26th Cong., 1st sess., Sen. Doc. No. 119, p. 6; RSPP, Petition 20484401, Series II, Part B, Reel 15, Washington, DC; Lord Goderich to Sir J.C. Smyth, October 20, 1831, p. 96, CO 23/92, NAUK (first quotation); *Bahama Argus*, reprinted in *Evening Post*, October 5, 1831 (second and third quotations). Morse stated in his letter of October 7 that the House of Assembly conducted a valuation of the *Comet* captives that underestimated their total value "by more than $50,000." This appraisement must be different from the one ordered by the Vice Admiralty Court, which put their values lower still. It seems there were at least two, and possibly as many as three, valuations completed.

3. Proslavery Exertions

1. Jeff Forret, *Slave Against Slave: Plantation Violence in the Old South* (Baton Rouge: Louisiana State University Press, 2015), chaps. 2–3; Thomas D. Morris, *Southern Slavery and the Law, 1619–1860* (Chapel Hill: University of North Carolina Press, 1996), 147–58; John Fabian Witt, *The Accidental Republic: Crippled Workingmen, Destitute Widows, and the Remaking of American Law* (Cambridge: Harvard University Press, 2004), 52.

2. Edward Livingston to Martin Van Buren, December 5, 1831, *Register of Debates*, 25th Cong., 1st sess., Appendix, p. 251.

3. William A. DeGregorio, *The Complete Book of U.S. Presidents*, 4th ed. (New York: Barricade, 1993), 123; Martin Van Buren to Edward Livingston, February 28, 1832, *Register of Debates*, 25th Cong., 1st sess., Appendix, p. 253.

4. Martin Van Buren to Lord Viscount Palmerston, February 25, 1832, *Register of Debates*, 25th Cong., 1st sess., Appendix, pp. 253 (first through fifth quotations), 254 (sixth quotation).

5. Van Buren to Palmerston, February 25, 1832, p. 254.

6. Van Buren to Palmerston, February 25, 1832, p. 254.

7. Van Buren to Palmerston, February 25, 1832, p. 255.

8. Van Buren to Palmerston, February 25, 1832, p. 255.

9. Van Buren to Palmerston, February 25, 1832, p. 256.

10. Van Buren to Palmerston, February 25, 1832, p. 256; The Duke of Wellington to the Earl of Aberdeen, January 12, 1835, p. 50, CO 23/95 Correspondence, Original–Secretary of State, NAUK.

11. The Duke of Wellington to the Earl of Aberdeen, January 12, 1835, p. 50 (quotations); James Stephen to George Grey, September 10, 1834, p. 309, CO 23/92, Secretary of State Correspondence, NAUK.

12. Edward Livingston to Aaron Vail, February 26, 1833, *Register of Debates*, 25th Cong., 1st sess., Appendix, p. 251; Aaron Vail to Edward Livingston, July 15, 1832, *Register of Debates*, 25th Cong., 1st sess., Appendix, p. 256; Chief Clerk of the Department of State to Aaron Vail, September 28, 1832, *Register of Debates*, 25th Cong., 1st sess., Appendix, p. 251 (first quotation); Aaron Vail to Edward Livingston, November 14, 1832, *Register of Debates*, 25th Cong., 1st sess., Appendix, p. 256 (second quotation).

13. Edward Livingston to Aaron Vail, February 26, 1833, *Register of Debates*, 25th Cong., 1st sess., Appendix, p. 252.

14. Robert Remini, *The Life of Andrew Jackson* (New York: HarperPerennial, 2009), 5, 33, 51, 20, 71, chap. 9, 215–19.

15. A. Vail to Viscount Palmerston, March 25, 1833, p. 195, CO 23/92, NAUK (first quotation); Lord Palmerston to Aaron Vail, March 30, 1833, *Register of Debates*, 25th Cong., 1st sess., Appendix, p. 257; Aaron Vail to Edward Livingston, March 30, 1833, *Register of Debates*, 25th Cong., 1st sess., Appendix, p. 256 (second quotation).

16. A. Vail to Viscount Palmerston, April 4, 1833, pp. 198 (first quotation), 199 (second through sixth quotations), CO 23/92, NAUK.

17. A. Vail to Viscount Palmerston, April 4, 1833, pp. 199 (first quotation), 200 (second through fourth quotations); Aaron Vail to Lord Palmerston, April 4, 1833, *Register of Debates*, 25th Cong., 1st sess., Appendix, p. 258 (fifth quotation).

18. A. Vail to Viscount Palmerston, April 4, 1833, p. 200 (first and second quotations), 200–201 (third quotation), 201 (fourth and fifth quotation).

19. Aaron Vail to Edward Livingston, April 6, 1833, *Register of Debates*, 25th Cong., 1st sess., Appendix, p. 257 (first through fourth quotations); Lord Palmerston to Aaron Vail, April 24, 1833, 24th Cong., 2d sess., Sen. Doc. 174, p. 21 (fifth quotation); Aaron Vail to Edward Livingston, April 29, 1833, 24th Cong., 2d sess., Sen. Doc. 174, p. 20 (sixth quotation).

20. Nicholas Draper, *The Price of Emancipation: Slave-Ownership, Compensation and British Society at the End of Slavery* (New York: Cambridge University Press, 2010), 100, 106, 114; Keith Hamilton and Farida Shaikh, "Introduction," in *Slavery, Diplomacy and Empire: Britain and the Suppression of the Slave Trade, 1807–1975*, ed. Keith Hamilton and Patrick Salmon (Brighton, UK: Sussex Academic Press, 2009), 14; Robert Elder, *Calhoun: American Heretic* (New York: Basic Books, 2021), 312; Jeffrey R. Kerr-Ritchie, *Rebellious Passage: The* Creole *Revolt and America's Coastal Slave Trade* (New York: Cambridge University Press, 2019), 161. An ongoing, contentious

debate over the length of apprenticeship between 1836 and 1838 led to a shortening of its duration. All apprenticeships ended in 1838. See Draper, *Price of Emancipation*, 21, 67.

21. Aaron Vail to Louis McLane, September 28, 1833, 24th Cong., 2d sess., Sen. Doc. 174, p. 21 (first, second, and fifth quotations); Aaron Vail to Louis McLane, January 14, 1834, *Register of Debates*, 25th Cong., 1st sess., Appendix, p. 258 (third and fourth quotations).

22. Herbert Jenner, J. Campbell, and C.C. Pepys to Viscount Palmerston, April 9, 1834, pp. 203, 204 (quotations), CO 23/92, NAUK.

23. Lord Palmerston to the Lords Commissioners of His Majesty's Treasury, May 10, 1834, pp. 207–8, CO 23/92, NAUK; James Stephen to George Grey, September 10, 1834, p. 310 (quotation).

24. Report of William Rothery, May 30, 1834, pp. 369 (first quotation), 373 (second through fourth quotations), 374 (fifth quotation), CO 23/92, NAUK.

25. Report of William Rothery, May 30, 1834, p. 375.

26. Report of William Rothery, May 30, 1834, pp. 376 (first through third quotations), 380 (fourth through sixth quotations). Rothery invoked the case of *Forbes v. Cochrane* (1824), which involved a group of thirty-eight enslaved people who fled a plantation in East Florida in 1815 and found refuge onboard the British warship *Terror*. Sir George Cockburn permitted Forbes, the former owner, to try to persuade the fugitives to return home but would not surrender them to him. See pp. 379–80.

27. Report of William Rothery, May 30, 1834, p. 381.

28. The Duke of Wellington to the Earl of Aberdeen, January 12, 1835, p. 51; James Stephen to George Grey, September 10, 1834, p. 310.

29. John Forsyth to Aaron Vail, August 2, 1834, *Register of Debates*, 25th Cong., 1st sess., Appendix, p. 252 (first through fourth quotations); Aaron Vail to Lord Palmerston, August 1, 1834, *Register of Debates*, 25th Cong., 1st sess., Appendix, p. 259 (fifth through seventh quotations).

30. Aaron Vail to John Forsyth, *Register of Debates*, August 6, 1834, 25th Cong., 1st sess., Appendix, p. 259 (first through third quotations); G. Shee to the lords commissioners, August 9, 1834, pp. 399–400 (fourth quotation p. 400), CO 23/92, NAUK; [Illegible] to J.G.S. Lefevre, August 22, 1834, p. 388, CO 23/92, NAUK; James Stephen to George Grey, September 10, 1834, p. 310 (fifth quotation); Aaron Vail to John Forsyth, August 14, 1834, *Register of Debates*, 25th Cong., 1st sess., Appendix, p. 259 (sixth quotation).

4. The *Encomium* Runs Aground

1. *Charleston (SC) Courier*, February 1, 1834 (first and second quotations); Walter Johnson, *River of Dark Dreams: Slavery and Empire in the Cotton Kingdom* (Cambridge: Belknap Press of Harvard University Press, 2013), 100.

2. Affidavit of Antonio Della Torre to Roger Heriot, November 9, 1837, T 1/3556 Treasury Long Papers, bundle 133, part 2, NAUK (first through fourth quotations); "Negroes Wanted," *Charleston (SC) Mercury*, July 7, 1835; Alexandra J. Finley, "A Gentleman and a Scoundrel?: Alexander McDonald, Financial Reputation, and Slavery's Capitalism," in *Southern Scoundrels: Grifters and Graft in the Nineteenth Century*, ed. Jeff Forret and Bruce Baker (Baton Rouge: Louisiana State University Press, 2021), chap. 2; Affidavit of Noah B. Sisson to Roger Heriot, May 15, 1837, T 1/3556 (fifth quotation). For more on John Hagan, see Alexandra J. Finley, *An Intimate Economy: Enslaved Women, Work, and America's Domestic Slave Trade* (Chapel Hill: University of North Carolina Press, 2020), 102–11.

3. Manuscript Census Returns, Seventh Census of the United States, 1850, St. Michael and St. Phillip, Charleston, South Carolina, Schedule 1, Free Population, NAMS M-432, reel 850, p. 312A; *Charleston (SC) Mercury*, August 3, 1858; *American Farmer* (Baltimore), January 6, 1826; Ira Berlin and Herbert G. Gutman, "Natives and Immigrants, Free Men and Slaves: Urban Workingmen in the Antebellum American South," *American Historical Review* 88, no. 5 (December 1983): 1176n2; Jerre Mangione and Ben Morreale, *La Storia: Five Centuries of the Italian American Experience* (New York: HarperPerennial, 1993), 14; Paolo Giordano, "Italian Immigration in the State of Louisiana: Its Causes, Effects, and Results," *Italian Americana* 5, no. 2 (Spring/Summer 1979): 164. On Italians in Louisiana, see A.V. Margavio and Jerome J. Salomone, *Bread and Respect: The Italians of Louisiana* (Gretna, LA: Pelican, 2002). The Mexican territory of Texas contained an estimated twenty-four Italian immigrants in 1821, and by 1839, the independent Republic of Texas contained approximately thirty-two. See Valentine J. Belfiglio, *The Italian Experience in Texas: A Closer Look* (Austin: Eakin Press, 1995), 15.

4. *Charleston (SC) Daily Courier*, October 29, 1819; *Charleston (SC) Daily Courier*, October 23, 1820; *Charleston (SC) Mercury*, April 9, 1823; *City Gazette* (Charleston, SC), October 28, 1823; *Southern Patriot* (Charleston, SC), November 27, 1823 (quotation); No. 6 Ruins of St. Finbar's Cathedral, Charleston, SC (Charleston: Quinby and Co., c. 1865), Housworth Stereographs Collection, University of South Carolina, South Carolina Library, Columbia, SC, digital.tcl.sc.edu/digital/collection/stereo/id/2584; *Charleston (SC) Courier*, October 28, 1826.

5. *Charleston (SC) Mercury*, August 19, 1823; *American Farmer* (Baltimore), January 6, 1826; *Charleston (SC) Mercury*, December 7, 1825 (quotation).

6. James William Hagy, *Charleston, South Carolina City Directories for the Years 1816, 1819, 1822, 1825, and 1829* (Clearfield, 2009), 106; *Charleston (SC) Daily Courier*, October 18, 1830; *Charleston (SC) Daily Courier*, July 26, 1832; *Charleston (SC) Daily Courier*, March 1, 1830.

7. *Charleston (SC) Daily Courier*, January 15, 1828 (first through fifth quotations); July 20, 1831; May 8, 1832; January 8, 1833 (sixth quotation); May 17, 1831;

October 25, 1830 (seventh quotation); November 25, 1833; August 18, 1831; August 28, 1833; July 7, 1832 (eighth quotation).

8. *Charleston (SC) Daily Courier*, October 18, 1830; *Charleston (SC) Daily Courier*, December 14, 1830; Manuscript Census Returns, Fifth Census of the United States, 1830, Charleston Ward 1, Charleston, South Carolina, NAMS M-19, reel 170, p. 13.

9. Affidavit of Noah B. Sisson, May 15, 1837, T 1/3556; Sixth Census of the United States, 1840, Fairfield, Fairfield County, Connecticut, NAMS M-704, reel 22, p. 375; *Charleston (SC) Daily Courier*, March 31, 1830; *Charleston (SC) Daily Courier*, January 24, 1832; *Charleston (SC) Daily Courier*, July 23, 1832; *Charleston (SC) Daily Courier*, January 3, 1833 (first quotation); *Evening Post* (New York), June 17, 1833 (second quotation); Manifest of Slaves, Passengers, on board the Brig *Encomium*, P. Sheffield, Master, February 1, 1834, T 1/3556, NAUK; *Charleston (SC) Daily Courier*, May 22, 1833; *Charleston (SC) Courier*, January 4, 1834; *Royal Gazette* (Nassau), February 12, 1834; *Charleston (SC) Courier*, February 20, 1834; Protest of the Master, Mate, a Seaman and 3 Passengers of the *Encomium*, February 12, 1834, T 1/3556, NAUK; *Charleston (SC) Courier*, February 3, 1834 (third quotation).

10. *Southern Patriot* (Charleston, SC), February 20, 1834 (first quotation); Protest of the Master (second through fifth quotations); *New Orleans Bee*, March 4, 1834, reprinted in *Charleston (SC) Courier*, reprinted in *United States' Telegraph* (Washington, DC), March 27, 1834; *Royal Gazette* (Nassau), February 12, 1834. The protest states that the *Encomium* departed on Sunday, February 2, with the wreck at midnight between Tuesday and Wednesday. I have relied on newspaper sources stating that the ship left on Saturday, February 1.

11. Protest of the Master (first and second quotations); *Royal Gazette* (Nassau), February 12, 1834; *Southern Patriot* (Charleston, SC), February 20, 1834 (third, fourth, seventh, and eighth quotations); *New Orleans Bee*, March 4, 1834, reprinted in *Charleston (SC) Courier*, reprinted in *United States' Telegraph* (Washington, DC), March 27, 1834 (fifth and sixth quotations). Italics in original.

12. *New Orleans Bee*, March 4, 1834, reprinted in *Charleston (SC) Courier*, reprinted in *United States' Telegraph* (Washington, DC), March 27, 1834 (first and fifth quotations); *Southern Patriot* (Charleston, SC), February 20, 1834 (second through fourth and sixth quotations); Protest of the Master (seventh quotation).

13. *Southern Patriot* (Charleston, SC), February 20, 1834 (first and second quotations); *New Orleans Courier*, March 5, 1834, reprinted in the *American and Commercial Daily Advertiser* (Baltimore), March 24, 1834 (third quotation); *New Orleans Bee*, March 4, 1834, reprinted in *Columbian Centinel* (Boston), March 26, 1834 (fourth quotation); Protest of the Master (fifth and seventh quotations); *Charleston (SC) Courier*, February 20, 1834 (sixth quotation); *Royal Gazette* (Nassau), February 12, 1834 (eighth quotation); *Commercial Advertiser* (New York), March 1, 1834 (ninth quotation).

14. *Royal Gazette* (Nassau), February 12, 1834; *Southern Patriot* (Charleston, SC), February 20, 1834 (quotation); Protest of the Master; *People's Press and Wilmington*

(NC) Advertiser, April 23, 1834; *New Orleans Bee*, reprinted in *Charleston (SC) Courier*, May 2, 1834.

15. Petition, John Waddell to the General Assembly of North Carolina, December 8, 1834, RSPP, Petition 11283408, Series I, Reel 6, North Carolina; *New Orleans Courier*, March 5, 1834, reprinted in *American and Commercial Daily Advertiser* (Baltimore), March 24, 1834 (quotations); *New Orleans Bee*, March 4, 1834, reprinted in *Charleston (SC) Courier*, reprinted in *United States' Telegraph* (Washington, DC), March 27, 1834; *People's Press and Wilmington (NC) Advertiser*, April 23, 1834.

16. *New Orleans Bee*, March 4, 1834, reprinted in *Charleston (SC) Courier*, reprinted in *United States' Telegraph* (Washington, DC), March 27, 1834; Protest of the Master; Manifest of the *Encomium*, February 1, 1834; *Royal Gazette* (Nassau), February 12, 1834.

17. John Forsyth to Aaron Vail, August 2, 1834, *Register of Debates*, 25th Cong., 1st sess., Appendix, p. 252; Protest of the Master (first, second, fourth, and fifth quotations); *Journal of the House of Representatives of the State of Ohio*, 484 (third quotation).

18. *New Orleans Courier*, March 5, 1834, reprinted in the *American and Commercial Daily Advertiser* (Baltimore), March 24, 1834.

19. *New Orleans Courier*, March 5, 1834, reprinted in the *American and Commercial Daily Advertiser* (Baltimore), March 24, 1834 (first and second quotations); Protest of the Master (third quotation).

20. *New Orleans Courier*, March 5, 1834, reprinted in the *American and Commercial Daily Advertiser* (Baltimore), March 24, 1834 (first quotation); Protest of the Master; Petition, John Waddell to the General Assembly of North Carolina, December 8, 1834 (second and third quotations); *Royal Gazette* (Nassau), February 12, 1834 (fourth quotation); *Charleston (SC) Courier*, reprinted in *United States' Telegraph* (Washington, DC), March 27, 1834; *New Orleans Bee*, reprinted in *Charleston (SC) Courier*, May 2, 1834; *People's Press and Wilmington (NC) Advertiser*, April 23, 1834.

21. B.T. Balfour to G.G. Stanly, February 18, 1834, folio 54, reel 47, CO 23/91, BNAN (first and second quotations); Protest of the Master (third quotation); George Huyler to Louis McLane, February 24, 1834, T 1/3556, NAUK; Petition, John Waddell to the General Assembly of North Carolina, December 8, 1834 (fourth quotation); *Alexandria (DC) Gazette*, March 22, 1834 (fifth quotation). Italics in original.

22. B.T. Balfour to G.G. Stanly, February 18, 1834, folio 54 (first through fourth quotations); Protest of the Master (fifth quotation); *Journal of the House of Representatives of the State of Ohio*, 484.

23. Protest of the Master; Protest of Henry Reilly, John Waddell, Amedee Gardanne Jr., and William Dalzell, March 11, 1834, T 1/3556, NAUK. Some surname spellings differ across the documents consulted for this study. I have standardized them in the text but listed them here as spelled in the protest.

24. *New Orleans Courier*, March 5, 1834, reprinted in the *American and Commercial Daily Advertiser* (Baltimore), March 24, 1834 (quotations); Manuscript Census

Returns, Fifth Census of the United States, 1830, Charleston Neck, Charleston, South Carolina, NAMS M-19, reel 170, p. 145.

25. *New Orleans Courier*, March 5, 1834, reprinted in the *American and Commercial Daily Advertiser* (Baltimore), March 24, 1834 (first through fourth quotations); *Journal of the House of Representatives of the State of Ohio*, 485; George Huyler to Blayney Townley Balfour, February 13, 1834, T 1/3556, NAUK (fifth quotation); C.N. Nesbitt to George Huyler, February 13, 1834, p. 249, CO 23/92 Secretary of State Correspondence, NAUK (sixth quotation).

26. Certificate of George Huyler, February 15, 1834, T 1/3556; B.T. Balfour to G.G. Stanley, March 17, 1834, Governor's Despatches, 1831–1835, box 5, no. 83, BNAN (first and second quotations); George Huyler to Lewis [*sic*] McLane, February 24, 1834, p. 237, CO 23/92, NAUK (third quotation); Valuation of the 22 Negroes shipped by John Waddell, T 1/3556, NAUK. Huyler asked Secretary of State Louis McLane if he was authorized to secure passage for any of the formerly enslaved people who had elected to remain in the Bahamas but who later changed their minds and wanted to return to the United States. "Will any risk attend the vessel, or penalty be attached to the master on their Landing[?]" Huyler asked, thinking that doing so would violate prohibitions against the importation of enslaved people from abroad. Ultimately, this was not a problem, since none of the freedpeople in the Bahamas are known to have later expressed a desire to return to slavery. See Huyler to McLane, February 15, 1834, p. 237.

27. George Huyler to Lewis [*sic*] McLane, February 24, 1834, p. 237; Stephanie McCurry, *Masters of Small Worlds: Yeoman Households, Gender Relations, and the Political Culture of the Antebellum South Carolina Low Country* (New York: Oxford University Press, 1995), 43–55. As late as 1860, by which time slave holding across the South had become concentrated among fewer and fewer people, only 4 percent of all Missouri slave owners qualified as planters, enslaving twenty or more bondpeople. Close to 90 percent of slaveholders in Missouri owned ten or fewer enslaved people. See Diane Mutti Burke, *On Slavery's Border: Missouri's Small-Slaveholding Households, 1815–1865* (Athens: University of Georgia Press, 2010), 314n7, 9–10, 128, 57, 102.

28. George Huyler to Lewis [*sic*] McLane, February 24, 1834, p. 237; *Charleston (SC) Courier*, March 12, 1834 (first quotation); *Commercial Advertiser* (New York), March 22, 1834 (second quotation); *Charleston (SC) Courier*, reprinted in *United States' Telegraph* (Washington, DC), March 27, 1834; *New Orleans Bee*, March 4, 1834, reprinted in *Charleston (SC) Courier*, reprinted in *United States' Telegraph* (Washington, DC), March 27, 1834 (third quotation).

29. George Huyler to Lewis [*sic*] McLane, February 24, 1834, p. 237; George Huyler, Certificate as to 8 of the Slaves from the Encomium having embarked on board the American Vessel the Sarah Jane for America, February 19, 1834, T 1/3556, NAUK; Valuation of the 22 Negroes shipped by John Waddell (quotations).

30. *American* (New York), March 3, 1834; *Commercial Advertiser* (New York), March 1, 1834.

31. *New Orleans Bee*, March 4, 1834, reprinted in *Columbian Centinel* (Boston), March 26, 1834 (first quotation); *New Orleans Bee*, March 4, 1834, reprinted in *Charleston (SC) Courier*, reprinted in *United States' Telegraph* (Washington, DC), March 27, 1834 (second and fourth through tenth quotations); *Commercial Advertiser* (New York), March 22, 1834 (third quotation); *New Orleans Bee*, reprinted in *Charleston (SC) Courier*, May 2, 1834.

32. Protest of Henry Reilly, John Waddell, Amedie Gardanne Jr., and William Dalzell, March 11, 1834.

33. Amédée Gardanne, assignment of right, title, and interest to the Charleston Fire and Marine Insurance Company, April 3, 1834, T 1/3556, NAUK; Negroes by the Brig Encomium. The property of Amedee Gardanne fils, T 1/3556, NAUK; Robert Eagar, assignment of right, title, and interest to the Charleston Fire and Marine Insurance Company, October 31, 1834, T 1/3556, NAUK; Alexander McDonald, certificate of value of slaves, April 27, 1837, T 1/3556, NAUK; Finley, "A Gentleman and a Scoundrel?"; T.N. Gadsden, certificate of value of slaves, April 20, 1837, T 1/3556, NAUK. The Charleston Fire and Marine Insurance Company was incorporated in 1818. See Karen Kotzuk Ryder, "'Permanent Property': Slave Life Insurance in the Antebellum Southern United States" (PhD diss., University of Delaware, 2012), 53.

34. Policy of Insurance, No. 6139, Charleston Fire and Marine Insurance Company to Amedie Gardanne, January 30 ,1834, T 1/3556, NAUK (first quotation); Policy of Insurance, No. 6145, Charleston Fire and Marine Insurance Company to Robert Eagar, February 1, 1834, T 1/3556, NAUK (second quotation).

35. Policy of Insurance, No. 6139.

36. *Charleston (SC) Courier*, February 20, 1834 (first quotation); Gardanne, assignment of right, title, and interest, April 3, 1834 (second through fourth quotations); Eagar, assignment of right, title, and interest, October 31, 1834; Affidavit of John Haslett, April 27, 1837, T 1/3556, NAUK (fifth quotation).

37. Affidavit of John Haslett, April 27, 1837, T 1/3556, NAUK; Policy of Insurance, No. 6139; Policy of Insurance, No. 6145; Charleston Fire and Marine Insurance Company, financial statement as of December 31, 1833, January 7, 1834, Andrew Wallace Papers, SCL; John Haslett to Lewis [*sic*] McLane, April 3, 1834, T 1/3556, NAUK (quotation).

38. Charles Harrod to Louis McLane, February 22, 1834, T 1/3556, NAUK (first quotation); *New Orleans Courier*, March 5, 1834, reprinted in the *American and Commercial Daily Advertiser* (Baltimore), March 24, 1834 (second and third quotations).

5. British Indecision

1. *Alexandria (DC) Gazette*, March 22, 1834 (first quotation); *New Orleans Bee*, March 4, 1834, reprinted in *Charleston (SC) Courier*, reprinted in *United States' Telegraph* (Washington, DC), March 27, 1834 (second and third quotations); *Baltimore Gazette*

and Daily Advertiser, March 26, 1834 (fourth and sixth quotations); B.T. Balfour to George Huyler, May 22, 1834, p. 255, CO 23/92, NAUK (fifth quotation).

2. George Huyler to Blayney Townley Balfour, May 21, 1834, p. 254, CO 23/92 Secretary of State Correspondence, NAUK; George Huyler to Lewis [*sic*] McLane, May 22, 1834, p. 253, CO 23/92, NAUK; B.T. Balfour to George Huyler, May 22, 1834, p. 255 (first, second, and fourth quotations), 256 (third quotation).

3. B.T. Balfour to G.G. Stanley, March 17, 1834, Governor's Despatches, 1831–1835, box 5, no. 83, BNAN (first quotation); B.T. Balfour to George Huyler, May 22, 1834, p. 255 (second quotation).

4. B.T. Balfour to George Huyler, May 22, 1834, p. 255 (first quotation); *Raleigh Register*, reprinted in *The Harbinger* (Chapel Hill, NC), June 5, 1834 (second through seventh quotations). See also *Lynchburg Virginian*, June 12, 1834.

5. John Forsyth to Aaron Vail, August 2, 1834, *Register of Debates*, 25th Cong., 1st sess., Appendix, p. 252.

6. John Forsyth to Aaron Vail, August 2, 1834, *Register of Debates*, 25th Cong., 1st sess., Appendix, p. 252.

7. Aaron Vail to Lord Palmerston, September 20, 1834, *Register of Debates*, 25th Cong., 1st sess., Appendix, p. 260.

8. Aaron Vail to Lord Palmerston, September 20, 1834, *Register of Debates*, 25th Cong., 1st sess., Appendix, p. 260.

9. Aaron Vail to Lord Palmerston, September 20, 1834, *Register of Debates*, 25th Cong., 1st sess., Appendix, pp. 261 (quotation), 225–26.

10. Aaron Vail to Lord Palmerston, September 20, 1834, pp. 226 (first quotation), 227 (second quotation).

11. Aaron Vail to Lord Palmerston, September 20, 1834, pp. 226 (first and second quotations), 227 (third quotation); Jeff Forret, *Slave Against Slave: Plantation Violence in the Old South* (Baton Rouge: Louisiana State University Press, 2015), 9, 82–87; Andrew T. Fede, *Homicide Justified: The Legality of Killing Slaves in the United States and the Atlantic World* (Athens: University of Georgia Press, 2017).

12. Aaron Vail to Lord Palmerston, September 20, 1834, p. 227.

13. Aaron Vail to Lord Palmerston, September 20, 1834, pp. 224 (first quotation), 228 (second through fifth quotations), 229 (sixth and seventh quotations).

14. Aaron Vail to Lord Palmerston, September 20, 1834, p. 231.

15. Aaron Vail to Lord Palmerston, September 20, 1834, p. 232.

16. Aaron Vail to Lord Palmerston, September 20, 1834, pp. 232 (first and second quotations), 233 (third quotation).

17. Aaron Vail to Lord Palmerston, September 20, 1834, pp. 233 (first through fifth quotations), 233–34 (sixth quotation), 234 (seventh quotation).

18. Aaron Vail to Lord Palmerston, September 20, 1834, p. 234.

19. Aaron Vail to Lord Palmerston, September 20, 1834, p. 234.

20. Aaron Vail to Lord Palmerston, September 20, 1834, pp. 235 (first quotation), 236 (second through fourth quotations).

21. The Duke of Wellington to the Earl of Aberdeen, January 12, 1835, p. 52, CO 23/95 Correspondence, Original—Secretary of State, NAUK (first quotation); J. Backhouse to R. W. Hay, September 30, 1834, p. 216, CO 23/92, NAUK (second quotation).

22. T. Spring Rice to the Lords of the Treasury, October 17, 1834, pp. 393 (first and second quotations), 394 (third quotation), CO 23/92, NAUK.

23. Nicholas Draper, *The Price of Emancipation: Slave-Ownership, Compensation and British Society at the End of Slavery* (New York: Cambridge University Press, 2010), 76; T. Spring Rice to the Lords of the Treasury, October 17, 1834, pp. 395 (first and second quotations), 396 (third through fifth quotations).

24. T. Spring Rice to the Lords of the Treasury, October 17, 1834, p. 397.

25. T. Spring Rice to the Lords of the Treasury, October 17, 1834, pp. 397 (first and second quotations), 398 (third quotation).

26. Lords of the Treasury report, November 20, 1834, pp. 139, 140 (quotations), TS 25/2047 Treasury Solicitor and HM Procurator General: Law Officers' and Counsel's Opinions, NAUK.

27. *Charleston (SC) Daily Courier*, March 3, 1834; *Commercial Bulletin, Price Current and Shipping List* (New Orleans), February 28, 1835; *Charleston (SC) Daily Courier*, December 9, 1834 (first through fourth quotations); *Charleston (SC) Daily Courier*, October 28, 1835; *Charleston (SC) Daily Courier*, November 10, 1835; *Charleston (SC) Mercury*, November 3, 1835 (fifth quotation).

28. *Charleston (SC) Daily Courier*, April 5, 1836; *Charleston (SC) Daily Courier*, May 16, 1836; *Charleston (SC) Daily Courier*, June 6, 1836; *Charleston (SC) Daily Courier*, March 2, 1837; *Times-Picayune* (New Orleans), December 9, 1840 (first quotation); Manuscript Census Returns, Seventh Census of the United States, 1850, St. Michael and St. Phillip, Charleston, South Carolina, Schedule 1, Free Population, NAMS M-432, reel 850, page 312A; Manuscript Census Returns, Seventh Census of the United States, 1850, Charleston District, South Carolina, Schedule 2, Slave Population, NAMS M-432, reel 862, image 16; *New-York Freeman's Journal and Catholic Register*, August 14, 1858; *Charleston (SC) Mercury*, August 3, 1858 (second through fourth quotations).

29. William Rothery to T.F. Baring, February or March 23, 1839, T 1/3556 Treasury Long Papers, bundle 133, part 2, NAUK.

6. John Waddell, Slave Owner

1. Manuscript Census Returns, Seventh Census of the United States, 1850, Natchitoches, Louisiana, NAMS M-432, reel 233, page 10B; *Fayetteville (NC) Weekly Observer*, November 25, 1824; *Cape-Fear Recorder* (Wilmington, NC), April 11,

1827 (quotation); Manuscript Census Returns, Fifth Census of the United States, 1830, Brunswick County, North Carolina, NAMS M-19, reel 118, p. 311; *Fayetteville (NC) Weekly Observer*, March 3, 1831; *North-Carolina Free Press* (Halifax), September 18, 1832; *Weekly Standard* (Raleigh, NC), May 29, 1844.

2. Manuscript Census Returns, Fifth Census of the United States, 1830, Natchitoches Parish, Louisiana, NAMS M-19, reel 44, p. 67; *Journal of the House of Representatives of the State of Ohio; Being the First Session of the Thirty-Third General Assembly: Begun and Held in the City of Columbus. Monday, December 1, 1834, and in the Thirty-Third Year of Said State* (Columbus: James B. Gardiner, 1834), 484; Petition, John Waddell to the General Assembly of North Carolina, December 8, 1834, RSPP, Petition 11283408, Series I, Reel 6, North Carolina; Affidavit of Sylvester Bossier, March 24, 1834, T 1/3556 Treasury Long Papers, bundle 133, part 2, NAUK (first and second quotations); Aaron Vail to Lord Palmerston, May 11, 1835, *Register of Debates*, 25th Cong., 1st sess., Appendix, p. 265 (third quotation).

Like his brother, Haynes Waddell lived in Brunswick County, North Carolina. He married Mary Flemming in 1826, the same year he served as a lieutenant colonel in the militia. He owned eleven enslaved people in 1830. *Weekly Raleigh (NC) Register*, August 19, 1825; *Fayetteville (NC) Weekly Observer*, January 19, 1826; *North-Carolina Star* (Raleigh), July 21, 1826; Manuscript Census Returns, Fifth Census of the United States, 1830, Brunswick County, North Carolina, NAMS M-19, reel 118, p. 311.

3. Valuation of the 22 Negroes shipped by John Waddell, T 1/3556, NAUK; Protest of the Master, Mate, a Seaman and 3 Passengers of the *Encomium*, February 12, 1834, T 1/3556, NAUK.

4. Protest of the Master.

5. B.T. Balfour to G.G. Stanley, March 17, 1834, Governor's Despatches, 1831–1835, box 5, no. 83, BNAN; *People's Press and Wilmington (NC) Advertiser*, April 23, 1834.

6. B.T. Balfour to G.G. Stanley, March 17, 1834.

7. B.T. Balfour to G.G. Stanley, March 17, 1834.

8. Policy of Insurance, No. 6139, Charleston Fire and Marine Insurance Company to Amedie Gardanne, January 30 ,1834, T 1/3556, NAUK.

9. *New Orleans Bee*, March 4, 1834, reprinted in *Charleston (SC) Courier*, reprinted in *United States' Telegraph* (Washington, DC), March 27, 1834; Protest of Henry Reilly, John Waddell, Amedie Gardanne Jr., and William Dalzell, March 11, 1834, T 1/3556, NAUK.

10. Valuation of the 22 Negroes; *Charleston (SC) Daily Courier*, July 21, 1834; *Philadelphia Inquirer*, July 25, 1834. No direct evidence confirms that Waddell's nine enslaved people ever made it to Louisiana at all. Newspapers reported that the Waddell captives from the *Encomium* arrived back in Charleston from Key West via the pilot boat *Washington* on Saturday, July 19. A voyage with their owner from the Bahamas to Key West and then to New Orleans would explain the almost five-month

delay between leaving Nassau in late February and reaching Charleston in mid-July. The press stated that only seven of the Waddell bondpeople reached Charleston in July, leaving two of the enslaved unaccounted for. If the papers did not simply undercount, the other two may have died or fled or been hired out, sold, or otherwise left behind in Louisiana.

11. Valuation of the 22 Negroes (quotation); George Huyler, Certificate as to 8 of the Slaves from the Encomium having embarked on board the American Vessel the Sarah Jane for America, February 19, 1834, T 1/3556, NAUK; www.measuringworth.com.

12. Affidavit of Sylvester Bossier, March 24, 1834.

13. *Southern Patriot* (Charleston, SC), April 4, 1834 (quotation); *Richmond (VA) Enquirer*, April 8, 1834; *Weekly Raleigh (NC) Register*, October 15, 1829; *Weekly Raleigh (NC) Register*, January 2, 1829; *Weekly Raleigh (NC) Register*, July 8, 1830; *Roanoke Advocate* (Halifax, NC), August 23, 1832; *Weekly Raleigh (NC) Register*, December 3, 1833; *Roanoke Advocate* (Halifax, NC), November 4, 1830; *North Carolina Spectator and Western Advertiser* (Rutherfordton), August 27, 1830; *Fayetteville (NC) Weekly Observer*, August 19, 1834; Manuscript Census Returns, Fifth Census of the United States, 1830, New Hanover County, North Carolina, NAMS M-19, reel 123, pp. 160A (Holmes, 11 slaves), 141B (Anderson, 16), 160 (Meares, 8). The Gabriel Holmes discussed here was not the former North Carolina governor and congressman of the same name, who had died in 1829. According to the *Cape-Fear Recorder* (Wilmington, NC), January 13, 1830, the Gabriel Holmes of this chapter was a junior, but with multiple Gabriel Holmeses in eastern North Carolina, he does not appear to have been the son of the ex-governor, either.

14. *Southern Patriot* (Charleston, SC), April 4, 1834.

15. B.T. Balfour to George Huyler, May 22, 1834, p. 255, CO 23/92, NAUK (quotation); *North- Carolina Star* (Raleigh), May 22, 1834.

16. *Richmond (VA) Enquirer*, April 8, 1834 (first and second quotations); *Evening Star* (New York), April 8, 1834.

17. *Charleston (SC) Courier*, April 5, 1834; *New-Orleans Commercial Bulletin*, April 24, 1834.

18. *Charleston (SC) Courier*, April 5, 1834.

19. *Charleston (SC) Courier*, April 5, 1834.

20. *Charleston (SC) Courier*, April 5, 1834.

21. *Baltimore Gazette and Daily Advertiser*, April 12, 1834 (quotations); Kenneth S. Greenberg, *Honor & Slavery: Lies, Duels, Noses, Masks, Dressing as a Woman, Gifts, Strangers, Humanitarianism, Death, Slave Rebellions, the Proslavery Argument, Baseball, Hunting, and Gambling in the Old South* (Princeton: Princeton University Press, 1996); *People's Press and Wilmington (NC) Advertiser*, April 23, 1834.

22. *People's Press and Wilmington (NC) Advertiser*, April 23, 1834.

23. *Charleston (SC) Courier*, April 5, 1834 (first through fourth quotations); *People's Press and Wilmington (NC) Advertiser*, April 23, 1834 (fifth and sixth quotations).

24. *People's Press and Wilmington (NC) Advertiser*, April 23, 1834.

25. *Charleston (SC) Courier*, April 29, 1834.

26. *New Orleans Bee*, reprinted in *Charleston (SC) Courier*, May 2, 1834.

27. *New Orleans Bee*, reprinted in *Charleston (SC) Courier*, May 2, 1834 (quotations); *Commercial Advertiser* (New York), March 1, 1834.

28. *New Orleans Bee*, reprinted in *Charleston (SC) Courier*, May 2, 1834.

29. *New Orleans Bee*, reprinted in *Charleston (SC) Courier*, May 2, 1834 (first through fifth quotations); *Evening Star* (New York), May 1, 1834 (sixth quotation). Reilley also confirmed that the lifeboat used to evacuate the sinking ship was a jolly boat, not a "first rate long boat." Reilley left the wreckage in it and knew for certain. Once in Nassau, he added, it was "sold as a jolly boat." See *New Orleans Bee*, reprinted in *Charleston (SC) Courier*, May 2, 1834.

30. *New Orleans Bee*, reprinted in *Charleston (SC) Courier*, May 2, 1834; Protest of the Master (first and third quotations); Aaron Vail to Lord Palmerston, September 20, 1834, *Register of Debates*, 25th Cong., 1st sess., Appendix, p. 260 (second quotation).

31. *Evening Post* (New York), April 10, 1834; *Evening Star* (New York), May 2, 1834 (quotations); *Charleston (SC) Daily Courier*, August 28, 1834; *Charleston (SC) Daily Courier*, December 18, 1834; Manuscript Census Returns, Sixth Census of the United States, 1840, Fairfield, Fairfield County, Connecticut, NAMS M-704, reel 22, p. 375; Manuscript Census Returns, Seventh Census of the United States, 1850, Fairfield, Fairfield County, Connecticut, Schedule 1, Free Population, NAMS M-432, reel 38, p. 23A; Manuscript Census Returns, Eighth Census of the United States, 1860, Fairfield, Fairfield County, Connecticut, Schedule 1, Free Population, NAMS M-653, reels 73–76, p. 1003; Manuscript Census Returns, Ninth Census of the United States, 1870, Fairfield, Fairfield County, Connecticut, Schedule 1, General Population, NAMS M-593, reel 97, p. 452A; www.measuringworth.com.

32. *Fayetteville (NC) Observer*, reprinted in *The Harbinger* (Chapel Hill, NC), April 3, 1834 (first quotation); *Newbern (NC) Spectator*, April 4, 1834 (second and third quotations); *Charleston (SC) Courier*, April 5, 1834 (fourth quotation); *Charleston (SC) Courier*, April 29, 1834 (fifth quotation).

33. *Charleston (SC) Daily Courier*, September 15, 1832; *Charleston (SC) Courier*, April 29, 1834 (quotations).

34. *Newbern (NC) Spectator*, November 28, 1834; *Hillsborough (NC) Recorder*, December 12, 1834; *Weekly Standard* (Raleigh, NC), December 12, 1834 (quotation).

35. Petition, John Waddell to the General Assembly of North Carolina, December 8, 1834, RSPP, Petition 11283408, Series I, Reel 6, North Carolina.

36. D.L. Swain to Robert Lucas, January 12, 1835, *Journal of the House of Representatives of the State of Ohio; Being the First Session of the Thirty-Third General Assembly:*

Begun and Held in the City of Columbus. Monday, December 1, 1834, and in the Thirty-Third Year of Said State (Columbus: James B. Gardiner, 1834), 485.

37. D.L. Swain to Robert Lucas, January 12, 1835, *Journal of the House of Representatives of the State of Ohio*, 486.

38. D.L. Swain to Robert Lucas, January 12, 1835, *Journal of the House of Representatives of the State of Ohio*, 486.

39. Aaron Vail to John Forsyth, January 14, 1835, *Register of Debates*, 25th Cong., 1st sess., Appendix, pp. 263 (first quotation), 264 (second through fifth quotations).

40. Aaron Vail to John Forsyth, January 22, 1835, *Register of Debates*, 25th Cong., 1st sess., Appendix, p. 264; Aaron Vail to John Forsyth, March 14, 1835, *Register of Debates*, 25th Cong., 1st sess., Appendix, p. 264 (quotation).

41. *People's Press and Wilmington (NC) Advertiser*, December 17, 1834; *Mississippi Free Trader* (Natchez), June 10, 1836 (quotation); *Alexandria Gazette*, August 26, 1835; *Fayetteville (NC) Weekly Observer*, September 8, 1835; Manuscript Census Returns, Seventh Census of the United States, 1850, Natchitoches, Louisiana, NAMS M-432, reel 233, p. 10B; *Daily National Intelligencer* (Washington, DC), June 15, 1839.

42. Manuscript Census Returns, Sixth Census of the United States, 1840, Natchitoches, Louisiana, NAMS M-704, reel 127, p. 143; *Semi-Weekly Natchitoches (LA) Times*, December 15, 1866; Manuscript Census Returns, Seventh Census of the United States, 1850, Natchitoches, Louisiana, NAMS M-432, reel 233, p. 10B; Manuscript Census Returns, Eighth Census of the United States, 1860, Winn Parish, Louisiana, Schedule 1, Free Population, NAMS M-653, reel 426, p. 945; *Daily Advocate* (Baton Rouge), March 6, 1858; www.measuringworth.com. In 1860, John Waddell owned another $10,000 in personal property. By then, he lived with his third wife, Diana Spencer, a thirty-five-year-old native of Texas with $2,000 of real estate and $3,500 in personal estate of her own.

43. *Times-Picayune* (New Orleans), March 4, 1841; *New Orleans Bee*, May 18, reprinted in *New York Daily Herald*, May 27, 1846; *Natchez (MS) Daily Courier*, August 24, 1847; *The South-Western* (Shreveport, LA), May 14, 1856.

44. *People's Press and Wilmington (NC) Advertiser*, September 20, 1839.

45. *Mississippi Free Trader* (Natchez), June 10, 1836 (quotations); Manifest of 22 Slaves shipped by John Waddell, February 1, 1834, T 1/3556, NAUK.

7. Emancipation from the *Enterprise*

1. Manifest of the *Enterprise*, January 22, 1835, unpaginated, T 1/3556 Treasury Long Papers, bundle 133, part 2, NAUK.

2. Manifest of the *Enterprise*, January 22, 1835; *Daily National Intelligencer* (Washington, DC), October 27, 1831 (quotations).

3. *Daily National Intelligencer* (Washington, DC), October 18, 1832; Jeff Forret, *Williams' Gang: A Notorious Slave Trader and His Cargo of Black Convicts* (New York:

Cambridge University Press, 2020), 44; *Daily National Intelligencer* (Washington, DC), October 24, 1825 (quotation); *Daily National Intelligencer* (Washington, DC), July 20, 1832. Robey's tavern was situated on block 407, encompassing lots 17, 18, and part of 5. The property included a stable. See *Daily National Intelligencer* (Washington, DC), July 20, 1832. Robey also kept a stable on Eighth Street, suggesting that he also bought, sold, and/or rented horses. See *Daily National Intelligencer* (Washington, DC), September 6, 1830.

4. *Daily National Intelligencer* (Washington, DC), July 20, 1832; *Daily National Intelligencer* (Washington, DC), October 9, 1832 (quotation); *Daily National Intelligencer* (Washington, DC), April 24, 1827; Forret, *Williams' Gang*, 124, 48; *The Liberator* (Boston), August 9, 1834.

5. E. S. Abdy, *Journal of a Residence and Tour in the United States of North America, from April, 1833, to October, 1834*, vol. 2 (London: John Murray, 1835), 96 (first and second quotations), 97 (third and fourth quotations); *The Liberator*, November 15, 1834 (fifth through seventh quotations).

6. *The Liberator*, November 15, 1834.

7. Abdy, *Journal of a Residence and Tour*, 96–97; *United States' Telegraph* (Washington, DC), October 9, 1832 (quotations); *Daily Globe* (Washington, DC), February 27, 1834.

8. *Daily Globe* (Washington, DC), June 4, 1834; *The Liberator* (Boston), August 9, 1834 (first quotation); *Daily National Intelligencer* (Washington, DC), January 2, 1835; *Daily Globe* (Washington, DC), January 21, 1835 (second quotation).

9. Manifest of the *Enterprise*, January 22, 1835; Nellie Eileen Musson, *Mind the Onion Seed: Black "Roots" Bermuda Presented During Bermuda's First Heritage Week, May, 1979* (Hamilton, Bermuda: Musson's, 1979), 66. Gerald Horne, *Negro Comrades of the Crown: African Americans and the British Empire Fight the U.S. Before Emancipation* (New York: New York University Press, 2012), 107, 108, suggests that the "copper" designation indicated Indigenous ancestry.

10. Musson, *Mind the Onion Seed*, 66 (quotation); Richard Bell, *Stolen: Five Free Boys Kidnapped into Slavery and Their Astonishing Odyssey Home* (New York: Simon and Schuster, 2019); Jonathan Daniel Wells, *The Kidnapping Club: Wall Street, Slavery, and Resistance on the Eve of the Civil War* (New York: Bold Type Books, 2020); W. Caleb McDaniel, *Sweet Taste of Liberty: A True Story of Slavery and Restitution in America* (New York: Oxford University Press, 2019); Jeff Forret, *Race Relations at the Margins: Slaves and Poor Whites in the Antebellum Southern Countryside* (Baton Rouge: Louisiana State University Press, 2006), 143, 145–46; Manifest of the *Enterprise*, January 22, 1835.

11. Manifest of the *Enterprise*, January 22, 1835; *Simpson v. Charleston Fire & Marine Ins. Co.*, Dudl 239 (1838), 23 S.C.L. 239; Manuscript Census Returns, Seventh Census of the United States, 1850, Van Vorst Township, Hudson County, New

Jersey, NAMS M-432, reel 452, p. 404B. The census states that Elliot Smith was born about 1802 in Maine. By 1850, he lived in Van Vorst Township, Hudson County, New Jersey (now part of Jersey City). His wife, Sarah A., was Irish-born and eighteen years younger than her husband. Capt. Smith's occupation was still listed in 1850 as "Seaman." The couple had three children: Sarah J., born in Florida about 1839; Margaret A., born in New York about 1843; and Lewis J., born in New Jersey about 1846.

12. Outward Manifest of the *Enterprise*, Bermuda Archives, Hamilton; *Newark (NJ) Daily Advertiser*, March 17, 1835; Manifest of the *Enterprise*, January 22, 1835 (first and fourth quotations); Letter of William Rothery, undated and unpaginated, T 1/3556 and HCA 30/895 Papers Relating to Services of W. Rothery, Slave Trade Adviser to the Treasury, NAUK (second and third quotations); *Simpson v. Charleston Fire & Marine Ins. Co.*, Dudl 239 (1838), 23 S.C.L. 239 (fifth quotation); *Charleston (SC) Courier*, March 16, 1835. The precise tons burthen listed in the *Enterprise* manifest was 127 27/95ths.

13. *Tarboro' (NC) Press*, January 16, 1835; *Fayetteville (NC) Weekly Observer*, January 13, 1835; *Tarboro' (NC) Press*, January 31, 1835; *Weekly Raleigh (NC) Register*, January 20, 1835; *Weekly Standard* (Raleigh, NC), January 16, 1835; *Charleston (SC) Daily Courier*, January 6, 1835; *Charleston (SC) Mercury*, February 2, 1835; *Charleston (SC) Daily Courier*, February 2, 1835; *Weekly Standard* (Raleigh, NC), February 6, 1835 (first quotation); *Fayetteville (NC) Weekly Observer*, February 10, 1835 (second quotation); *People's Press and Wilmington (NC) Advertiser*, February 4, 1835; *Charleston (SC) Mercury*, February 9, 1835 (third and fourth quotations).

14. *Charleston (SC) Courier*, March 16, 1835 (first quotation); Aaron Vail to Lord Palmerston, May 11, 1835, *Register of Debates*, 25th Cong., 1st sess., Appendix, p. 264 (second quotation); 34th Cong., 1st sess., Senate, Ex. Doc. No. 103, p. 236 (third quotation); *Charleston (SC) Courier*, May 27, 1837 (fourth and seventh quotations); *Oliver Simpson v. Charleston Fire and Marine Insurance Co.*, Judgment Roll, Charleston District (L10018), June 10, 1837, Item 109A, SCDAH (fifth quotation); *Simpson v. Charleston Fire & Marine Ins. Co.*, Dudl 239 (1838), 23 S.C.L. 239 (sixth quotation).

15. Peter Kolchin, *American Slavery 1619–1877* (New York: Hill and Wang, 1999), 114; *Savannah Republican*, quoted in *People's Press and Wilmington (NC) Advertiser*, January 21, 1835 (first and second quotations); *Tarboro' (NC) Press*, January 16, 1835 (third through fifth quotations). A pair of captains later testified that Capt. Elliot Smith's "log book of the voyage was . . . badly kept," not recording "the distances made by the ship each day, . . . except the first." They noted that, when Smith bore for Bermuda on February 5, the *Enterprise* was no more than twenty miles north of the latitude of Charleston. See *Simpson v. Charleston Fire & Marine Ins. Co.*, Dudl 239 (1838), 23 S.C.L. 239.

16. Virginia Bernhard, *Slaves and Slaveholders in Bermuda, 1616–1782* (Columbia: University of Missouri Press, 2016); Michael Bradshaw, "True But Brief History of

the Friendly Societies and Development of Black Bermudian Communities After Emancipation: Black People Seek Pride and Power in a Post-slavery and Post-emancipation World, the Bermuda Experience," *Africology: Journal of Pan African Studies* 12, no. 1 (September 2018): 564, 565.

17. Elliot Smith, reply to the writ of *habeas corpus*, February 18, 1835, Proceedings of the Court of Assizes 1832–1849, A2/102/15, Bermuda National Archives, Hamilton (first quotation); Letter of William Rothery (second through fourth quotations); John Forsyth to Andrew Stevenson, March 27, 1837, 25th Cong., 3d sess., Sen. Doc. No. 216, p. 7; *Register of Debates*, 25th Cong., 1st sess., Appendix, p. 267.

18. 34th Cong., 1st sess., Senate, Ex. Doc. No. 103, p. 236 (quotations); *Bermuda Royal Gazette*, February 24, 1835.

19. Letter of William Rothery (first through third quotations); 34th Cong., 1st sess., Senate, Ex. Doc. No. 103, p. 236; *Bermuda Royal Gazette*, February 24, 1835 (fourth quotation).

20. 34th Cong., 1st sess., Senate, Ex. Doc. No. 103, p. 236.

21. Bermuda National Trust, *Black History in Bermuda* (Bermuda National Trust, 2019), 14, www.bnt.bm/images/News%20Articles/Black%20History%20Book.pdf (first quotation); Letter of William Rothery; 34th Cong., 1st sess., Senate, Ex. Doc. No. 103, p. 236 (second through fourth quotations).

22. 34th Cong., 1st sess., Senate, Ex. Doc. No. 103, p. 236; Smith, reply to the writ of *habeas corpus*, February 18, 1835; Bradshaw, "True But Brief History of the Friendly Societies," 560–61, 566, 569; Bermuda National Trust, *Black History in Bermuda*, 23; Kenneth E. Robinson, *Heritage: Including an Account of Bermudian Builders, Pilots and Petitioners of the Early Post-abolition Period 1834–1859* (London: Macmillan Education, 1979), 152. As Bradshaw explained it, "Friendly societies were started among the formerly enslaved Black individuals who were turned out into the capitalist world with no resources or compensation from the British government."

23. Robinson, *Heritage*, 88–90, 152–53, 203; Bradshaw, "True but Brief History of the Friendly Societies," 566, 569; Meredith Ebbin, "Two Luminaries Who List the Way for Freedom and Equality," February 1, 2012, bermudasun.bm/Content/Mobile-Site-Home/Mobile/Article/Two-luminaries-who-lit-the-way-for-freedom-and-equality/-5/-5/56512; 34th Cong., 1st sess., Senate, Ex. Doc. No. 103, p. 236 (first quotation); *Bermuda Royal Gazette*, February 24, 1835 (second quotation).

24. 34th Cong., 1st sess., Senate, Ex. Doc. No. 103, p. 237; *Bermuda Royal Gazette*, February 24, 1835 (quotations).

25. *Bermuda Royal Gazette*, February 24, 1835; *The Observer* (London), April 19, 1835; 34th Cong., 1st sess., Senate, Ex. Doc. No. 103, p. 237 (quotation); Anita Rupprecht, "'All We Have Done, We Have Done for Freedom': The *Creole* Slave-Ship Revolt (1841) and the Revolutionary Atlantic," *International Review of Social History* 58 (2013): 267.

26. *Bermuda Royal Gazette*, February 24, 1835 (first, third, fourth, and seventh quotations); *Charleston (SC) Courier*, March 16, 1835 (second quotation); *The Observer* (London), April 19, 1835; *Camden (NJ) Mail and General Advertiser*, April 8, 1835 (fifth and sixth quotations). One source suggests that Capt. Smith was arrested and detained by the authorities in Bermuda, on the orders of Judge Butterfield, but it is not clear if or when this happened. See *Oliver Simpson v. Charleston Fire and Marine Insurance Co.*, Judgment Roll, Charleston District (L10018), June 10, 1837, Item 109A, SCDAH.

27. *Camden (NJ) Mail and General Advertiser*, April 8, 1835.

28. Ebbin, "Two Luminaries"; *Bermuda Royal Gazette*, February 24, 1835 (quotations).

29. Letter of William Rothery (first quotation); *The Observer* (London), April 19, 1835 (second through seventh quotations).

30. *Bermuda Royal Gazette*, reprinted in *Alexandria (DC) Gazette*, March 17, 1835.

31. *Bermuda Royal Gazette*, reprinted in *Alexandria Gazette*, March 17, 1835.

32. Manifest of the *Enterprise*, January 22, 1835; Calvin Schermerhorn, *Money over Mastery, Family over Freedom: Slavery in the Antebellum Upper South* (Baltimore: Johns Hopkins University Press, 2011); Emily West, *Family or Freedom: People of Color in the Antebellum South* (Lexington: University Press of Kentucky, 2012); Ted Maris-Wolf, *Family Bonds: Free Blacks and Re-enslavement Law in Antebellum Virginia* (Chapel Hill: University of North Carolina Press, 2015); Ben Adamson and Jeffrey Elkinson, *The Supreme Court of Bermuda: 400 Years, 1616–2016*, 13, bda.bm/wp-content/uploads/2016/06/Supreme-Court-400.pdf.

33. Manifest of the *Enterprise*, January 22, 1835; *The Observer* (London), April 19, 1835 (quotation); Harriet A. Jacobs, *Incidents in the Life of a Slave Girl, Written by Herself*, ed. Jean Fagan Yellin (Cambridge: Harvard University Press, 2000), chap. 10; Marisa J. Fuentes, *Dispossessed Lives: Enslaved Women, Violence, and the Archive* (Philadelphia: University of Pennsylvania Press, 2016), 9–10, chaps. 2–3; Alexandra J. Finley, *An Intimate Economy: Enslaved Women, Work, and America's Domestic Slave Trade* (Chapel Hill: University of North Carolina Press, 2020), 76; Sowande' M. Mustakeem, *Slavery at Sea: Terror, Sex, and Sickness in the Middle Passage* (Urbana: University of Illinois Press, 2016), chap. 4; Edward E. Baptist, "'Cuffy,' 'Fancy Maids,' and 'One-Eyed Men': Rape, Commodification, and the Domestic Slave Trade in the United States," *American Historical Review* 100 (December 2001): 1619–50; Edward E. Baptist, *The Half Has Never Been Told: Slavery and the Making of American Capitalism* (New York: Basic Books, 2014), 233–44.

34. *Bermuda Royal Gazette*, reprinted in *Alexandria Gazette*, March 17, 1835.

35. *Bermuda Royal Gazette*, reprinted in *Alexandria Gazette*, March 17, 1835 (first, second, and fifth quotations); Robinson, *Heritage*, 153; *Bermuda Royal Gazette*,

February 24, 1835 (third and fourth quotations); Musson, *Mind the Onion Seed*, 66; Manifest of the *Enterprise*, January 22, 1835.

36. *Charleston (SC) Courier*, March 16, 1835 (quotations); *Bermuda Royal Gazette*, February 24, 1835; Letter of William Rothery. On December 20, 1837, less than two years after piloting the *Enterprise* from Bermuda to Charleston, Capt. Elliot Smith helped rescue U.S. troops and supplies from the ship *Charles Wharton* "when stranded upon the bar at Tampa bay." See H.R. 1101 (Rep. No. 239), 25th Cong., 3d sess., February 6, 1839.

8. Britain's Decision

1. *New York Journal of Commerce*, March 17, 1835.

2. *Alexandria (DC) Gazette*, March 23, 1835 (first and third quotations); *New York Journal of Commerce*, reprinted in *The Liberator* (Boston), April 4, 1835 (second quotation).

3. *Bermuda Royal Gazette*, reprinted in *Newark (NJ) Daily Advertiser*, March 17, 1835 (first and second quotations); *Tarboro' (NC) Press*, May 9, 1835; *New York Journal of Commerce*, March 17, 1835 (third quotation).

4. *Baltimore Gazette and Daily Advertiser*, March 26, 1835 (first quotation); *Charleston (SC) Courier*, March 16, 1835 (second, third, and fifth quotations); *New York Journal of Commerce*, March 17, 1835 (fourth quotation). British reporting on the *Enterprise* may be found in such newspapers as the *Hampshire Telegraph and Naval Chronicle* (Portsmouth, England), April 20, 1835; *Aberdeen Journal, and General Advertiser for the North of Scotland*, May 6, 1835; *Weekly Standard and Express* (Blackburn, Lancashire, England), September 16, 1835; and *Bristol Mercury and Daily Post, Western Countries and South Wales Advertiser* (Bristol, England), September 19, 1835.

5. *New York Journal of Commerce*, reprinted in *The Liberator* (Boston), April 4, 1835 (first through fifth quotations); *New Hampshire Sentinel* (Keene), March 26, 1835 (sixth quotation).

6. *New York Journal of Commerce*, reprinted in *The Liberator* (Boston), May 30, 1835.

7. *Baltimore Gazette and Daily Advertiser*, March 26, 1835 (first and second quotations); *Southern Christian Herald* (Columbia, SC), reprinted in *New York Evangelist*, December 26, 1835 (third quotation); *New York Evangelist*, December 26, 1835 (fourth and fifth quotations); *Republican Farmer, and Democratic Journal* (Wilkes Barre, PA), July 23, 1835 (sixth quotation).

8. *Baltimore Gazette and Daily Advertiser*, March 26, 1835 (first through fourth quotations); *New York Journal of Commerce*, reprinted in *The Liberator* (Boston), April 4, 1835 (fifth through seventh quotations).

9. *Charleston (SC) Courier*, March 16, 1835 (first and second quotations); *New York Journal of Commerce*, reprinted in *The Liberator* (Boston), April 4, 1835 (third quotation).

10. Letter of John Dodson, Fred. Pollock, and W.W. Follett, February 3, 1835, p. 140, TS 25/2047 Treasury Solicitor and HM Procurator General: Law Officers' and Counsel's Opinions, NAUK.

11. John Forsyth to Aaron Vail, March 28, 1835, *Register of Debates*, 25th Cong., 1st sess., Appendix, p. 252.

12. Aaron Vail to Lord Palmerston, May 11, 1835, *Register of Debates*, 25th Cong., 1st sess., Appendix, p. 264.

13. Aaron Vail to Lord Palmerston, May 11, 1835, *Register of Debates*, 25th Cong., 1st sess., Appendix, pp. 264 (first quotation), 265 (second and third quotations); Aaron Vail to John Forsyth, May 14, 1835, *Register of Debates*, 25th Cong., 1st sess., Appendix, p. 264 (fourth quotation).

14. William Rothery to James Stephen, August 26, 1835, p. 213, CO 23/95 Correspondence, Original—Secretary of State, NAUK; Aaron Vail to John Forsyth, November 6, 1835, *Register of Debates*, 25th Cong., 1st sess., Appendix, p. 266 (quotation).

15. Aaron Vail to John Forsyth, November 6, 1835, *Register of Debates*, 25th Cong., 1st sess., Appendix, p. 266.

16. Aaron Vail to John Forsyth, November 6, 1835, *Register of Debates*, 25th Cong., 1st sess., Appendix, p. 266; Lord Palmerston to Aaron Vail, November 13, 1835, 24th Cong., 2d sess., Sen. Doc. No. 174, p. 40; Aaron Vail to John Forsyth, November 14, 1835, *Register of Debates*, 25th Cong., 1st sess., Appendix, p. 266.

17. Aaron Vail to John Forsyth, November 6, 1835, *Register of Debates*, 25th Cong., 1st sess., Appendix, p. 266.

18. John Forsyth to Andrew Stevenson, May 19, 1836, *Register of Debates*, 25th Cong., 1st sess., Appendix, p. 253; Manuscript Census Returns, Fifth Census of the United States, 1830, Richmond Monroe Ward, Richmond (independent city), Virginia, NAMS M-19, reel 195, p. 399.

19. John Forsyth to Andrew Stevenson, May 19, 1836, *Register of Debates*, 25th Cong., 1st sess., Appendix, pp. 252 (first and second quotations), 253 (third quotation).

20. Andrew Stevenson to John Forsyth, July 14, 1836, *Register of Debates*, 25th Cong., 1st sess., Appendix, p. 266; Andrew Stevenson to John Forsyth, July 29, 1836, *Register of Debates*, 25th Cong., 1st sess., Appendix, p. 266 (first quotation); Andrew Stevenson to John Forsyth, August 6, 1836, *Register of Debates*, 25th Cong., 1st sess., Appendix, p. 267 (second quotation).

21. Andrew Stevenson to John Forsyth, August 6, 1836, *Register of Debates*, 25th Cong., 1st sess., Appendix, pp. 267 (first through fourth quotations), 268 (fifth quotation), 269 (sixth through eleventh quotations).

22. Andrew Stevenson to John Forsyth, August 6, 1836, *Register of Debates*, 25th Cong., 1st sess., Appendix, pp. 269 (first quotation), 270 (third and fourth quotations); Jennifer Pitts, *Boundaries of the International: Law and Empire* (Cambridge: Harvard University Press, 2018), 70 (second quotation), 80, 6; Alice L.

Baumgartner, *South to Freedom: Runaway Slaves to Mexico and the Road to the Civil War* (New York: Basic Books, 2020), 72. In the 1830s, Emmerich de Vattel's *Le Droit des Gens* (1758) remained the "authoritative source of legal principles for interstate relations throughout Europe, [and] in the . . . United States." See Pitts, *Boundaries of the International*, 119, 120 (quotation). What Stevenson was discussing was the issue of comity, discussed later in this chapter, without using the term explicitly.

23. Pitts, *Boundaries of the International*, 6; Lauren Benton and Lisa Ford, *Rage for Order: The British Empire and the Origins of International Law, 1800–1850* (Cambridge: Harvard University Press, 2016), 26, 125, 180, 190.

24. Andrew Stevenson to John Forsyth, August 6, 1836, *Register of Debates*, 25th Cong., 1st sess., Appendix, p. 271.

25. Andrew Stevenson to John Forsyth, August 6, 1836, *Register of Debates*, 25th Cong., 1st sess., Appendix, pp. 271 (first through sixth quotations), 272 (seventh and eighth quotations).

26. John Forsyth to Andrew Stevenson, September 14, 1836, 25th Cong., 3d sess., Sen. Doc. No. 216, p. 3.

27. Andrew Stevenson to John Forsyth, August 22, 1836, *Register of Debates*, 25th Cong., 1st sess., Appendix, p. 273; Andrew Stevenson to John Forsyth, October 5, 1836, *Register of Debates*, 25th Cong., 1st sess., Appendix, p. 273; Andrew Stevenson to John Forsyth, November 19, 1836, 24th Cong., 2d sess., Sen. Doc. 174, p. 56 (quotation).

28. Andrew Stevenson to John Forsyth, December 14, 1836, *Register of Debates*, 25th Cong., 1st sess., Appendix, p. 273 (first quotation); Andrew Stevenson to Lord Palmerston, December 13, 1836, *Register of Debates*, 25th Cong., 1st sess., Appendix, pp. 273 (third quotation), 274 (second quotation).

29. Letter of J. Dodson, J. Campbell, and R.M. Rolfe, October 31, 1836, p. 488, TS 25/2047, NAUK. John Dodson served as the King's advocate, John Campbell as attorney general, and R.M. Rolfe as solicitor general.

30. Letter of J. Dodson, J. Campbell, and R.M. Rolfe, October 31, 1836, p. 488.

31. Letter of J. Dodson, J. Campbell, and R.M. Rolfe, October 31, 1836, pp. 488 (first through third quotations), 488–89 (fourth quotation), 489 (fifth through ninth quotations); Mark V. Tushnet, *The American Law of Slavery, 1810–1860: Considerations of Humanity and Interest* (Princeton: Princeton University Press, 1981).

32. Letter of J. Dodson, J. Campbell, and R.M. Rolfe, October 31, 1836, pp. 489–90 (quotations 490). Years later, Sen. John C. Calhoun of South Carolina blamed Britain's providing compensation for two ships but not the third on British politics. The split decision balanced out the competing factions with the government, one of which was a powerful "abolition interest," he said. See *Weekly Standard* (Raleigh, NC), April 15, 1840.

33. Lord Palmerston to Andrew Stevenson, January 7, 1837, 25th Cong., 3d sess., Sen. Doc. No. 216, p. 13.

34. Lord Palmerston to Andrew Stevenson, January 7, 1837, 25th Cong., 3d sess., Sen. Doc. No. 216, pp. 14 (first quotation), 15 (second and third quotations).

35. Andrew Stevenson to Lord Palmerston, January 14, 1837, 25th Cong., 3d sess., Sen. Doc. No. 216, p. 16 (quotations); Andrew Stevenson to John Forsyth, January 22, 1837, 25th Cong., 3d sess., Sen. Doc. No. 216, p. 13.

9. The Law of Nations

1. Resolution, January 28, 1837, 24th Cong., 2d sess., in *Daily National Intelligencer* (Washington, DC), January 30, 1837 (first quotation); Robert Elder, *Calhoun: American Heretic* (New York: Basic Books, 2021), 335–40 (second quotation 335; third quotation 338).

2. Senate, *Register of Debates*, February 7, 1837, 24th Cong, 2d sess., 725. The final text read, "Resolved, That the President be requested to communicate to the Senate, if not incompatible with the public interest, a copy of the correspondence with the Government of Great Britain in relation to the outrage committed on our flag, and the rights of our citizens, by the authorities of Bermuda and New Providence, in seizing the slaves on board of the brigs Encomium and Enterprize, engaged in the coasting trade, but which were forced by shipwreck and stress of weather into the ports of those islands." See *Senate Journal*, February 7, 1837, 24th Cong., 2d sess., 217.

3. Elder, *Calhoun*, 24, 25, 75; Irving H. Bartlett, *John C. Calhoun: A Biography* (New York: Norton, 1993).

4. *Register of Debates*, February 13, 1837, 25th Cong., 1st sess., Appendix, pp. 250–51; Message from the President of the United States, February 13, 1837, 24th Cong., 2d sess., Sen. Doc. No. 174, unnumbered p. 1; John Forsyth to Andrew Jackson, February 13, 1837, 24th Cong., 2d sess., Sen. Doc. No. 174, unnumbered p. 1; Senate, *Register of Debates*, March 2, 1837, 24th Cong., 2d sess., 1016 (quotations).

5. Senate, *Register of Debates*, March 2, 1837, 24th Cong., 2d sess., 1016; Elder, *Calhoun*, 99, 118.

6. Elder, *Calhoun*, 335, 338; Jeff Forret, *Williams' Gang: A Notorious Slave Trader and His Cargo of Black Convicts* (New York: Cambridge University Press, 2020), 218–20.

7. Elder, *Calhoun*, 345–46, 114–15; Senate, *Register of Debates*, March 2, 1837, 24th Cong., 2d sess., 1017 (quotations).

8. Joseph T. Murphy, "The British Example: West Indian Emancipation, the Freedom Principle, and the Rise of Antislavery Politics in the United States, 1833–1843," *Journal of the Civil War Era* 8, no. 4 (December 2018): 621–22, 624, 625; Mark Weston Janis, *America and the Law of Nations 1776–1939* (New York: Oxford University Press, 2010), 96–98; Elder, *Calhoun*, 17, 312; Willem Theo Oosterveld, *The Law of Nations in Early American Foreign Policy: Theory and Practice from the Revolution to the Monroe*

Doctrine (Boston: Brill Nijhoff, 2016), 46 (quotation); J.L. Brierly, *The Law of Nations: An Introduction to the International Law of Peace*, 6th ed., ed. Sir Humphrey Waldock (New York: Oxford University Press, 1963), 306–7; *Weekly Raleigh (NC) Register*, April 15, 1834 (quotations).

John C. Calhoun was not the first to raise the issue of the law of nations. Newspaper editorials recognized that the interpretation of the law of nations was at stake from the spring of 1835, although contributors disagreed about whether the judge in Bermuda had acted in conformity with it in deciding the case of the *Enterprise*. See the pieces by "A Looker On" in the *Evening Post* (New York), April 9, 1835; and "J.S." in the *New York Journal of Commerce*, reprinted in *The Liberator* (Boston), May 30, 1835. U.S. Minister Andrew Stevenson also invoked the law of nations in his early communications with Great Britain but pressed the issue more strenuously in 1837, after Calhoun's January resolution and the denial of compensation for the *Enterprise*.

9. Murphy, "British Example," 622, 624, 625, 626.

10. Senate, *Register of Debates*, March 2, 1837, 24th Cong., 2d sess., 1017 (quotations); Elder, *Calhoun*, 312. The *Southern Christian Herald* (Columbia, SC) anticipated Calhoun's arguments in late 1835. Reporting on the "BRITISH OUTRAGES" committed against the *Encomium* and the *Enterprise*, the newspaper noted that the law of nations was at issue, but so was the question, "Can man become the property of man?" "It will no doubt be a subject of great interest in Congress," the *Herald* reported. "We shall then have an opportunity of knowing who are the friends of the south and who are not." See *Southern Christian Herald* (Columbia, Cheraw, SC), reprinted in *New York Evangelist*, December 26, 1835.

11. Senate, *Register of Debates*, March 2, 1837, 24th Cong., 2d sess., 1018.

12. John Forsyth to Andrew Stevenson, March 27, 1837, 25th Cong., 3d sess., Sen. Doc. No. 216, p. 3.

13. Lord Palmerston to Andrew Stevenson, January 7, 1837, 25th Cong., 3d sess., Sen. Doc. No. 216, p. 14.

14. Lord Palmerston to Andrew Stevenson, January 7, 1837, 25th Cong., 3d sess., Sen. Doc. No. 216, p. 14; Murphy, "British Example," 627.

15. *Richmond (VA) Enquirer*, December 21, 1841 (first quotation); John Forsyth to Andrew Stevenson, March 27, 1837, 25th Cong., 3d sess., Sen. Doc. No. 216, p. 4 (second and third quotations).

16. John Forsyth to Andrew Stevenson, March 27, 1837, 25th Cong., 3d sess., Sen. Doc. No. 216, pp. 4–5 (first quotation), 5 (second through seventh quotations).

17. John Forsyth to Andrew Stevenson, March 27, 1837, 25th Cong., 3d sess., Sen. Doc. No. 216, pp. 5 (first through fourth quotations), 6 (fifth and sixth quotations).

18. John Forsyth to Andrew Stevenson, March 27, 1837, 25th Cong., 3d sess., Sen. Doc. No. 216, p. 7.

19. John Forsyth to Andrew Stevenson, March 27, 1837, 25th Cong., 3d sess., Sen. Doc. No. 216, p. 8.

20. John Forsyth to Andrew Stevenson, March 27, 1837, 25th Cong., 3d sess., Sen. Doc. No. 216, pp. 9 (first and second quotations), 10 (third quotation).

21. John Forsyth to Andrew Stevenson, March 27, 1837, 25th Cong., 3d sess., Sen. Doc. No. 216, p. 10.

22. Andrew Stevenson to Lord Palmerston, May 12, 1837, 25th Cong., 3d sess., Sen. Doc. No. 216, pp. 17, 24.

23. Lord Palmerston to Andrew Stevenson, December 11, 1837, 25th Cong., 3d sess., Sen. Doc. No. 216, p. 26.

24. Letter of William Rothery, undated and unpaginated, HCA 30/895 Papers Relating to Services of W. Rothery, Slave Trade Adviser to the Treasury, NAUK.

25. Lord Palmerston to Andrew Stevenson, December 11, 1837, 25th Cong., 3d sess., Sen. Doc. No. 216, p. 26.

26. Lord Palmerston to Andrew Stevenson, December 11, 1837, 25th Cong., 3d sess., Sen. Doc. No. 216, pp. 27 (first quotation), 28 (second quotation).

27. Andrew Stevenson to Lord Palmerston, December 23, 1837, 25th Cong., 3d sess., Sen. Doc. No. 216, pp. 28 (first quotation), 30 (second through fifth quotations); John Forsyth to Andrew Stevenson, March 27, 1837, 25th Cong., 3d sess., Sen. Doc. No. 216, p. 10 (sixth quotation).

28. *People's Press and Wilmington (NC) Advertiser*, April 14, 1837. Italics in original.

29. *People's Press and Wilmington (NC) Advertiser*, April 14, 1837.

10. Compensation

1. Lord Palmerston to Andrew Stevenson, January 7, 1837, 25th Cong., 3d sess., Sen. Doc. No. 216, p. 15 (first through third, seventh, and eighth quotations); *People's Press and Wilmington (NC) Advertiser*, April 14, 1837 (fourth through sixth quotations).

2. *Edenton (NC) Gazette*, March 16, 1831 (first through sixth quotations); www.measuringworth.com; Martin Van Buren to Lord Viscount Palmerston, February 25, 1832, *Register of Debates*, 25th Cong., 1st sess., Appendix, p. 256 (seventh quotation); John Forsyth to Andrew Stevenson, March 27, 1837, 25th Cong., 3d sess., Sen. Doc. No. 216, p. 10.

3. John Forsyth to Andrew Stevenson, March 27, 1837, 25th Cong., 3d sess., Sen. Doc. No. 216, p. 10 (quotation); *Comet* Document N, Statement of 36 Slaves insured in the Louisiana State Marine Office, New Orleans. Also of 5 Slaves insured in said Office, and also of 16 Do. Do., T 1/3556, Treasury Long Papers, bundle 133, part 2, NAUK; *Comet* Document L, Certificate that 40 Slaves had been insured in the Mississippi Marine Insurance Office, New Orleans, T 1/3556, NAUK; No. 1. Mississippi Marine & Fire In Co. Statement, T 1/3556, NAUK; Manifest of the *Comet*, December 17, 1830, pp. 187–91, CO 23/92, Secretary of State Correspondence, NAUK; *Comet* Document M, Statement of 49 Slaves Insured in the Merchants Insurance Office, New Orleans, T 1/3556, NAUK. In 1840, the Louisiana State Marine and Fire Insurance

Company and Mississippi Marine and Fire Insurance Company were each capitalized at $300,000. See *Historical Epitome of the State of Louisiana, with an Historical Notice of New-Orleans, Views and Descriptions of Public Buildings, &c., &c.* (New Orleans, 1840), 351.

4. Ironically, one of the surviving policies listing the value of each slave is with the Charleston Fire and Marine Insurance Company, for Oliver Simpson's captives aboard the *Enterprise*. That ship was not included in the negotiations of 1837. See *Oliver Simpson v. Charleston Fire and Marine Insurance Co.*, Judgment Roll, Charleston District (L10018), June 10, 1837, Item 109A, SCDAH.

5. *Comet* Document D, Certificate of Sundry Planters of the State of Louisiana, May 16, 1837, T 1/3556, NAUK (quotations); Jeff Forret, *Williams' Gang: A Notorious Slave Trader and His Cargo of Black Convicts* (New York: Cambridge University Press, 2020), 192; *Comet* Document K, Amount of Claims stated to be due to the Mississippi Marine, Louisiana State, and Merchants Insurance Companies in New Orleans, T 1/3556, NAUK.

6. *Comet* Document K (quotation); John Storr[']s Bill at Nassau, April 4, 1831, p. 175, CO 23/92, NAUK.

7. *Encomium* Document D, Valuation of the 22 Negroes shipped by John Waddell, May 20, 1837, T 1/3556, NAUK (first through third quotations); *Encomium* Document E, Certificate of the Governor of the State of Louisiana, May 20, 1837, T 1/3556, NAUK (fourth quotation).

8. Statement, Shewing the value of the Slaves landed at the Bahamas from the American Vessels the Comet and Encomium, February 8, 1838, T 1/3556, NAUK.

9. Andrew Stevenson to Lord Palmerston, May 12, 1837, 25th Cong., 3d sess., Sen. Doc. No. 216, p. 24 (quotation); John Forsyth to Andrew Stevenson, August 4, 1837, 25th Cong., 3d sess., Sen. Doc. No. 216, p. 10; Statement, Shewing the value of the Slaves landed at the Bahamas from the American Vessels the Comet and Encomium, February 8, 1838, T 1/3556, NAUK; Andrew Stevenson to Lord Palmerston, December 4, 1838, 25th Cong., 3d sess., Sen. Doc. No. 216, p. 46; *Comet* Document K.

10. Andrew Stevenson to Lord Palmerston, December 4, 1838, 25th Cong., 3d sess., Sen. Doc. No. 216, p. 46; Statement, Shewing the value of the Slaves landed at the Bahamas from the American Vessels the Comet and Encomium, February 8, 1838, T 1/3556, NAUK.

11. Lord Palmerston to Andrew Stevenson, September 13, 1838, 25th Cong., 3d sess., Sen. Doc. No. 216, pp. 40, 41 (quotations).

12. Lord Palmerston to Andrew Stevenson, September 13, 1838, 25th Cong., 3d sess., Sen. Doc. No. 216, pp. 41 (first through fifth quotations), 42 (sixth quotation).

13. Lord Palmerston to Andrew Stevenson, September 13, 1838, 25th Cong., 3d sess., Sen. Doc. No. 216, p. 42.

14. John Forsyth to Andrew Stevenson, November 28, 1838, 25th Cong. 3d sess., Sen. Doc. No. 216, p. 12; Andrew Stevenson to Lord Palmerston, October 30, 1838,

25th Cong., 3d sess., Sen. Doc. No. 216, p. 42 (quotations); Andrew Stevenson to Lord Palmerston, December 4, 1838, 25th Cong., 3d sess., Sen. Doc. No. 216, p. 46.

15. Andrew Stevenson to Lord Palmerston, October 30, 1838, 25th Cong., 3d sess., Sen. Doc. No. 216, p. 42 (first through fourth quotations); Andrew Stevenson to Lord Palmerston, December 4, 1838, 25th Cong., 3d sess., Sen. Doc. No. 216, pp. 47 (fifth and seventh quotations), 48 (sixth and eighth quotations).

16. Andrew Stevenson to Lord Palmerston, December 4, 1838, 25th Cong., 3d sess., Sen. Doc. No. 216, pp. 48 (first quotation), 49 (second through fourth quotations).

17. Andrew Stevenson to Lord Palmerston, December 4, 1838, 25th Cong., 3d sess., Sen. Doc. No. 216, pp. 49–55 (quotation 49).

18. Andrew Stevenson to Lord Palmerston, January 10, 1839, 26th Cong., 1st sess., Sen. Doc. No. 119, pp. 3 (first and second quotations), 3–4 (third quotation); Andrew Stevenson to John Forsyth, January 24, 1839, 26th Cong., 1st sess., Sen. Doc. No. 119, p. 3 (fourth and fifth quotations).

19. *Senate Journal*, February 1, 1839, 25th Cong., 3d sess., vol. 29, p. 182 (quotation); John Forsyth to Martin Van Buren, February 12, 1839, 25th Cong., 3d sess., Sen. Doc. No. 216, unnumbered p. 1; Martin Van Buren to the Senate, February 13, 1839, 25th Cong., 3d sess., Senate Doc. No. 216, unnumbered p. 1.

20. Lord Palmerston to Andrew Stevenson, September 13, 1838, 25th Cong., 3d sess., Sen. Doc. No. 216, p. 42; William Rothery to T. F. Baring, February 23, 1839, T 1/3556, NAUK (quotations).

21. William Rothery to T.F. Baring, February 23, 1839; Andrew Stevenson to John Forsyth, February 5, 1839, 26th Cong., 1st sess., Sen. Doc. No. 119, p. 4.

22. William Rothery to T.F. Baring, February 23, 1839.

23. William Rothery to T.F. Baring, February 23, 1839.

24. William Rothery to T.F. Baring, February 23, 1839; Sixth Census of the United States, 1840, District 1, Anne Arundel County, Maryland, NAMS M-704, reel 157, p. 130; Sixth Census of the United States, 1840, Upper District, Chesterfield County, Virginia, NAMS M-704, reel 554, p. 204.

25. Andrew Stevenson to John Forsyth, February 5, 1839, 26th Cong., 1st sess., Sen. Doc. No. 119, p. 4 (first quotation); William Rothery to T.F. Baring, February 23, 1839 (second through sixth quotations).

26. William Rothery to T.F. Baring, February 23, 1839.

27. William Rothery to T.F. Baring, February 23, 1839 (quotations); William Rothery to T.F. Baring, March 23, 1839, T 1/3556, NAUK.

28. *Comet* Document K; Sixth Census of the United States, 1840, Opelousas, St. Landry Parish, Louisiana, NAMS M-704, reel 128, p. 234; RSPP, Petition 20484401, Series II, Part B, Reel 15, Washington, DC, January 17, 1844; William Rothery to T.F. Baring, February 23, 1839 (quotations).

29. William Rothery to T.F. Baring, February 23, 1839 (first and second quotations); William Rothery to T.F. Baring, March 23, 1839 (third quotation).

30. William Rothery to T.F. Baring, February 23, 1839 (first and second quotations); William Rothery to T.F. Baring, March 23, 1839 (third and fourth quotations).

31. *Rochester (NY) Freeman*, July 17, 1839.

32. Andrew Stevenson to John Forsyth, March 18, 1839, 26th Cong., 1st sess., Sen. Doc. No. 119, pp. 4 (quotations), 5.

33. William Rothery to T.F. Baring, March 23, 1839.

34. William Rothery to T.F. Baring, March 23, 1839.

35. Royal Commission on Fugitive Slaves, *Report of the Commissioners. Minutes of the Evidence. And Appendix, with General Index, of Minutes of Evidence and Appendix* (London: George Edward Eyre and William Spottiswoode, 1876), 231.

36. Andrew Stevenson to John Forsyth, April 27, 1839, 26th Cong., 1st sess., Sen. Doc. No. 119, p. 5 (first quotation); J. Backhouse to the Secretary to Her Majesty & Treasury, May 2, 1839, T 1/3556, NAUK; Lord Palmerston to Andrew Stevenson, May 2, 1839, 26th Cong., 1st sess., Sen. Doc. No. 119, pp. 7 (second quotation), 8 (third through fifth quotations); Royal Commission on Fugitive Slaves, *Report of the Commissioners*, 231.

37. Andrew Stevenson to John Forsyth, May 8, 1839, 26th Cong., 1st sess., Sen. Doc. No. 119, p. 5; www.measuringworth.com.

38. *Rochester (NY) Freeman*, July 17, 1839 (first and second quotations); *Richmond (VA) Enquirer*, June 28, 1839; Andrew Stevenson to John Forsyth, May 8, 1839, 26th Cong., 1st sess., Sen. Doc. No. 119, p. 6 (third through sixth quotations).

39. *People's Press and Wilmington (NC) Advertiser*, June 14, 1839.

40. *Rochester (NY) Freeman*, July 17, 1839; *Commercial Advertiser* (New York), June 28, 1839; *Charleston (SC) Mercury*, April 9, 1839 (first through third quotations); *Charleston (SC) Mercury*, April 11, 1839 (fourth quotation).

11. An Alarm of Fire

1. *Charleston (SC) Courier*, March 16, 1835; *Bermuda Royal Gazette*, reprinted in *Alexandria (DC) Gazette*, March 17, 1835; Manifest of the *Enterprise*, January 22, 1835, unpaginated, T 1/3556 Treasury Long Papers, bundle 133, part 2, NAUK; *The Observer* (London), April 19, 1835.

2. Seventh Census of the United States, 1850, Edgefield District, South Carolina, NAMS M-432, reel 852, p. 120B; Fourth Census of the United States, 1820, Rockingham County, North Carolina, NAMS M-33, reel 82, p. 620; Fifth Census of the United States, 1830, Rockingham County, North Carolina, NAMS M-19, reel 124, p. 314; *United States' Telegraph* (Washington, DC), October 9, 1832; *Daily Globe* (Washington, DC), February 27, 1834.

3. *Smith, Mowry & Son v. Schroder* (December 1, 1849), Court of Appeals of Law of South Carolina, 35 S.C.L. 69, 4 Strob. 69, 1849 WL 2704; *Edgefield (SC) Advertiser*, December 27, 1838; Charles G. Cordle, "Henry Shultz and the Founding of

Hamburg, South Carolina," in *Studies in Georgia History and Government*, ed. James C. Bonner and Lucien E. Roberts (Athens: University of Georgia Press, 1940), 79–82; John A. Chapman, *History of Edgefield County from the Earliest Settlements to 1897* (Newberry, SC: Elbert H. Aull, 1897), 236–39; Orville Vernon Burton, *In My Father's House Are Many Mansions: Family and Community in Edgefield, South Carolina* (Chapel Hill: University of North Carolina Press, 1985), 6, 29–30. As Burton explains, Shultz's grudge toward Augusta continued even in death. He had himself buried standing up, with his back facing the city.

4. Burton, *In My Father's House*, 30; Cordle, "Henry Shultz," 93; Chapman, *History of Edgefield County*, 237; *Edgefield (SC) Advertiser*, December 27, 1838.

5. *Edgefield (SC) Advertiser*, December 27, 1838; *Edgefield (SC) Advertiser*, November 18, 1841 (first quotation); *Duncan v. S. D. Clark & Co.* (May 1, 1846), Court of Appeals of Law of South Carolina, 2 Rich. 587, 31 S.C.L. 587, 1846 WL 2250 (second quotation); *Lamar's Ex'rs v. Simpson* (December 1, 1844), Court of Appeals of Equity of South Carolina, 1 Rich.Eq. 71, 18 S.C. Eq. 71, 1844 WL 2664, 42 Am.Dec. 345; *Camden (SC) Weekly Journal*, March 19, 1836; *Charleston (SC) Daily Courier*, December 31, 1835; *Charleston (SC) Daily Courier*, May 14, 1836; Jeff Forret, *Williams' Gang: A Notorious Slave Trader and His Cargo of Black Convicts* (New York: Cambridge University Press, 2020), 89–90, chap. 6; Jeff Forret, "'How Deeply They *Weed* into the Pockets': Slave Traders, Bank Speculators, and the Anatomy of a Chesapeake Wildcat, 1840–1843," *Journal of the Early Republic* 39 (Winter 2019): 709–36; Alexandra J. Finley, "A Gentleman and a Scoundrel?: Alexander McDonald, Financial Reputation, and Slavery's Capitalism," in *Southern Scoundrels: Grifters and Graft in the Nineteenth Century*, ed. Jeff Forret and Bruce Baker (Baton Rouge: Louisiana State University Press, 2021), chap. 2.

6. *New York Journal of Commerce*, reprinted in *The Liberator* (Boston), April 4, 1835 (first quotation); 34th Cong., 1st sess., Sen. Ex. Doc. No. 103, p. 236; *Charleston (SC) Courier*, March 16, 1835; *Oliver Simpson v. Charleston Fire and Marine Insurance Co.*, Judgment Roll, Charleston District (L10018), June 10, 1837, Item 109A, SCDAH; Manifest of the *Enterprise*, January 22, 1835, unpaginated, T 1/3556 Treasury Long Papers, bundle 133, part 2, NAUK (second quotation); *Simpson v. Charleston Fire & Marine Ins. Co.*, Dudl 239 (1838), 23 S.C.L. 239.

7. *Oliver Simpson v. The Augusta Insurance and Banking Company* (1837), Richmond County, Georgia, Superior Court, Minutes, vol. 14, GA; *Charleston (SC) Mercury*, January 10, 1835.

8. *Oliver Simpson v. Charleston Fire and Marine Insurance Co.* (first quotation); *Charleston (SC) Courier*, May 27, 1837 (second quotation).

9. *Charleston (SC) Courier*, May 27, 1837; *Oliver Simpson v. Charleston Fire and Marine Insurance Co.*; *Simpson v. Charleston Fire & Marine Ins. Co.*, Dudl 239 (1838), 23 S.C.L. 239 (quotations).

10. Eight of the twelve jurors still lived in Charleston District three years later, when census takers arrived in 1840. At that time, they owned a total of 118 enslaved people, an average of almost 15 per juror. Foreman John F. Poppenheim alone owned 42. Sixth Census of the United States, 1840, St. James Goose Creek Parish, Charleston District, South Carolina, NAMS M-704, reel 509, pp. 149, 153; Sixth Census of the United States, 1840, Christ Church, Charleston District, South Carolina, NAMS M-704, reel 509, p. 183; Sixth Census of the United States, 1840, Charleston, Charleston District, South Carolina, NAMS M-704, reel 509, pp. 40, 49, 80; Sixth Census of the United States, 1840, St. Thomas and St. Dennis, Charleston District, South Carolina, NAMS M-704, reel 509, p. 191; *Oliver Simpson v. Charleston Fire and Marine Insurance Co.*; *Simpson v. Charleston Fire & Marine Ins. Co.*, Dudl 239 (1838), 23 S.C.L. 239; www.measuringworth.com. *Charleston (SC) Courier*, May 27, 1837 (quotation).

11. *Charleston (SC) Courier*, May 27, 1837 (quotation); *Oliver Simpson v. The Augusta Insurance and Banking Company.*

12. *Simpson v. Charleston Fire & Marine Ins. Co.*, Dudl 239 (1838), 23 S.C.L. 239.

13. *Simpson v. Charleston Fire & Marine Ins. Co.*, Dudl 239 (1838), 23 S.C.L. 239 (quotations); *Charleston (SC) Courier*, June 11, 1838; *Oliver Simpson v. Charleston Fire and Marine Insurance Co.*; Charleston Fire and Marine Insurance Company, financial statement as of July 1, 1838, July 5, 1838, Andrew Wallace Papers, SCL.

14. Andrew Stevenson to Lord Palmerston, May 6, 1839, 26th Cong., 1st sess., Senate Doc. No. 119, pp. 8–9 (first quotation); Royal Commission on Fugitive Slaves, *Report of the Commissioners. Minutes of the Evidence. And Appendix, with General Index, of Minutes of Evidence and Appendix* (London: George Edward Eyre and William Spottiswoode, 1876), 231; Andrew Stevenson to John Forsyth, March 18, 1839, 26th Cong., 1st sess., Sen. Doc. No. 119, p. 5 (second through fourth quotations).

15. Fifth Census of the United States, 1830, Richmond Monroe Ward, Richmond City, Virginia, NAMS M-19, reel 195, p. 399; *Morning Post* (London), September 20, 1838 (first through fourth and seventh through eleventh quotations); Gregory D. Smithers, *Slave Breeding: Sex, Violence, and Memory in African American History* (Gainesville: University Press of Florida, 2012); Daina Ramey Berry, *"Swing the Sickle for the Harvest Is Ripe": Gender and Slavery in Antebellum Georgia* (Urbana: University of Illinois Press, 2007), 77–83; Kenneth S. Greenberg, *Honor & Slavery: Lies, Duels, Noses, Masks, Dressing as a Woman, Gifts, Strangers, Humanitarianism, Death, Slave Rebellions, the Proslavery Argument, Baseball, Hunting, and Gambling in the Old South* (Princeton: Princeton University Press, 1996), 62; *Southern Sun* (Jackson, MS), October 13, 1838 (fifth and sixth quotations).

16. *The Standard* (London), August 6, 1839.

17. *The Standard* (London), August 6, 1839; Randolph B. Campbell, *An Empire for Slavery: The Peculiar Institution in Texas, 1821–1865* (Baton Rouge: Louisiana State University Press, 1989), 51; Andrew J. Torget, *Seeds of Empire: Cotton, Slavery, and the*

Transformation of the Texas Borderlands, 1800–1850 (Chapel Hill: University of North Carolina Press, 2015), 182–83, 194–96; Forret, *Williams' Gang*, 112–13.

18. *The Standard* (London), August 6, 1839 (first quotation); Andrew Stevenson to John Forsyth, August 6, 1839, 26th Cong., 1st sess., Sen. Doc. No. 119, p. 9 (second and third quotations); Matthew Karp, *This Vast Southern Empire: Slaveholders at the Helm of American Foreign Policy* (Cambridge: Harvard University Press, 2016).

19. Andrew Stevenson to John Forsyth, August 6, 1839, 26th Cong., 1st sess., Sen. Doc. No. 119, p. 9; Andrew Stevenson to John Forsyth, September 14, 1839, 26th Cong., 1st sess., Sen. Doc. No. 119, p. 9 (first quotation); John Forsyth to Andrew Stevenson, September 16, 1839, 26th Cong., 1st sess., Sen. Doc. No. 119, p. 10 (second through fifth quotations). Stevenson had first requested "instructions as to the disposition of the amount" in May, "should they prefer paying it here [in England], and not in the United States." See Andrew Stevenson to John Forsyth, May 8, 1839, 26th Cong., 1st sess., Sen. Doc. No. 119, p. 6.

20. John Forsyth to Andrew Stevenson, September 19, 1839, 26th Cong., 1st sess., Sen. Doc. No. 119, p. 10 (first and second quotations); John Forsyth to Andrew Stevenson, October 30, 1839, 26th Cong., 1st sess., Sen. Doc. No. 119, pp. 10 (third through fifth quotations), 11 (sixth quotation); *Morning Post* (London), March 5, 1841.

21. Marcus Rediker, *The Amistad Rebellion: An Atlantic Odyssey of Slavery and Freedom* (New York: Penguin, 2012).

22. Senate, *Register of Debates*, February 7, 1837, 24th Cong., 2d sess., 725 (first quotation); *Senate Journal*, January 13, 1840, 26th Cong., 1st sess., vol. 30, p. 101 (second quotation); *Senate Journal*, January 14, 1840, 26th Cong., 1st sess., vol. 30, p. 108; Message from the President of the United States, in Compliance with a resolution of the Senate in relation to the seizure and detention of the brigs, Enterprise, Encomium, and Comet, January 27, 1840, 26th Cong., 1st sess., Sen. Doc. No. 119, unnumbered p. 1 (third quotation).

23. *Weekly Standard* (Raleigh, NC), February 5, 1840; House of Representatives, *Congressional Globe*, 26th Cong., 1st sess., February 10, 1840, p. 180; Joseph T. Murphy, "The British Example: West Indian Emancipation, the Freedom Principle, and the Rise of Antislavery Politics in the United States, 1833–1843," *Journal of the Civil War Era* 8, no. 4 (December 2018): 631; Robert Elder, *Calhoun: American Heretic* (New York: Basic Books, 2021), 378; *Senate Journal*, March 4, 1840, 26th Cong., 1st sess., vol. 30, p. 216 (quotations).

24. Senate, *Congressional Globe*, 26th Cong., 1st sess., March 13, 1840, p. 267; *New York Spectator*, March 19, 1840 (first, second, and fourth through sixth quotations); *North American* (Philadelphia), March 16, 1840 (third quotation).

25. *Weekly Standard* (Raleigh, NC), April 15, 1840 (quotations); *American and Commercial Daily Advertiser* (Baltimore), March 14, 1840; *New York Spectator*, March 19, 1840. The full text of Calhoun's extensive speech appeared in the *Weekly Standard* more than a month after he gave it. Ironically, British historians are picking up on cues from

Calhoun as they show renewed interest in British slavery outside the Atlantic basin. See, for example, the papers by Kathleen Wilson, "Slavery, Coercion and Marronage in British Sumatra, 1685–1816," and Jessica Hanser, "Britain, China and Slavery in the Eighteenth Century" (North American Conference on British Studies Annual Conference, Vancouver, British Columbia, November 16, 2019).

26. *Weekly Standard* (Raleigh, NC), April 15, 1840 (first and second quotations); *Vicksburg (MS) Tri-Weekly Sentinel*, April 17, 1840; *New York Journal of Commerce*, quoted in *New-York Observer*, March 21, 1840 (third quotation); *St. Johnsbury (VT) Caledonian*, March 24, 1840 (fourth quotation); *North American* (Philadelphia), March 16, 1840 (fifth quotation); *Evening Post* (New York), March 16, 1840 (sixth quotation).

27. Senate, *Congressional Globe*, 26th Cong., 1st sess., March 13, 1840, p. 267; *Senate Journal*, March 13, 1840, 26th Cong. 1st sess., vol. 30, p. 244; Senate, *Congressional Globe*, 26th Cong., 1st sess., April 13, 1840, p. 320; *Senate Journal*, April 13, 1840, 26th Cong., 1st sess., vol. 30, p. 303; Doc. No. 378, *Public Documents Printed by Order of the Senate of the United States, During the First Session of the Twenty-Sixth Congress, Begun and Held at the City of Washington, December 2, 1839*, vol. 6 (Washington: Blair and Rives, 1840); Senate, *Congressional Globe*, 26th Cong., 1st sess., April 15, 1840, p. 328 (quotation).

28. Senate, *Congressional Globe*, 26th Cong., 1st sess., April 15, 1840, pp. 327 (first quotation), 328 (second and third quotations).

29. Senate, *Congressional Globe*, 26th Cong., 1st sess., April 15, 1840, p. 328.

30. Senate, *Congressional Globe*, 26th Cong., 1st sess., April 15, 1840, p. 328.

31. Senate, *Congressional Globe*, 26th Cong., 1st sess., April 15, 1840, p. 328.

32. Senate, *Congressional Globe*, 26th Cong., 1st sess., April 15, 1840, p. 328.

33. Senate, *Congressional Globe*, 26th Cong., 1st sess., April 15, 1840, pp. 328 (sixth and seventh quotations), 329 (first through fifth quotations).

34. *Senate Journal*, April 15, 1840, 26th Cong., 1st sess., vol. 30, p. 311; Senate, *Congressional Globe*, 26th Cong., 1st sess., April 15, 1840, p. 329.

35. *Mississippi Free Trader* (Natchez), April 30, 1840 (first quotation); *Weekly Standard* (Raleigh, NC), April 15, 1840 (second through fourth quotations); *Vicksburg (MS) Tri-Weekly Sentinel*, April 17, 1840; *New Orleans Bee*, reprinted in *North-Carolinian* (Fayetteville), February 13, 1841 (fifth and sixth quotations).

36. *Charleston (SC) Courier*, May 27, 1837. Oliver Simpson's former business partner and associate, Washington, DC, slave trader Joseph W. Neal, sued him in the Rockingham County, North Carolina Court of Pleas and Quarter Sessions in the August 1845 term. It is not clear whether the suit was related to the captives Neal consigned to Simpson aboard the *Enterprise* or to another shipment of enslaved people. Although Simpson maintained plantations in both Rockingham County, North Carolina, and in Edgefield County, South Carolina, in 1840, he seems to have left North Carolina sometime prior to the fall of 1845. Having failed to appear for his November

court date, Simpson lost the case and was ordered to pay Neal $2,054.13, plus interest from June 1845. See *James* [sic] *W. Neal vs. Oliver Simpson* (August 1845), Rockingham County, North Carolina, Court of Pleas and Quarter Sessions, in *Greensboro (NC) Patriot*, September 20, 1845; *Joseph W. Neal v. Oliver Simpson* (August 1845), Rockingham County, North Carolina, County Court of Pleas and Quarter Sessions, Minutes, 1786–1868, NCDAH; *Joseph W. Neal v. Oliver Simpson* (November 1845), Rockingham County, North Carolina, County Court of Pleas and Quarter Sessions, Minutes, 1786–1868, NCDAH; Sixth Census of the United States, 1840, Rockingham County, North Carolina, NAMS M-704, reel 369, p. 150; Sixth Census of the United States, 1840, Edgefield District, South Carolina, NAMS M-704, reel 511, p. 54. By 1850, either Simpson's economic fortunes had soured or he had already distributed much of his wealth to his children. He appeared in the census as a sixty-four-year-old farmer living in the household of a husband-less adult daughter and her eight children ranging in age from twenty-one to one. Simpson's reputation was damaged before 1850, perhaps through unscrupulous slave trades. His character was described as "bad or doubtful" and unworthy of belief, certainly when "he had an interest" at stake "or was prejudiced." See Seventh Census of the United States, 1850, Edgefield District, South Carolina, NAMS M-432, reel 852, p. 120B; *Smith, Mowry & Son v. Schroder* (December 1, 1849), Court of Appeals of Law of South Carolina, 35 S.C.L. 69, 4 Strob. 69, 1849 WL 2704.

12. The Wreck of the *Hermosa*

1. John Forsyth to Andrew Stevenson, March 12, 1838, 25th Cong., 3d sess., Sen. Doc. No. 216, p. 11.

2. Andrew Stevenson to Lord Palmerston, April 17, 1838, 25th Cong., 3d sess., Sen. Doc. No. 216, p. 36.

3. Lord Palmerston to Andrew Stevenson, April 28, 1838, 25th Cong., 3d sess., Sen. Doc. No. 216, p. 37; Andrew Stevenson to John Forsyth, May 5, 1838, 25th Cong., 3d sess., Sen. Doc. No. 216, p. 37; Lord Palmerston to Andrew Stevenson, May 19, 1838, 25th Cong., 3d sess., Sen. Doc. No. 216, p. 38 (quotations).

4. John Forsyth to Andrew Stevenson, June 6, 1838, 25th Cong., 3d sess., Sen. Doc. No. 216, p. 12.

5. Andrew Stevenson to Lord Palmerston, July 10, 1838, 25th Cong., 3d sess., Sen. Doc. No. 216, p. 39; Lord Palmerston to Andrew Stevenson, September 10, 1838, 25th Cong., 3d sess., Sen. Doc. No. 216, pp. 43 (fourth quotation), 44 (first through third and fifth quotations).

6. Lord Palmerston to Andrew Stevenson, September 10, 1838, 25th Cong., 3d sess., Sen. Doc. No. 216, p. 44.

7. Lord Palmerston to Andrew Stevenson, September 10, 1838, 25th Cong., 3d sess., Sen. Doc. No. 216, p. 44.

8. Lord Palmerston to Andrew Stevenson, September 10, 1838, 25th Cong., 3d sess., Sen. Doc. No. 216, p. 44.

9. Lord Palmerston to Andrew Stevenson, September 10, 1838, 25th Cong., 3d sess., Sen. Doc. No. 216, pp. 44–45 (quotations, 45).

10. Andrew Stevenson to Lord Palmerston, October 30, 1838, 25th Cong., 3d sess., Sen. Doc. No. 216, p. 45; Andrew Stevenson to John Forsyth, November 5, 1838, 25th Cong., 3d sess., Sen. Doc. No. 216, p. 43.

11. *Richmond (VA) Whig*, September 29, 1840 (quotation); Manifest of the *Hermosa*, October 10, 1840, reel 59, folio 367, CO 23/107, BNAN; *Richmond (VA) Whig & Public Advertiser*, February 2, 1836.

12. Department of Commerce, Bureau of the Census, *Fourteenth Census of the United States State Compendium Virginia* (Washington, DC: Government Printing Office, 1925), 8; Michael Tadman, *Speculators and Slaves: Masters, Traders, and Slaves in the Old South* (Madison: University of Wisconsin Press, 1989), 57, 62; Calvin Schermerhorn, *The Business of Slavery and the Rise of American Capitalism, 1815–1860* (New Haven: Yale University Press, 2015), 179, 127; Steven Deyle, *Carry Me Back: The Domestic Slave Trade in American Life* (New York: Oxford University Press, 2005), 115.

13. *Richmond (VA) Compiler*, November 19, 1840, reprinted in *American and Commercial Daily Advertiser* (Baltimore), November 20, 1840; Manifest of the *Hermosa*, October 10, 1840; Manuscript Census Returns, Seventh Census of the United States, 1850, New York Ward 9, District 3, New York, New York, NAMS M-432, reel 544, p. 390B; Jeff Forret, *Williams' Gang: A Notorious Slave Trader and His Cargo of Black Convicts* (New York: Cambridge University Press, 2020), 44.

14. *Richmond (VA) Whig*, September 29, 1840; Manifest of the *Hermosa*, October 10, 1840 (quotation); Manuscript Census Returns, Seventh Census of the United States, 1850, New Orleans Municipality 1, Ward 1, Orleans Parish, Louisiana, NAMS M-432, reel 235, p. 10B; *Richmond (VA) Enquirer*, April 21, 1840; *Richmond (VA) Enquirer*, August 18, 1840; *Vicksburg (MS) Tri-Weekly Sentinel*, November 6, 1843; *New-Orleans Directory for 1842* (New Orleans: Pitts and Clarke, 1842), 242.

15. *Richmond (VA) Compiler*, November 19, 1840, reprinted in *American and Commercial Daily Advertiser* (Baltimore), November 20, 1840; Manuscript Census Returns, Eighth Census of the United States, 1860, Richmond Ward 3, Henrico County, Virginia, NAMS M-653, reel 1353, p. 516; *Republican Star* (Easton, MD), October 30, 1827; Robert H. Gudmestad, *A Troublesome Commerce: The Transformation of the Interstate Slave Trade* (Baton Rouge: Louisiana State University Press, 2003), 30; Schermerhorn, *Business of Slavery*, 56; *Constitutional Whig* (Richmond, VA), November 26, 1830 (quotations).

16. *Richmond (VA) Enquirer*, June 24, 1834; Hank Trent, *The Secret Life of Bacon Tait, a White Slave Trader Married to a Free Woman of Color* (Baton Rouge: Louisiana State University Press, 2017), 92; Schermerhorn, *Business of Slavery*, 56, 203, 127; *Richmond (VA) Whig & Public Advertiser*, September 2, 1834 (quotations); Forret, *Williams' Gang*, 60–61; Deyle, *Carry Me Back*, 115.

17. Manifest of the *Hermosa*, October 10, 1840 (quotations); *H.N. Templeman v. Louisiana State Marine & Fire Insurance Company*, case #3261, December 24, 1840, p. 15, New Orleans Commercial Court, NOPL; Jeff Forret, "'Deaf & Dumb, Blind, Insane, or Idiotic': The Census, Slaves, and Disability in the Late Antebellum South," *Journal of Southern History* 82 (August 2016): 540–46. Templeman paid $17 apiece to ship thirty-five of his thirty-eight captives, and $10 for each of the other three, "without primage and average accustomed." "Primage" referred to "the small payment allowed to the master of the vessel for his care and attention to the cargo." "Average" referred to "the right reserved to divide pro rata between the owners of the ship and the proprietors of the cargo any small items of expense for towage, pilotage, &c." See Charles Putzel and H.A. Bähr, *Commercial Precedents Selected from the Column of Replies and Decisions of the New York Journal of Commerce, Also Selected Decisions from Other Sources*, rev. ed. (Hartford, CT: S.S. Scranton, 1900), 56.

18. *Richmond (VA) Compiler*, November 19, 1840, reprinted in *American and Commercial Daily Advertiser* (Baltimore), November 20, 1840 (first, second, fifth, and sixth quotations); *Boston Post*, November 23, 1840; Francis Cockburn to Lord John Russell, December 1, 1840, reel 59, folio 363, CO 23/107, BNAN (third and fourth quotations); 34th Cong., 1st sess., Senate, Ex. Doc. No. 103, p. 239; *H.N. Templeman v. Louisiana State Marine & Fire Insurance Company*, p. 2. Capt. Chattin reported that the ship *Wellington*, of Bath, Maine, wrecked near the *Hermosa* the same night. See *Richmond Compiler*, November 19, 1840, reprinted in *American and Commercial Daily Advertiser* (Baltimore), November 20, 1840.

19. *H.N. Templeman v. Louisiana State Marine & Fire Insurance Company*, pp. 19 (first and seventh quotations), 2 (second, fourth, and sixth quotations), 20; 34th Cong., 1st sess., Senate, Ex. Doc. No. 103, p. 239 (third quotation); Lord Aberdeen to Edward Everett, May 20, 1842, in *Washington (DC) Globe*, January 2, 1843; Francis Cockburn to Lord John Russell, December 1, 1840, folio 363; *New York Herald*, reprinted in *Jacksonville (AL) Republican*, February 3, 1841 (fifth quotation).

20. Francis Cockburn to Lord John Russell, December 1, 1840, folios 364 (first quotation), 363 (second through seventh quotations); *New York Herald*, quoted in *Jacksonville (AL) Republican*, February 3, 1841 (eighth and ninth quotations); Michael Craton, "The Ambivalences of Independency: The Transition Out of Slavery in the Bahamas, c. 1800–1850," in *West Indies Accounts: Essays on the History of the British Caribbean and the Atlantic Economy in Honour of Richard Sheridan*, ed. Roderick A. McDonald (Jamaica: Press University of the West Indies, 1996), 284.

21. Henry Wilson, *History of the Rise and Fall of the Slave Power in America*, vol. 1, 3rd ed. (Boston: James R. Osgood, 1875), 440 (quotation); Lorraine Sencicle, "Sir Francis Cockburn," *Dover Historian*, February 11, 2017, doverhistorian.com/2017/02/11/sir-francis-cockburn-canada-belize-bahamas-and-dover.

22. Francis Cockburn to Lord John Russell, December 1, 1840, folio 364 (first through third quotations); Despatch No. 80, letter to Colonel Cockburn, February 6, 1841, reel 59, folio 365, CO 23/107, BNAN (fourth quotation).

23. *Baltimore Sun*, November 20, 1840 (first quotation); *H.N. Templeman v. Louisiana State Marine & Fire Insurance Company*, p. 1 (second quotation). The court case states that the *Hermosa* left Richmond on October 12 rather than October 10. It also incorrectly lists the date of the policy as November 9, which would have been the month after the voyage. Presumably, Templeman took out the policy on October 9, the day preceding the schooner's departure.

24. *H.N. Templeman v. Louisiana State Marine & Fire Insurance Company*, pp. 2 (first and second quotations), 9 (third and fourth quotations), 1, 3 (fifth quotation).

25. *H.N. Templeman v. Louisiana State Marine & Fire Insurance Company*, pp. 8, 11 (first through third quotations), 12; *Historical Epitome of the State of Louisiana, with an Historical Notice of New-Orleans, Views and Descriptions of Public Buildings, &c., &c.* (New Orleans, 1840), 351.

26. *H.N. Templeman v. Louisiana State Marine & Fire Insurance Company*, pp. 6, 3, 18, 16, 22, 13 (quotation).

27. *H.N. Templeman v. Louisiana State Marine & Fire Insurance Company*, p. 13.

28. *H.N. Templeman v. Louisiana State Marine & Fire Insurance Company*, p. 13 (first and second quotations); *Richmond (VA) Compiler*, November 19, 1840, reprinted in *American and Commercial Daily Advertiser* (Baltimore), November 20, 1840 (third and fourth quotations); *Baltimore Sun*, November 21, 1840 (fifth quotation); *Detroit Free Press*, December 3, 1840 (sixth quotation); *Morning Post* (London), March 5, 1841 (seventh quotation). British papers remembered that remuneration for the *Francis and Eliza* remained unpaid.

29. John F. Bacon to Daniel Webster, November 17, 1841, 27th Cong., 2d sess., Sen. Doc. No. 51, p. 2; Matthew Karp, *This Vast Southern Empire: Slaveholders at the Helm of American Foreign Policy* (Cambridge: Harvard University Press, 2016), 23; Jeffrey R. Kerr-Ritchie, *Rebellious Passage: The* Creole *Revolt and America's Coastal Slave Trade* (New York: Cambridge University Press, 2019), 103, 107, 115, 122, 128 (quotation); Arthur T. Downey, *The* Creole *Affair: The Slave Rebellion That Led the U.S. and Great Britain to the Brink of War* (Lanham, MD: Rowman and Littlefield, 2014), 9–15; Phillip Troutman, "Grapevine in the Slave Market: African American Geopolitical Literacy and the 1841 *Creole* Revolt," in *The Chattel Principle: Internal Slave Trades in the Americas*, ed. Walter Johnson (New Haven: Yale University Press, 2004), 209, 210 (same quotation); Anita Rupprecht, "'All We Have Done, We Have Done for Freedom': The *Creole* Slave-Ship Revolt (1841) and the Revolutionary Atlantic," *International Review of Social History* 58 (2013): 265 (same quotation); Walter Johnson, "White Lies: Human Property and Domestic Slavery Aboard the Slave Ship *Creole*," *Atlantic Studies* 5, no. 2 (2008): 238 (same quotation), 254; Gerald Horne, *Negro Comrades of the Crown: African Americans and the British Empire Fight the U.S. Before Emancipation*

(New York: New York University Press, 2012), 133; Edward D. Jervey and C. Harold Huber, "The *Creole* Affair," *Journal of Negro History* 65, no. 3 (Summer 1980): 200.

30. Rupprecht, "'All We Have Done, We Have Done for Freedom,'" 267. Only five enslaved passengers aboard the *Creole* opted to continue on their original journey to New Orleans. See Bacon to Webster, November 17, 1841; Horne, *Negro Comrades*, 135; and Trent, *Secret Life of Bacon Tait*, 113.

31. *Richmond (VA) Enquirer*, December 21, 1841 (first through fourth quotations); *Mobile (AL) Register and Journal*, reprinted in *South-Western Farmer* (Raymond, MS), January 7, 1842 (fifth and sixth quotations).

32. Karp, *Vast Southern Empire*, 23; *Norwich (CT) Courier*, December 29, 1841 (first through fourth quotations); *Daily Madisonian* (Washington, DC), December 23, 1841 (fifth and sixth quotations); *Daily National Intelligencer* (Washington, DC), December 23, 1841; *Daily Pennsylvanian* (Philadelphia), December 24, 1841 (seventh quotation).

33. *Daily Madisonian* (Washington, DC), December 23, 1841 (first quotation); *Daily National Intelligencer* (Washington, DC), December 23, 1841 (second, seventh, and eighth quotations); *Norwich (CT) Courier*, December 29, 1841 (fifth and sixth quotations); *Mecklenburg Jeffersonian* (Charlotte, NC), January 4, 1842 (third and fourth quotations).

34. *Daily National Intelligencer* (Washington, DC), December 23, 1841 (first quotation); *Norwich (CT) Courier*, December 29, 1841; *Daily Madisonian* (Washington, DC), December 23, 1841 (second and third quotations); *Daily Pennsylvanian* (Philadelphia), December 24, 1841; *Mecklenburg Jeffersonian* (Charlotte, NC), January 4, 1842 (fourth quotation).

35. *Daily Madisonian* (Washington, DC), December 23, 1841 (first through fourth quotations); *Daily National Intelligencer* (Washington, DC), December 23, 1841 (fifth quotation).

36. *Daily Madisonian* (Washington, DC), December 23, 1841.

37. *Daily Madisonian* (Washington, DC), December 23, 1841 (first and third quotations); *Mecklenburg Jeffersonian* (Charlotte, NC), January 4, 1842 (second quotation).

38. *Norwich (CT) Courier*, December 29, 1841 (first and fifth quotations); *Daily National Intelligencer* (Washington, DC), December 23, 1841 (second and twelfth quotations); *Daily Madisonian* (Washington, DC), December 23, 1841 (third, fourth, sixth through eleventh, and thirteenth through sixteenth quotations).

39. *Daily Madisonian* (Washington, DC), December 23, 1841.

40. *Richmond (VA) Enquirer*, May 13, 1845; *Richmond (VA) Enquirer*, June 2, 1845; *Richmond (VA) Enquirer*, March 20, 1846; *Richmond Enquirer*, June 1, 1847 (first quotation); Frederic Bancroft, *Slave Trading in the Old South*, introduction by Michael Tadman (1931; Columbia: University of South Carolina Press, 1996), 97; Manuscript Census Returns, Eighth Census of the United States, 1860, Richmond Ward 3, Henrico County, Virginia, NAMS M-653, reel 1353, p. 516 (second quotation).

13. Relief

1. Sixth Census of the United States, 1840, Opelousas, St. Landry Parish, Louisiana, NAMS M-704, reel 128, p. 234.

2. St. Landry Parish, Louisiana, Genealogy and History, Genealogy Trails History Group, Biographies, Alexander Mouton, genealogytrails.com/lou/stlandry/bios.html; Louisiana Historical Association, Dictionary of Louisiana Biography, Alexandre Mouton, www.lahistory.org/resources/dictionary-louisiana-biography/dictionary-louisiana-biography-m; Sixth Census of the United States, 1840, Lafayette, Louisiana, NAMS M-704, reel 127; Stephanie E. Jones-Rogers, *They Were Her Property: White Women as Slave Owners in the American South* (New Haven: Yale University Press, 2019). I do not have letters from either Mrs. Mary E. Mudd to Sen. Mouton or from Sen. Mouton to Secretary Forsyth but can infer that is what happened from John Forsyth to Alexander Mouton, April 20, 1840, 27th Cong., 2d sess., Indemnities for Slaves on Board the Comet and Encomium [To accompany bill H.R. No. 483], House Doc. No. 242, p. 4.

3. Indemnity for slaves per the Comet and Encomium, 27th Cong., 2d sess., House Doc. No. 242, p. 3.

4. Manifest of the *Comet*, December 17, 1830, T 1/3556 Treasury Long Papers, bundle 133, part 2, NAUK; John Forsyth to Alexander Mouton, April 20, 1840, p. 4 (quotations); John Forsyth to the Presidents of the Louisiana State Insurance, Mississippi Marine and Fire, and the Merchants' Insurance Companies, N. Orleans, April 20, 1840, 27th Cong., 2d sess., Indemnities for Slaves on Board the Comet and Encomium [To accompany bill H.R. No. 483], House Doc No. 242, p. 5; Indemnity for slaves per the Comet and Encomium, 27th Cong., 2d sess., House Doc. No. 242, p. 3.

5. John Forsyth to the Presidents of the Louisiana State Insurance, Mississippi Marine and Fire, and the Merchants' Insurance Companies, N. Orleans, April 20, 1840, p. 5.

6. John Forsyth to Alexander Mouton, April 20, 1840, p. 4.

7. Indemnity for slaves per the Comet and Encomium, 27th Cong., 2d sess., House Doc. No. 242, p. 3.

8. Indemnity for slaves per the Comet and Encomium, 27th Cong., 2d sess., House Doc. No. 242, p. 3; Senate, *Congressional Globe*, 26th Cong., 1st sess., April 15, 1840, p. 329 (quotations); George Huyler to Lewis [*sic*] McLane, February 24, 1834, p. 237, CO 23/92 Secretary of State Correspondence, NAUK. See also *Richmond (VA) Enquirer*, December 1, 1840.

9. *Richmond (VA) Enquirer*, December 1, 1840.

10. Indemnity received from the British, [*sic*] Government for slaves per the Comet and Encomium, in account with John Forsyth, March 3, 1841, 27th Cong., 2d sess., House Doc. No. 242, p. 2; Indemnity for slaves per the Comet and Encomium,

27th Cong., 2d sess., House Doc. No. 242, p. 3. These two sources differ by 3¢ in the total amount of money distributed, at $107,484.34 and $107,484.31, respectively.

11. *Daily Madisonian* (Washington, DC), February 24, 1842.

12. Edward Everett to Lord Aberdeen, May 3, 1842, in *Washington (DC) Globe*, January 2, 1843.

13. Edward Everett to Lord Aberdeen, May 3, 1842.

14. Edward Everett to Lord Aberdeen, May 3, 1842.

15. Lord Aberdeen to Edward Everett, May 20, 1842, in *Washington (DC) Globe*, January 2, 1843.

16. *Daily Madisonian* (Washington, DC), December 23, 1841 (quotation); *Norwich (CT) Courier*, December 29, 1841; *Morning Post* (London), March 5, 1841; Keith Hamilton and Farida Shaikh, "Introduction," in *Slavery, Diplomacy and Empire: Britain and the Suppression of the Slave Trade, 1807–1975*, ed. Keith Hamilton and Patrick Salmon (Brighton, UK: Sussex Academic Press, 2009), 9; Arthur T. Downey, *The* Creole *Affair: The Slave Rebellion That Led the U.S. and Great Britain to the Brink of War* (Lanham, MD: Rowman and Littlefield, 2014), 66, 56–62.

17. The Webster-Ashburton Treaty, Avalon Project, Yale Law School, Lillian Goldman Law Library, avalon.law.yale.edu/19th_century/br-1842.asp; *Washington (DC) Globe*, January 2, 1843; *Washington (DC) Globe*, December 15, 1842; Downey, Creole *Affair*, 113, 118–27, 195 (quotation); Jeffrey R. Kerr-Ritchie, *Rebellious Passage: The* Creole *Revolt and America's Coastal Slave Trade* (New York: Cambridge University Press, 2019), 186–87. Abolitionist Joshua R. Giddings later observed in his American Piracy speech of June 7, 1858, that Great Britain could not have provided compensation without violating the terms of article ten of the Treaty of Ghent, by which both countries pledged to abolish the "traffic in slaves." See *Anti-Slavery Bugle* (Lisbon, OH), August 14, 1858.

18. *Senate Journal*, August 18, 1842, 27th Cong., 2d sess., vol. 33, Appendix, pp. 695–96; *Senate Executive Journal*, August 18, 1842, 27th Cong., 2d sess., p. 126; *Washington (DC) Globe*, November 28, 1842.

19. *Washington (DC) Globe*, January 2, 1843.

20. *Washington (DC) Globe*, January 2, 1843. Italics in original.

21. *Washington (DC) Globe*, January 2, 1843. Italics in original.

22. *Washington (DC) Globe*, January 2, 1843.

23. *Washington (DC) Globe*, December 15, 1842.

24. *Washington (DC) Globe*, December 15, 1842.

25. *Washington (DC) Globe*, December 15, 1842. Italics in original.

26. *Washington (DC) Globe*, December 15, 1842.

27. *Washington (DC) Globe*, December 15, 1842.

28. *Washington (DC) Globe*, December 15, 1842.

29. *Independent Democrat* (Canton, MS), January 21, 1843.

30. *Washington (DC) Globe*, January 5, 1843 (quotations); *Senate Journal*, August 19, 1842, 27th Cong., 2d sess., vol. 33, Appendix, p. 696; Richard N. Current, "Webster's Propaganda and the Ashburton Treaty," *Mississippi Valley Historical Review* 34, no. 2 (September 1947): 193–94.

31. William M. King, "An Essay on the Webster-Ashburton Treaty of 1842" (master's thesis, Loyola University Chicago, 1957), 78; *Morning Post* (London), May 3, 1843; *Morning Chronicle* (London), March 22, 1843 (first and second quotations); *Calendonian Mercury* (Edinburgh, Scotland), March 25, 1843 (third quotation); *Times* (London), April 8, 1843 (fourth and fifth quotations).

14. Opposition

1. *Daily Madisonian* (Washington, DC), March 11, 1842; *New York Tribune*, March 12, 1842; *The Liberator* (Boston), April 1, 1842; *Niles National Register* (St. Louis), March 19, 1842 (first and third quotations); *Madisonian* (Washington, DC), March 12, 1842 (second and fourth quotations). The House was meeting as a Committee of the Whole at the time.

2. James Brewer Stewart, *Joshua R. Giddings and the Tactics of Radical Politics* (Cleveland: Press of Case Western Reserve University, 1970), 4–10, 25–26.

3. William Jay, *A View of the Action of the Federal Government, in Behalf of Slavery*, 2nd ed. (New York: American Anti-Slavery Society, 1839), 70–73 (first quotation, 71), 61 (second and third quotations). Abolitionist literature in the 1840s continued to mention the U.S. government's efforts on behalf of the domestic slavers. See, for example, Loring Moody, *Facts for the People; Showing the Relations of the United States Government to Slavery, Embracing a History of the Mexican War, Its Origin and Objects* (Boston: Anti-Slavery Office, 1847), 30–33.

4. *New York American*, reprinted in *Pittsburgh Gazette*, April 10, 1839. See also *The Liberator* (Boston), April 12, 1839; and *Emancipator* (New York), May 9, 1839.

5. *Cincinnati Gazette*, July 19, 1839, reprinted in *Emancipator* (New York), July 25, 1839.

6. *Republican Banner* (Nashville, TN), March 9, 1842 (quotation); *Fayetteville (NC) Weekly Observer*, March 9, 1842; Jeff Forret, *Williams' Gang: A Notorious Slave Trader and His Cargo of Black Convicts* (New York: Cambridge University Press, 2020), 221.

7. *Richmond (VA) Enquirer*, March 15, 1842 (first and second quotations); *New York Tribune*, March 12, 1842 (third and fourth quotations); Manisha Sinha, *The Slave's Cause: A History of Abolition* (New Haven: Yale University Press, 2016), 414.

8. *Evening Post* (New York), March 12, 1842 (first, second, and fifth quotations); *Richmond (VA) Enquirer*, March 15, 1842 (third, fourth, sixth, and seventh quotations).

9. *Evening Post* (New York), March 12, 1842 (first quotation); *Madisonian* (Washington, DC), March 12, 1842; *Richmond (VA) Enquirer*, March 15, 1842 (second through fourth quotations).

10. *Richmond (VA) Enquirer*, March 15, 1842 (first and second quotations); *New York Tribune*, March 12, 1842 (third quotation).

11. *Richmond (VA) Enquirer*, March 15, 1842; *Evening Post* (New York), March 12, 1842; *Madisonian* (Washington, DC), March 12, 1842.

12. Sinha, *Slave's Cause*, 415.

13. House, *Congressional Globe*, 27th Cong., 2d sess., March 21, 1842, p. 342.

14. House, *Congressional Globe*, 27th Cong., 2d sess., March 21, 1842, p. 343.

15. House, *Congressional Globe*, 27th Cong., 2d sess., March 21, 1842, p. 343; James Brewer Stewart, *Abolitionist Politics and the Coming of the Civil War* (Amherst: University of Massachusetts Press, 2008), 113.

16. House, *Congressional Globe*, 27th Cong., 2d sess., March 22–23, 1842, pp. 345–46, 349; *House Journal*, vol. 37, 27th Cong., 2d sess., March 22–23, 1842, pp. 573–86; *The Liberator* (Boston), April 1, 1842 (quotations); Stewart, *Joshua R. Giddings*, 73–74.

17. *Salem (MA) Register*, reprinted in *The Liberator* (Boston), April 1, 1842 (first through fifth quotations); *Boston Courier*, reprinted in *The Liberator* (Boston), April 1, 1842 (sixth and seventh quotations).

18. Daniel Webster to Millard Fillmore, May 6, 1842, 27th Cong., 2d sess., House Doc. No. 242, unnumbered p. 1 (quotations); Indemnity received from the British, [*sic*] Government for slaves per the Comet and Encomium, in account with John Forsyth, March 3, 1841, 27th Cong., 2d sess., House Doc. No. 242, p. 2.

19. Daniel Webster to Millard Fillmore, May 6, 1842 (quotation); H.R. 483, June 10, 1842, 27th Cong., 2d sess., House Doc. No. 242; *House Journal*, vol. 37, 27th Cong., 2d sess., June 10, 1842, pp. 939–40; Indemnities for Slaves on Board the Comet and Encomium. [To accompany bill H.R. No. 483.], 27th Cong., 2d sess., House Doc. No. 242, unnumbered p. 1.

20. Senate, Bills and Resolutions, S. 11, 27th Cong., 3d sess., December 13, 1842; *Senate Journal*, vol. 34, 27th Cong., 3d sess., December 14, 1842, p. 29; Senate, *Congressional Globe*, 27th Cong., 3d sess., December 14, 1842, p. 50; Senate, *Congressional Globe*, 27th Cong., 3d sess., December 30, 1842, p. 100; *Senate Journal*, vol. 34, 27th Cong., 3d sess., December 30, 1842, p. 64; *Daily Madisonian*, December 31, 1842; Senate, *Congressional Globe*, 27th Cong., 3d sess., January 6, 1843, p. 128; *Senate Journal*, vol. 34, 27th Cong., 3d sess., January 6, 1843, p. 80; *Daily Madisonian* (Washington, DC), January 7, 1843; *Senate Journal*, vol. 34, 27th Cong., 3d sess., January 9, 1843, p. 84; Senate, *Congressional Globe*, Senate, 27th Cong., 3d sess., January 9, 1843, p. 133; *Daily Madisonian* (Washington, DC), January 10, 1843. The Senate was meeting as a Committee of the Whole.

21. *The Liberator* (Boston), January 20, 1843.

22. Stewart, *Joshua R. Giddings*, 76.

23. *House Journal*, vol. 38, 27th Cong., 3d sess., January 10, 1843, p. 167; *The Liberator* (Boston), January 20, 1843 (first through fourth quotations); Senate, *Congressional Globe*, 27th Cong., 3d sess., January 12, 1843, p. 157; *House Journal*, vol. 38,

27th Cong., 3d sess., January 12, 1843, p. 176 (fifth quotation); *House Journal*, vol. 38, 27th Cong., 3d sess., January 14, 1843, p. 189.

24. *House Journal*, vol. 38, 27th Cong., 3d sess., February 3, 1843, pp. 312, 314; Forret, *Williams' Gang*, 308; Senate, *Congressional Globe*, 27th Cong., 3d sess., February 10, 1843, p. 267. According to Joshua Giddings and David L. Child, the Senate struck out all House amendments and restored the bill to its original form. Other newspaper accounts stated that the bill returned from the Senate with "a very slight amendment," "merely changing the phraseology." The mixed use of the singular and plural in the *Congressional Globe* and *House Journal* does not make clear whether there was one amendment or more. One definitive change was a modification to the title of the bill. See *Speech of Mr. Giddings, of Ohio, on His motion to reconsider the vote taken upon the final passage of the "Bill for the relief of the owners of slaves lost from on board the* Comet *and* Encomium, House of Representatives, February 13, 1843, p. 2; *The Liberator* (Boston), February 24, 1843; *New York Daily Herald*, February 15, 1843 (first quotation); *Daily Madisonian* (Washington, DC), February 14, 1843 (second quotation); House, *Congressional Globe*, 27th Cong., 3d sess., February 13, 1843, p. 276; *House Journal*, vol. 38, 27th Cong., 3d sess., February 13, 1843, p. 357; *Senate Journal*, vol. 34, 27th Cong., 3d sess., February 15, 1843, p. 176.

25. *New York Daily Herald*, February 15, 1843 (first, second, fifth, and sixth quotations); *Daily Madisonian* (Washington, DC), February 14, 1843 (third and fourth quotations); House, *Congressional Globe*, 27th Cong, 3d sess., February 13, 1843, p. 276.

26. *Speech of Mr. Giddings*, 2 (first quotation); *New York Daily Herald*, February 15, 1843 (second quotation); *Daily Madisonian* (Washington, DC), February 14, 1843 (third quotation); House, *Congressional Globe*, 27th Cong, 3d sess., February 13, 1843, p. 276 (fourth and fifth quotations); *Ohio Statesman* (Columbus), February 18, 1843 (sixth quotation).

27. *Speech of Mr. Giddings*, 1 (first and second quotations); Joshua R. Giddings, *Speeches in Congress* (Boston: Jewett, 1853), 49 (third through fifth quotations).

28. *Speech of Mr. Giddings*, 1 (first quotation), 2 (second and third quotations); Giddings, *Speeches in Congress*, 33 (fourth quotation).

29. *Speech of Mr. Giddings*, 2 (first and second quotations), 3 (third through fifth quotations).

30. *Speech of Mr. Giddings*, 3 (first, second, and sixth quotations); Giddings, *Speeches in Congress*, 39 (third through fifth quotations).

31. *Speech of Mr. Giddings*, 4 (first quotation), 3 (second quotation), 5, 7 (third quotation), 6 (fourth and fifth quotations). Italics in original.

32. *Speech of Mr. Giddings*, 7, 8 (quotations). Italics in original.

33. *New York Tribune*, February 15, 1843 (first quotation); *New York Daily Herald*, February 15, 1843 (second through fifth quotations); *Daily Madisonian* (Washington, DC), February 14, 1843 (sixth quotation).

34. *The Liberator* (Boston), February 24, 1843 (first quotation); Joanne B. Freeman, *The Field of Blood: Violence in Congress and the Road to Civil War* (New York: Farrar, Straus and Giroux, 2018), 48, 68 (second quotation), 115–16; *Ohio Statesman* (Columbus), February 18, 1843 (third quotation); *New York Daily Herald*, February 15, 1843 (fourth and fifth quotations); Stewart, *Joshua R. Giddings*, 5.

35. *New York Daily Herald*, February 15, 1843, recounts the verbatim conversation. House, *Congressional Globe*, 27th Cong, 3d sess., February 13, 1843, p. 277; *Ohio Statesman* (Columbus), February 18, 1843; and *The Liberator* (Boston), February 24, 1843, summarize this portion of the exchange.

36. *Ohio Statesman* (Columbus), February 18, 1843; James Brewer Stewart, *Abolitionist Politics and the Coming of the Civil War* (Amherst: University of Massachusetts Press, 2008), 133; Kenneth S. Greenberg, *Honor & Slavery: Lies, Duels, Noses, Masks, Dressing as a Woman, Gifts, Strangers, Humanitarianism, Death, Slave Rebellions, the Proslavery Argument, Baseball, Hunting, and Gambling in the Old South* (Princeton: Princeton University Press, 1996), 62; *New York Daily Herald*, February 15, 1843 (quotation).

37. *New York Daily Herald*, February 15, 1843 (first quotation); *The Liberator* (Boston), February 24, 1843 (second quotation); *Ohio Statesman* (Columbus), February 18, 1843 (third and fourth quotations). Stewart, *Abolitionist Politics*, 135, writes that Giddings dismissed Dawson as "a 'perfectly harmless' drunkard who deserved 'pity' instead of a thrashing," although the Ohio abolitionist also expressed confidence of victory in any physical encounter with the Louisiana representative.

38. *Daily Madisonian* (Washington, DC), February 14, 1843; House, *Congressional Globe*, 27th Cong, 3d sess., February 13, 1843, p. 277 (quotations).

39. House, *Congressional Globe*, 27th Cong, 3d sess., February 13, 1843, p. 277; *New York Daily Herald*, February 15, 1843 (first, second, fourth, and fifth quotations); *Daily Madisonian* (Washington, DC), February 14, 1843 (third quotation). In *The Liberator* (Boston), February 24, 1843, David L. Child reported that Rep. Arnold did withdraw his motion so that Stanly could speak, under a promise from Stanly to renew the motion. Stanly renewed the motion but then, with Arnold's permission, withdrew it so that others could speak.

40. House, *Congressional Globe*, 27th Cong, 3d sess., February 13, 1843, p. 277; *Daily Madisonian* (Washington, DC), February 14, 1843; *House Journal*, vol. 38, 27th Cong., 3d sess., February 13, 1843, pp. 357–59; *Bangor (ME) Daily Whig and Courier*, August 29, 1843.

41. House, *Congressional Globe*, 27th Cong, 3d sess., February 13, 1843, p. 277 (first quotation); *New York Daily Herald*, February 15, 1843 (second, third, fifth, and sixth quotations); *The Liberator* (Boston), February 24, 1843 (fourth quotation).

42. *The Liberator* (Boston), February 24, 1843 (first and second quotations); House, *Congressional Globe*, 27th Cong, 3d sess., February 13, 1843, p. 277 (third quotation); *New York Daily Herald*, February 15, 1843.

43. *New York Daily Herald*, February 15, 1843 (first, fourth, seventh, eighth, and tenth through thirteenth quotations); House, *Congressional Globe*, 27th Cong, 3d sess., February 13, 1843, p. 277 (second, third, fifth, and sixth quotations); *The Liberator* (Boston), February 24, 1843 (ninth quotation); *Ohio Statesman* (Columbus), February 18, 1843; Freeman, *Field of Blood*, 70. Two years later, after another abolitionist speech, Dawson pulled his pistol on Giddings and cocked it, sparking a standoff on the House floor between proslavery and antislavery members.

44. *New York Daily Herald*, February 15, 1843; House, *Congressional Globe*, 27th Cong, 3d sess., February 13, 1843, p. 277 (first quotation); *The Liberator* (Boston), February 24, 1843 (second quotation).

45. *House Journal*, vol. 38, 27th Cong., 3d sess., February 18, 1843, pp. 400–401, 407–8; *Senate Journal*, vol. 34, 27th Cong., 3d sess., February 21, 1843, p. 201; *House Journal*, vol. 39, 28th Cong., 1st sess., January 22, 1844, p. 278. The full text of the law, available in *Statutes at Large*, vol. 5, 27th Cong., 3d sess., p. 601, reads

> *An act for the relief of the owners of the fund received from the British Government as an indemnity for slaves lost from on board the Comet and Encomium at Nassau, Bahamas. Be it enacted by the Senate and House of Representatives of the United States of America in Congress assembled*, That the sum of seven thousand nine hundred and sixty-five dollars and twenty-eight cents, a balance of the indemnities received from the British Government for loss of slaves from on board the Comet and the Encomium, at Nassau, paid into the treasury by the late John Forsyth, be paid, on the order of the Secretary of State, to the persons or companies entitled thereto, or to their representatives; and that, for that purpose, the aforesaid sum be, and it is hereby, appropriated, to be paid out of any moneys in the treasury not otherwise appropriated. APPROVED, February 18, 1843.

See also *Daily Madisonian* (Washington, DC), February 22, 1843.

15. The Trials of Widowhood

1. Indemnity for slaves per the Comet and Encomium, 27th Cong., 2d sess., House Doc. No. 242, p. 3; Manifest of the *Comet*, December 17, 1830, pp. 187–91, CO 23/92 Secretary of State Correspondence, NAUK; Manifest of the *Comet*, December 17, 1830, T 1/3556 Treasury Long Papers, bundle 133, part 2, NAUK; Indemnity received from the British, [*sic*] Government for slaves per the Comet and Encomium, in account with John Forsyth, March 3, 1841, 27th Cong., 2d sess., House Doc. No. 242, p. 2; John Forsyth to Alexander Mouton, April 20, 1840, 27th Cong., 2d sess., Indemnities for Slaves on Board the Comet and Encomium [To accompany bill H.R. No. 483], House Doc. No. 242, p. 4.

2. Ernest F. Dibble, *Ante-Bellum Pensacola and the Military Presence* (Pensacola: Mayes, 1974), 3–4, 9, chap. 5; Navy Department Library—Naval History and Heritage Command, *U.S. Navy and Marine Corps Directory, 1831* (Washington, DC), 66;

John Lee Williams, *View of West Florida*, in *Andrew Jackson and Pensacola*, ed. James R. McGovern (Pensacola: Jackson Day Sesquicentennial Committee of the City of Pensacola, Florida, 1971), 28 (quotation). On the development of the Pensacola Navy Yard, see George F. Pearce, *The U.S. Navy in Pensacola: From Sailing Ships to Naval Aviation (1825–1930)* (Pensacola: University Presses of Florida, 1980), chap. 1. He mentions Col. Tutt on pp. 19 and 23.

3. Manuscript Census Returns, Fifth Census of the United States, 1830, Leesburg Township, Loudoun County, Virginia, NAMS M-19, reel 193, p. 38; U.S., War of 1812 Service Records, 1812–1815, Index to the Compiled Military Service Records for the Volunteer Soldiers Who Served During the War of 1812, NARA M-602, reel 213; Ann M. Tutt, War of 1812 Pension Applications, NARA M-313, reel 94, pension number WO 9509; Navy Department Library—Naval History and Heritage Command, *Navy Register: Officers of the U.S. Navy and Marine, 1832* (Washington, DC), 37; Manuscript Census Returns, Fifth Census of the United States, 1830, Escambia County, Florida, NAMS M-19, reel 15, p. 62; *Ann M. Tutt v. Robt. G. Bowie and Wm. T.T. Mason Exers & Trustees of George M. Chichester*, January 29, 1844, bill in equity, RSPP, Petition 20484401, Series II, Part B, Reel 15, Washington, DC; *Daily National Intelligencer* (Washington, DC), November 2, 1832; *Lynchburg Virginian*, November 5, 1832. Tutt was replaced as Navy agent at Pensacola by loyal Jacksonian Byrd C. Willis, a onetime resident of Fredericksburg, Virginia, then living in Tallahassee, Florida. The other ten U.S. Navy agents were stationed at New York, Philadelphia, Baltimore, Norfolk, Savannah, Boston, Portsmouth, Charleston, Marseilles, and London.

The 1830 U.S. census for Loudoun County listed one more enslaved person in Col. Tutt's household than the nine that were placed aboard the *Comet* later that year. One bondwoman, listed as twenty-four to thirty-five years old on the census, is unaccounted for on the *Comet* manifest. It is unclear if she had been sold, run away, or died. The Escambia County census indicates that she did not accompany Col. Tutt to Florida. Manifest of the *Comet*, December 17, 1830, pp. 187–91, CO 23/92 Secretary of State Correspondence, NAUK.

4. Manuscript Census Returns, Eighth Census of the United States, 1860, Allegany County, Maryland, NAMS M-653, reel 456, p. 685; Manuscript Census Returns, Ninth Census of the United States, 1870, Bath, Morgan County, West Virginia, NAMS M-593, reel 1695, p. 120B; Manuscript Census Returns, Third Census of the United States, 1810, Fauquier County, Virginia, NAMS M-252, reel 68, p. 247; Kirsten E. Wood, *Masterful Women: Slaveholding Widows from the American Revolution Through the Civil War* (Chapel Hill: University of North Carolina Press, 2004), 79; Marylynn Salmon, *Women and the Law of Property in Early America* (Chapel Hill: University of North Carolina Press, 1986), 14; Stephanie E. Jones-Rogers, *They Were Her Property: White Women as Slave Owners in the American South* (New Haven: Yale University Press, 2019), 33–34, 60–80. Whereas

Jones-Rogers stresses white women's complicity in slaveholding, Marli F. Weiner, "Mistresses, Morality, and the Dilemmas of Slaveholding: The Ideology and Behavior of Elite Antebellum Women," in *Discovering the Women in Slavery: Emancipating Perspectives on the American Past*, ed. Patricia Morton (Athens: University of Georgia Press, 1996), 278–98, suggests that, despite differences in race and class, white women felt "a degree of sympathy" with enslaved women but were limited in their ability to act upon those sentiments. For more on marriage settlements, see Marylynn Salmon, "Women and Property in South Carolina: The Evidence from Marriage Settlements," *William and Mary Quarterly*, 3rd ser. 39, no. 4 (October 1982): 655–85.

5. Wood, *Masterful Women*, 4, 193, 31; Salmon, *Women and the Law of Property*, 5, 141; Marie S. Molloy, *Single, White, Slaveholding Women in the Nineteenth-Century American South* (Columbia: University of South Carolina Press, 2018), 10.

6. Ann Mason Tutt, bill of complaint, Circuit Court of the District of Columbia for the County of Washington, January 17, 1844, RSPP, Petition 20484401, Series II, Part B, Reel 15, Washington, DC; Memorial, Ann Mason Tutt to Secretary of State John Forsyth, n.d., RSPP, Petition 20484401, Series II, Part B, Reel 15, Washington, DC (quotations). The details of Col. Charles P. Tutt's indebtedness are shared in Memorial, William T.T. Mason and Robert G. Bowie, n.d., RSPP, Petition 20484401, Series II, Part B, Reel 15, Washington, DC; Indenture, Charles Tutt, July 29, 1823, RSPP, Petition 20484401, Series II, Part B, Reel 15, Washington, DC; Robert Bowie and William T.T. Mason, answer to Ann M. Tutt, Circuit Court of the District of Columbia, Washington County, June 14, 1844, in equity, RSPP, Petition 20484401, Series II, Part B, Reel 15, Washington, DC; Charles P. Tutt to [George] Mason [Chichester], January 30, 1831, RSPP, Petition 20484401, Series II, Part B, Reel 15, Washington, DC; and *Ann M. Tutt v. Robt. G. Bowie and Wm. T.T. Mason*, January 29, 1844.

7. Ann Mason Tutt, bill of complaint, Circuit Court of the District of Columbia for the County of Washington, January 17, 1844 (quotations); Deposition of John A. Carter, June 24, 1840, *Ann M. Tutt v. Robt. G. Bowie and Wm. T.T. Mason Exers & Trustees of George M. Chichester*, January 29, 1844, bill in equity, RSPP, Petition 20484401, Series II, Part B, Reel 15, Washington, DC; Deposition of William P. Swarm, June 24, 1840, *Ann M. Tutt v. Robt. G. Bowie and Wm. T.T. Mason Exers & Trustees of George M. Chichester*, January 29, 1844, bill in equity, RSPP, Petition 20484401, Series II, Part B, Reel 15, Washington, DC. Although George M. Chichester went by "Mason" among his family and friends, I refer to him throughout the chapter as either "Chichester" or "George" to avoid confusing him with his coexecutor William T.T. Mason.

8. Ann Mason Tutt, bill of complaint, Circuit Court of the District of Columbia for the County of Washington, January 17, 1844; Memorial, William T.T. Mason and Robert G. Bowie (first quotation); George Mason Chichester to Ann Tutt, Decem-

ber 28, 1830, RSPP, Petition 20484401, Series II, Part B, Reel 15, Washington, DC (second through fifth quotations); Charles P. Tutt to George M. Chichester, January 30, 1831, in Robert Bowie and William T.T. Mason, answer to Ann M. Tutt, June 14, 1844 (sixth quotation).

9. Ann Mason Tutt, bill of complaint, Circuit Court of the District of Columbia for the County of Washington, January 17, 1844 (quotation); Memorial, Ann Mason Tutt to Secretary of State John Forsyth.

10. Ann Mason Tutt, bill of complaint, Circuit Court of the District of Columbia for the County of Washington, January 17, 1844.

11. Catherine Clinton, *The Plantation Mistress: Woman's World in the Old South* (New York: Pantheon, 1982), 76–77; Molloy, *Single, White, Slaveholding Women*, 18, 19, 38, 80, 87; Ann Mason Tutt, bill of complaint, Circuit Court of the District of Columbia for the County of Washington, January 17, 1844.

12. Ann Mason Tutt, bill of complaint, Circuit Court of the District of Columbia for the County of Washington, January 17, 1844 (quotation); Last Will and Testament, George Mason Chichester, December 5, 1835, RSPP, Petition 20484401, Series II, Part B, Reel 15, Washington, DC; Manuscript Census Returns, Sixth Census of the United States, 1840, District 1, Loudoun County, Virginia, NAMS M-704, reel 564, pp. 216–17; Manuscript Census Returns, Fifth Census of the United States, 1830, Middleburg, Loudoun County, Virginia, NAMS M-19, reel 193, p. 26; Memorial, Ann Mason Tutt to Secretary of State John Forsyth.

13. Ann Mason Tutt, bill of complaint, Circuit Court of the District of Columbia for the County of Washington, January 17, 1844 (first quotation); Memorial, Ann Mason Tutt to Secretary of State John Forsyth (second and third quotations).

14. Deposition of William P. Swarm, June 24, 1840 (quotation); deposition of William H. Clowe, June 24, 1840; deposition of John Martin, auctioneer, June 27, 1840; deposition of John T. Mason, July 1, 1840; Josiah Colston to C. Cox, March 11, 1844; deposition of Josiah Colston, March 14, 1844; deposition of Mrs. Throckmorton, May 21, 1844, all in *Ann M. Tutt v. Robt. G. Bowie and Wm. T.T. Mason*, January 29, 1844.

15. Affidavit of Charles Bonnycastle, July 6, 1840, RSPP, Petition 20484401, Series II, Part B, Reel 15, Washington, DC; *Ann M. Tutt v. Robt. G. Bowie and Wm. T.T. Mason*, January 29, 1844 (quotations); Wood, *Masterful Women*, 62; Molloy, *Single, White, Slaveholding Women*, 157.

16. Molloy, *Single, White Slaveholding Women*, 10, 24; Wood, *Masterful Women*, 148; Salmon, *Women and the Law of Property*, 153–55.

17. Ann Mason Tutt, bill of complaint, Circuit Court of the District of Columbia for the County of Washington, January 17, 1844; *Ann M. Tutt v. Robt. G. Bowie and Wm. T.T. Mason*, January 29, 1844.

18. Robert Bowie and William T.T. Mason, answer to Ann M. Tutt, June 14, 1844 (quotations); *Ann M. Tutt v. Robt. G. Bowie and Wm. T.T. Mason*, January 29, 1844.

19. Memorial, William Mason and Robert Bowie to John Forsyth, n.d., RSPP, Petition 20484401, Series II, Part B, Reel 15, Washington, DC (quotations); Robert Bowie and William T.T. Mason, answer to Ann M. Tutt, June 14, 1844.

20. Ann M. Tutt to [George] Mason [Chichester], January 29, 1831, RSPP, Petition 20484401, Series II, Part B, Reel 15, Washington, DC (quotations); Memorial, William Mason and Robert Bowie to John Forsyth; Robert Bowie and William T.T. Mason, answer to Ann M. Tutt, June 14, 1844.

21. Robert Bowie and William T.T. Mason, answer to Ann M. Tutt, June 14, 1844 (quotations) (emphases in original); Memorial, William Mason and Robert Bowie to John Forsyth.

22. *Ann M. Tutt v. Robt. G. Bowie and Wm. T.T. Mason*, January 29, 1844. President John Adams had first nominated Cranch, his nephew, to the court in 1801, and despite the political gulf that separated Adams from his successor as commander in chief, Thomas Jefferson elevated Cranch to chief judge in 1806, a testament to the jurist's talents.

23. *Ann M. Tutt v. Robt. G. Bowie and Wm. T.T. Mason*, January 29, 1844.

24. *Ann M. Tutt v. Robt. G. Bowie and Wm. T.T. Mason*, January 29, 1844.

25. *Ann M. Tutt v. Robt. G. Bowie and Wm. T.T. Mason*, January 29, 1844.

26. *Ann M. Tutt v. Robt. G. Bowie and Wm. T.T. Mason*, January 29, 1844.

27. *Ann M. Tutt v. Robt. G. Bowie and Wm. T.T. Mason*, January 29, 1844 (first and second quotations); Auditor's Report, November 25, 1844, *Ann M. Tutt v. Robt. G. Bowie and Wm. T.T. Mason*, January 29, 1844 (third quotation).

28. Auditor's Report, November 25, 1844.

29. Ann M. Tutt to [George] Mason [Chichester], January 29, 1831 (first and fifth quotations); deposition of John T. Mason, July 1, 1840 (second through fourth quotations).

30. Josiah Colston to C. Cox, March 11, 1844 (first quotation); Wood, *Masterful Women*, 150; Manuscript Census Returns, Eighth Census of the United States, 1860, Allegany County, Maryland, NAMS M-653, reel 456, p. 685; Manuscript Census Returns, Ninth Census of the United States, 1870, Bath, Morgan County, West Virginia, NAMS M-593, reel 1695, p. 120B; www.measuringworth.com.

16. Unsettled Claims

1. William Rothery to T.F. Baring, February 23, 1839, T 1/3556, NAUK; *House Journal*, vol. 39, 28th Cong., 1st sess., January 22, 1844, p. 278.

2. *Oliver Simpson v. Charleston Fire and Marine Insurance Co.*, Judgment Roll, Charleston District (L10018), June 10, 1837, Item 109A, SCDAH; *Simpson v. Charleston Fire & Marine Ins. Co.*, Dudl 239 (1838), 23 S.C.L. 239; *Charleston (SC) Courier*, June 11, 1838; *Charleston (SC) Mercury*, April 30, 1838; *Charleston (SC) Daily Courier*, April 30, 1838; Charleston Fire and Marine Insurance Company, financial statement as of July 1, 1838, July 5, 1838, Andrew Wallace Papers, SCL. Sixth Census of the

United States, 1840, Charleston, Charleston District, South Carolina, NAMS M-704, reel 509, p. 70, shows Strohecker as owning eight enslaved people.

3. John Strohecker, Petition, ND 2917, Box 21, S165015, SCDAH (quotations); *Charleston Daily Courier*, December 20, 1844. See also RSPP, Petition 11384205, Series I, Reel 11, South Carolina.

4. *House Journal*, vol. 40, 28th Cong., 2d sess., December 30, 1844, p. 145 (quotation); *Senate Journal*, vol. 36, 28th Cong., 2d sess., January 7, 1845, p. 74.

5. *Senate Journal*, vol. 36, 28th Cong., 2d sess., February 20, 1845, p. 188.

6. *Daily Union* (Washington, DC), January 9, 1846; *House Journal*, vol. 41, 29th Cong., 1st sess., January 9, 1846, p. 220 (quotation); *Senate Journal*, vol. 37, 29th Cong., 1st sess., January 20, 1846, p. 108; *Senate Journal*, vol. 37, 29th Cong., 1st sess., July 1, 1846, p. 382; *Senate Journal*, vol. 37, 29th Cong., 1st sess., July 2, 1846, p. 384; *House Journal*, vol. 43, 30th Cong., 1st sess., January 25, 1848, p. 290.

7. RSPP, Petition 21385340, Series II, Part D, Reel 21, South Carolina; U.S. Census Mortality Schedules, South Carolina, 1850–1880, reel 3, 1850, St. James, Goose Creek Parish, Charleston District, South Carolina, p. 139; Henrietta Strohecker, Charleston District, Equity Bills, 1853, no. 95, Box 79, L10090, SCDAH (quotations).

8. *Washington (DC) Globe*, May 23, 1844.

9. Ephraim Douglass Adams, ed., "Correspondence from the British Archives Concerning Texas, 1837–1846," *Quarterly of the Texas State Historical Association* 15, no. 3 (January 1912): 224, 230–31, 238, 239; Lelia M. Roeckell, "Bonds over Bondage: British Opposition to the Annexation of Texas," *Journal of the Early Republic* 19, no. 2 (Summer 1999): 267, 268.

10. Roeckell, "Bonds over Bondage," 268; Speech of Col. W.R. Hill, July 4, 1844, in *Independent Democrat* (Canton, MS), August 7, 1844.

11. Speech of Col. W.R. Hill, July 4, 1844, in *Independent Democrat*, August 7, 1844 (quotations); *South-Western Farmer* (Raymond, MS), March 22, 1839; Edward B. Rugemer, "Robert Monroe Harrison, British Abolition, Southern Anglophobia and Texas Annexation," *Slavery and Abolition* 28, no. 2 (August 2007): 169, 177, 179.

12. William A. DeGregorio, *The Complete Book of U.S. Presidents*, 4th ed. (New York: Barricade, 1993), 180–81.

13. *Hartford (CT) Courant*, July 13, 1848.

14. *Richmond (VA) Enquirer*, October 13, 1848.

15. House, *Congressional Globe*, 27th Cong., 2d sess., April 22, 1842, pp. 438–39; *Richmond (VA) Enquirer*, October 13, 1848 (quotations).

16. *Wilmington (NC) Chronicle*, October 18, 1848 (quotations); *Newbernian and North Carolina Advocate* (New Bern, NC), October 17, 1848.

During the presidential election year of 1852, an anonymous "PENNSYLVANIA DEMOCRAT" wrote an editorial to a Washington, DC, newspaper endorsing Virginia's Andrew Stevenson as his party's "nominee for vice president, should the

Democrats nominate for president a candidate from a nonslaveholding state." While touting Stevenson's long political career, seven distinguished years as Speaker of the House, and leadership of the "harmonious" 1848 Democratic National Convention, the unnamed Pennsylvania Democrat saved special commendation for the Virginian's tenure as U.S. minister to Great Britain from 1836 to 1841. The country was indebted to Stevenson, he argued, for "his fortunate adjustment of the cases of the Comet, [and] Encomium, . . . in which upwards of one hundred thousand dollars were recovered from the British government as compensation to the owners of the slaves . . . wrecked on board those vessels off the Bahamas." When the Democrats indeed nominated a Northerner, Franklin Pierce of New Hampshire, for president in 1852, Stevenson was bypassed for the vice-presidential slot in favor of a different Southerner, William R. King of Alabama. Still, Stevenson's prominent role in securing reparations for Southern slave owners did earn him notice. See *Washington (DC) Union*, January 25, 1852.

17. Robert Elder, *Calhoun: American Heretic* (New York: Basic Books, 2021), 298, 308, 344, 499, 505; Irving H. Bartlett, *John C. Calhoun: A Biography* (New York: Norton, 1993), 368.

18. *Evening Post* (New York), June 12, 1849 (quotations); Elder, *Calhoun*, 511; Bartlett, *John C. Calhoun*, 368.

19. *Washington (DC) Globe*, December 15, 1842.

20. *New York Daily Herald*, July 21, 1849.

21. *New York Daily Herald*, July 21, 1849.

22. *Richmond (VA) Enquirer*, June 29, 1849 (first through fourth quotations); *Richmond (VA) Enquirer*, August 24, 1849; *The Southron* (Jackson, MS), September 28, 1849; *New York Daily Herald*, July 21, 1849 (fifth and sixth quotations).

23. *New York Daily Herald*, July 21, 1849 (first quotation); *Richmond (VA) Enquirer*, June 29, 1849 (second and third quotations); *Richmond (VA) Enquirer*, August 24, 1849 (fourth and fifth quotations); Bartlett, *John C. Calhoun*, 368.

24. *National Era* (Washington, DC), reprinted in *Anti-Slavery Bugle* (Lisbon, OH), March 26, 1847. For an example of Giddings's comments delivered outside the House chamber, see *Green Mountain Freeman* (Montpelier, VT), July 22, 1847.

25. House, *Congressional Globe*, 30th Cong., 2d sess., December 23, 1848, p. 96 (first quotation), House, *Congressional Globe*, 30th Cong., 2d sess., December 29, 1848, p. 126 (second quotation). The story of Lewis (as he was called in congressional documents), Luis, or Louis Pacheco is recounted in greater detail in the posthumously published Kenneth W. Porter, *The Black Seminoles: History of a Freedom-Seeking People* (1996; Gainesville: University Press of Florida, 2013), 40–43. Most accounts of Lewis appear in articles dating to the mid-twentieth century. See Albert Hubbard Roberts, "The Dade Massacre," *Florida Historical Quarterly* 5, no. 3 (January 1927): 126; Eugene Portlette Southall, "Negroes in Florida Prior to the Civil War," *Journal of Negro History* 19, no. 1 (January 1934): 85–86; Kenneth W. Porter, "Three Fighters for Freedom," *Journal of Negro History* 28, no. 1 (January 1943): 65–72; Kenneth Wiggins

Porter, "Florida Slaves and Free Negroes in the Seminole War, 1835–1842," *Journal of Negro History* 28, no. 4 (October 1943): 393, 419; Kenneth W. Porter, "The Early Life of Luis Pacheco né Fatio," *Negro History Bulletin* 7, no. 3 (December 1943): 52, 54, 62, 64; Edwin L. Williams Jr., "Negro Slavery in Florida," *Florida Historical Quarterly* 28, no. 2 (October 1949): 104–5; Mark F. Boyd and Joseph W. Harris, "The Seminole War: Its Background and Onset," *Florida Historical Quarterly* 30, no. 1 (July 1951): 105–7; Kenneth Wiggins Porter, "Negroes and the Seminole War, 1835–1842," *Journal of Southern History* 30, no. 4 (November 1964): 433, 447. A more recent account is Alcione M. Amos, *The Life of Luis Fatio Pacheco: Last Survivor of Dade's Battle*, Pamphlet Series 1, no. 1 (Dade City, FL: Seminole Wars Foundation, 2006), seminolewars.org/wp-content/uploads/2018/05/Life-of-Luis-Pacheco.pdf.

26. House, *Congressional Globe*, 30th Cong., 2d sess., January 6, 1849, pp. 172 (first and second quotations), 175 (third through sixth and tenth quotations); House, *Congressional Globe*, 30th Cong., 2d sess., January 16, 1849, p. 241 (seventh and eighth quotations); House, *Congressional Globe*, 30th Cong., 2d sess., December 29, 1848, p. 126 (ninth and eleventh through thirteenth quotations).

27. Bills and Resolutions, House of Representatives, 27th Cong., 2d sess., April 1, 1842; H.R. 322 (Rep. No. 472), 27th Cong., 2d sess., April 1, 1842; Bills and Resolutions, House of Representatives, 28th Cong., 1st sess., June 7, 1844; *House Journal*, vol. 41, 29th Cong., 1st sess., March 2, 1846, p. 474; Bills and Resolutions, House of Representatives, 30th Cong., 1st sess., February 9, 1848; H.R. 197 (Rep. No. 187), 30th Cong., 1st sess., February 9, 1848; *House Journal*, vol. 44, 30th Cong., 2d sess., December 29, 1848, p. 165; *House Journal*, vol. 44, 30th Cong., 2d sess., January 19, 1849, p. 277.

A mistake in recording the votes created some confusion before the bill's eventual passage. See *House Journal*, vol. 44, 30th Cong., 2d sess., January 6, 1849, pp. 207–9; January 8, 1849, p. 211, Appendix pp. 689–90; and January 19, 1849, pp. 276–78.

28. *House Journal*, vol. 44, 30th Cong., 2d sess., December 29, 1848, p. 166; House, *Congressional Globe*, 30th Cong., 2d sess., December 23, 1848, p. 95 (first and second quotations); House, *Congressional Globe*, 30th Cong., 2d sess., January 6, 1849, pp. 173–74; House, *Congressional Globe*, 30th Cong., 2d sess., January 12, 1849, p. 239 (third quotation). See also the letter from David L. Child, March 11, 1843, in *The Liberator* (Boston), March 17, 1843.

29. *Green Mountain Freeman* (Montpelier, VT), January 18, 1849 (first quotation); H.R. 351 (Rep. No. 558), 27th Cong., 2d sess., April 12, 1842 (second through fifth quotations); House, *Congressional Globe*, 30th Cong., 2d sess., January 6, 1849, p. 174.

30. House, *Congressional Globe*, 30th Cong., 2d sess., January 6, 1849, p. 174; House, *Congressional Globe*, 30th Cong., 2d sess., December 23, 1848, p. 95 (quotation).

31. House, *Congressional Globe*, 30th Cong., 2d sess., January 6, 1849, p. 174.

32. House, *Congressional Globe*, 30th Cong., 2d sess., January 6, 1849, pp. 172, 174; *Senate Journal*, vol. 40, 30th Cong., 2d sess., February 5, 1849, p. 183. Pacheco's heirs

sought reparations again later, also unsuccessfully. See *House Journal*, vol. 45, 31st Cong., 1st sess., January 24, 1850, p. 396; Amos, *Life of Luis Fatio Pacheco*, 10.

33. *Daily Republic* (Washington, DC), November 10, 1852; *Weekly Raleigh (NC) Register*, November 24, 1852; *Charleston (SC) Mercury*, November 22, 1852; *New York Journal of Commerce*, reprinted in *The Liberator* (Boston), November 19, 1852.

34. *Charleston (SC) Mercury*, November 22, 1852; *Daily Republic* (Washington, DC), November 10, 1852.

35. Manuscript Census Returns, Seventh Census of the United States, 1850, District 8, Bath County, Virginia, NAMS M-432, reel 935, p. 130B; *New York Journal of Commerce*, reprinted in *The Liberator* (Boston), November 19, 1852 (quotations).

36. *New York Journal of Commerce*, reprinted in *The Liberator* (Boston), November 19, 1852 (quotations); *Daily Republic* (Washington, DC), November 10, 1852.

37. *Weekly Raleigh (NC) Register*, November 24, 1852; *New York Journal of Commerce*, reprinted in *The Liberator* (Boston), November 19, 1852 (quotation).

38. *Lowell (MA) Journal*, reprinted in *The Liberator* (Boston), December 3, 1852; *Charleston (SC) Mercury*, November 22, 1852 (first through third quotations); *Southern Reveille* (Port Gibson, MS), December 15, 1852; *Richmond (VA) Enquirer*, December 31, 1852; *Evening Star* (Washington, DC), December 16, 1852 (fourth quotation); *Planters' Banner* (Franklin, LA), December 11, 1852; *Times-Picayune* (New Orleans), December 24, 1852.

The New York Supreme Court and the New York Court of Appeals each affirmed the decision of Judge Payne's Superior Court. The Civil War intervened before an appeal before the U.S. Supreme Court could be made. The case would have forced the court to revisit its monumentally wrongheaded *Dred Scott v. Sandford* decision of 1857. See *Lemmon v. People ex rel. Napoleon*, 26 Barb. 270 (1857) and *Lemmon v. People*, 6 E.P. Smith 562 (1860).

39. *Washington (DC) Union*, November 25, 1852.

40. *Washington (DC) Union*, November 25, 1852.

41. *Daily National Intelligencer* (Washington, DC), March 29, 1850.

42. John G. Whitter, "The Branded Hand," in *Voices of the True-Hearted* (Philadelphia: Merrihew and Thompson, 1846), 287 (quotation); *Pensacola (FL) Gazette*, July 22, 1844; *Edgefield (SC) Advertiser*, January 1, 1845.

Conclusion

1. For reports on the British refusal to provide compensation for enslaved people liberated from the *Creole*, see *Morning Chronicle* (London), February 15, 1842; and *The Standard* (London), February 18, 1842. Four different New Orleans companies insured enslaved people aboard the *Creole*: the Merchants, New Orleans, Firemen's, and Ocean insurance companies. All four resisted paying on their policies. In 1845, the Louisiana Supreme Court sided with the insurance companies by holding them not liable in five of the seven lawsuits filed by owners against them for nonpayment. The

court determined that mutiny, rather than foreign interference, caused the losses. Three of the insurers' policies included a clause that exempted losses occasioned by insurrection, but the Merchants Insurance Company's did not. The ruling forced it to pay hefty claims. It later dissolved, leaving liquidator John Pemberton of New Orleans to attempt to recoup the money paid out. The *Creole* claims heard by the Anglo-American commission discussed in this chapter therefore came from individuals rather than from insurance companies, as in the cases of the *Enterprise* and *Hermosa*. On the *Creole*, see Jeffrey R. Kerr-Ritchie, *Rebellious Passage: The* Creole *Revolt and America's Coastal Slave Trade* (New York: Cambridge University Press, 2019), 223, 246–48, 257; Arthur T. Downey, *The* Creole *Affair: The Slave Rebellion That Led the U.S. and Great Britain to the Brink of War* (Lanham, MD: Rowman and Littlefield, 2014), 146–47; and Karen Kotzuk Ryder, "'Permanent Property': Slave Life Insurance in the Antebellum Southern United States" (PhD diss., University of Delaware, 2012), 43.

2. *Washington (DC) Sentinel*, February 2, 1855; Kerr-Ritchie, *Rebellious Passage*, 252; 34th Cong, 1st sess., Senate, Ex. Doc. No. 103, *Message of the President of the United States, Communicating the Proceedings of the Commissioners for the Adjustment of Claims Under the Convention with Great Britain of February 8, 1853* (Washington, DC: A.O.P. Nicholson, 1856), iv; *New York Tribune*, November 21, 1856.

3. *New York Tribune*, November 21, 1856.

4. 34th Cong, 1st sess., Senate, Ex. Doc. No. 103, pp. i–ii, 13, 26; Kerr-Ritchie, *Rebellious Passage*, 250–51.

5. *New York Tribune*, November 21, 1856; Kerr-Ritchie, *Rebellious Passage*, 252; Downey, Creole *Affair*, 142.

6. Nicholas Draper, *The Price of Emancipation: Slave-Ownership, Compensation and British Society at the End of Slavery* (New York: Cambridge University Press, 2010), 246; Downey, Creole *Affair*, 142 (first quotation); 34th Cong, 1st sess., Senate, Ex. Doc. No. 103, pp. ii, 82 (second and third quotations); Kerr-Ritchie, *Rebellious Passage*, 251–52; Calvin Schermerhorn, *The Business of Slavery and the Rise of American Capitalism, 1815–1860* (New Haven: Yale University Press, 2015), chap. 4.

7. 34th Cong., 1st sess., Senate, Ex. Doc. No. 103, pp. 26, 31 (first quotation), 33, 38 (second quotation), 57. For Thomas's remarks, see 34th Cong., 1st sess., Senate, Ex. Doc. No. 103, pp. 189–201. For Hannen's, see 34th Cong., 1st sess., Senate, Ex. Doc. No. 103, pp. 187–88.

8. 34th Cong, 1st sess., Senate, Ex. Doc. No. 103, pp. 40, 57, 238 (quotations).

9. N.G. Upham, *Opinion in the Case of the Enterprise, Pending Before the Mixed Commission, Under the Convention of 1853, for the Settlement of Claims Between Great Britain and the United States* (London: John Edward Taylor, 1854), 11 (first and second quotations), 2 (third through sixth quotations), 13, 10. For Upham, see also 34th Cong., 1st sess., Senate, Ex. Doc. No. 103, pp. 202–19.

10. Upham, *Opinion*, 6–8, 15 (first and second quotations), 16, 22 (third quotation).

11. 34th Cong, 1st sess., Senate, Ex. Doc. No. 103, pp. 221 (first through third quotations), 223 (fourth and fifth quotations).

12. Upham, *Opinion*, 6; 34th Cong, 1st sess., Senate, Ex. Doc. No. 103, p. 225 (quotations).

13. 34th Cong., 1st sess., Senate, Ex. Doc. No. 103, pp. 221 (first and second quotations), 226 (third quotation), 229 (fourth quotation), 230 (fifth quotation), 235.

14. 34th Cong., 1st sess., Senate, Ex. Doc. No. 103, pp. 45, 57, 237 (quotations).

15. 34th Cong., 1st sess., Senate, Ex. Doc. No. 103, pp. 45, 57, 237 (quotation); www.measuringworth.com.

16. 34th Cong., 1st sess., Senate, Ex. Doc. No. 103, pp. 47, 57, 238–40 (quotation 240); *Washington (DC) Sentinel*, February 2, 1855.

17. 34th Cong., 1st sess., Senate, Ex. Doc. No. 103, pp. 47, 52, 78; *New York Tribune*, November 21, 1856 (quotations).

18. *New York Tribune*, November 21, 1856; www.measuringworth.com; 34th Cong, 1st sess., Senate, Ex. Doc. No. 103, pp. iii, iv, 78. Bates "refused to receive any remuneration whatever" for his role as umpire. See 34th Cong, 1st sess., Senate, Ex. Doc. No. 103, p. 82.

19. *New York Evening Post*, reprinted in *Daily National Intelligencer* (Washington, DC), January 27, 1855; *Baltimore Sun*, reprinted in the *Daily Union* (Washington, DC), January 28, 1855; *Washington (DC) Sentinel*, February 2, 1855; *National Era* (Washington, DC), February 8, 1855; *Charleston (SC) Courier*, January 30, 1855 (first quotation); *Richmond (VA) Dispatch*, reprinted in *Macon (GA) Weekly Telegraph*, February 6, 1855 (second quotation).

20. *The Liberator* (Boston), May 26, 1837 (quotation); *The Liberator* (Boston), December 14, 1833.

21. *The Liberator* (Boston), May 26, 1837.

22. *Anti-Slavery Bugle* (Lisbon, OH), August 14, 1858 (first quotation); Joshua R. Giddings, *Speeches in Congress* (Boston: John P. Jewett and Company, 1853), 361 (second and third quotations).

23. *Green Mountain Freeman* (Montpelier, VT), July 22, 1847 (first quotation); Giddings, *Speeches in Congress*, 360 (second and third quotations); *Anti-Slavery Bugle* (Lisbon, OH), August 14, 1858 (fourth through eighth quotations).

24. Giddings, *Speeches in Congress*, 42 (first quotation), 42–43 (third quotation), 43 (fourth quotation), 360, (fifth and sixth quotations) *Anti-Slavery Bugle* (Lisbon, OH), August 14, 1858 (second, seventh, and eighth quotations).

25. *Daily Union and American* (Nashville, TN), November 3, 1860. On squatters and their importance to Democrats like Douglas, see John Suval, *Dangerous Ground: Squatters, Statesmen, and the Antebellum Rupture of American Democracy* (New York: Oxford University Press, 2022).

26. *Daily Union and American* (Nashville, TN), November 3, 1860.

27. *Daily Constitutionalist* (Augusta, GA), December 15, 1860.

28. Giddings, *Speeches in Congress*, 290. Longstreet's nephew James went on to serve as a Confederate general during the Civil War.

29. Jeff Forret, *Slave Against Slave: Plantation Violence in the Old South* (Baton Rouge: Louisiana State University Press, 2015), 130–35; Daina Ramey Berry, *The Price for Their Pound of Flesh: The Value of the Enslaved, from Womb to Grave, in the Building of a Nation* (Boston: Beacon, 2017), 100, 111–14.

30. Jeff Forret, *Williams' Gang: A Notorious Slave Trader and His Cargo of Black Convicts* (New York: Cambridge University Press, 2020), 327–31. For the full text of the Emancipation Act of 1862, see www.archives.gov/exhibits/featured-documents/dc-emancipation-act/transcription.html. As Tera W. Hunter has written, "although the District of Columbia Emancipation Act marked the only time the federal government would compensate slaveowners, there is a longer history of slaveowners requesting and receiving indemnification for the loss of their chattel." That history includes occasions "when enslaved women and men ran away, participated in rebellions or were executed for crimes." See Tera W. Hunter, "When Slaveowners Got Reparations," *New York Times*, April 16, 2019.

31. Draper, *Price of Emancipation*, 138, 6n15, 138n2. Using Draper's definition found on p. 139, the British West Indies includes Anguilla, Antigua, Barbados, British Guiana, Dominica, Grenada, Honduras, Jamaica, Montserrat, Nevis, St. Kitts, St. Lucia, St. Vincent, Tobago, Trinidad, and the Virgin Islands. There, 30,227 awards for 655,780 enslaved people totaled £16,356,668 3s 1d. See also Kris Manjapra, *Black Ghost of Empire: The Long Death of Slavery and the Failure of Emancipation* (New York: Scribner, 2022), 97–111. Statistically, "more than 50% of the total compensation money went to just 6% of the total number of claimants." See Kris Manjapra, "When Will Britain Face Up to Its Crimes Against Humanity?" *The Guardian* (London), March 29, 2018.

32. Manjapra, "When Will Britain Face Up to Its Crimes Against Humanity?"; Thomas Craemer, "There Was a Time Reparations Were Actually Paid Out—Just Not to Formerly Enslaved People," *The Conversation*, February 26, 2021, theconversation.com/there-was-a-time-reparations-were-actually-paid-out-just-not-to-formerly-enslaved-people-152522.

33. Manjapra, *Black Ghost of Empire*, 57–68; Craemer, "There Was a Time."

34. Manjapra, *Black Ghost of Empire*; Frédérique Beauvois, *Between Blood and Gold: The Debates over Compensation for Slavery in the Americas* (New York: Berghahn, 2016).

Epilogue

1. William A. Darity Jr. and Dania Frank, "The Economic of Reparations," in *African Americans in the U.S. Economy*, ed. C.A. Conrad, J. Whitehead, P. Mason, and J. Stewart (Lanham, MD: Rowman and Littlefield, 2005), 334; Tracy Jan, "Reparations Mean More than Money for a Family Who Endured Slavery and Japanese American Internment," *Washington Post*, January 24, 2020; Marcia Chatelain,

William A. Darity Jr., Roy E. Finkenbine, and Stephanie E. Jones-Rogers, "What Americans Need to Know About Reparations Ahead of This Week's Big Hearing," *Slate*, June 18, 2019.

2. Patricia Cohen, "What Reparations for Slavery Might Look Like in 2019," *New York Times*, May 23, 2019; Joel Edward Goza, "Opening the Door to Reparations for Black Americans," *North Star*, August 14, 2019, www.thenorthstar.com/p/opening-the-door-to-reparations-for-black-americans; Arica L. Coleman, "The House Hearing on Slavery Reparations Is Part of a Long History. Here's What to Know on the Idea's Tireless Early Advocates," *Time*, June 18, 2019; Jan, "Reparations Mean More than Money"; Ta-Nehisi Coates, "The Case for Reparations," *The Atlantic*, June 2014 (quotation).

3. As the U.S. government was focused on repaying slave owners, and even before, the formerly enslaved struggled for reparations throughout the Atlantic world. On that transatlantic history of reparations, see Ana Lucia Araujo, *Reparations for Slavery and the Slave Trade: A Transnational and Comparative History* (New York: Bloomsbury, 2017).

4. John Torpey, *Making Whole What Has Been Smashed: On Reparation Politics* (Cambridge: Harvard University Press, 2006), 8 (first quotation), 45 (second quotation), 159; Araujo, *Reparations for Slavery*, 1–2. Araujo notes that slaves and freed slaves did not typically use the word "reparation" themselves, despite their firsthand experiences in bondage and their acute awareness of the harm they suffered.

5. W. Caleb McDaniel, *Sweet Taste of Liberty: A True Story of Slavery and Restitution in America* (New York: Oxford University Press, 2019) examines the lawsuit filed by Henrietta Wood.

6. Mary Frances Berry, *My Face Is Black Is True: Callie House and the Struggle for Ex-Slave Reparations* (New York: Vintage Books, 2006); Erin B. Logan, "In a Year of Reckoning, Slavery Reparations Bill Moves Forward in the House," *Los Angeles Times*, April 14, 2021; Coleman, "House Hearing on Slavery Reparations"; Adam Harris, "Everyone Wants to Talk About Reparations. But for How Long?," *The Atlantic*, June 19, 2019.

7. Robert S. Lecky and Elliott Wright, eds., *Black Manifesto: Religion, Racism, and Reparations* (New York: Sheed and Ward, 1969).

8. Coates, "The Case for Reparations."

9. Thomas Craemer, "There Was a Time Reparations Were Actually Paid Out—Just Not to Formerly Enslaved People," *The Conversation*, February 26, 2021, theconversation.com/there-was-a-time-reparations-were-actually-paid-out-just-not-to-formerly-enslaved-people-152522; P.R. Lockhart, "What Slavery Reparations from the Federal Government Could Look Like," NBC News, May 12, 2021.

10. Morgan Gstalter, "Most Oppose Cash Reparations for Slavery: Poll," *The Hill*, June 29, 2019; Lockhart, "What Slavery Reparations"; Tom Huddleston Jr., "The Debate over Slavery Reparations: Where Things Stand to How Much It Could Cost,"

CNBC, June 19, 2021; Errin Haines Whack, "Danny Glover to Testify at House Slavery Reparations Hearing," AP News, June 13, 2019; Logan, "Year of Reckoning." On the fight over Confederate monuments, see Karen L. Cox, *No Common Ground: Confederate Monuments and the Ongoing Fight for Racial Justice* (Chapel Hill: University of North Carolina Press, 2021); and Adam H. Domby, *The False Cause: Fraud, Fabrication, and White Supremacy in Confederate Memory* (Charlottesville: University of Virginia Press, 2020).

11. Craig Steven Wilder, *Ebony and Ivy: Race, Slavery, and the Troubled History of America's Universities* (New York: Bloomsbury, 2013); Jennifer Oast, *Institutional Slavery: Slaveholding Churches, Schools, Colleges, and Businesses in Virginia, 1680–1860* (New York: Cambridge University Press, 2016); Leslie M. Harris, James T. Campbell, and Alfred L. Brophy, eds., *Slavery and the University: Histories and Legacies* (Athens: University of Georgia Press, 2019); Jesús A. Rodríguez, "This Could Be the First Slavery Reparations Policy in America," *Politico*, April 9, 2019; Adeel Hassan, "Georgetown Students Agree to Create Reparations Fund," *New York Times*, April 12, 2019; Miranda Bryant, "Catholic Order Pledges $100m in Reparations to Descendants of Enslaved People," *The Guardian*, March 16, 2021 (quotation).

12. Safia Samee Ali, "Chicago Suburb to Become First City to Give Black Residents Reparations," NBC News, March 11, 2021; Lockhart, "What Slavery Reparations."

13. Huddleston, "Debate over Slavery Reparations"; Logan, "Year of Reckoning"; Michael D'Orso, *Like Judgement Day: The Ruin and Redemption of a Town Called Rosewood* (New York: G.P. Putnam's Sons, 1996); William A. Darity Jr. and Kirsten Mullen, *From Here to Equality: Reparations for Black Americans in the Twenty-First Century* (Chapel Hill: University of North Carolina Press, 2020), 16–17.

As in the United States, British universities such as Cambridge are exploring their ties to the institution of slavery, as are financial institutions such as the Bank of England, the Royal Bank of Scotland, and Barclays. Insurance market Lloyd's of London and brewer Greene King have already pledged reparations. Like the U.S. government, the Crown itself has been slower to acknowledge its complicity with slavery and the slave trade. See Catherine Hall, Nicholas Draper, Keith McClelland, Katie Donlington, and Rachel Lang, *Legacies of British Slave-Ownership: Colonial Slavery and the Formation of Victorian Britain* (Cambridge: Cambridge University Press, 2014); Brooke Newman, "Throne of Blood: It's Time for the British Royal Family to Make Amends for Centuries of Profiting from Slavery," *Slate*, July 28, 2020; David Olusaga, "Why Are So Many Afraid to Confront Britain's Historical Links with the Slave Trade?" *The Guardian*, May 5, 2019; Myriam François, "It's Not Just Cambridge University—All of Britain Benefited from Slavery," *The Guardian*, May 7, 2019; Catherine Hall, "There Are British Businesses Built on Slavery. This Is How We Make Amends," *The Guardian*, June 23, 2020; Kevin Rawlinson, "Lloyd's of London and Greene King to Make Slave Trade Reparations," *The Guardian*, June 17, 2020.

14. Cohen, "What Reparations for Slavery Might Look Like"; Logan, "Year of Reckoning"; Jan, "Reparations Mean More than Money"; Gstalter, "Most Oppose Cash Reparations."

15. Cohen, "What Reparations for Slavery Might Look Like"; Lockhart, "What Slavery Reparations"; Huddleston, "Debate over Slavery Reparations"; Jan, "Reparations Mean More than Money"; Darity and Frank, "Economics of Reparations," 336.

16. Joshua D. Rothman, *The Ledger and the Chain: How Domestic Slave Traders Shaped America* (New York: Basic Books, 2021), 356, 358, gives two examples of slave-trading families successfully filing appeals to the U.S. government to recover property after the Civil War.

17. "Ta-Nehisi Coates Revisits the Case for Reparations," *The New Yorker*, June 10, 2019 (first quotation); Ibram X. Kendi, "There Is No Middle Ground on Reparations," *The Atlantic*, June 19, 2019 (second quotation). Kendi contends that it is racist to oppose reparations and that the antiracist position is to embrace them.

18. Logan, "Year of Reckoning."

19. Tera W. Hunter, "When Slaveowners Got Reparations," *New York Times*, April 16, 2019.

Illustration Credits

Cover

"Wreck of the Slave Ship," in Richard Hildreth, *The White Slave; Or, Memoirs of a Fugitive* (London: Ingram, Cooke, 1852), 80. Library Company of Philadelphia.

Introduction

Page 2: Map by Joe LeMonnier.

Chapter 1

Page 16: Henry Schenck Tanner, "Map of the West India and Bahama Islands" (Philadelphia: H.S. Tanner, 1831). David Rumsey Map Collection, David Rumsey Map Center, Stanford Libraries.

Page 21: "Entrance to Port Nassau," in "The Bahamas," *Harper's New Monthly Magazine* 49, no. 294 (November 1874): 764.

Page 24: "Government House," in "The Bahamas," *Harper's New Monthly Magazine* 49, no. 294 (November 1874): 762.

Page 27: "Nassau from Hog Island," in Charles Ives, *The Isles of Summer; Or, Nassau and the Bahamas* (New Haven, CT: printed by the author, 1880), facing p. 160.

Page 30: "Old Gunnybags," in "The Bahamas," *Harper's New Monthly Magazine* 49, no. 294 (November 1874): 763.

Chapter 3

Page 57: Conrad L'Allemand (lithographer Carl Wildt), *Lord Palmerston*. Acc. #2683. Government Art Collection, The National Archives.

Chapter 4

Page 77: "Bay Street, West End of Nassau," in Charles Ives, *The Isles of Summer; Or, Nassau and the Bahamas* (New Haven, CT: printed by the author, 1880), facing p. 312.

Page 78: "Street in Nassau," in "The Bahamas," *Harper's New Monthly Magazine* 49, no. 294 (November 1874): 770.

Chapter 7

Page 112: F.C. De Krafft, Mrs. W.I. Stone, and William M. Morrison, *Map of the City of Washington* (Wm. M. Morrison, 1840). Library of Congress, Geography and Map Division.

Page 114: "Slave House of J. W. Neal & Co.," from the broadside *Slave Market of America* (New York: American Anti-Slavery Society, 1836). Library of Congress, Rare Book and Special Collections Division.

Page 117: Johnson Savage, *The Road Leading to Hamilton and Hunt's Island.* National Museum of Bermuda.

Page 118: Johnson Savage, *The Flatts and Its Bridge, Under Which Is the Entrance to Harrington Sound.* National Museum of Bermuda.

Page 119: Johnson Savage, *The Building Used as a Barrack for Royal Artillery.* National Museum of Bermuda.

Page 125: Portrait of Mary Warfield with her grandson Brownlow Charles Williams, c. 1890. National Museum of Bermuda/Patricia Ferguson.

Chapter 9

Page 142: Library of Congress, Prints and Photographs Division.

Chapter 14

Page 221: Library of Congress, Prints and Photographs Division.

Index

About the Author

Jeff Forret is University Professor of History at Lamar University in Beaumont, Texas. He has authored or edited seven books, including the award-winning *Slave Against Slave: Plantation Violence in the Old South* and *Williams' Gang: A Notorious Slave Trader and His Cargo of Black Convicts*. He lives in Lumberton, Texas.

Publishing in the Public Interest

Thank you for reading this book published by The New Press; we hope you enjoyed it. New Press books and authors play a crucial role in sparking conversations about the key political and social issues of our day.

We hope that you will stay in touch with us. Here are a few ways to keep up to date with our books, events, and the issues we cover:

- Sign up at www.thenewpress.com/subscribe to receive updates on New Press authors and issues and to be notified about local events
- www.facebook.com/newpressbooks
- www.twitter.com/thenewpress
- www.instagram.com/thenewpress

Please consider buying New Press books not only for yourself, but also for friends and family and to donate to schools, libraries, community centers, prison libraries, and other organizations involved with the issues our authors write about.

The New Press is a 501(c)(3) nonprofit organization; if you wish to support our work with a tax-deductible gift please visit www.thenewpress.com/donate or use the QR code below.